I0878254

THE SAINTS OF PROGRESS

THE SAINTS OF PROGRESS

A History of Coffee, Migration, and Costa Rican National Identity

CARMEN KORDICK

The University of Alabama Press
Tuscaloosa

The University of Alabama Press
Tuscaloosa, Alabama 35487-0380
uapress.ua.edu

Copyright © 2019 by the University of Alabama Press
All rights reserved.

Inquiries about reproducing material from this work should be addressed to the University of Alabama Press.

Typeface: Minion and Arial

Cover image: Civic parade in San Marcos de Tarrazú, 1960s; courtesy of Juan Mora
Cover design: David Nees

Library of Congress Cataloging-in-Publication Data

Names: Kordick, Carmen, 1980– author.
Title: The saints of progress : a history of coffee, migration, and Costa Rican national identity / Carmen Kordick.
Description: Tuscaloosa : The University of Alabama Press, [2019] | Includes bibliographical references and index.
Identifiers: LCCN 2018021215| ISBN 9780817320027 (cloth) | ISBN 9780817392093 (ebook)
Subjects: LCSH: Costa Rica—History. | Coffee industry—Political aspects—Costa Rica.
Classification: LCC F1546 .K67 2019 | DDC 972.86—dc23
LC record available at https://lccn.loc.gov/2018021215

For Alexandra and Nidia

Contents

Illustrations

MAPS

FIGURES

Preface

As the daughter of a Costa Rican immigrant in the 1980s, many of my childhood afternoons were punctuated with stories about the country where my mother was born and raised. I longed to know the idyllic world she vividly described. In the Costa Rica of her memory, children played without a care in the countryside, the government disbanded the military as part of a historic commitment to peace, and many Costa Ricans slept with their doors unlocked. The society she evoked was very far removed from my own existence as a young girl in an upper-middle-class neighborhood in Colorado, where my parents' concerns for my safety restricted playtime to fenced yards or the public park under adult supervision.

While the Costa Rica of my mother's childhood was a universe away from my everyday existence in the United States, it seemed equally distant from what I experienced during our annual vacations at my maternal grandmother's home. Indeed, each summer we were met with warm hugs from family, followed by news about how a cousin or other family member suffered a violent mugging, a carjacking, or a home robbery. Additionally, it seemed that each time we visited Costa Rica, the walls around the houses in my grandmother's neighborhood were higher, the barbed-wire coils thicker; eventually, electric fences were installed around most homes to deter intruders. With my grandmother's home a virtual fortress, most of my playtime with cousins was restricted to the walled-in yard my grandmother shared with my aunt. Even in the face of these realities, for most of my childhood, the faith in Costa Ricans' inherent peacefulness espoused by my mother rarely wavered. Certainly, she was not alone; in fact, in the years since I first began researching Costa Rica's historical development, I have met few Costa Ricans (outside of academia) who question the image of their nation as a uniquely peaceful paradise in the Americas.

Additionally, while conducting fieldwork, I was repeatedly confronted with the fact that my Costa Rican informants' aspirations and actions were deeply shaped by their faith in a multifaceted official national narrative, which celebrates Costa Rica as an outlier in the isthmus. This myth holds that Costa Rica is not only Central America's most peaceful but also its most democratic, egalitarian, and "white" (i.e., not indigenous or racially mixed, but, exclusively, European) republic. Costa Ricans view their allegedly untainted Iberian heritage as critical to their ability to forge a law-abiding and democratically oriented society much more rapidly than their mixed-race Central American neighbors. Geneticists, social scientists, and other scholars have questioned this ahistorical and racist narrative for decades.[1] Additionally, the evening news offers daily reports of high-profile corruption schemes, and newspaper headlines often have dramatic exposés of violent crime scenes. Still, most Costa Ricans, including many of my informants for this project, continue to see their nation as the product of this official national narrative.

Many perceive contemporary issues dealing with crime, violence, and corruption as a consequence of changing demographics, in particular the influx of large numbers of Nicaraguan laborers since the early 1980s.[2] In recent decades, it has become common to hear politicians, journalists, and public service administrators blame immigrants for inaugurating Costa Rica's present social ills and for destroying the society's exceptionalist past. Most social scientists, however, attribute the nation's rising levels of urban poverty, decreasing quality of human services, and increasing crime rates not to immigrants' penchant for crime and (ab)use of social services but to larger policy shifts, namely, a series of neoliberal policies enacted since the 1990s.[3] Regardless of believed and real causes, most Costa Ricans have been personally impacted by an uptick in crime, a decline in the number of job opportunities, and declining quality of state-sponsored healthcare and educational services.[4] In this context, arguably, the exceptionalist national past of shared prosperity and peace, which the official national narrative celebrates, has become an increasingly powerful source of national pride and hope for ordinary Costa Ricans. Indeed, if the nation's past was exceptional because Costa Ricans are an innately egalitarian, peaceful, and democratic people, then Costa Ricans can nostalgically imagine that the exceptionalism celebrated in the official national narrative is recoverable. As patriotically potent a symbol as the narrative is for Costa Ricans in the capital of San José, it even more powerfully shapes the lives of Costa Ricans in the rural Tarrazú Valley.

In 2005, when I first visited this rural region, I was struck by both this coffee region's idyllic beauty and its seeming timelessness. Global coffee prices plummeted in the mid-1970s due to overproduction, and consequentially, farmers in many of the nation's traditional coffee-producing regions abandoned this crop by the 1990s.[5] The reductions in profits are striking. In 1977, the average coffee producer in Costa Rica was earning $1.39 per pound of Arabica coffee produced. In 1983, this was down to 56¢ per pound, and by 2004, the year before I embarked on my research project, farmers were earning just 59.44¢ per pound.[6] Taking inflation into consideration, the decrease in price per pound of coffee is substantial. Moreover, since the cost of seedlings, transportation to market, and pesticides increased during this same period, local farm owners in Tarrazú have been continually forced to cut costs wherever possible. Harvester's wages have suffered in this context. Indeed, for the past couple of decades, they have been insufficient to entice most local residents to pick up a harvester's basket.[7]

Given these economic realities, it would seem that residents would discontinue coffee production. The hills in Tarrazú, however, have not been abandoned. In fact, they were as neatly tended in 2005, when I first arrived in the region, as they were in the 1970s, when coffee prices were high.[8] Additionally, at the region's numerous small bars, like Santa María's Taberna El Arbolito, it was common to overhear local men discussing global coffee market values, precipitation levels, and the effectiveness of different herbicide and pesticide varieties. Equally curious was the apparent wealth of the region. The streets were lined with well-kept homes with many shiny new trucks parked in front.[9] These images and conversations suggested a local economy that not only was tied to the land but seemingly exemplified a charming vision of Costa Rican rural life from before the collapse of global coffee prices.

Although the rural economy was thriving, local farm families had a very different relationship to the land than their parents and grandparents had. The area managed to remain a rural coffee-growing region by establishing tight connections to transnational webs of capital and labor. These webs are delineated in the following way: local farm families rely on remittances from family members in the United States not only to purchase new equipment, like trucks, and to increase landholdings but to subsidize the cost of seedlings, herbicides, pesticides, and other basic farm expenses. Remittances also allow farmers to pay the wages of foreign agricultural laborers from Nicaragua and Panama who spray, weed, and pick the coffee.[10]

It quickly was clear that the transnational movement of capital and labor permitted Tarrazú to survive as a coffee-growing region in the face of tumbling coffee prices, but it raised the question of why local families clung to coffee production even as this crop's value declined steadily and showed no signs of improvement. I first thought that perhaps the overhead costs of crop conversion were deterring local families. This, however, seemed a weak argument, given the inflow of remittances and farmers' reliance on relatively inexpensive foreign labor.

My conversations with coffee farmers and their families both in Tarrazú and in the United States soon revealed that, for many, coffee was not an exclusively economic venture; rather, its real value was cultural. Coffee plays a key role in the official national narrative as the celebrated "Golden Bean" that brought the nation economic wealth. Moreover, historically, coffee is associated with progress, modernity, and civilization. In the nineteenth century, when coffee production began, Eurocentric elites and policy makers in San José used coffee export taxes to build libraries, museums, schools, railroads, and an opera house. By the 1880s, coffee and wealthy *cafetaleros*, or large-scale coffee farmers—like the structures and institutions that they helped fund and design—came to embody modernity and civilization. In contrast, subsistence farmers, or *maiceros*, were quickly becoming the cafetalero's mythic opposite and a symbol of this agrarian republic's uneducated, impoverished, and uncultured past.[11]

Tarrazú Valley farmers began planting coffee at the turn of the twentieth century, and by the 1920s, it was the region's principal cash crop. Many in the region associate the introduction of coffee to Tarrazú with progress, modernity, and civilization. Indeed, in the years after coffee farming began, many residents purchased their first pair of shoes, electric irons, washing machines, and other material goods that not only improved their owners' quality of life but served as powerful local symbols of a family's commitment to and successful embrace of progressive national values. Tarrazúceños' faith in modernity and progress, which have traditionally been tied symbolically to the procurement of particular objects and coffee production, is striking. Indeed, residents continually speak of particular objects that they acquired through coffee profits to demonstrate their commitment to modernity and progress. Many of my older informants, for instance, made special mention of the day they purchased their first pair of shoes. For many, their shoes, which they purchased with coffee profits, literally permitted them to walk into the world of civilized modernity.[12]

The Tarrazú Valley is commonly known throughout Costa Rica as La Zona de los Santos, or the Saints' Region, as all of the communities in the valley are named after Catholic saints, such as San Marcos de Tarrazú. This fact, coupled with the widespread popular fixation on progress, inspired this book's title, *The Saints of Progress*. Indeed, it emerged from a repeated trope in almost all of my interviews where folks would sooner or later ask me whether I wanted to know when progress arrived or how they helped bring progress to their community or what it was like before the region "progressed." In sum, the people of the region clearly saw a before and an after date, which coincided with the establishment of the cooperatives at the start of the Second Republic.

Coffee's introduction to the region did not provide all Tarrazú families with the chance to enjoy the fruits of modernity. In fact, for many of the region's landless laborers, coffee profits served to widen the socioeconomic division between themselves and their neighbors who owned small parcels of land. Immigration to the United States, which began in the late 1960s, provided landless families in Tarrazú with an avenue to reduce or even eliminate that gap. Families who sent husbands or other family members to work in the United States used remittances to purchase farmlands and coffee seedlings and also to build themselves modern homes.[13] By the early 1980s, the global downturn in coffee prices also made emigration an attractive option for traditional landholding families hoping to retain or improve their family farms in the face of decreasing profits. In this context, where large numbers of emigrants had both entered into the landholding class and retained that position through remittances, such emigration has ironically become a means by which local families can remain in Tarrazú, as this rural region offers few economic opportunities outside of agriculture. Moreover, emigration has permitted once impoverished families to "buy into" the national mythos as not only hardworking coffee farmers but also good Costa Rican citizens committed to the ideals of progress, modernity, and civilization through their remittance-earned material wealth.[14]

This book is, in many ways, the product of my desire to understand the relationship between migratory flows and coffee production in the Tarrazú Valley. However, as I have come to realize, it has also provided me with insight into the mythic Costa Rica that my mother spoke of so lovingly when I was a child. This is all to express that while this study is intellectually driven, it too is very personally shaped.

Acknowledgments

My quest to understand, question, and ultimately break apart Costa Rica's national mythology was made possible by the assistance and support of a large number of people and several institutions that provided me with academic, financial, and moral support over the past decade.

For their unwavering commitment to my work as a scholar since meeting me as a first-year graduate student, I am deeply indebted to my graduate school mentors: Patricia Pessar, Gil Joseph, Lillian Guerra, Lowell Gudmundson, and Stuart Schwartz. Sadly, Patricia passed away in 2013; however, this project would not have been possible without the sound advice and astute observations she so generously shared with me from the very start. I am forever indebted to her and feel blessed to have had the chance to have known and worked with such a brilliant and kind scholar. I am tremendously grateful to Lowell for graciously committing to serve as an outside reader and for offering thoughtful comments on early drafts of each of this book's chapters. As a leader in the field of Costa Rican history, Lowell's insights have greatly strengthened this work. Stuart merits special thanks for not only agreeing to be a reader but also for introducing me to his former student Lowell. I wish to make special mention of Lily, who pushed me to move beyond shallow observations and to seek precision and clarity in my analysis. My greatest intellectual debt is to my principal mentor, Gil, for his calm reassurance and unfaltering support. Since meeting Gil in the fall of 2004, he has proven himself to be a model mentor through not only his generous support of my scholarship throughout the years but also his genuine and caring friendship in both times of joy and hardship. I am a stronger scholar and writer thanks to the comments, questions, patience, and words of wisdom of all my intellectual mentors.

I am also deeply indebted to my graduate school colleagues and Yale history faculty members who shared insights and criticisms and who raised questions about this work. I am particularly thankful to Daniel Brueckenhaus, Sarah Cameron, Haydon Cherry, Lisa Pinley Covert, Seth Fein, Caitlin Fitz, Kathryn Gin, Mary Greenfield, Jennifer Lambe, Christine Mathias, Nick Rutter, and Kate Unterman, who not only provided me with moral support but took time out of their busy schedules to read and comment on (often very rough) chapter drafts. I would also like to thank Sarah Cameron, Andrew Conroe, and Kylea Liese for punctuating my days in Sterling Memorial Library with a healthy dose of conversation and cheer in my final summer in New Haven.

I especially want to thank Juan Bautista Chanto Méndez, Fany Jiménez Solís, Lorena Naranjo Monge, and all the Tarrazúceños, who generously welcomed me into their homes and shared their memories and perspectives alongside family photographs and homemade sweet breads, tortillas, and coffee. I am particularly thankful to Juan de Dios Mora Córdoba for sharing copies of his impressive collection of historical photographs of the region for this project. My deepest gratitude in Tarrazú, however, extends to Doña Berta Monge Umaña, who passed away in June 2015. I am deeply saddened to have lost a dear friend, whose hospitality, wisdom, and patience made me feel so much at home during my many months in Tarrazú. Moreover, Doña Berta's personal connections and her knowledge of the community ensured my research's success in Tarrazú.

In northern New Jersey, I am indebted to all the Costa Ricans who filled out surveys and allowed me to interview and work beside them and even attend their children's birthday parties. I am particularly grateful to Catalina Muñoz (pseud.), who eagerly introduced me to her family and friends and who taught me how to make *picadillo de arracache*, one of my favorite Costa Rican dishes. I am also very thankful to the staff and management at both La Montaña and El Típico for not only allowing me to leave surveys in their restaurants but also encouraging their clients to fill them out. I am equally thankful to the management at Mi Pueblo in Bloomfield, Tucanes in Prospect Park, and La Bahía in Paterson, who allowed me to use their restaurants to meet and converse with Costa Ricans. I am also very grateful to Rev. Donald J. Sella of Paterson's Our Lady of Lourdes Roman Catholic Church for affording me the opportunity to introduce myself to the community during Sunday mass and for personally introducing me to a number of his Costa Rican parishioners.

In San José, I am indebted to a number of people and institutions that made research and writing possible. Above all, I am grateful to the investigators in the Programa de Cultura at the University of Costa Rica's Insituto de Investigaciones Sociales, especially Carlos Sandoval García and Carmen Caamaño, who both encouraged and supported this project from its earliest stages. I would also like to thank the staff at the Biblioteca Nacional for facilitating my access to historic newspapers, and the librarians at the University of Costa Rica's Biblioteca Carlos Meléndez, who time and again helped me secure special permission to check out secondary sources despite my not being a student at their institution. At the Archivo Nacional de Costa Rica, archivists Franklin Álvarado Q., Jafeth Campos R., Eduardo Hidalgo S., Vinicio Méndez M., and Xinia Trejos R. were incredibly patient and helpful. I owe particular thanks to Adolfo Chacón, a retired public servant, whose passion for Costa Rican political history and all things related to José "Pepe" Figueres Ferrer proved particularly helpful as I sought out sources on Costa Rica's 1948 Civil War. I am most thankful to my cousin, close friend, and fellow historian Ana Lucía Barboza Hernández for sharing her passion for the profession in our discussions about Costa Rican historiography and for her sincere interest in my work.

I also wish to thank my history professors at the University of Colorado at Boulder, who excited my interest in the past and taught me to read critically. I am particularly thankful to my undergraduate advisor, Fred Anderson, who taught me how to conduct archival research and encouraged me to continue my studies. I am also very grateful to Camile Guerín-González, who first sparked my interest in migration and took a personal interest in my development as a young scholar.

I would also like to thank my former colleagues, Sunita Manian and Jim Winchester, at Georgia College and State University for sharing so many lovely evenings discussing the past and present over bottles of wine during my two years in Middle Georgia. I must also make special note of my former colleague, Doug Oetter, who generously shared his time and talents to produce the maps in this book.

I also wish to extend my gratitude to my Roosevelt University colleagues for their camaraderie, kindness, and encouragement over the years. I am particularly thankful to Celeste Chamberland, Chris Chulos, Heather Dalmage, Sarah Elliott, Sandra Frink, Erik Gellman, Phil Holquist, Brad Hunt, Zarco Minkov, Margie Rung, and Stuart Werner. I am delighted too to be able to thank my newest colleagues in the History Department at Southern Connecticut State University for welcoming me into their supportive and dynamic intellectual community.

Additionally, I appreciate the chance to acknowledge the generous financial support I received from the following institutions, without which this project would not have been possible: the Yale Graduate School of Arts and Sciences, the MacMillan Center for International and Area Studies, and the Andrew W. Mellon Foundation.

The University of Alabama Press's editor in chief, Dan Waterman, showed early interest in this project and generously put me in contact with the wonderfully efficient Wendi Schnaufer, who has proven herself to be an exceedingly patient and understanding editor. I thank you both, alongside the academic editorial board, Susan Harris, Kelly Finefrock-Creed, and everyone at the University of Alabama Press, for your clear direction and support throughout this process. Additionally, I am indebted to the two anonymous readers who carefully read my manuscript and provided me with insightful feedback that deeply shaped and strengthened this work. Thank you.

All translations, unless otherwise noted, are mine. So too, any shortcomings of this book are mine alone.

Finally, I want to thank my dearest friends and my family for their unfaltering love and encouragement. I could not have completed this project without the laughter, distraction, and love that my dearest friends outside of academia, Molly Lubin, Dede and Sonny Santana, Susan Shepard Niemeier, and Amber Williams, have provided me in varying measure throughout the years. Though he entered late in this book's production, I want to acknowledge the loving support, enthusiasm, and joy that my most treasured friend, favorite adventure partner, and closest confidant, Edward, has provided since entering into my life. My greatest and never-ending thanks, however, go to my family. In many ways this work is a testament to my father, Lloyd; from an early age, he inspired in me a passion for learning, reading, and the past. This work would not have been possible were it not for the unrelenting interest he took in my academic success until the day he passed away. I am equally thankful to the two most important women in my life, my mother, Nidia, and my younger sister, Alexandra, who have both in their own way been constant sources of strength and inspiration for as long as I can remember. I feel nothing short of blessed to have shared the first chapters of my life exploring and learning beside my brilliant, beautiful, and beloved Alexandra, who has been a constant source of calm, compassion, and clarity. I am similarly indebted to Nidia, whose love for the nation of her birth first inspired my work. I am deeply thankful to her not only for sparking my love and interest in Costa Rica but for most generously allowing me as well as my piles of books, photocopies, and photographs to stay with her while I was researching in the Central Valley.

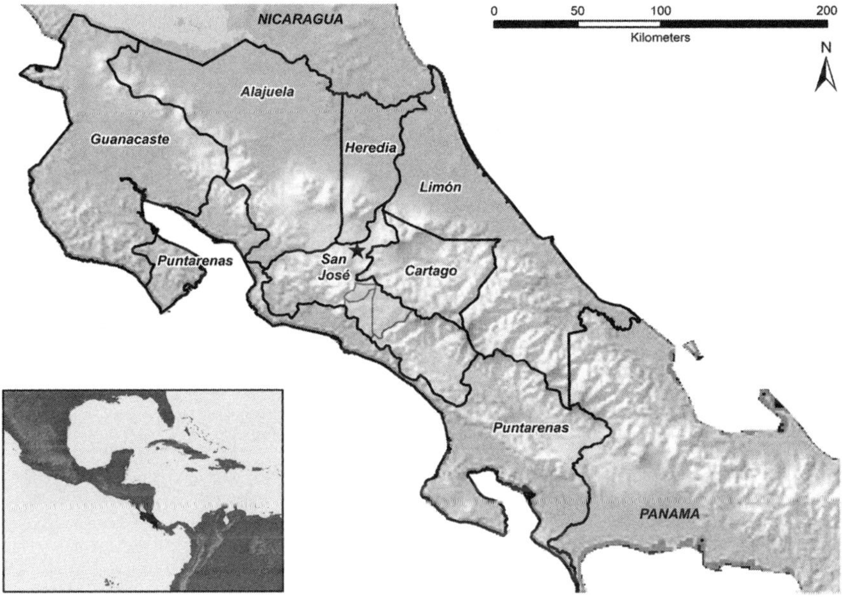

Map of Costa Rica. (Courtesy of Doug Oetter)

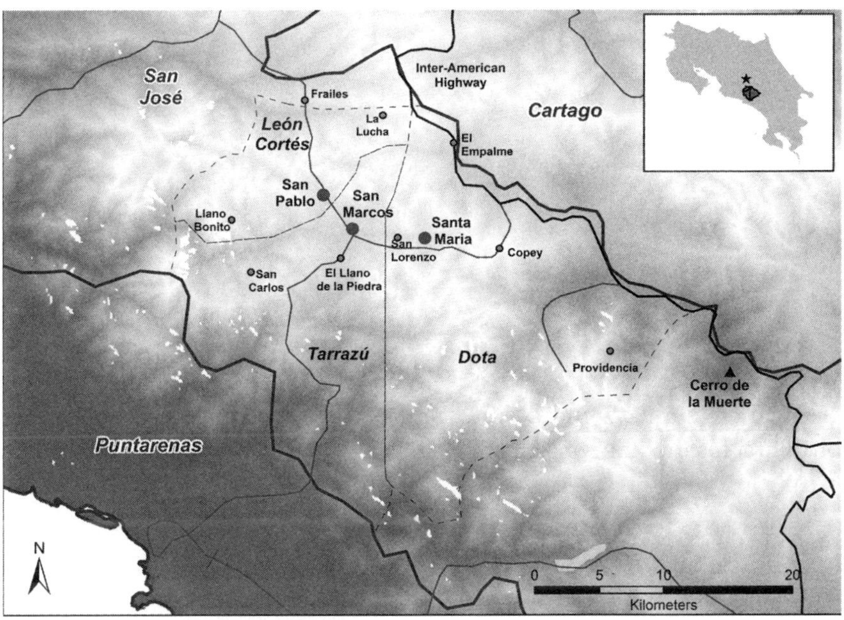

Map of Tarrazú. (Courtesy of Doug Oetter)

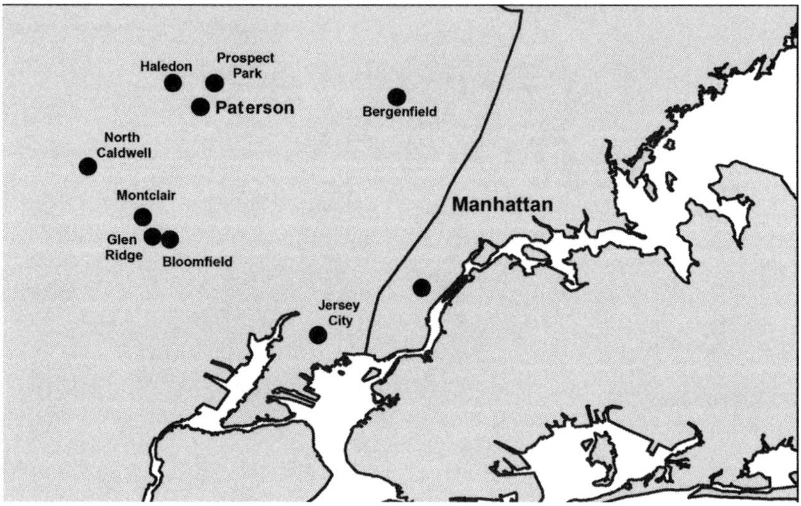

Map of New Jersey communities with Costa Rican immigrant populations. (Courtesy of Doug Oetter)

THE SAINTS OF PROGRESS

Introduction

Tarrazú

A Place, a Coffee, and a People

The highest point of the Inter-American Highway, the Cerro de Buena Vista, or Good View Mountain, is located some 90 kilometers south of the Costa Rican capital of San José. At 3,491 meters above sea level, this mountain section of the highway has earned its name as one of the few places in the Americas where on a clear day it is possible to glimpse both the Atlantic and Pacific Oceans.[1] Just 35 kilometers to the north of this awe-inspiring point, there is a winding two-lane road that descends west into the verdant Tarrazú Valley (fig. I.1). Fields planted with blackberry bushes and fruit groves greet travelers at the higher elevations of this mountain valley. At slightly lower elevations, this colorful array gives way to a profusion of coffee bushes that neatly line the valley's steep hillsides.

For the past 130 years, the valley's well-cared-for coffee fields have shaped the socioeconomic reality of the men, women, and children who have lived and died in this place. Indeed, Tarrazú is not just a place; it is also the name of one of the world's most-renowned coffee varieties and has been recognized internationally as Costa Rica's premier coffee region.[2]

This is a social history of a small rural region, which throws into sharp relief the everyday struggles of the men and women whose actions helped transform Tarrazú from a subsistence-centered community founded in the 1820s to a world-renowned coffee exporting region by the early twentieth century and more recently into a transnational migratory hub—a sending and receiving community of migrants. The region's socioeconomic transformations over the past 190 years and the increasing linkages between Tarrazú and the global economy in many ways echo changes that have taken place in communities throughout Central America during the national period.[3] Moreover, the region's shift to coffee monoculture was part of a larger

Figure I.1. Santa María de Dota from the road linking the Inter-American Highway to Tarrazú, 2008. (Carmen Kordick)

economic, social, and cultural pattern that swept the isthmus beginning in Costa Rica's Central Valley in the 1830s.[4]

The region's transition to coffee capitalism is of particular interest because of the critical role that this crop's introduction plays in the way that Costa Rican elites and intellectuals have defined their nation's economic and political development. This remarkably durable, multilayered, official national narrative celebrates Costa Rica as the isthmus's peaceful, democratic, white, and egalitarian republic. The narrative holds that during the colonial period Costa Ricans, who were of "pure" European extraction, forged a peaceful, egalitarian, though impoverished society far away from the colonial centers of power. Capitalism supposedly arrived after independence, with the introduction of coffee in the mid-nineteenth century. In stark contrast, however, to the rest of the isthmus—where coffee capitalism saw rigid colonial-era class and race hierarchies strengthened, Costa Rica allegedly followed a different path. Costa Rica's colonial position, as an isolated backwater supposedly settled by a homogenous white population, forged a society free of class distinctions, where shared poverty was the norm. Coffee is thus celebrated for establishing a new socioeconomic order based on a large class of thriving small-scale, or yeoman, coffee farmers. In the twentieth century, then, peace, democracy, whiteness, and small-scale coffee production, in combination, are credited for the nation's relative stability that would encourage migrant workers to enter (rather than leave) the nation in search of opportunity.

Like all national mythologies, Costa Rica's exceptionalist rendition draws upon some undeniable realities. During the Cold War, as revolution, civil war, military dictatorship, and state violence plagued much of Central America, Costa Rica eliminated its standing army in 1948 and, for the most part, remained a stable democracy. The widely embraced master narrative, however, distorts as much as it illuminates the experience of contemporary and historical actors. From the vantage point of the Tarrazú Valley, this book examines local, national, and transnational processes—including the onset of massive out-migration to the United States—to present a more adequate and textured national narrative. Tarrazú is an ideal locale from which to (re)consider Costa Rica's historical development, not only because of the region's tight linkages to coffee production, which played a central role in the national mythos, but because of the critical part that the region played in the formation of the Second Republic. In fact, the Tarrazú Valley was the locus of a successful armed revolt in 1948 against the national government; the winners forged the current political regime. In sum, Tarrazúceños' actions put into place the political framework out of which Costa Rica's celebrated national narrative emerged. Additionally, because of the region's more recently developed relationship to the United States via massive out-migration, a study of Tarrazú and its current and past residents' experiences is the ideal source to produce a more suitable and multifaceted national narrative.

Remapping Costa Rican History

Although the Tarrazú Valley has played a critical role in Costa Rica's political and economic development, its location, outside of the nation's densely populated political core centered in San José and the Central Valley, encouraged scholars to neglect this region and elide its role within the master narrative.[5] For decades, academics have embraced one of two geographical foci: the Central Valley and, to a lesser extent, the Atlantic coast, with its West Indian community and the United Fruit Company, which dominated the coastal economy during the late nineteenth and early twentieth centuries. These two scholarly trends have produced a bifurcated image of Costa Rica's economic, social, cultural, and political development. Costa Rican historiography suggests the existence of a white, Hispanic, coffee-growing Central Valley and a black, English-speaking, banana-producing Atlantic coast.[6]

Costa Rica, however, is much more than these two geographical spaces. In fact, for most of the nation's history a majority of the population lived in rural areas outside of the Central Valley and the Atlantic coast, in regions such as Tarrazú.[7] In fact, while in 2010 59 percent of Costa Ricans lived in urban areas, just thirteen years earlier, in 1997, a full 55.6 percent of the population inhabited rural areas. These changing demographics reflect increased urban migration but also highlight that until recently most Costa Ricans lived in the countryside. Given that Costa Rican society has historically been largely rural, this monograph's emphasis on a coffee-growing region beyond the Central Valley seeks to redraw Costa Rica's historical map.[8]

In addition to reshaping the geographical bounds of Costa Rican studies, *The Saints of Progress* contributes to a larger conversation among Costa Ricanists that questions Costa Rica's exceptionalist national mythology. Historian Lowell Gudmundson initiated this conversation in the 1980s with his groundbreaking work *Costa Rica before Coffee*, which rejected the master narrative's assertion that capitalism and class divisions arrived with coffee. Using property records, Gudmundson demonstrates that Costa Rican society has been historically divided along clearly demarcated class lines and that coffee profits benefited most smallholders. As Gudmundson's work (and a basic knowledge of modern societies) predicts, clear class divisions that predated commercial coffee production defined Tarrazú society. Unlike in the Central Valley, however, Tarrazú area farmers had only a few local processing options for their coffee, which allowed processors to set rates to their advantage, decreasing the benefit to individual farmers. Tarrazú's coffee revolution thus serves as a clear counterexample that adds nuance to traditional understandings of how coffee reshaped Costa Rican society.[9]

In the 1990s, scholars Fabrice Lehoucq and Iván Molina took pains to highlight the historical fragility of Costa Rican democracy before 1948. They cite electoral fraud allegations in the historical record to reject the widely held belief that Costa Rica's democratic stability dated back to the nineteenth century.[10] Around the same time, historian Mercedes Muñoz Guillén's analysis of the nation's three civil wars (of 1823, 1835, and 1948) and seven successful coups d'état during the nineteenth and twentieth centuries question the master narrative's depiction of Costa Rica as a historically pacific republic.[11] More recently, Kirk Bowman's *Militarization, Democracy, and Development: The Perils of Praetorianism in Latin America* explores how and why the Costa Rican government chose to demilitarize, convincingly arguing that even after 1948 the nation's leaders were not fully committed to the democratic process and at various points considered using force to override electoral outcomes.[12] Together, these three studies demonstrate that Costa Rica's stable democratic government and nonmilitary traditions emerged not, as the master narrative would suggest, in the nineteenth century thanks to the nation's forward-thinking, civilized, and white founders but rather starting in 1948 after the short-lived but violent Civil War that was partially sparked by electoral fraud. Yet, none of these works provide a detailed analysis of the Civil War itself, nor do they consider the site where the Civil War broke out: the Tarrazú Valley.

Given the centrality of the 1948 Civil War in shaping contemporary Costa Rican political, economic, and social realities, a study that considers the conditions that prompted hundreds of men and boys in the Tarrazú Valley to take up arms against the state and successfully overthrow the state is arguably overdue. *The Saints of Progress* fills this vacuum; indeed, it (re)inserts the birthplace of the Second Republic into the larger national narrative. In particular, this study argues that while electoral fraud was the norm, male suffrage, which was established in the late nineteenth century, had by the 1940s converted the right to vote into a measure of manhood. Consequentially, when local men opposed the ruling party, they fell victim to blatant electoral fraud and political violence during the 1940s, a decade marked by an increasingly polarized political environment, and they often came to feel that violence alone could ensure that their political voices were heard. Interestingly, the state's declared commitment to the democratic process, though historically not honored, created expectations that poor peasants and farmers in the Tarrazú Valley forced elites to meet, by taking up arms against the state. Thus, Costa Rica's current democratic system and its armyless state are rooted in the events of 1948 that unfolded in Tarrazú.

The final element of Costa Rica's exceptionalist mythology underscores that, unlike their Central American neighbors, Costa Ricans have not immigrated to the United States and, indeed, celebrate the conditions that have engendered Costa Rica as a receiving nation of both political and economic refugees. Independently conducting work in both Costa Rica and the United States, Costa Rican scholar Carmen Caamaño and I have led attempts to interrogate the myth that Costa Rica does not export labor. This volume and Caamaño's *Entre "arriba" y "abajo": La experiencia transnacional de la migración de costarricenses hacia Estados Unidos* draw attention to the flow of money, ideas, goods, and people across borders. As the first transnational monograph on Costa Rican emigration, Caamaño's pathbreaking work provides an excellent snapshot of cross-border cultural, economic, and human exchange through an exclusively ethnographic approach. Missing, however, from this first work on Costa Rican emigration is a historical approach that can explain how and why Tarrazú became a major sending community of immigrants to the United States in the 1960s. The present volume provides that historical framing.

Contemporary Proponents of Costa Rican Exceptionalism

Although Costa Rican scholars have long questioned the various elements of Costa Rica's exceptionalist mythology, the national master narrative continues to be very much alive within certain sectors of Costa Rican and Central American studies. In 2001, political scientist Mitchell A. Seligson penned an article aptly titled "Costa Rican Exceptionalism: Why the 'Ticos' Are Different," in which he uncritically repeats Costa Rica's official national narrative before declaring that this mythic past had established "a stable democracy" that was so well established that "no observer sees any serious threat to its continuation."[13] Seligson's ahistorical celebratory assertions of Costa Rica's deep-seated democratic past have proven just as problematic as his faith in its continuation. In 2003, just two years after the publication, Costa Ricans would see three former presidents accused of corruption.

This scandal severely shook Costa Ricans' faith in their nation's democratic leaders.[14] It would not, however, dampen John A. Booth, Christine J. Wade, or Thomas W. Walker's praise for Costa Rica's commitment to the democratic system or to its pacifist traditions. In 2009, these political scientists published *Understanding Central America: Global Forces, Rebellion, and Change*, in which they repeatedly describe Costa Rica in exceptionalist terms. For example, when referring to the Spanish conquest of the isthmus, the authors write that in most of Central America the Spanish "steadily drained resources from the region. Subjugated masses of indigenous peons (workers and peasants), mestizos (people of mixed white and Indian descent), and eventually black slaves . . . supplied most of the labor."[15] In stark contrast to the rest of the isthmus, Costa Rica was allegedly the only place where "with few easily exploitable resources and not many native people . . . a few Spaniards came to till the soil."[16] The authors then assert that Costa Rica did not have "many native people," but they provide no evidence or explanation for this assertion. Yet, it is this claim that explains Costa Rica's difference for these authors, who declare, "Small wonder . . . that nearly five centuries later, the four northern countries of Central America had severe mass poverty and huge class disparities, whereas Costa Rica had developed a relatively more democratic, egalitarian, and socially just system."[17] While these authors are largely in agreement with Seligson's idyllic portrait of Costa Rica, they suggest that Costa Rica's exceptionalism came to an end in the 1990s, when all five Central American republics could claim they had democratic governments in place.[18]

The works of these political scientists fully ignore the efforts of Costa Ricanists such as Lowell Gudmundson, who spent decades interrogating the nation's master narrative. One reason, arguably, for their continued use of the myth is the broader objectives of their field. Since the 1970s, political scientists' studies of the isthmus have been principally concerned with explaining the root causes of the region's political instability and violence. In this context, explaining how and why Costa Rica avoided the military dictatorships and civil wars that defined the Cold War for the rest of the isthmus was a topic that required attention. Given the violence the rest of the region experienced during the Cold War, this question merits consideration; the response of these political scientists inevitably suggests Costa Rica is an outlier within the isthmus. Unfortunately, rather than delving into the reasons why in 1948 Costa Ricans broke with their historical traditions to eliminate their nation's military, this handful of US-based political scientists has preferred to adopt without question an ahistorical nationalistic narrative. By simply adopting the official narrative without question, these scholars, dismiss the need to investigate Costa Rica, to instead dedicate their energies to investigating the sources and consequences of the extreme political violence that plagued the rest of the isthmus during the Cold War.

Because the official national narrative serves clear pro-US political goals, the US Department of State promulgates this mythology on its web page on Costa Rica, claiming that "unlike many of their Central American neighbors . . . Costa Ricans are largely of European . . . descent. . . . Few of the native Indians survived European contact; the indigenous population today is less than 1% of the population."[19] Here again, Costa Rica's white myth is asserted without providing sources for its statistical claims, which suggests that this information is an established fact. Additionally, the website provides a nice summary of the classless and democratic aspects of Costa Rica's official national narrative: "Finding little gold . . . the Spanish turned to agriculture. The small landowner's relative poverty, the lack of a large indigenous labor force, the population's ethnic and linguistic homogeneity, and Costa Rica's isolation from the Spanish colonial centers . . . contributed to the development of an autonomous and individualistic agrarian society."[20]

Putting forward this myth, with its emphasis on Costa Rica's historical commitment to peace and democracy as a *natural* consequence of the nation's alleged European cultural and ethnic heritage, serves a clear political function for the US State Department and, likely, for patriotic US scholars who are arguably interested in asserting that culpability for the region's politically motivated violence in the twentieth century falls entirely on Central American shoulders. In fact, Costa Rica's exceptionalism has been put forward consistently as a counterpoint to critics of US support of Latin American military dictators with terrible human rights records. The myth suggests that the ethnic makeup of the region's other republics—not US-supported militarization—has been responsible for the political instability and violence in the rest of the region.

Not surprisingly, Costa Rica's politicians also regularly make rhetorical use of Costa Rica's official national narrative and the tenets of national identity in their political speeches. Their motivations, however, are not related to US public image but center squarely on plugging into deep-seated nationalistic sentiments among Costa Ricans that are tied to the narrative. Take for instance former president Oscar Arias's second inaugural speech of 2006, titled "I Choose Life, Democracy, and the Challenge to Change in Peace." The title underscores two central points of Costa Rica's official national narrative—democracy and peace—that he developed throughout the speech. Arias asserted that his administration's foreign policy would "be based on the principles and values profoundly rooted in Costa Rican history, namely: the defense of democracy, the . . . promotion of human rights, the struggle for peace . . . and the pursuit of human development."[21] Arias's successor, Laura Chinchilla, would embrace these mythologies to an even greater extent in her 2010 inaugural speech, stating: "We celebrate . . . democracy in the oldest democracy in Latin America, which by the nineteenth century converted education, paid for by the state, into a universal right, and which in this same century eliminated the death penalty as a gesture exalting life, and 61 years ago, abolished the army to declare peace on the world."[22] Chinchilla went beyond Arias, who clearly celebrated Costa Rica's democratic and pacifist "traditions," to root these aspects of the Costa Rican national character in the nineteenth century. While Chinchilla is correct in noting that Costa Rica did away with the death penalty in the nineteenth century and the military in 1948, she would be hard-pressed to demonstrate that the nation's commitment to pacifism and democracy date back to the nineteenth century. As noted earlier, before 1948, Costa Rica experienced heavy moments of militarization, electoral fraud was common, and, in much of the region, the military exercised a heavy hand in politics.[23]

The continued espousal of this mythic vision of Costa Rica's past reflects the durability of Costa Rica's official national narrative. Additionally, as with all resilient mythologies, Costa Rica's is based on a kernel of truth. Certainly, Costa Rica experienced a different historical trajectory during the second half of the twentieth century than its neighbors. The issue is what are the roots of that distinction? Is it, as the mythic narrative would suggest, a question of genetic composition? Or, is it the product of a series of circumstances that came together in the late 1940s, as I and many other historians would argue? If it is the latter, then the events leading up to the outbreak of the 1948 Civil War in Tarrazú require sustained scholarly attention.

In this book, I expose the varied textures of the official national narrative by examining change and continuity in the Tarrazú Valley, from the nineteenth century into the twenty-first century. In particular, this book inserts this important region into the larger national narrative. More than a standard regional history, this volume draws attention not only to how national and international developments impacted the region but also to how local events shaped national and transnational realities. This work's broad temporal focus, which encompasses the entire length of Costa Rica's national period, coupled with its tight geographical focus on the Tarrazú Valley as well as the small enclave of Tarrazúceños in northern New Jersey, allows a detailed examination of economic development, social change, state formation, and international migration.

Central Contributions and Arguments

This volume makes three significant interventions into the fields of Costa Rican, Central American, and Latin American history and migration studies. The first is the only historical examination, so far, of burgeoning Costa Rican immigration to the United States. Beyond revealing the deep historical factors that converted the Tarrazú Valley into a major sending community of immigrants to the US Northeast beginning in the 1960s, this study uncovers how emigration has ironically strengthened many Tarrazúceños' sense of national belonging. Many once-landless Tarrazú families have used money earned abroad to purchase land, exit the ranks of landless laborers, and, in turn, assert themselves for the first time as yeoman coffee farmers. In other words, remittances have provided local farmers with opportunities to assert themselves not only as members of the nation-state but as the epitome of the national archetype.

Second, this study is the first to cover the span of Costa Rica's national period, from the 1820s to the recent past. By embracing such a broad temporal field, it demonstrates the evolution of long-term historical processes, including changing gendered relationships, the roots and consequences of a transnational migration chain, and the development of Costa Rica's national mythology. This book's temporal breadth and geographical focus permit a deep interrogation of Costa Rica's official national narrative and a critical exploration of how national ideals and myths reflect and contradict the lived realities of historical actors. This work effectively questions the validity of each of the elements that compose Costa Rica's exceptionalist national mythology.

Last, this book elucidates the critical role that local socioeconomic hierarchies have played in the production of individual understandings of themselves and their relationship to the Costa Rican nation. In particular, this project suggests that Tarrazúceños embraced Costa Rica's official national narrative in response to three economically driven transformations: (1) the rise of a coffee economy in the late nineteenth century, (2) the outflow of thousands of local laborers to the United States beginning in the middle of the twentieth century, and (3) the arrival of thousands of poor, indigenous coffee pickers (mostly from Panama) in recent decades.

A Note on Sources and Methods

In Costa Rica, I did extensive archival research, examining a wide assortment of traditional archival sources uncovered in Costa Rica's National Archives, National Library, and Judicial Archives, including census records; official reports and letters from local governmental officials to San José authorities; petitions from local residents to national political leaders; police, judicial, and electoral records; official teacher's reports to San José superiors; tax records; maps; San José newspaper articles and letters to the editor; and other records. Archival records proved helpful in understanding the official channels of power between the region and the national capital. Given, however, that one of the central aims of this work is to uncover the histories of ordinary men and women, who do not always make it into the official records, this study also integrates ethnographic methods, including participant observation, an anonymous survey, and the collection of oral histories. I collected 105 formal interviews in Tarrazú and 31 in a ten-mile area in and around Paterson, New Jersey, which I designate as "northern New Jersey" in this book.[24] Additionally, I collected 103 completed surveys from northern New Jersey. Moreover, countless informal conversations and hours of participant observation, in both Tarrazú and northern New Jersey, significantly shaped this book.

The survey I created and distributed through the restaurant staff at two Paterson restaurants, which cater primarily to Costa Rican clients, collected basic demographic information (age, gender, civil status, community of origin in Costa Rica, years living in the United States, and the respondents' town of residence within New Jersey).[25] Although the sample size for the surveys is too small to make any statistically significant conclusions, it is large enough to provide a snapshot of northern New Jersey's Costa Rican population alongside the oral histories collected in this same community.

I gathered three types of oral histories that were defined by specific research goals and types of informants. The first set of interviews consists of sixty-eight life histories (forty-four men's and twenty-four women's) of some of Tarrazú's more elderly residents. In the hopes of reflecting a multitude of

Figure I.2. San Marcos de Tarrazú's church, as viewed from the outskirts of town, 2008. (Carmen Kordick)

experiences, I intentionally sought out interviewees of both sexes, of varying socioeconomic positions, across multiple regional communities, with different levels of schooling, and of different political outlooks. The first life histories collected were of individuals whom I came across in the archival record and who appeared to have played a critical role in the region's development. Using these initial contacts, the snowball method was adopted, where initial informants were asked to suggest additional candidates who would be helpful for understanding particular historical processes, events, or experiences. Moreover, to ensure that the historical narrative reflected the experiences and memories of the larger community, and not just those whose voices were recorded in the archives, I also interviewed older residents whom I met through ordinary encounters at the local Catholic church and at municipal functions (fig. I.2). With a couple of exceptions, I collected these life histories within informants' homes; the visits oftentimes were punctuated with coffee, freshly prepared sweet breads, and tortillas that the informants generously shared.

The second group of oral histories also came from Tarrazú. Whereas in the first group the goal was the collection of life histories, this second group focused on more recent recollections and experiences that were closely tied to the processes of emigration and immigration. In total, I interviewed thirty-seven individuals (twenty-one men and sixteen women) within this second group. Every informant had either lived in the United States, had family members who currently or previously lived in the United States, had foreign laborers picking coffee on their farms, or were Ngöbe-Buglé (indigenous Panamanian) coffee pickers. As the aim with these interviews was to understand the social, economic, and political ramifications of emigration and immigration on the community, again I sought out individuals from all socioeconomic levels and sectors, including farmers, civil servants, shop owners, school teachers, school principals and counselors, physicians, parish priests, attorneys, and other professionals. I also spoke with one male seasonal agricultural laborer from Panama and a woman from Panama who has made Tarrazú her home.[26] During these conversations, I asked informants to speak about how emigration and immigration had impacted them, their families, and the region. I also requested that informants discuss how and why they believed emigration and immigration were taking place and whether they thought it was necessary for the region's economic well-being. A number of informants in this group were family members of Tarrazúceños I had met in northern New Jersey. Others I met through ordinary interactions in Tarrazú. All of these interviews took place at informants' homes.

Northern New Jersey was the site of the final group of interviews. Although the aim was to speak with and observe Tarrazúceños in the United States, this quickly proved difficult to do exclusively. This was largely due to the fact that Tarrazúceños make up a considerable portion of northern New Jersey's Costa Rican population, but they are subsumed within a larger Costa Rican community. Tarrazúceños work alongside, socialize with, and marry Tarrazúceños as well as individuals from other parts of Costa Rica, immigrants from throughout Latin America, and US Americans. Thus, it was necessary to speak with men and women from all over Costa Rica, as well as other Latinos, who had married, lived with, worked with, or socialized with individuals from Tarrazú. Thus, the conditions in New Jersey make it difficult to refer to a Tarrazúceño community in northern New Jersey; it is more accurate to refer to it as northern New Jersey's Costa Rican community.[27] As with the interviews in Tarrazú, informants of different ages, socioeconomic backgrounds, marital statuses, and from different sending communities in Tarrazú were sought out. In total, I interviewed thirty-one Costa Ricans (twenty men and eleven women, all but two of whom were Tarrazúceños) in New Jersey. Seeking principally to understand how Costa Ricans in northern New Jersey understood their position vis-à-vis the nation, I asked informants what they thought of Costa Rica, how they felt their family members and friends in both Costa Rica and in New Jersey perceived them, what their goals were in New Jersey, how they arrived, and if and/or when they planned to return to Costa Rica. I conducted many interviews in various Costa Rican restaurants in northern New Jersey; other oral histories were collected in migrants' homes.

Initially, I recorded all interviews, and in all of these cases, I asked interviewees for permission to record the conversation and made them aware that the conversation was being recorded; moreover, I told them that at any point they could ask to turn off the recorder. In all interviews, whether recorded or not, I made informants aware that they had the right to decline to answer any questions and to stop the interview at any time.[28] Additionally, I informed all interviewees that, if they wished, they could request a pseudonym in the book. The promise of anonymity proved crucial to securing the trust of informants in New Jersey, where the vast majority of informants were undocumented immigrants.[29] In addition, for a number of interviewees in Tarrazú who shared difficult memories about physical and sexual abuse, the knowledge that their names would not be associated with the recollections they shared encouraged their openness.[30]

Early in the project, I decided not to record my interviews. This decision was made after my recorder's batteries died during an interview and I removed the recorder from the table. Unexpectedly, what followed was the best interview (or portion of an interview), in terms of quality and quantity of helpful information shared. This experience encouraged me to attempt a couple of interviews without a recorder, taking notes instead. While a recorder certainly facilitated interview transcriptions each night, I observed that without a recorder present, individuals seemed more forthcoming with their opinions and their memories, as well as their jokes and anecdotes. And so, while this method could be physically exhausting in a multihour interview and required me to ask interviewees to repeat points and ideas, its success in soliciting information led to the decision not to record interviews. Without a recorder, I found it necessary to frequently read back my notes during the interview and to ask interviewees to verify that their words had been faithfully written down. At these points, interviewees were invited to edit my notes to better reflect their thoughts, memories, and opinions. Moreover, because I was cognizant that proximity to a conversation increased my memory and clarity, I made sure to transcribe all of my interview notes on the night interviews were recorded. If questions arose during the transcription process, the next day I would seek out interviewees to clarify their words and meaning.[31]

It is impossible to know precisely why the elimination of the recorder greatly improved interview quality; however, it likely reflects the region's history, which has engendered strong local distrust for outsiders. When I began this project, I was certainly an outsider to this community. In my first few weeks in the Tarrazú Valley, I sensed that many of the people I interacted with initially viewed me with suspicion (some did so for the duration of our interactions). Moreover, given recent media attention to the region's relationship to migration, which has been particularly negative, it seems likely that many informants were intimidated by the idea of being recorded.[32] Yet, as the oral histories that enrich this book show, I proceeded to secure the trust and confidence of many informants, in particular from women, both in Tarrazú and in New Jersey. Any success I had in collecting oral histories reflects my informants' readiness to share their life stories with someone who sincerely wanted to listen. Unfortunately, the reality of Costa Rican studies has been that no one has cared to ask what life was/is like for those who live outside of the Central Valley (and to a lesser extent Limón, on the Atlantic coast). Many of my informants were eager to have their ideas, their experiences, and their region noted. In fact, many told me that they knew that their experiences, and the experiences of their families, contradicted the master narrative. At first, many of my informants hesitated to share memories that they thought did not align with traditional ideas of the nation, but when they saw that the inconsistencies they shared did not spur me to question their memory, sanity, or honesty (something several of my older informants told me their children and grandchildren had done), they were quick to open up. In other words, when my informants realized I wanted to write a history of the region that took into account their voices and their experiences, rather than try to shape their words and memories to fit the contours of the official national narrative, they enthusiastically shared their stories with me.

Organization

Divided into seven chapters, which are organized in roughly chronological order, the book traces economic, political, and social transformation in the Tarrazú Valley for the length of Costa Rica's national history, from the 1820s to the present. After the first chapter, which orients readers geographically and grounds them in the early national period, the chapters each drive forward the narrative of Tarrazú's economic, political, and social development within a national and international context. Each chapter considers, as well, an aspect or two of Costa Rica's official national narrative from the vantage point of the Tarrazú Valley. As noted, the widely accepted myth that emerges from the master narrative holds that Costa Ricans are of pure European descent and their genetic composition engendered the formation of a democratic, peaceful, forward-thinking, and egalitarian—though capitalistic—republic. The history that follows interrogates this narrative by considering the role of coffee in defining local class boundaries, political and domestic violence in maintaining the social order, mass out-migration as a means of retaining familial coffee farms in the face of collapsing coffee prices on the global market, and the role of international migration in both confirming and questioning Costa Ricans' sense of themselves as a *white* nation. In the process, it highlights the contradictions between the extraordinarily durable national narrative and the actual experiences of historical and contemporary Costa Ricans.

Chapters 1 and 2 examine the settlement of the Tarrazú Valley and the way that coffee shaped economic, political, and social realities at both the local and national levels. Chapter 1 explores the region's initial settlement in 1824 within a broader national process of settlement outside the Central Valley during the nineteenth century. The nation's mid-nineteenth century coffee revolution drove up real estate prices and encouraged ambitious families to migrate to more remote areas of the republic, like the Tarrazú Valley. Coffee thus transformed the valley from an isolated familial settlement into a rural community. Chapter 2 observes changing class relationships in the Tarrazú Valley following the introduction of large-scale coffee production in the 1880s. Regional records and oral histories underscore how the inauguration of coffee capitalism led not to the development of small yeomanry, as the official national narrative would suggest, but rather to heightened class divisions and the concentration of lands in fewer hands.

Chapters 3, 4, and 5 consider the issue of violence in Costa Rican society, scrutinizing the most sacred and resilient element of Costa Rica's exceptionalist mythology. Additionally, these chapters bring into focus the causes and consequences of the nation's short-lived, though violent, 1948 Civil War. Chapter 3 examines how state violence against homemade liquor producers, whose actions reduced national liquor tax revenues, and domestic violence established and maintained local political and gendered power hierarchies. Given the social centrality and quotidian nature of violence in Tarrazú during the late nineteenth and early twentieth centuries this chapter complicates the official mythos's celebration of a peaceful national past. Chapter 4 interrogates the origins of Costa Rica's democratic political tradition, suggesting the nation's democratic system emerged not, as is commonly held, in the nineteenth century but in 1948. Events in Tarrazú, namely the violent suppression of the political opposition and blatant electoral fraud in national and local elections during the 1930s, helped ignite a successful armed rebellion in the region, which culminated in the formation of the nation's current political regime. Chapter 5 juxtaposes the violence Tarrazúceños experienced during the 1948 Civil War with the decision that same year to eliminate the nation's military to scrutinize the official narrative's celebration of Costa Rica's historically pacific society. The formulation of a master narrative, which has sought to downplay, if not ignore, historical violence, has also served to isolate the Tarrazú Valley, the epicenter of the rebellion, from a sense of national belonging in the Second Republic.

Chapters 6 and 7 employ a transnational framework to consider how large-scale emigration and immigration have impacted Tarrazúceños sense of national belonging. In addition to highlighting the fact that Costa Ricans immigrate to the United States to take advantage of economic opportunities, like their isthmian neighbors, these chapters examine how international migration has shaped racial identities at the local level and at once affirmed and questioned the image of Costa Rica as a *white* republic. Chapter 6 focuses on the large-scale out-migration of Tarrazúceño workers to the United States and the influx of indigenous Panamanian laborers into the region. This chapter considers how earnings made abroad have provided locals with the capital to purchase farms, thereby allowing many to identify with the national narrative as yeoman coffee farmers for the first time. Moreover, this chapter demonstrates how the nation's mythology of whiteness has been confirmed for Tarrazúceños through the annual arrival of foreign indigenous laborers whose physical appearance, culture, and poverty have served to affirm locals' sense of themselves as white, civilized, members of the nation-state. Chapter 7 looks at Tarrazúceños in New Jersey. In particular, this chapter scrutinizes how Costa Rica's exceptionalist mythology has made the Costa Rican government and its functionaries reluctant to acknowledge the needs of undocumented Costa Rican workers in the United States. The chapter particularly considers how the experience of living in the United States has shaped the way that Costa Rican migrants understand themselves and their nation racially. The book closes with a brief conclusion that delves into the basis for Costa Rica's exceptionalist mythology and also suggests areas for further study.

1
Tarrazú's Founding and Settlement

In 1825, just four years after Costa Rica gained independence from Spain, José Miguel Cascante requested a land grant from government authorities in San José, the capital of the republic.[1] Cascante explained to officials how, the year before, he and his family had left the rural Central Valley community of Escazú for an unpopulated mountain valley to the south of the capital in the Talamanca Mountain Range. The site was located at "the mouth of Dota Mountain."[2] The family's move to "Dota" would have required a four- to seven-day journey, depending on the condition of the oxcart road.[3] Likely, the family walked the entire length of the journey, herding the cattle and prodding the oxen that pulled their belongings in oxcarts up the steep mountain slopes. If the few papers that document the Cascante family in this remote homestead are correct, the family arrived at present-day San Marcos de Tarrazú during the dry season, sometime between January and May, of 1824.[4]

This chapter examines the colonization of Tarrazú through the Cascante family's move to and settlement of the region in the 1820s. The Cascante family's migration to Tarrazú is considered as part of a larger process of national settlement beyond the nation's more populated centers, which began just after Costa Rica was granted independence from Spain on September 15, 1821. State legislation promoted colonization, road construction, and settlement in places such as Tarrazú by families like the Cascantes. However, the colonization of Tarrazú and other regions of the country increased considerably in the mid-nineteenth century following the introduction of coffee production in the Central Valley.[5] Coffee ushered in dramatic changes for the Central Valley's economy and class relations, and it deeply impacted national identity formation.[6] Moving beyond the Central Valley, which has received scholarly attention, this chapter explains the cultural, social, and economic pull that Tarrazú farmers likely felt to start growing coffee locally. In addition, the chapter explores the pivotal role this community of origin had on settlement patterns in the region and on local identity formation. The chapter concludes with an examination of the region's infrastructure and population in the final decade of the nineteenth century, when coffee was introduced.

Homesteading on a Trade Route

The Cascante family built their home near the Paquita River on a small mesa, which today is the site of San Marcos de Tarrazú's soccer field. Homesteading near the river facilitated the family's ability to irrigate their fields and provide their livestock with water. Additionally, living alongside the river lightened the load of the women who would have carried large ceramic jugs of water from the river to their homes for cooking and also would have washed the family's laundry at the riverbed.[7] Until the 1850s, the Cascante family lived a rather isolated life in Tarrazú as subsistence farmers.[8] In the second half of the nineteenth century, however, the area's landscape and economy would be completely transformed by coffee. By 1900, the region's "Tarrazú" coffee beans would begin earning international recognition for their rich cacao flavor and aroma. While coffee would come to dominate Tarrazú's economy and society, when the Cascante family first arrived nearly two centuries ago, there were no homes, no coffee plants, just a dense forest with a rough oxcart road that cut a narrow line though the imposing wilderness.

This thoroughfare was a critical component of the Cascante family's move, providing the family with a means of arriving at their new home and affording them a source of income. Traders and merchants had traveled this same oxcart road since the colonial period to transport goods between Costa Rica and neighboring New Granada (the future Republic of Colombia). Following the Cascante family's arrival, travelers between these two nations likely would have stopped at the Cascante home for news on road conditions and perhaps even stayed with the family, paying for meals and a bed for the night. The Cascante family's move to present-day San Marcos de Tarrazú and their use of the trade road as a means of securing familial income put the family in direct alignment with the political visions of Costa Rica's leaders in the 1820s. In fact, the same year that the Cascantes abandoned Escazú for Tarrazú, 1824, the government issued Decree XXIV, which called for the collection of funds to pay for road improvements. This decree established a protocol by which squatters on state-owned lands could purchase the lands they were cultivating from the state. The monies from these sales were designated for road improvements.[9] Decree XXIV was the first of numerous decrees and laws that the Costa Rican state established in the nineteenth and early twentieth centuries to encourage infrastructure development and the farming of state-owned lands beyond the nation's populated centers.[10]

Cascante's land request preceded the passage of Decree XXIV. The contents of his letter, however, demonstrate that he was clearly aware of the government's interests in encouraging trade, improving roads, and settling uncultivated lands. He began his appeal for a land grant by pointing out that the nation would receive a "large benefit . . . [from] the traffic and commerce" that would result from improving "the road in . . . the Mountain of Dota which carries traders to Colombia." Cascante then explained that during his year living in "Dota" he had been "moved . . . by the great difficulties he ha[d] seen traders suffer" and from watching "many animals perish" because of the poor conditions of the mountainous trade route that passed by his home. To improve travelers' safety, Cascante and his sons began "the building and opening of a good road" that would link the community of Frailes to his home on the Paquita River's bank. At the time of his letter, Cascante claimed the work had "advanced" with "more than half of said road" being completed. Cascante then requested that the state compensate him for his "costs," which he estimated at "one hundred pesos . . . [for] peons' [salaries and] his work." He added that, if "in their consideration[,] these small services" merited more than just the payment of costs, he would like "a piece of National soil with personal rights of use."[11]

Cascante's request for remuneration was bold, especially since no one had charged him with improving the road. Nevertheless, his request made good political sense at the time. The new republic's leaders were interested in populating their country and encouraging trade, so Cascante's request that the state grant him the lands he had homesteaded because of the improvements he was making to the trade road fit well with early republican leaders' goals.

Before 1821, however, Cascante had few options for legalizing his land claim, since Spanish colonial laws sought to keep the nation's population concentrated within the Central Valley to facilitate tax collection and ensure easy access to cheap labor.[12] Moreover, for the length of colonial rule, the Spanish crown owned all uncultivated lands and resisted urban or rural expansion beyond the confines of the Central Valley.[13] Strict colonial management of lands meant that a majority of Costa Ricans during the colonial period had no lands and were either *peones* employed by Spanish ranchers or farmed communal lands. The colonial elites—Spaniards and their direct descendants—owned most of the cultivated lands and were dedicated primarily to cattle ranching and tobacco production.[14]

Like most of colonial Latin America, Costa Rica's class divisions were highly racialized, with land and power concentrated in the hands of wealthy Spaniards and their descendants (the creoles), with mulattos, mestizos, and poor creoles making up the laboring and landless classes.[15] No extant records reveal whether Cascante was creole, mulatto, or mestizo, or what types of economic activities he dedicated himself to in Escazú before moving his wife, Casilda Cascante, and an unspecified number of children to Tarrazú in 1824.[16] Despite the lack of abundant documentation, a number of inferences can be drawn. First, his decision to abandon the Central Valley suggests that he did not have large landholdings or much political power in the Central Valley. Cascante, however, was also unlikely to have been a landless peasant laborer, since he had the capital to undertake a large move with his family and his request for lands noted that he owned several head of cattle, which required considerable access to capital.[17] Additionally, the fact that he was a literate man, evidenced in his writing and signing of his land request, indicates that he received some level of education, which—in the days before public education—implies he came from a family of some means.[18] Lastly, his ability to dedicate one hundred pesos of labor, materials, and planning to construct an improved road suggests access to capital. So, it is likely that Cascante owned some land, where he raised cattle and basic foodstuffs, but not sufficient land to provide for the economic security of all of his children. It seems likely, then, that the Cascante family left the Central Valley not out of extreme necessity but out of a desire to improve their circumstances.

The Cascante family's economic and territorial ambitions coincided well with the young Costa Rican state's interests; however, shared goals were not sufficient to secure the Cascante family's land request. Indeed, Cascante's 1825 petition for land was denied. No documents have survived that explain why the Costa Rican state chose to deny his request, but the Cascante family does not appear to have been disheartened by this decision. In fact, it seems they remained on their homestead near the Paquita River, raising cattle and planting basic foodstuffs, namely beans, corn, and sugarcane.[19] Then in 1846, twenty-one years later, Cascante would make a second attempt, this time successfully, to legalize his family's farmstead under Decree XXVI, which was signed into law in 1840 and called for anyone who held and improved a property for five years to be given legal title over those lands.[20] Clearly the cattle, crops, and fine woods the Cascante family sold in the capital allowed them to amass a considerable fortune, since Cascante paid an impressive 442 pesos and half a real to the Costa Rican state to legalize his holdings.[21]

By the time of this second request in 1846, Cascante was an old man. His attorney noted that this "farmer and cattle breeder" was "older than seventy years" at the time.[22] Cascante and likely his wife, Casilda, returned to the "City" of San José and were no longer living in Tarrazú; nevertheless, the family farmstead had not been abandoned. Cascante noted that in Parrita, as he was now calling present-day San Marcos de Tarrazú, he held "some forty" head of cattle and had planted plantains and other crops including sugarcane.[23] It is uncertain who was caring for the cattle and crops; it is probable that it was his sons, Juan María and Juan de Jesús, who would eventually gain ownership of Cascante's 855 hectares land claim.

Coffee and Its Impact on National Identity and Class Relations in the Central Valley

In the interim between Cascante's two land claim requests, Costa Rica underwent dramatic changes. Politically, it had gained its second independence, this time not from Spanish colonial rule but from the failed Federal Republic of Central America in 1838.[24] However, perhaps the most important change in the everyday lives of the people came with the introduction of coffee as an export crop in the early 1830s.[25] In 1832, Costa Rica's first shipment of coffee arrived in Chile. This first shipment amounted to twenty-three thousand kilograms, and this was only the beginning.[26] By the end of the 1840s, Costa Rica was exporting a million kilograms annually, four million per year in the 1850s, eleven million a year in the 1870s, and an impressive twenty million kilograms annually on the eve of the twentieth century.[27]

Coffee export profits dramatically transformed this colonial backwater's economy, society, and culture. As coffee's profitability became clear, elites began abandoning cattle ranching and tobacco in favor of coffee.[28] The introduction of coffee attracted European, namely British, investors who married into some of Costa Rica's most elite families in the middle of the nineteenth century.[29] These foreigners provided farmers with cash and merchandise advances on future coffee crops, thus funding the transition to a coffee monoculture in the Central Valley.[30] Many European immigrants started planting their own coffee and became involved in the processing and export of this crop.[31] Increased contact with Europeans sparked a desire among Central Valley elites to construct an identity that mirrored their business alliances and consumption tastes and by denying their historic and social roots as a mixed-raced population.[32]

Coffee profits dramatically amplified existing class differentiations within Costa Rican society. Moreover, with the introduction of coffee came the construction of new spaces and ideas of leisure, which greatly reduced mixed-class interactions. In fact, it has been well documented that during the second half of the nineteenth century, mixed socioeconomic leisure spaces ceased to be the norm in the Central Valley. Coffee export duties funded infrastructure projects to foster trade and provide spaces worthy of the nation's new European tastes. In fact, taxes on coffee exports paid for the construction of railroad lines, roads, schools, and eventually theaters. Central America's first theater, the Teatro Mora, opened its doors in 1850. The theater was named after Costa Rica's then president Juan Rafael Mora Porras and encapsulated his commitment as a liberal to order, progress, and modernization. The theater, built in a neoclassical style replete with Greek columns, provided San José's elites with their first refined alternative to more traditional nocturnal activities: public cockfights and gambling. The impact of this theater on mixed-class socializing was evident in the 1860s, when foreign travelers noted that San José politicians and other elites were no longer attending cockfights.[33] After 1888, when an earthquake destroyed the Teatro Mora, a tax on coffee exports would help fund the construction of its replacement. The National Theater—a perfect copy, in miniature, of the Paris Opera House—is to this day Costa Rica's most celebrated cultural symbol and a clear reflection of the coffee-producing elites' desire to transform San José into a modern and European city.[34] Personal coffee wealth also increased socioeconomic divisions within the Central Valley. In point of fact, the coffee profits of the late nineteenth and early twentieth centuries funded the construction of large Victorian and Art Deco mansions in San José's celebrated Barrio Amón, where the nation's wealthiest coffee barons built their homes.[35]

Coffee exacerbated socioeconomic divisions within Central Valley society, providing elites with the capital necessary to construct spaces that helped better define class divisions. In general, pre-coffee-era elites retained their position of economic and political dominance, becoming the first to convert their landholdings to coffee farms.[36] Additionally, wealthy mercantile families followed their neighbors' crop selection shift, exporting coffee instead of brazilwood, cacao, tobacco, and sugar to European ports.[37] During the nineteenth century, coffee production became the measure of power in the Central Valley, and the wealthy cafetalero, or large-scale coffee farmer, who was also frequently involved in processing and exporting coffee, came to define Costa Rica's national identity.

While coffee transformed elite society and culture, it also provided the nation's lower classes with considerable economic opportunities. As historian Lowell Gudmundson has effectively argued, while coffee augmented socioeconomic divisions, it also created a rural middle class: the petty capitalist smallholder.[38] As nineteenth-century farmers moved into more remote parts of the Central Valley to grow coffee, the nation's population grew, reflecting the increased prosperity coffee brought to many smallholders.[39] Importantly, as coffee profits improved individual peasant family's socioeconomic expectations, migration into more remote regions of the republic was motivated by a desire to avoid downward mobility through increased coffee production. Most migrants sought new lands not to escape the coffee revolution but to participate within it as small-scale producers.[40]

Migration and Infrastructure Development in Tarrazú, 1850–1905

Coffee may have created a rural middle class that expanded the nation's coffee frontier, but not all of those who chose to leave the Central Valley in the second half of the nineteenth century went to areas where coffee production was possible, at least not initially. For instance, ten land grant requests in Tarrazú were made between 1858 and 1864.[41] By the time these settlers arrived, coffee was already dramatically changing Costa Rica's society and economy. It is difficult to know precisely what motivated these migrants to become the Cascantes' neighbors but a number of assumptions can be made. First, the desire to grow coffee was not the driving factor, since the lack of a processing plant in the area at the time made it infeasible to grow coffee for export. Coffee is a delicate crop and must be processed within forty-eight hours of being picked or the fruit will begin fermentation, destroying the bean's flavor. Hence, before a commercial processor was built in Tarrazú, it was impossible to grow coffee for export.[42]

The Cascante family's first neighbor, Manuel Piedra, who arrived in 1858 and made a successful land claim on the other side of the Paquita River, appears to have been a land speculator.[43] It seems Piedra remained for just the time necessary to clear lands, make a land claim, and sell for a profit in 1860. Piedra's buyers were the impressively extensive Zúñiga family from Desamparados, which consisted of Ramón Zúñiga Barahona and his fourteen adult children, from two marriages, and their eleven spouses.[44] With such a large family, Piedra's holdings in Desamparados were not sufficient for all of Zúñiga Barahona's offspring and their spouses, who made eight land claims in Tarrazú over the next several years. The Zúñiga clan likely left Desamparados, then a rural community just outside of the city of San José, for a remote area where the whole family could live in close proximity and support themselves.[45] Juan Chanto and his father Marcos Chanto Méndez, local historians of San Marcos de Tarrazú, both performed in-depth investigations into the origins of Tarrazú's families. In their mid-twentieth-century works, they assert that the extended Zúñiga family provided the population base of contemporary Tarrazú society as well as the region's most common last names: Barboza, Godínez, Mora, Navarro, Parra, Ureña, Valverde, and Zúñiga.[46]

Between 1865 and 1894, an additional 109 families would join the extended Zúñiga and Cascante families in Tarrazú. Most of these families would come from Desamparados, Guadalupe, and Alajuelita, all of which were sizable communities in San José provinces where the coffee revolution was in full swing and where residents had easy access to the capital city and its marketplaces. Most of these families would have selected uncultivated sections of the remaining rain forest as their homesteading site, where they would have planted corn, sugar cane, and beans for both subsistence and for sale in San José's markets.[47] These migrants would have traveled on the same trade route that José Miguel Cascante and his family followed decades earlier to make the region's first land claim.

The road itself, over time, was greatly improved and widened. Aside from Cascante's early improvements, the Costa Rican state provided Francisco Castro Valverde with a contract in 1874 to expand the road's width, converting the distance between Desamparados and San Marcos de Tarrazú into a "highway," which made the passage of oxcarts considerably easier than on the original rough trail. This project was completed in 1881, earning Castro Valverde an impressive 4,900 pesos worth of lands. It centered around what would first become the town of San Pablo de Tarrazú, but is today known as San Pablo de León Cortés.[48] This same route was declared a national highway in 1905, a reflection of the importance of the trade from this region to the national economy.[49] By this date, Tarrazú had become a major source of basic foodstuffs and timber for the Central Valley.[50] As coffee production provided farmers with much greater profits than other crops, farmers in the Central Valley gradually ceased growing basic foodstuffs in favor of coffee. Thus, as the Central Valley became increasingly rural—with coffee covering the hills, grown in Central Valley gardens, and in fields interspersed among homes even in the capital of San José—it became ever more dependent on rural regions outside the Central Valley, such as Tarrazú, for grains, livestock, and lumber.[51]

The improved Desamparados–San Marcos de Tarrazú highway likely encouraged migration into Tarrazú during the second half of the nineteenth century, which would reach its highpoint in the decade between 1895 and 1904, when 181 land claims were made in Tarrazú. The peak year was 1896, when 130 families petitioned the Costa Rican state for lands in the region. In fact, over 41 percent (41.53 percent) of all land claims made in the history of the region were made in this single year, according to historian Javier Agüero García's statistical analysis of land grant requests in Tarrazú.[52] Agüero maintains that the region's best lands were occupied by the beginning of the twentieth century; he effectively supports this claim with the fact that a mere twelve land grant requests were made in the next decade. Moreover, beginning in the 1920s, the region began to lose population as residents sought new opportunities in the southern valley of El General, in the present-day canton of Pérez Zeledón.[53]

All the migrants who arrived in the second half of the nineteenth century, whether they came from Desamparados, Guadalupe, or Alajuelita, were involved in similar economic activities, namely the felling of forests, the milling of wood, the planting of basic food crops, and the transportation of wood and foodstuffs to San José markets. These shared economic activities, however, did not immediately result in a shared sense of community. In fact, rivalries based on migrants' community of origin arose early on. The fiercest divisions occurred between individuals from Desamparados and Guadalupe, who together provided the region with most of its new population.

On January 20, 1895, one of San José's many short-lived daily newspapers, *El Diarito*, published a letter signed by "some Guadalupanos" from San Marcos de Tarrazú.[54] The letter accused Tarrazú's mayor, Antonio N. García, of "on more than one occasion . . . insulting" the town's residents from Guadalupe. García was accused of calling the Guadalupanos "vagabonds" who came to Tarrazú "because [they] do not fit" in Guadalupe. The writers wished to set the record straight, explaining "we have not come to populate these woods like [the] Mayor maliciously states, but in search of hard work which characterizes our natal community." Beyond defending the character of their natal town and their noble intentions, the writers sought to question the integrity of their detractor, describing García as "a man worse than a whore" and alluding to his being a drunkard, claiming that he is a "faithful follower of the God Bacchus."[55]

Although the letter writers do not specify from where García originated, it is likely he came from Desamparados, since Guadalupe and Desamparados provided Tarrazú with most of its original settlers.[56] Even if García had come from another section of San José, it is evident that the strength of this "Guadalupano" identity would hinder the possibility of forming a singular Tarrazú identity. Moreover, these divisions had an impact on the settlement pattern of the region, namely with the formation of the community of Guadalupe de Tarrazú, which is located just across the Paquita River from San Marcos de Tarrazú and, as the name indicates, was first populated by migrants from Guadalupe.[57]

Amid the political infighting between different settlers in the second half of the nineteenth century, Tarrazú's population increased, and the community's political and ecclesiastical position within the nation also grew. San Marcos had the largest population in the region, and as the first settlement in the area, it was the logical selection to be Tarrazú's municipal center in 1890. San Marcos was also the location for the region's first school, which began providing boys and girls with lessons in 1874, and the site of the region's first telegraph office, inaugurated in 1892. Also, in 1882, when government officials appointed Tarrazú's first *jefe político*, the highest government post in the region as this officeholder would have the power and functions of a regional mayor and justice of the peace, his offices would be in San Marcos.[58] When Tarrazú became the fifth canton of San José province in 1868, splitting from the canton of Desamparados, San Marcos was the most important population in the region. This is evident in the fact that, when the priests Raimundo Mora and Matías Zavaleta of Desamparados arrived in 1867 to provide the residents of Tarrazú with Lenten services, they selected San Marcos as the site for the region's first church (fig. 1.1). According to popular memory, the former cleric had spent considerable time as the priest in the town of San Marcos, Guatemala, and he decided to christen José Miguel Cascante's Parrita "San Marcos," the name it holds today.[59]

In 1867, two of Cascante's sons, Juan de Jesús and Juan María Cascante, inherited their parents' considerable land grant in the center of San Marcos.[60] The two brothers demonstrated their interest in local community development. In fact, in 1869, Juan de Jesús contributed a large plot of land in the center of San Marcos for the construction of the town's first church, and Juan María donated a bell for the new church. The Cascante family, however, was not the only family involved in the construction of San Marcos's first church; master craftsman Juan Umaña carved the wooden altar, confessionary, and pulpit. Umaña and his wife, Juana Jiménez, and their young family purchased land near the church from the Cascante brothers. As migration increased during the nineteenth century, the Cascante brothers would sell off much of the land they held in the center of San Marcos to families such as the Umaña Jiménez family.[61]

As San Marcos's population grew, other rural communities quickly developed in the region, namely Santa María, San Pablo, and San Lorenzo. José María Ureña, one of Ramón Zúñiga Barahona's sons-in-law, founded Santa María in 1863 after coming across the neighboring valley during a hunting trip.[62] Other families also sought to expand their opportunities by seeking out new lands a short distance from San Marcos's center; indeed the communities of San Pablo, to the northwest, and San Lorenzo, to the west of San Marcos, were both founded by colonists in the second half of the nineteenth century.[63] Once forests were cleared, crops planted, and lands claimed in these locations, subsequent waves of migrants would push the region's population farther and farther from San Marcos's center. As the canton's population grew and its infrastructure continued to develop, San

Figure 1.1. San Marcos de Tarrazú's church under construction, early twentieth century. (Courtesy of Juan Mora)

Marcos remained the population, economic, and political center of the region. Still, schools, churches, and roads linking the region's various communities together quickly developed in the towns nearest to San Marcos, namely Santa María, San Pablo, and San Lorenzo. In fact, by 1891, Santa María and San Pablo could both boast that their communities had elementary schools, which would in time make them the ideal municipal centers of the cantons of Dota and León Cortés, which would form out of Tarrazú through San José directives.[64]

In the final decades of the nineteenth century, Tarrazú not only experienced population growth and infrastructure development, it also saw the creation of new industries. In 1905, the first agricultural census of the canton of Tarrazú noted the presence of seven hydraulic sawmills, three cheese producers, two dairies, and thirty-nine sugar mills, which produced a crude sugar product, *tapa dulce*.[65] The quantity of sugar mills reflects the level of production in the region dedicated to sugarcane; in fact, a considerable 153 *manzanas*, or 267.75 acres, in Tarrazú were planted in cane in 1905.[66] The presence of different industries reveals that, aside from producing basic foodstuffs, such as corn for sale in San José, the population of Tarrazú was interested in sending processed products to market. This supports Gudmundson's assertion that Costa Rica's nineteenth-century migrants were not escaping San José in the hopes of leaving capitalism behind. Rather, migrants moved beyond the nation's populated center to expand the production radius and amass sufficient territory to participate as independent producers in the market economy.[67] Moreover, the agricultural census of 1905 reveals that, by this time, numerous residents in Tarrazú had sufficient capital to undertake costly processing ventures at the local level.

Initiating Tarrazú's Coffee Revolution

In a nation where coffee heralded considerable social, cultural, and economic change, it is unsurprising that Tarrazú's wealthiest citizens sought to create a local coffee niche once they had enough capital to purchase and transport the costly materials needed to build a local processing plant and drying patio.[68] The precise date that coffee was introduced to the region is unknown; however, one can safely assume that a significant quantity of coffee was planted locally during the 1890s. The 1905 agricultural census makes note of the existence of 222 manzanas, or approximately 388.5 acres, in the region growing coffee.[69] While coffee certainly was the dominant commercial crop, even surpassing the quantity of acres dedicated to sugarcane with its developed infrastructure, the region's coffee revolution was in its initial stages. In fact, the census shows that over 90 percent of the region's coffee in 1905 had been planted in the previous ten years.[70]

The region's earliest investors in coffee, reportedly, were master craftsman Juan Umaña's wife, Juana Jiménez, and their son, Julio Umaña Jiménez. This mother and son processed coffee in a primitive coffee roaster in their home in downtown San Marcos. According to popular memory, this small family processor was employed in providing coffee for local consumption; the earliest coffee grown in the region was not intended for export.[71] This, however, would change when Ramón Blanco Araya constructed a hydraulic-powered coffee processor, or *beneficio*, in San Pablo in 1902.[72] Blanco would soon be joined by Macario Arias Campos of Desamparados, who would invest in his own hydraulic-powered beneficio, in San Marcos. The precise dates when Umaña, Blanco, and Arias began processing coffee are unclear from the written record; however, it is likely that Blanco and Arias were the two beneficios noted in the 1905 census, since the Umaña Jiménez beneficio was likely too small to be taxed.[73] By 1907, Arias and Blanco were joined by Paulino Ardón Cáceres, who built a hydraulic coffee mill in El Rodeo of San Marcos, and by Pedro Rivera Araya, who started milling coffee with hydraulic power in San Marcos. With four beneficios, local coffee farmers had numerous options for securing credit and selling their crops.[74] It is noteworthy, however, that Santa María, one of the region's largest communities, did not have a beneficio, which meant that coffee farmers from this town had to transport their harvests to San Marcos, El Rodeo, or San Pablo for processing.

With only four processing plants and a mere 388.5 acres of coffee in production, Tarrazú was far from a major player in Costa Rica's massive coffee export economy. However, by 1900, Costa Rica was exporting over twenty million kilograms of its "golden bean."[75] Tarrazú's entrance into the coffee economy ushered in dramatic cultural and economic changes at the local level. In a nation where being a coffee farmer, or cafetalero, was becoming increasingly synonymous with ideas of progress, modernity, and wealth, to be a coffee farmer brought considerable prestige. In fact, as the independent cafetalero emerged as a national icon, his antithesis, the subsistence farmer, or maicero, became tantamount to the nation's uncultured and impoverished past. While the production of basic foodstuffs, including corn, beans, and sugarcane, was the basis of Tarrazú's rural economy and provided the capital to begin coffee processing, the farmers involved in these activities did not wish to remain corn farmers, or maiceros, forever. Thus, the desire to transition into coffee was motivated not only by the handsome profits that coffee sales brought but also by the desire to participate in and benefit from Costa Rica's modernization project.

Conclusion

Between 1824 and 1907, Tarrazú was witness to a series of dramatic changes in terms of population growth, infrastructure development, and economic activity. These shifts mirrored transformations on the national stage, namely in the Central Valley. Although for most of this period Tarrazú was more isolated from, than integrated with, the nation's capital, considerable migration into the region in the second half of the nineteenth century ensured that the region's residents were well aware of the symbolic, economic, and political importance coffee had come to hold in San José. This awareness did not automatically translate into coffee production, since the infrastructure simply was not available at the local level. For most of the nineteenth century, Tarrazú was little more than an isolated stop on a commercial road linking Costa Rica to its southern neighbor, Colombia. For the Cascante family, the region's first settlers, life in present-day San Marcos de Tarrazú meant extreme isolation for over two decades, with their nearest neighbors a two-day oxcart trip away. Living so far from the center, however, allowed for the Cascante family to claim and develop a considerable tract of land in what would become one of the nation's most celebrated coffee producing regions.

The Cascante family made San Marcos its home just under a decade before coffee production in far-off San José transformed Costa Rica's economy, society, and culture. So far from San José, the isolated Cascante family likely did not grasp during the nineteenth century the weight and importance that coffee production had come to hold in the Central Valley. The region's later migrants, however, were all too aware that coffee production and, more importantly, processing could create sizable fortunes. So, while the Cascante family certainly was in a position to dominate the local move to coffee production, as Tarrazú's primary landholders, they made no move to establish themselves as cafetaleros. Almost certainly, the Cascante family did not recognize the economic potential of coffee production in Tarrazú's high mountain valleys until it was too late. Indeed, the Cascante family's decision to not jump on the coffee bandwagon early on would mark the end of the Cascante family as local power holders in the region.

2

Coffee, Downward Mobility, and Political Power in Tarrazú

In 1946, one of the University of Costa Rica's first graduates, Gabriela Monge Álvarado described San Marcos de Tarrazú as a community whose resident's lives revolved around the production of a single crop: coffee.[1] In her undergraduate thesis about this small rural town, Monge asserts that Tarrazúceños "tend to plant . . . [coffee] to the extent possible . . . since this crop provides admirable monetary compensation." Economics may have driven Tarrazúceños to grow coffee, but she portrays their harvest of this crop as a cooperative and festive event: "Young and old go to the coffee fields from . . . [four] . . . in the morning until six in the evening. . . . The coffee is [then] transported to . . . the processing mills by oxcarts, . . . [as] the [farmers] return tired and satisfied to their homes . . . smell[ing] of the earth." Adding to her idyllic depiction of these farmers, she describes the region's humble farmers as men of an earlier era who had "yet to be influenced by the modern age."[2]

While Monge's description of Tarrazú families picking and loading coffee into oxcarts is bucolically romantic, she also reveals the clear socioeconomic divisions within the region's coffee-centered economy. She contrasts the wholesome portrayal of family labor with a description of Tobías Umaña Jiménez, who at the time was Tarrazú's largest coffee producer, largest landholder, and sole beneficio owner. She portrays Umaña not as a farmer but rather as an "industrialist," whom she critiques for exploiting "his harvesters" by not only paying them low wages but paying them "with scrip."[3] Her depiction of him as an "industrialist" squarely places him within the modern era and in opposition to the region's humble small-scale coffee farmers and landless farmhands, who had yet to "enter . . . the modern age." This contrast between him and his neighbors means that when she describes how his peons "recognize the harm . . . [he] does them" but "do not dare protest," she accuses him of ruthlessly preying on his poor neighbors with modern exploitation methods that they are unprepared to resist.[4] At the root of her unrelenting criticism is a class argument, based on the idea that Umaña, as the proprietor of the local coffee mill and as the region's largest landowner, exploits the region's landless laborers as well as smaller coffee farm owners.

Monge's portrait of Tarrazú's socioeconomic relations during the first half of the twentieth century at once shatters and affirms traditional representations of Costa Rica as Central America's egalitarian republic.[5] Central American historians have regularly celebrated the persistence of smallholding coffee farmers following Costa Rica's transition to a coffee-centered economy in the mid-nineteenth century. It is certainly easy to make comparisons to nearby Nicaragua, El Salvador, and Guatemala, where the transition to coffee sooner or later led to elites establishing a near monopoly over landownership. This, coupled with the passage and enforcement of repressive labor and vagrancy laws, served to create a bifurcated society. To be sure, for most of Central America the transition to coffee saw the creation of a powerful coffee oligarchy that exercised considerable economic and political power due in large part to their near monopoly over landholdings.[6]

In contrast, in Costa Rica, coffee production spread through the persistence of small-scale landholders who lived and worked alongside a large number of landless laborers, primarily employed by large-scale landholders, whose lives had much in common with their counterparts in other Central American nations, including Nicaragua, Guatemala, and El Salvador. Therefore, the perseverance of Costa Rica's much-celebrated small-scale coffee farming class should not be read as evidence that rural Costa Rica was an agricultural utopia free of class tensions. Instead, Costa Rican elites invested heavily in setting up large milling and processing facilities to prepare the coffee beans raised by other farmers for export. Processors were also frequently exporters and thus tended to bring in the highest profits within the nation's coffee-centered export economy. For much of the first half of the twentieth century, continual strife existed over the price the coffee-processing sector paid coffee producers for their crops.[7]

A considerable body of literature centers on how in Nicaragua, Guatemala, and El Salvador, under liberal regimes, most rural residents found themselves trapped in unfree labor relationships.[8] To date, however, little work has been done to understand labor and class relationships beyond Costa Rica's populated Central Valley. This chapter considers the role that capital and debt played in creating exploitative socioeconomic relations after coffee's introduction to the Tarrazú Valley. This region's transition to coffee production during the first half of the twentieth century paralleled the socioeconomic rise of this region's most powerful resident: Tobías Umaña Jiménez.

In the following pages, I examine Tarrazú's transition to coffee production. In particular, I explain how, between 1900 and 1948, Umaña came to be Tarrazú's largest landholder, sole coffee processor, and the owner of several local businesses. While my focus is on Umaña, I do not piece together a biography of him so much as provide a critical examination of local, national, and international events that allowed this man to dominate the region's economy, society, and culture for over fifty years. Critical global events, namely the Great Depression and World War II, played essential roles in his rise to economic power. While he (and other Tarrazú elites) accumulated landholdings, businesses, and economic positions, many in the region saw their holdings decrease dramatically. On the national level, growing tensions between coffee mill owners—such as Umaña—and independent farmers throughout the countryside and high unemployment in the Central Valley forced the state to reconsider its role in the economy. This chapter examines how these conflicts impacted class relations and laborers in Tarrazú.

Coffee and Socioeconomic Relations in Tarrazú

Coffee production, initiated in the late nineteenth century, created a new socioeconomic order in Tarrazú. While Tarrazúceños had a steady income before coffee, it paled dramatically in comparison to what coffee farmers in the nation's Central Valley were earning.[9] As discussed in detail in chapter 1, the high prices Central Valley coffee producers received for their annual crop made many Tarrazúceños seek to plant coffee in the hopes of improving their families' socioeconomic position. Although local farmers welcomed the introduction of coffee to their region, profitable coffee production in Tarrazú could not begin until extensive infrastructure development was realized. The primary obstacle to local farmers' ability to transition to coffee before 1890 was the lack of a local coffee mill, where the coffee could be washed, dried, and packed into burlap sacks ready for export. The need for a local beneficio cannot be overstated, given the delicacy of the coffee fruit.[10] While today the Central Valley is only a two-hour drive on the Inter-American Highway from Tarrazú, as late as the 1940s the trip between San José and San Marcos de Tarrazú could take an oxcart driver four days. The region's first hydraulic-powered beneficios began functioning between 1902 and 1907.

Aside from beneficios, access to capital was essential to make the transition to coffee production. Coffee farmers required loans to purchase coffee seedlings. More importantly, with just a single annual harvest (unlike with other traditional crops, which provided multiple harvests), monocultural coffee farmers needed credit throughout the year to purchase food, fabrics, medications, and other goods that they did not produce at home. In Tarrazú, as in the rest of Costa Rica, beneficio owners, or *beneficiadores*, provided loans throughout the year to farmers who agreed to sell their harvest to them.[11] Beneficiadores were also frequently exporters who sold processed coffee beans to markets in Europe and the United States. So, while Costa Rican farmers secured higher profits growing coffee than they could producing any other crop, it was the exporters, processors, and moneylenders, or beneficiadores, such as Umaña, who made the most tangible profits in Costa Rica's coffee economy.[12]

Perhaps the best way to measure the local social class structure of this period is through Umaña's accounting books. Fortunately, one of these ledgers has survived. The book dates back to 1948, when his bookkeeper recorded a list of seventy-six coffee producers and the advances given to them for the coffee harvest.[13] In Tarrazú, as in most of rural Costa Rica, as his records reflect, there were four basic socioeconomic groups: beneficiadores, independent coffee producers who employed wage laborers, independent coffee producers who occasionally labored for other producers or beneficiadores, and landless wage laborers. In total, he would extend ₡23,979.20 in advances that year, with the largest advance being that granted to Jeremías Ureña Ch. for a hefty ₡4,077.25.[14] Umaña made five advances for ₡1,000 or more, putting into perspective his considerable economic position in the region. Clearly, the farmers who received advances of over ₡1,000 were among the largest landholders in the region and likely required a considerable number of wage laborers to help run their coffee farms. On the other end of the spectrum, fourteen producers—such as Marcos Camacho A., who secured an advance for just ₡1.35—were given advances of fewer than ₡10. Another fourteen producers were extended advances of between ₡10 and ₡49. In other words, twenty-eight producers were extended fewer than ₡49 in advances for 1948. Given the size of the loans, these twenty-eight men likely owned very small coffee farms and would have almost certainly had to seek wage labor on a regular basis to make ends meet. But it was Tarrazú's landless peons, many of whom were employed by Umaña, who most certainly had the most precarious position in the region. Unfortunately, this single accounting book does not include a list of his peons or their wages.

Between these two economic poles, however, there existed medium-scale producers, whose coffee production was their family's main form of sustenance but who perhaps did wage labor during the coffee harvest to supplement their incomes. Indeed, eighteen coffee producers, or 24 percent of all producers who were given an advance in 1948, were granted between ₡100 and ₡500. Moreover, sixteen producers received advances in the ₡501 to ₡999 range. In sum, using Umaña's recorded loans to coffee farmers in 1948, we can extrapolate that roughly 41.8 percent of the region's farmers were smallholders, who owned their own coffee plots but were dependent on wealthier neighbors for salaried work to supplement their family income. About half (50.7 percent) of the area's farmers were members of the rural middle class, meaning that they likely worked on neighbors' farms seasonally but were primarily able to make ends meet by laboring on their own farms. Additionally, a small number (7.5 percent) of wealthy farm owners likely did little in the way of farming their own lands but instead relied heavily on the labors of poorer neighbors. Of course, a small number of landless laborers did not make it into these numbers.

Despite the absence of the region's poorest residents, these numbers provide an outline of the socioeconomic geography of the region in 1948 and coincidentally align with Javier Agüero's socioeconomic analysis of the region in 1895, which he compiled from collected road repair taxes by the municipal government. In fact, he found that there were roughly 404 small- or medium-scale farm owners in the region in 1895 and 35 largeholders. In other words, a little fewer than 8 percent (7.9 percent) of the region's farmers owned relatively large farms, and an overwhelming 92 percent of the region's farm owners had small- or medium-sized farms. The conformity between sources from 1895 and 1948 suggests that class relations remained relatively steady for this long period. However, there was considerable diversity within the community's middling farm core. Some landowners barely broke even on small tracts of marginal land that required them to work considerable hours on neighbors' farms, while others who counted on excellent soil and employed poorer neighbors lived relatively comfortable lives on their small farms. This large and heterogeneous middle stratum of farmers appears to have had a strong presence in Tarrazú from the region's inception. In fact, Agüero's statistical analysis of land claims suggests that over half of all claims filed between 1827 and 1913 were for twenty-five hectares or fewer. In other words, colonists from the Central Valley arrived to the region to establish themselves as small- and medium-scale producers and landowners.[15] The economic and numeric strength of this rural middle class should not be underestimated. In fact, it seems that in 1920, small- and medium-sized farm owners as a group paid more municipal taxes than did their coffee mill counterparts.[16] It seems that the first settlers of the region sought to imitate the socioeconomic relations that defined the nation's Central Valley, from whence they had emigrated, forging a society with a large middle class and small elite and impoverished classes.

As mentioned, class relations in Costa Rica's coffee fields in the early twentieth century varied from those in other Central American coffee-producing countries. Costa Rican coffee farmers were a diverse group: some farmers owned just a handful of coffee plants, whereas others had sizable plots that required year-round labor to maintain. In much of the rest of Central America, however, coffee was produced almost exclusively on large coffee farms that almost always had an on-site beneficio.[17] While this system ensured greater control over the entire production of the crop, it required coffee elites to provide for a considerable labor pool year-round. Moreover, members of the coffee oligarchy in these countries felt the full brunt of dips in the price of coffee on the world market as producers, processors, and also exporters. In contrast, Costa Rican coffee elites ensured their profitability as the owners of beneficios, which received the coffee that small- and medium-scale coffee farmers harvested each year. Costa Rica's coffee society spread the risk of crop losses and declines on the world market among beneficiadores and independent coffee producers. To be sure, when demand for coffee declined, Costa Rica's beneficiadores could minimize their losses by purchasing just the coffee they could place on the market for sale abroad. Moreover, independent producers supported themselves and their families throughout the year, thereby lowering the economic burden on Costa Rica's coffee elites.

Tobías Umaña Jiménez's Political Career

As we have narrowed our focus from a region to a crop, so now will we narrow it even more to a man, one who eventually became the center of power in Tarrazú and in the region's coffee industry. In 1892, twelve-year-old Tobías Umaña Jiménez began a life of politics and public service in San Marcos as the telegrapher's assistant.[18] In 1904, he replaced his first employer as Tarrazú's official telegrapher, a post he held until 1910. Later, he would become the jefe político and municipal president (fig. 2.1).[19] In fact, he held both of these posts simultaneously in 1928.[20] As a government functionary, he earned not only local recognition but also a monthly salary that implied a level of financial security unlike that of his neighbors, since their reliance on agriculture forced them to contend with the ups and downs of market prices, droughts, floods, and pestilences. Retired schoolteacher Fany Jiménez Solís of San Marcos de Tarrazú recalls that "since he was a [government] functionary, Don Tobías had money and he would give loans to people, and if they could not pay off the loan, they had to give him their farm or a horse or whatever collateral available to back their debt."[21]

Figure 2.1. Tobías Umaña Jiménez (*center*), his son Humberto Umaña Parra (*right*), and one of Umaña's foremen (*left*), likely in Umaña's coffee fields before a celebration (note the decorative arch), circa early 1950s. This serves as a record of the region's clear socioeconomic divisions, evident in the barefoot peon as he walks behind the others. (Courtesy of Juan Mora)

Perhaps because of the connections he made early in life in local politics, Umaña found profitable labor opportunities in the region, namely as a *perito*, an independent property assessor measuring farms for the national registry. As farmers increasingly grew coffee, the use of credit in the months before and after the coffee harvest gradually became the norm. This meant that few farmers who employed Umaña's services as a perito were able to pay him in cash. Instead, farmers paid for his services with a piece of the land he assessed.[22] Many of the small belts of land that he received were located far from San Marcos, San Pablo, or any other settled community in the region. In fact, his son would recall that many of the lands his father assessed were in the community of Copey, which would become the second district of the newly formed canton of Dota in 1925.[23] As a perito, Umaña helped the coffee frontier to spread into remote areas of the canton of Tarrazú by dividing up larger land grants and defining new ones. Over the years, he came to own a sizable number of smallholdings throughout Tarrazú. He, however, did not keep many of these small landholdings for long but quickly resold them.[24] He reportedly used the cash from these sales to make loans to farmers, businessmen, and even the municipality.[25] At the same time, he was also busy purchasing prime real estate in the heart of San Marcos and in the hills around this community.[26]

Class Conflict in the Costa Rican Countryside in the 1920s and 1930s

While Umaña was busy working his way up Tarrazú's political and socioeconomic ladder, conflict between coffee farmers and beneficiadores broke out throughout the Costa Rican countryside. Coffee farmers in the 1920s began organizing themselves to protest the prices beneficios paid them for their coffee. Simultaneously, farmers began pressing the government to provide them with alternatives to privately owned beneficios—aside from state-run beneficios—and state-set prices for coffee.

Tensions between farmers and beneficiadores reached a pitch in 1928, in large part because of record coffee prices on the world market. Throughout the 1920s, coffee prices increased. From 1924 to 1928, the price of coffee experienced a 50 percent upturn in the world market.[27] This rise in coffee prices created economic prosperity for beneficiadores and coffee exporters in the 1920s. As coffee farmers watched beneficiadores/exporters grow increasingly wealthier without experiencing a correlating increase in profits, tensions mounted. In 1928, farmers in the Central Valley community of Turrialba introduced the idea of creating a local beneficio run by a cooperative of coffee farmers, and they implemented a massive publicity campaign where producers wrote letters to the editors and sought outside support for their efforts. That same year, producers in Hatillo, located just outside of the nation's capital, unsuccessfully organized themselves in an attempt to increase the price paid for their coffee by local beneficiadores.[28]

The tensions of 1928 were not limited to the Central Valley. To be sure, conflict broke out in Tarrazú over the price local beneficios were offering for that year's crop. Local producers successfully forced beneficiadores to provide them with a price similar to that given to Central Valley producers. *El Diario de Costa Rica*, one of the nation's most important dailies in this period, published an article on March 29, 1928, that discussed the prices different beneficios were paying producers throughout the country. The article took special note of Tarrazú, reporting that "there have been struggles over the price [of coffee] and they have arrived at [₡]100 per *fanega*, [approximately 200 kilograms], without subtracting the ₡5 of transport [costs] for each sack."[29] The article indicates that Tarrazú's coffee farmers secured a decent rate for their crop. In fact, the article states that throughout the nation, fanegas of "regular classes [of coffee] have been paid at [₡]100 and [₡]105."[30] Given the failure of coffee farmers in the Central Valley communities of Hatillo and Turrialba to obtain their demands, the success of Tarrazú's farmers to ensure a competitive price for their crops is striking.

Although beneficiadores and exporters earned tremendous returns on coffee for most of the 1920s, this changed dramatically in 1929. Costa Rica's economy in the early twentieth century was almost entirely dependent on coffee exports. When the world economy nosedived in 1929, European and US consumers were forced to cut back on household expenses; this meant that prices for nonessential goods, such as coffee, declined dramatically on the world market. In fact, from 1929 to 1931, Costa Rica saw the value of all its exports reduced by an incredible 21 percent (or ₡15,675,000).[31] While this statistic refers to all export goods, coffee was the dominant export crop and thus the primary component of the decline.[32] Moreover, the price of coffee declined from 1928 to 1930 by nearly 50 percent, then fell another 40 percent from 1930 to 1936. In other words, in eight years coffee prices experienced a catastrophic decrease on the world market.[33]

The economic downturn of the 1930s not only impacted Costa Rica's coffee producers, mill operators, and exporters, it also left many urban workers unemployed and dramatically decreased banana exports, the nation's second-largest export crop.[34] In 1933, the streets of San José were filled by thousands of the nation's unemployed.[35] In 1934, banana workers and the Communist Party organized a successful strike on the Atlantic coast that effectively halted all banana exports.[36] The dramatic reduction in coffee and banana exports during the 1930s created a severe deficit for the Costa Rican state, which depended greatly on customs revenues.[37] Since the 1880s, Costa Rica's different governments encouraged unrestrained capitalism, placing their faith in the idea that an economy based on agricultural exports would create economic prosperity.[38] Nevertheless, civil unrest, high unemployment, and the growing political strength of the nation's Communist Party during the 1930s encouraged the Costa Rican state to take a dramatic step away from traditional liberal ideals.[39]

The Costa Rican government began to take a more active role in the national economy during the 1930s. In 1933, it created the Institute for the Defense of Coffee, charged with protecting small growers from exploitative beneficiadores. Each year, the institute set legal limits on profit margins—in other words, it determined the maximum price a beneficiador could sell coffee for, based on the price he paid producers for the crop.[40] Two years later, the nation's first minimum wage for agricultural laborers became law.[41] Perhaps the most significant change was the dramatic increase in public works. Between 1932 and 1939, the Costa Rican state tripled its investment in infrastructure in an attempt to reduce the number of unemployed.[42] President León Cortés Castro (1936–40) dedicated considerable state funds to building and improving bridges and roads, and public works would define his administration.[43] Although a majority of the infrastructure built during his administration benefited the Central Valley, a couple of bridges were replaced on the road that connected Tarrazú to San José.[44]

Although government spending helped reduce unemployment levels during the 1930s, public works and the Institute for the Defense of Coffee could not undo the impact of lower coffee prices on the national economy. As exporters/beneficiadores quickly reduced the rates they paid producers for their coffee to contend with the lower prices they were being paid for the processed product, low coffee prices impacted all levels of the coffee economy. While it would be reasonable to assume that declines on the world market would have discouraged coffee production, the opposite was true. In fact, the number of fanegas exported in these years rose as farmers increased production in an attempt to counter their losses in the face of lower prices for their crops.[45] The low prices for coffee on the world market did, however, greatly reduce the amount of capital beneficio owners had on hand, and in many cases, they were unable to provide farmers with the loans they had given in years past on the promise of new crops.[46] Not only were beneficios forced to reduce the credit they could offer farmers but many also needed credit themselves to pay their large overheads in the face of low coffee prices.[47] In sum, all levels of Costa Rica's coffee economy were badly hit by the economic downturn.[48] For those few individuals who had liquid capital, however, the 1930s provided ample opportunities for amassing a fortune.

Tarrazú in the Great Depression and the Rise of Tobías Umaña Jiménez's Beneficio Monopoly

In Tarrazú, Tobías Umaña Jiménez was one of the few local residents who had access to large amounts of cash, thanks to his real estate ventures and moneylending. Umaña would use his capital to purchase lands, beneficios, and businesses in San Marcos, San Lorenzo, and San Pablo from cash-strapped farmers and beneficiadores.[49] By the close of the decade, he was unquestionably the wealthiest and most powerful man in Tarrazú.[50] In a 1999 interview with historian Javier Agüero, Umaña's son Tobías Umaña Parra recalled that his father purchased his first beneficio in 1933 from Ramón Blanco in San Pablo. A year later, Umaña bought Eduardo Bonilla's beneficio, also in San Pablo.[51] Between 1939 and 1941, Umaña purchased Alberto

Chavarría Escalante's beneficio located within San Marcos' city limits on the road to San Lorenzo. By January 1941, Umaña had effectively bought out all of his competition in Tarrazú, becoming the sole beneficiador in the region.[52]

His beneficio monopoly concerned many of the region's farmers. This is evident in the January 1941 request made by San Marcos's jefe político Marcos Chanto to the municipality, imploring the National Bank to build a patio for drying and processing coffee. Certainly Chanto, who was also an independent coffee farmer, recognized the economic advantage competition meant for farmers.[53] Umaña's final acquisition, Chavarría's beneficio, not only gave him a monopoly, it also made Chanto his debtor. Alongside the beneficio machinery, Umaña purchased the contracts and debts the former owners had with individual farmers. Juan Chanto, Marcos's son, recalled that his father processed his coffee with Chavarría and signed a contract guaranteeing him a determined price. Umaña paid farmers considerably less than Chavarría. After buying out Chavarría, Umaña attempted to rescind the contracts farmers made earlier and to pay these farmers the rate he was paying at his other beneficios. Chanto and the other farmers fought back, seeking the validation of their contracts with Chavarría.[54] According to Chanto's son, his father and other farmers successfully forced Umaña to pay them in accordance with Chavarría's terms for that year.

Tarrazú's coffee farmers, under the leadership of Chanto, also successfully secured funding from the National Bank to form two beneficios in the region, one in San Marcos and another in Santa María.[55] While these beneficios represented a clear challenge to Umaña's beneficio monopoly, this did not improve the price given to coffee producers for their harvests. As state-owned industries, these beneficios were prohibited from competing with private businesses such as Umaña's.[56] This meant that the National Bank's beneficios were legally required to pay precisely what Umaña paid farmers for their harvests.[57] Hence, the opening of the bank's beneficios was more a symbolic than a real change for local farmers. Coffee farmers, such as Chanto, who chose to sell their harvests at the National Bank's beneficio were motivated by nothing more or less than the desire not to sell to Umaña.[58]

Debt Peonage and the Construction of a Circular Economy in Tarrazú

During the 1930s, Umaña purchased beneficios and also began taking a number of calculated steps to ensure that he would fully dominate the local economy. By 1950, he was the region's single largest landholder, holding nearly one thousand hectares.[59] With such large holdings, he was fully dependent on *jornaleros*, or day laborers, to weed, fertilize, prune, and pick his coffee.

Umaña's business interests were not limited to farms and beneficios. In fact, his first commercial venture was the opening of *comisariatos* (similar to a US general store) in San Marcos, San Lorenzo, and San Pablo. The precise date that these comisariatos were opened is unknown; nevertheless, given his reliance on labor for his sizable coffee farms and later beneficios, he quickly created a circular economy by paying his laborers not in cash but in scrip that was only recognized in his stores.[60] He ensured himself comisariato patrons, and he also guaranteed himself laborers, since his workers had no access to cash and were therefore dependent on his stores to feed and clothe their families. Umaña's grip over his jornaleros was strengthened by the geographical distance between the region and San José and by the lack of alternative employment options in the region. With multiple beneficios, comisariatos, and farms in different communities, Umaña fast became the most powerful man in Tarrazú. Of course, his business model, relying on dependent labor relationships, was employed in various rural communities throughout Costa Rica and was part and parcel of coffee agriculture in most of Central America.[61] In neighboring Nicaragua, for instance, debt peonage appears to have been the preferred means by which the coffee oligarchy secured labor in this same period.[62]

Coffee elites in Nicaragua, like Umaña in Tarrazú, employed debts as a contract between themselves and local peasants.[63] The use of debt provided men with considerable power over their peons, who were obligated by their debt to labor until they could repay their loans. Varying degrees of labor coercion were employed throughout the isthmus during the late nineteenth and early twentieth centuries in different communities. In Nicaragua, El Salvador, Honduras, and Guatemala, members of the coffee oligarchies colluded with government officials to pass vagrancy laws and privatize communal lands to secure access to a ready labor force. In these nations, there was a very small nonelite coffee-growing class. In fact, most coffee production took place on large haciendas that were cared for by a combination of landless peons and subsistence farmers who labored for part of the year. A small group of people controlled the whole coffee industry, evident by the fact that in these countries coffee farmers had on-site beneficios where they processed and readied the coffee they produced for export.[64]

In contrast, Costa Rica's coffee oligarchy and the state were less interested in monopolizing coffee production and landownership than in dominating the processing and exporting of this crop. So, whereas Tarrazú's poorest landholders were often indebted peons and subsistence farmers, like their counterparts in Nicaragua, Guatemala, Honduras, and El Salvador, many of

Tarrazú's small landholders were also growing a few coffee bushes on their farms. Unlike in the rest of the isthmus, where debt peonage was almost always an exclusively coercive means to secure labor, in Tarrazú this was not always the case. In fact, some indebted families who grew coffee on lands rented from Umaña managed to escape debt servitude and purchase small plots of land with their coffee earnings. Moreover, Umaña appears to have used debt less as a means of coercion and more as a means of securing consent to his monopoly over the local economy.

In fact, Umaña and other Costa Rican coffee elites often extended loans and sold off small portions of their large landholdings as a means to spread the risk of low prices on the world market and poor harvests to the middle and lower classes. These elites encouraged small-scale coffee production while ensuring themselves the largest profits as beneficiadores and lenders. Umaña was involved in this type of activity even while purchasing farms from some of the region's less fortunate residents. His great grandson Juan Bosco Umaña Abarca explained that "as a business strategy, [my great-grandfather] decided to sell some of his farms to different people who . . . [did not always have the money to pay for the land]. . . . But he planned the sale in such a way that the person could pay for the farm. [This generally was made possible] with comfortable . . . long-term . . . payments. [Some of the farms were] even [paid for] . . . with the coffee the farm produced."[65]

Unlike in the rest of Central America, small- and medium-scale producers were the backbone of Costa Rica's coffee economy. While elites and the state colluded in other parts of the region to keep a majority of their nation's rural poor landless, in Costa Rica these powerholders used a different tactic. In fact, governmental policies throughout the nineteenth and twentieth centuries encouraged this development through laws that benefited squatters who could demonstrate that they had both occupied and improved on fallow lands.[66] Similarly, elites, such as Umaña, commonly sold small portions of their farms to some of their less well-to-do neighbors to reduce the amount of lands they were responsible for cultivating, harvesting, and maintaining. This reality, however, does not mean that profits were equally spread in this community.[67] As Monge's depiction of Tarrazú's coffee harvest in 1946 suggests, there was a clear socioeconomic gap separating independent producers, landless peons, and Umaña (the region's sole private beneficiador).

Downward Mobility in Tarrazú

The economic downturn of the 1930s forced many families to sell their farms and to take out loans from the region's few residents, such as Umaña, who had the capital to lend and buy. The lives of those farmers and their families changed dramatically as many became landless peons, fully dependent on wage labor on the large farms of their wealthier neighbors.

Perhaps the most dramatic case of downward mobility in this period is that of the Cascante family, the descendants of Tarrazú's founding father José Miguel Cascante. Juana Fernández, whose husband was Umaña's nephew, recalled that the Cascante family fell on tough times before she was born in 1934 and sold off all their lands and worked as peons on Umaña's hacienda.[68] Fernández related that "Mr. Cascante was very humble, with just one shirt and one pair of pants, and he became ill."[69] She remembered that at some point in her childhood, Cascante's clothes became wet while he was suffering from pneumonia. As Cascante had no other clothes to change into, he was forced to seek Umaña's aid. Fernández related that Cascante "asked Don Tobías to sell him another pair of pants and a shirt on credit because he did not have the money to buy it. The man was very sick and very cold, but Don Tobías did not want to give it to him. Don Tobías said that Cascante was too sick to repay the loan for the clothes."[70] Fernández quickly added that Umaña's actions toward Cascante were not only "unjust" but bordered on homicide, since "the next day that poor man died of pneumonia and cold."[71]

This narrative is among the most moving stories told in the region regarding the control Umaña exercised over other residents' lives, yet it is just one of many. Still, it is important to take into account that, although no one in Tarrazú could compete with Umaña's buying and lending power, other residents in Tarrazú also wielded economic power. In fact, Jeremías Ureña in Santa María, Antolín Gamboa in Carrizal, and Manuel Castro in San Pablo also purchased farms from less fortunate residents of the region who fell on hard times before, during, and after the Great Depression.[72] Umaña and these men provided individual farmers with loans, and they also extended credit to the local government to repair roads and improve schools and for other infrastructure projects.[73] It seems clear that in the 1930s, the fortunes of Tarrazú's most economically viable families rose at the same time the region's humblest inhabitants experienced extreme downward mobility.

The decreased coffee prices of the Great Depression impacted all of the region's small- and medium-scale farmers. However, not all farmers were as unfortunate as the Cascante family, which lost all of its landholdings. Also, though Umaña cornered a considerable sector of the local market with his comisariatos and the use of scrip on his farms and in his beneficios, there were other businesses in the region. A number of small stores, bakeries, and billiard parlors competed with Umaña for clients among the region's independent coffee farmers, artisans, and other business owners. Many of these businesses predated Umaña's entrance into commerce. In fact, San Marcos had on the tax rolls as early as 1911 four independently owned *pulperías*, or small general stores, which sold rice, flour, pasta, salt, soap, fabric, and other goods not locally produced.[74] In 1925, the canton of Tarrazú would lose a considerable portion of its territory as the canton of Dota was formed from the eastern half of Tarrazú.[75] The largest community in this newly formed canton, Santa María, became the political center. Upon becoming a canton capital, Santa María boasted six pulperías, eight butcher shops, six carpenter shops, and four barbershops.[76]

Umaña may not have been the only business owner or wealthy landowner in Tarrazú in the 1930s, but he was the only beneficiador. Dominating the beneficio sector of the regional economy meant that he could determine the price he paid coffee farmers for their harvests. Many of the region's residents felt that he abused his financial powers by not only paying low prices for coffee but also by not paying coffee farmers promptly for their harvests. Elías Montero of El Llano de la Piedra remembered, "Here, earlier there were two businessmen [Alberto Chavarría and Tobías Umaña], and they paid what they liked without reason. . . . They [often] did not pay until the end of the year."[77] Given that the coffee harvest runs from late November to early March, receiving payment at the end of the year meant families were paid a full year after they picked and delivered their first coffee harvest to the beneficio. While Montero did not distinguish between Chavarría and Umaña, many of the region's residents remembered that the situation worsened when Umaña bought out all of his competitors. As Kiko Vargas recalled, "Don Tobías was the only [coffee] receiver in those times. . . . He was . . . wealthy and powerful. . . . It does not serve me to say if he was good or bad, [but] he was not good."[78]

Tarrazú in the Economic Decline of the 1940s

While Umaña was expanding his financial hold on the region, the nation's economy began to rebound in 1936. The upturn is evident in the stabilization of coffee prices and expanded banana production that year.[79] Unfortunately, when World War II broke out in 1939, Costa Rica's primary market for coffee and bananas dried up almost overnight. The nation's coffee exporters were quick to reroute European-bound shipments of coffee to the United States. While this meant that not all of the nation's coffee income was lost, as the North American coffee market was flooded with imports from throughout Central and South America, coffee prices decreased.[80] Exporting exclusively to the United States diminished coffee profits, which at the time formed the nation's primary economic sector.[81] Imports subsided dramatically as well in this period, since Europe was not exporting machinery and other goods that Costa Ricans traditionally imported from the other

Figure 2.2. Political cartoon puts into focus the scarcity of tires, gasoline, and spare car parts during World War II. The caption declares that the horse and buggy will be 1943's new model car. "Volverán los viejos rocinantes," *La Tribuna*, May 1, 1942, 1. (Carmen Kordick, from Costa Rica's National Library)

side of the Atlantic. While many business owners, farmers, and laborers suffered great losses in the 1940s, just as in the 1930s, individuals with accumulated capital increased their holdings. In Tarrazú, Tobías Umaña Jiménez would once again be the primary beneficiary in this time of economic woe.

According to Juan Bosco Umaña, his great-grandfather made a fortune in the 1940s speculating on tires and *manta*, a raw cotton fabric primarily used for clothing in Tarrazú.[82] According to the younger Umaña, his great-grandfather recognized weeks before World War II began that war was imminent and that it would mean a decline in exports to and imports from Europe. Knowing that Costa Rica did not manufacture tires or manta and did not have the machinery to produce either of these essential goods, Umaña saw a tremendous opportunity. He reportedly went to all of San José's fabric and tire suppliers and "purchased all the manta and tires that existed in the country."[83] He purportedly employed "a hundred oxcarts," or an incredible two hundred oxen, just to transport all of the manta back to Tarrazú. The considerable size of his purchases made it possible for him to negotiate and secure a competitive price for both of these items.[84]

When World War II broke out, the very men who sold Umaña their tires and manta came to San Marcos de Tarrazú to negotiate the repurchase of their former merchandise. According to Umaña Abarca, his great-grandfather made "a good profit" with the resale of these goods.[85] World War II provided Umaña with tremendous economic opportunity both through speculation and as a lender. However, for most of the region's independent coffee producers and those who had no lands, this was a period of great necessity (fig. 2.2).

Labor and Gender at the Hacienda and the Cafetalera

To manage and maintain his considerable landholdings and run his various comisariatos, stables, and, most importantly, beneficios, Umaña required a sizable labor force year-round. Moreover, the coffee harvest each summer required a considerable number of seasonal employees as well. The region's landless men and young boys, such as the Cascante family, made up a majority of his full-time labor force; however, many other men and boys whose families had smaller landholdings, such as Nino Vargas Picado, were required to work for Umaña during the harvest season to ensure that their families could cover basic expenses.[86] Vargas's father inherited a considerable sixty manzanas (approximately forty-two hectares); yet, with twenty-one children, it was often difficult to make ends meet, particularly during the 1930s and 1940s.[87] In fact, during this period, Vargas's father's economic travails forced him to sell off large portions of the family's farm to purchase fabric for clothes, rice, flour, salt, medications, and other necessities that they could not produce for themselves. Alongside his brothers and father, Nino Vargas labored as a peon for Umaña on a farm known as the hacienda. Vargas recalled, "We all went barefooted, and we earned a colón each day at the hacienda. We worked hard weeding, planting." Laboring for Umaña provided the Vargas family with a meager income in scrip, which could not help the family eliminate the debt it had on its farm. However, "at one point Don Tobías saved us from losing the farm entirely in exchange for all of the coffee we had planted on the farm." Vargas remembered that Umaña paid the small debt the family had on their remaining lands in exchange for the entire coffee crop that year. This forced the already poor family to suffer extreme deprivation: that year, the family was unable to purchase enough fabric to dress the whole family. Many of the younger children dressed in simple outfits made from flour bags. Vargas and three older brothers shared a single pair of decent pants, and therefore, not all of the brothers could attend the annual civic festivities in San Marcos.[88]

While the weeding, fertilizing, planting, and other labors in the coffee fields that boys and men like Vargas did were considered "men's labor," given the considerable increase in laborers during the harvest, it is unsurprising that coffee picking incorporated women and children (fig. 2.3). Coffee pick-

Figure 2.3. Juan Rafael Umaña Jiménez (*left, with basket*), Tobías Umaña Jiménez's brother, and his children, four with their wicker coffee baskets tied to their waists, circa late 1910s or early 1920s. (Courtesy of Luz Berta Monge Umaña)

ers were not paid hourly but by the amount of coffee they picked. The coffee fruit was picked off the bushes, placed in wicker baskets that the pickers tied to their waists, and then poured into large burlap sacks. At the end of each workday, harvesters carted their filled sacks of coffee to the oxcarts or trucks to be measured before loading the sacks' contents into the truck bed or oxcart for processing of the coffee. The coffee harvest provided many children with an opportunity to earn money to help pay for their school supplies, shoes, and uniforms, and perhaps they even had a few extra colones for candy, a soda, or other treats.[89] For women workers, the coffee harvest provided extra cash to purchase rice, salt, fabric for clothes, and other items that the family could not always afford.[90]

Men and boys made up the majority of Umaña's workforce in the cafetalera, as the Umaña beneficio was popularly known, running the machinery that washed the coffee fruit, spreading the cleaned seeds on the tiled patio floors to dry in the sun, packing the dry seeds into large burlap sacks, and finally transporting the packed coffee to San José by oxcarts or trucks for export. However, one task was open to women and girls. The critical job of coffee "selecting" was held exclusively by female laborers such as Margarita Mora (fig. 2.4), who worked selecting coffee for Umaña and later for his two

Figure 2.4. Women sorting coffee beans at Tobías Umaña Jiménez's beneficio, the cafetalera, late 1950s. Margarita Mora is the second woman from the right. (Courtesy of Juan Mora)

sons, Tobías and Humberto Umaña Parra.[91] Mora began working at the cafetalera as a young woman, sorting coffee beans on large wooden tables. She was one of a hundred or so young women who worked in a large hall. The women would separate the small beans from the medium and large beans for packaging and shipping. However, perhaps the most important category to be sorted was that of the peaberries. These occur when the two seeds in the coffee fruit merge, forming a larger curled bean. Peaberries received the highest price in the European markets and were painstakingly sorted out regardless of their size.[92]

Women were considered better selectors than men because they were seen as more detail oriented and patient. This is why "only women worked [selecting] and the men worked in the patios or bringing us the coffee, but not selecting." While gendered ideas prompted the notion that women were ideal selectors, these same ideas led to the conclusion that women needed to work under male supervision and authority. Mora remembered that "a few men walked between us to check our work."[93] Aside from ensuring that the women were correctly separating coffee beans, male supervisors scolded the women workers for chatting among themselves.[94] While the men were in a

Figure 2.5. Young women wearing their Sunday best near San Marcos's central plaza, early 1950s. (Courtesy of Juan Mora)

position of authority, the fear of being reprimanded did not end the conversations between workers. Instead, as Mora recalled, "one would speak every once in a while with the worker beside you, but always in a soft voice, because if they [the management] heard us they would scold us, they would say, that [when] talking, it was not possible to work well."[95] For rural women, like Mora, selecting coffee beans was a highly cherished job. After the coffee harvest was complete, very few avenues of respectable employment outside of the household existed for women in rural areas. Besides selecting coffee, working as domestic servants in the houses of wealthier neighbors or family members or in San José was the only option available to women in the region.

Mora, who had small children and was not married, could not take a position as a domestic servant, since domestic workers slept in the home where they worked. Moreover, working as a selector was preferable because, as one of the local women recalled, "selecting" was understood to be among the only "clean labor" opportunities in the community.[96] Illustrating this idea, Luz Berta Monge Umaña recalled that she and the other selectors wore their "nicest clothing and shoes" to work (fig. 2.5).[97] In contrast, working as a domestic servant was considered "dirty" labor because women not only cleaned but also frequently became dirty in the process of washing clothes, baking, cooking, and scrubbing floors. Therefore, they arrived in their poorest attire to spare their nicest clothing items from the rigors of domestic labor. Also, domestic labor was a job that consumed a worker's entire existence. Whereas a selector would clock in and out and therefore had considerable autonomy both in and out of work, domestic servants were expected to labor for the family that employed them from the moment they woke until they were permitted to go to bed.

Perhaps, however, what made selecting most attractive was that it largely spared women from verbal, physical, and even sexual abuse—something that was all too common for domestic servants. In fact, it was not uncommon for employers to disparage, yell at, and slap domestic servants if they did something incorrectly or took longer than expected to complete a task.[98] I examine these abuses closely in the next chapter. Nonetheless, it is important to recognize that women had limited employment opportunities, and many women of humble origins were forced to seek this type of work after the coffee harvest was complete.

Social Reform on the National Stage in the 1930s and 1940s and Its Impact on Tarrazú

In the early 1940s, while Umaña was in the process of consolidating his economic position as the region's primary employer, lender, and only beneficiador, a number of key political transformations were taking place in San José that would dramatically affect Tarrazúceños in the years to come. The move toward increased governmental control in the economy that began under León Cortés Castro's presidency (1936–40) was augmented when Pres. Rafael Ángel Calderón Guardia (1940–44) established the nation's Social Guarantees in 1941, which were added to the nation's constitution in 1942, and to the new Labor Code, enacted in 1943.[99]

The Labor Code established clear employment regulations that largely favored laborers. For businessmen, such as Umaña, whose ventures required a considerable workforce, the Labor Code promised to impact profits negatively. Perhaps the most noticeable change came in the form of Articles 70 and 165, which banned employers from forcing their employees to purchase goods from a particular store and from paying employees in scrip or merchandise.[100] These two articles legally obliged Umaña to pay his laborers in colones and in turn allowed workers to shop around for the best price for fabric, medicines, foods, and other goods. In addition, the Labor Code, in concert with the Social Guarantees, established a social security system that provided workers with disability, retirement, and maternity benefits via the creation of a new state institution: the Caja Costarricense de Seguro Social. The government, employers, and workers, in equal share, would fund the Caja.[101] Additionally, employers were required to provide their laborers with workmen's compensation insurance, funded exclusively by the employer.[102] While this legislation provided workers with benefits, it saddled employers with more expenses and no noticeable gains.

Like any good businessman, Umaña was quick to look over the new legislation in search of loopholes to reduce his expenses. He discovered that Article 22 of the Labor Code specifically designated that workers employed for fewer than ninety days did not require a contract and that their employers did not need to register them with the Caja.[103] While Umaña required year-round labor to maintain his hacienda, beneficios, comisariatos, and other businesses in the region, he strategically began to employ individual workers for two months at a time, after which he would let them go, then rehire them a month later for another two months.[104] By rotating workers in and out, he freed himself from having to register workers with the Caja and, in turn, eliminated his obligation to pay workers' retirement, disability, and other funds sanctioned in the new legislation. Clearly, all of his workers lost out, since they could not reap the benefits of the new legislation. Still, for those in the region with no lands, the inability to secure year-round employment caused particular hardships.

Tobías Umaña, Tarrazú's Generous Patriarch

Although Umaña clearly put economic gain before the interests of his workers, numerous residents deeply respected and admired him. Herminía Muñoz Estrada's recollections of Umaña as a benevolent patriarchal figure provide a case in point: "For me, Don Tobías was a grand man. You see, he fed all the poor in this region, he gave us food by giving us work, and he paid us well. He paid us ten colones a week and we were girls—that is what he paid the women—if you selected coffee well in the beneficio."[105] For Muñoz, the fact that Umaña did not make a distinction between girls, such as herself and her sisters, and older women, so long as they worked equally hard, demonstrated his generosity.

Perhaps more important to Muñoz was the fact that later on in life, Umaña showed benevolence to her and her husband, who were among Tarrazú's landless families and relied entirely on wage labor to make ends meet. Muñoz's husband was a peon at Umaña's hacienda and at some point was injured on the job. According to Muñoz, Umaña "signed the little paper" that provided her husband with a pension after the injury. Because her husband had not worked "three months in his [Umaña's] farm that year" when he was injured, Umaña's willingness to provide him with benefits was an act of generosity. While she praised his kindness to her family, she quickly noted, "I cannot speak ill of him, although many others can."[106] Curiously, Muñoz did not question the fact that Umaña had consistently taken actions to avoid paying benefits to employees, such as her husband. The precarious nature of Muñoz's husband's situation, upon being injured, was constructed by Umaña's own practices to avoid paying his employees benefits.

Muñoz's positive recollection of her former boss was shared by many of the women in the region who, at one time or another, labored for Umaña selecting coffee. Margarita Mora was quick to state that while Umaña and later his sons "had a lot—they were the owners of almost everything," what mattered most to her was that the Umaña family "gave [her] work."[107] Additionally, as workers within the cafetalera, selectors were provided the opportunity to forge personal paternalistic relationships with Umaña (and later his sons), based on their selecting skills and years of service, which these selectors could call upon in tough times. Muñoz related that when her husband was injured, it was she who spoke to Umaña and secured the paper that provided her husband with a pension. When she asked for Umaña's aid, her former employer offered to pay her husband's pension not only because her injured husband had been a "good worker" but because he "respected all the years of work my sister and I had done for him."[108] Women selectors' ability to call upon the same patriarchal bonds that traditionally linked men of means to their laborers, coupled with selectors' increased economic position within the household as wage earners, potentially made women less dependent on their familial patriarchs.

Although Umaña's beneficio monopoly provided the region's women with an attractive employment opportunity, his dominance of the region's economy cost men dearly. As his grip on the local economy strengthened, he managed to turn back the clock on the capacity of men to provide for their families. Although coffee's introduction to the region at the close of the nineteenth century initially ushered in an era of increased profitability for a majority of the region's farmers, the economic security coffee offered farmers came to an abrupt end during the Great Depression. In the 1930s, coffee prices collapsed, and, in addition, Umaña became the region's sole coffee processer, which meant he had absolute discretion to determine what to pay local coffee farmers for their annual harvest and the amount of credit to extend to them. Thus, by the 1930s, he held the power to determine whether individual coffee farmers would retain their lands and the ability to provide for their families or whether they would need to find employment as peons.

Of course, not all men in Tarrazú were farmers or peons, nor was Umaña's dominance limited to the region's coffee sector. In fact, while a majority of the region's men who were not landowners secured employment as agricultural laborers, many also found work as government functionaries or independent transporters or in cottage industries such as shoemaking, baking, and blacksmithing. While the relationship between these different industries was less direct than in the region's coffee sector, since Umaña also came to own most of the sawmills, bakeries, and comisariatos, he competed directly with both existing and potential new businesses and industries. Additionally, as the region's primary lender, he also had the power to determine who did and did not have access to employment, loans, and other opportunities. Men who lost their businesses and farms to Umaña because of their inability to repay loans often found themselves laboring as his peons, making the probability that their economic situation would improve slim. Moreover, Umaña often determined their economic fate based on the hours, pay, jobs, loans, and opportunities that he provided them. The men who experienced this downward mobility likely felt that their masculinity was being questioned, since they no longer held the power to decide their family's economic situation. The full consequences of men's declining ability to provide for their families in this period—namely heavy drinking, brawling, and domestic violence—are discussed in detail in chapter 3.

Conclusion

Whether Umaña's former employees and beneficio clients saw his business practices as just or unjust and whether the foresight of a half century has led them to reconsider Umaña as a generous patriarch or cruel exploiter, in his lifetime no employee openly questioned his firing and rehiring policies or his recalcitrance to pay for his employees' access to the Caja and other benefits in the courts. Moreover, his workers do not appear to have ever organized a strike to improve working conditions, wages, or benefits.[109] Indeed, his former political and economic power is palpable even today, as Tarrazúceños retell stories that paint him in a negative light only with the promise of anonymity and in hushed voices.

In the first four decades of the twentieth century, Tobías Umaña Jiménez managed to become the most important figure in Tarrazú's economy as the only private beneficiador and as the region's largest landowner. His rise to economic dominance was the result of both calculated steps taken by this politician turned lender, farmer, and entrepreneur and of dramatic economic changes at the national and international level. While the economic downturn of the 1930s and World War II created considerable hardships for small- and medium-scale farmers, beneficiadores, and wage laborers in San José and Tarrazú, it created substantial opportunity for those individuals with considerable capital on hand. During these two decades, Umaña purchased beneficios, farms, tires, and manta in a calculated fashion that ensured him considerable profits in the long term. His fortunes did not, however, grow simply because he had foresight and world and national events aligned in his favor. As shown, he was not above seeking loopholes in legislation to make a better profit.

By the close of the 1940s, Umaña was unquestionably the most powerful man in the region. This would begin to change, however, after the 1948 Civil War, which broke out in Tarrazú. Although Umaña sided with the winning camp, led by fellow hacendado José "Pepe" Figueres, and did not lose any of his lands, beneficios, comisariatos, his soda factory, or sawmills, the conflict would weaken his economic position in the region. The postwar Costa Rican republic would encourage cooperatives and strengthen the Social Guarantees, and this in turn would chip away at Umaña's once-firm hold over the local economy. This conflict and its consequences for Umaña, his peons, and independent coffee farmers are the subject of chapters 4 and 5. Before discussing the Civil War, it is necessary to examine the role the state played in the lives of the region's residents, which is the subject of chapter 3.

3

Maintaining the Order

Gender, Class, State Authority, and Violence

> We always knew someone had tattled when . . . [the Resguardo Fiscal] arrived. Almost always, there were six or seven men on horseback . . . [who] would group up the men and boys . . . but they never touched the women or girls. . . . Those men were very rude. They would do anything to get someone to admit they had produced contraband [liquor]. Dad used to say they would mistreat them with needles. They used to say that the Resguardos would choke the men and boys to see who would say "yes" first. If that did not work, they would tie their fingers to repress the blood. They would torture them into saying "yes." Some [members of the Resguardo Fiscal] were more violent than others, but they all came to haul someone off to jail. In San Andrés, many people produced contraband in the crevices [of the hillsides] for sale, but those men were only interested in hauling off a single "guilty" [man] to prison in San José. . . . I certainly was scared of them, but they never messed with me because I was a girl.
>
> —Flora Villa, San Pablo de León Cortes, April 21, 2008

Flora Villa's description of the interrogation methods of the Treasury Department's policing agents, called the Resguardo Fiscal Guards, poignantly recalled the fear their visit to her community of San Andrés de Tarrazú elicited and it suggests a frightening vision of governmental authority in Tarrazú. Villa, who was born in 1928, attempted to excise herself (and all of San Andrés's women and girls) from this violence, but the fact that she recalled what her father and other men told her decades ago implies that women and girls almost certainly suffered psychologically as they were left to ponder what was or was not taking place with their husbands, sons, and fathers.

The Resguardo Fiscal were charged with protecting the financial interests of the Costa Rican state, which in the case of Tarrazú primarily meant seeking out and arresting local producers and consumers of homemade liquor to protect the state's extremely lucrative monopoly on liquor production.[1] The level of violence invoked by Resguardo Fiscal guards to determine who was involved in the production of homemade liquors suggests that the Costa Rican state saw bootlegging as a serious offense.[2] To fully understand why authorities thought it necessary to be so violent, I examine Tarrazú's masculine drinking culture, the reasons locals produced and consumed contraband liquor, and the rationale behind the Resguardo Fiscal's mandate to arrest producers and consumers of homemade liquors. The oral histories I collected in the region from both men and women make evident that clandestine liquor production and consumption were not only a part of daily life in the region but also an act of resistance against the authority of the state and the local socioeconomic order (headed by men such as Tobías Umaña Jiménez, whose grip on the local economy was the focus of the previous chapter).

Moving beyond the very visible power struggle over liquor production and consumption, this chapter places into focus the often-hidden exercise of power that took place in the homes of Tarrazúceños. In particular, it spotlights the role that physical and sexual violence against women and children played in the struggle for authority and manhood in the region during this period. By examining state violence against men and men's violence against women and children together, this chapter provides critical context to the next two chapters, which interrogate the causes and consequences of Costa Rica's 1948 Civil War. Moreover, chapters 3, 4, and 5 together scrutinize different types of historic violence that when considered together serve to dismantle Costa Rica's most hallowed exceptionalist myth, which portrays Costa Ricans as an inherently nonviolent people. In sum, this chapter begins the process of questioning the mythic vision of Costa Rica as a historically peaceful republic by examining the function of violence in asserting and preserving federal political authority and the patriarchal order in Tarrazú.

The State's Liquor Monopoly and the Resguardo Fiscal

The long history of the Costa Rican state's interests in liquor centers on the economic profitability of liquor sales and stretches back well into the nineteenth century. Beginning in the late 1820s, the Costa Rican state attempted to tax liquor sales and to require producers and sellers to pay a licensing fee. Motivated by a desire to increase liquor revenues, in 1850 the state outlawed the production of liquors, wine, and beer by private industry and became the sole legal producer of alcoholic beverages.[3] It also attempted to strictly control the sale of both national and imported spirits through the sale of liquor licenses and taxes levied on imported liquors.[4] Costa Rica's treasury depended heavily on the revenue produced from the sale of state-produced liquors and liquor licenses to restaurants, casinos, bars, and hotels.[5] The economic revenues produced through liquor sales were substantial. Between 1851 and

1861, the state-owned Fábrica Nacional de Licores, or National Liquor Factory (hereafter FNL), provided the state treasury with between ₡200,000 and ₡300,000 annually. Given the fact that the Costa Rican treasury's annual revenue in 1868 was ₡356,308.93, it is evident that the FNL was a primary source of income for the state.[6] These dates do not precisely align and exact figures of FNL income for subsequent decades are not available. However, according to the FNL, they were the second most important source of income for the Costa Rican treasury—just below coffee export taxes—in the first four decades of the twentieth century.[7]

To protect the state's monopoly over alcohol production, a body of law enforcement was needed to ferret out and arrest producers, consumers, and distributors of homemade liquors and untaxed imported spirits. The Resguardo Fiscal was that body. Commissioned by the state to "seek out all that is clandestine or not clandestine that harms the Treasury," officers and guards of the Resguardo Fiscal had military authority.[8] Although the Resguardo was initially formed in the 1820s to decommission unlicensed tobacco growers, the state decreed in 1837 that the Resguardo Fiscal expand its duties and root out unlicensed liquor producers and sellers.[9] The Resguardo's military powers gave lower-level members known as guards the right to conduct searches in private residences, businesses, and vehicles, without permission from local police or judicial authorities.

The Resguardo Fiscal still engaged in their primary role of seeking out "bootleggers" of spirits as late as the 1960s. The passage of time did not result in a decrease in its authority. Indeed, in the 1950s, an instruction manual issued by the Resguardo to all its guards attested that "*suspicion is enough* (emphasis in original) . . . to solicit the owner of a private domicile . . . to open the door."[10] Moreover, in cases where a member of the Resguardo Fiscal located evidence that liquors were being illegally distilled or sold, guards had the authority to confiscate evidence and arrest and transport suspects to San José for trial. Historically, Resguardo Fiscal guards could also serve as court witnesses for whatever they uncovered in their searches. However, following the 1948 Civil War, searches had to be conducted with two non-Resguardo witnesses to verify what was or was not found during a search.[11] Resguardo guards ensured their safety and the authority of their office by means of the revolver and knife (along with a whistle and badge) that they carried on their persons at all times.[12]

Thus, it is unsurprising that Tarrazúceños recalled that the sight of the Resguardo Fiscal could make women faint, children cry, and men quiver.[13] Víctor Manuel Mata remembered that as a child in Santa María de Dota, whenever he and his friends would pass the office of the Resguardo Fiscal in San Marcos de Tarrazú, they would "stand up straight and look to the ground, because they [the Resguardo guards] were men who required respect."[14]

The Historical Importance of *Chicha* and *Guarapo* in Costa Rican Society

The production of guarapo (a fermented sugarcane drink) and chicha (a fermented corn drink) has a very long history in Costa Rican society. In fact, long before Columbus "discovered" Central America, Costa Rica's indigenous populations produced and consumed chicha, and since the sixteenth century, members of the plebian classes had been producing guarapo throughout the kingdom of Guatemala, to which present-day Costa Rica belonged.[15] These homemade liquors were traditionally a critical source of economic stimulus for different sectors of the population. During the colonial era and early republic, it was customary for travelers throughout Central America to purchase guarapo and chicha from rural families whose houses they passed to relieve travelers' fatigue.[16] Aside from the benefit to the travelers, the sale of these drinks was a source of income for many families who lived in less populated regions of the country.[17] Similarly, the sale of guarapo and chicha was a major source of income for municipalities and churches during civic and religious festivities.[18]

In light of the economic benefits that families, the Catholic Church, and municipalities traditionally received from the sale of homemade spirits, the Costa Rican state's attempt to tax and license this home industry in the 1820s was ill received. The cultural importance of homemade liquors is apparent in a November 1839 resolution, which called for "ending the sale of guarapo and chicha" by way of increased vigilance on the part of Resguardo Fiscal.[19] Legislators were, nevertheless, sensitive to the fact that these alcoholic beverages were customarily produced for home consumption, since the final line of the resolution reads "but when the chicha are destined for individual consumption, . . . they will not be sought . . . since the sale is [what is] prohibited."[20]

Although the Costa Rican state provided the Resguardo Fiscal with considerable authority, their job was dangerous and difficult. While legislators initially sought only to prohibit the unlicensed sale of homemade liquors, it likely proved too difficult for guards to determine if an unlicensed producer was distilling solely for his family's consumption or also for sale. The amount of liquor considered acceptable for home consumption was never determined. The language in the 1839 resolution remained vague, only stipulating that "large portions" of chicha and/or guarapo were "sufficient evidence that a producer intended to sell."[21] Given the obvious difficulty that this entailed, the Costa Rican state decided to outlaw home liquor production entirely in 1850, making itself the sole legal producer of liquors, beers, and other distilled drinks throughout the nation. The complete prohibition of liquor distillation outside of the FNL did not mark the end of the state's battle to curb contraband production. Instead, it simply inaugurated a new phase. In fact, the amount of contraband on the market fluctuated considerably in relation to two crucial variables: the price of coffee on the world market and the price of FNL liquors. In 1941, historian Francisco María Núñez examined the sales of the FNL between 1868 and 1941 for an unpublished report he assembled for then president Prospero Guardia. Nuñez's detailed description of alcohol sales for this period demonstrates that whenever coffee prices on the world market declined and liquor prices increased, sales at the FNL would decrease. These two shifts tended to coincide with an increase in the number of contraband liquor producers the Resguardo Fiscal apprehended as well as the quantities of illegal liquors confiscated. In other words, liquor demand did not decline. However, in times of economic distress, consumers were more likely to purchase homemade liquors. And when a downturn in coffee prices destabilized their families' economic situation, perhaps more individuals were willing to risk the chance of jail time and fines for illegally producing liquor. Likewise, if the price of FNL liquors were high enough, homemade liquors could fetch a pretty penny, encouraging farmers who cultivated sugarcane as a cash crop to produce illegal liquor at home for profitable sales to neighbors.

The Local Economy of Guarapo and Chicha in Tarrazú

The state's primary interest in halting the production of homemade liquors was economic, and the families in Tarrazú (and other communities) who disobeyed the prohibition—both producing and purchasing chicha and guarapo—did so mainly for economic reasons as well. The main economic drive to produce liquors at home was tied to the fact that Tarrazú's consumers paid higher prices than did their counterparts in San José for rice, textiles, shoes, FNL-produced liquors, and all other goods that came from the Central Valley. This was largely due to the high cost of transporting goods into the region from the capital.[22]

As seen, between 1890 and 1948, the Tarrazú region's economy and society became increasingly linked to coffee production. The annual harvest provided producers with larger profits than were possible with other cash crops. However, because coffee produced only one harvest per year, many coffee farmers required access to credit or advances for the nine months of the year that they were not harvesting coffee and receiving an income. Such heavy reliance on credit also laid the groundwork for ambitious businessman Tobías Umaña Jiménez to create a circular economy in the 1930s and 1940s. As noted in chapter 2, Umaña was one of the region's chief lenders, the owner of all of Tarrazú's private beneficios, as well as its principal employer. Moreover, Umaña's use of scrip, which was only recognized at his numerous businesses, ensured that he would have both customers in his stores and workers in his fields, businesses, and beneficios. Similarly, Umaña frequently provided coffee farmers with advances on next year's crop not in the form of cash loans but credit in his stores. This also meant that a majority of the FNL-produced liquors that were sold in the region outside of licensed bars were sold in Umaña's stores.

Though farmers in Tarrazú were incapable of producing their own textiles or growing rice (the region's high elevation made it impossible to produce this crop), they could produce their own liquors. All that was needed to make homemade guarapo was sugarcane, abundant firewood, water, several pots, and barrels.[23] Families who produced their own liquors not only saved money by not purchasing liquor from Umaña but also made money if they were able to produce enough to sell to their neighbors.

The production of homemade liquors was seen by the state and its agents, Resguardo guards, as a financial crime against the national treasury, but for many struggling peasant families, the production, purchase, and consumption of homemade liquors were acts of defiance against both the state and Umaña's economic hold over their lives. According to Arturo Valverde Navarro, who started working for Umaña at the age of nine, most farmers considered the state and Umaña one and the same: Umaña "owned Tarrazú. . . . He was the jefe político, he was the municipal president, he was the telegrapher, he owned the beneficios, he owned the farms, he owned everything, and he was everywhere. Tarrazú was his."[24] While Valverde is indeed correct that Umaña owned all of the region's beneficios and did hold all of those political offices during his lifetime, Umaña did not do all of these things simultaneously. In fact, as Umaña began increasing his business ventures in the 1930s, he also started the process of retiring from public office. But even though Umaña was not jefe político and the region's only beneficiador at the same time, his considerable economic power, combined with his political know-how and his extensive network of politicians and government functionaries (both in San José and in the region), made it easy for people to continue to conflate Umaña with the Costa Rican state. Moreover, when families chose to buy homemade spirits from neighbors or make their own, they were not only cutting out state profits but also reducing their purchases at Umaña's comisariatos. In this way, their illicit behavior represented a conscious subversion of Umaña's economic dominance.

Cantinas, Pool Halls, Street Brawls, and Tarrazú's Masculine Culture

Most of the spirits purchased at Umaña's comisariatos, as well as those made by families in the region, were intended for consumption *within* the home. Yet, while men certainly drank at home, as drinking was considered a strictly masculine activity, drinking socially was a critical component of masculine culture.[25] Tarrazú had a number of cantinas and pool halls where men could purchase spirits and engage in sometimes-heated discussions of local and national politics, familial strife, the price of coffee, and other issues of prime interest (fig. 3.1).

Local conditions, namely the radical socioeconomic impact of the coffee monoculture and the deep-seated linkage between social drinking and masculinity, coupled with state attempts to eliminated homemade spirits, seem to have made violent confrontations between local men and state authorities an almost inevitable outcome. Coffee cultivation made smallholders reliant on creditors, such as Umaña, and in turn, this decreased the socioeconomic agency individual men exercised over their own households and farms. Moreover, in periods of worldwide economic decline, such as the Great Depression, many men lost part or all of their landholdings and were transformed almost overnight into landless wage laborers. As their traditional roles as breadwinners became threatened, many men thought that this raised doubts about their masculinity.[26] No doubt these socioeconomic transformations, which tended to emasculate men, converted such traditionally masculine activities as drinking, boisterous participation in politics, and street fights into an increasingly necessary outlet. Moreover, the actions of the Resguardo Fiscal not only threatened the economic activity of local liquor distillers, their abuses signaled an attack on the region's poorest men's ability to assert their masculinity via the consumption of spirits.[27] This generated considerable anger against state authorities, often leading to greater incidents of localized violence among men and *between* them and state authorities.

Physical encounters between men often began with fists but could quickly escalate as they used machetes, knives, sticks, rocks, broken bottles, and, on rare occasions, firearms. Many of these conflicts ended with the spilling of blood and with heavy bruises, broken limbs, and a night in prison. Moreover, there was always the potential for death, which was a rare occurrence.

Figure 3.1. Men and boys standing in front of the entrance of a San Marcos de Tarrazú cantina, 1920s. (Courtesy of Juan Mora)

Alcohol-induced behavior and the poor judgment and decision making that come with drunkenness exacerbated these situations, yet drinking was such a significant aspect of the culture that it also served to excuse (partially or completely) even the most drastic and tragic behaviors.[28]

In July 1954, for example, seventy-four-year-old Gregorio Barboza Muñoz made a petition for clemency on behalf of his son, José María "Macho" Barboza Blanco, who had been sentenced to ten years imprisonment after murdering his close friend Silvano de Jesús Navarro Fernández (fig. 3.2).[29] According to the elder Barboza, the "great friendship" between his son and the victim, the lack of premeditation, and the inebriated state of both parties were reasons for reducing his son's prison time.[30] According to several witnesses, after a night of drinking, the younger Barboza bumped into a group of friends, among them Navarro. The men began to antagonize one another lightheartedly and in the sporting spirit of the encounter Barboza dismounted his horse, pulled out his pocketknife, and challenged his friend to do the same. Apparently, Barboza only intended to nick his friend with his pocketknife as an inducement for a fight. Unfortunately for both men, Barboza miscalculated and his knife made a fatally deep incision in his friend's chest.[31] The sight of Navarro's blood seeping through his shirt and his cry "you screwed me up" failed to make the drunken Barboza realize the gravity of the situation. So impaired was Barboza's judgment of his friend's condition that rather than seek medical aid, Barboza galloped into the center of

Figure 3.2. Gregorio "Goyo" Barboza dancing joyfully, 1940s. Barboza is remembered warmly as one of the region's happiest residents and also the owner of a small cantina. Barboza knew sadness, too, after his son's arrest for murder. (Courtesy of Juan Mora)

San Marcos calling out "I screwed Silvano up" to anyone he met, while brandishing the unintended murder weapon in the air.[32] Because Barboza never denied his guilt, the courts sentenced him to prison in San José's penitentiary. Barboza never completed his ten-year sentence, as his father's request for clemency was granted. In the view of the courts, and of Barboza and his family, what had taken place was the tragic consequence of men's drinking but not a serious crime.[33]

Oftentimes, men fought over various issues, such as the honor of a woman or the merits of a political candidate. However, when liquor was involved, the intervention of other men in the ensuing conflict often backfired, escalating the violence and obscuring its cause. As retired schoolteacher Fany Jiménez of San Marcos recalled, "when my father was young, there were fights where men would take two hundred meters [roughly two city blocks] of the street to fight."[34] These street fights could become so large and heated that it sometimes proved dangerous for the police to intercede. Jiménez's memory is born out in the archival evidence of this period. On April 28, 1912, San Marcos police officer José Vargas Retana accused four men of attacking him. According to Vargas Retana's sworn testimony, the incident began when he encountered "Guillermo Campos, . . . Dolores Sánchez and Rafael Rivera fighting" on San Marcos's main street. In an attempt to fulfill his duty and maintain peace, Vargas Retana interceded and asked the three inebriated men to accompany him to the local jail. In response, "Campos took out the knife he was carrying." The sight of Campos's blade reportedly disquieted some in the crowd, and a struggle soon broke out between Campos and several unnamed members of the crowd. During the commotion, Vargas Retana lost consciousness after receiving "a strong blow to the head." One witness told Vargas Retana that it was "Malaquías Zúñiga who had hit [him] various times in the head, though . . . [Vargas Retana] only felt one" blow. Subsequent examination revealed that Vargas Retana's injuries were considerable but impermanent. According to the report, Vargas Retana had sustained "a wound on the upper part of his head that was six centimeters long . . . and one millimeter deep."[35]

The physical attacks leveled against Officer Vargas Retana point up the fact that Tarrazú's police exercised restricted rather than absolute authority in the region. Moreover, drunken men did not always take seriously the threat of arrest by a local policeman. Perhaps this had something to do with the limitations of the local legal system. Thus, even though Officer Vargas Retana's accused attackers were brought to trial, the case was eventually dismissed.

The Tarrazú police's feeble authority contrasts greatly with that of the Resguardo Fiscal. Although the Costa Rican state granted both police officers and Resguardo Fiscal its authority, only the Resguardo had military authority. Moreover, while the Resguardo would take accused bootleggers immediately to San José for trial, individuals arrested by the local police were tried in local courts.[36] Although it might seem to have been in the state's interest to allow the Resguardo to assist local law enforcement, their function in the community was actually limited to the arrest of unsanctioned liquor producers, consumers, sellers, and anyone who placed in danger the *economic* interests of the Costa Rican state.[37] This meant that if a drunken mob were openly drinking homemade liquors or cutting down state-owned forests without a license, the Resguardo could intervene, but under any other circumstances, the local police were on their own in cases of drunken disorder.[38]

Men's social activities went beyond drinking and brawling, however, and particularly in years of presidential elections, local men formed and participated actively in political clubs.[39] These clubs typically were formed with the goal of promoting a single candidate or political party. Members would come together on a regular basis to discuss their candidate's platform and formulate an invitation for their candidate to visit the region and make a speech. Drinking was strictly prohibited within political clubs, and it was unheard of for men within the same political club to engage in a fight with one another.[40] Political discussions could become violent, when men continued their political discussions at a bar or pool hall, where those of different political stripes might be itching to come to blows with them.[41] In the 1940s, a number of political shifts and episodes of electoral fraud at both the local and national levels would make political discussions increasingly tense and impassioned.[42]

In 1947, politics spurred one of the largest street fights in Tarrazú's history. Decades later, prominent coffee farm owner Manuel Castro, of San Pablo de León Cortés, remembered how, on Christmas Eve of 1947, a political discussion about the validity of the upcoming year's elections became so intense that the entire plaza of San Pablo was filled with brawling men, all shouting out "death" to one another as they threw sticks, stones, and glass bottles.[43] The size of the mayhem was such that Castro claimed "the police came, but there were too many [violent] men and the police left running."[44] Castro alone recalled the date of this politically charged scuffle; however, numerous men and women in San Pablo remembered the violent political encounter that took place in the heart of their town.[45] As in the case of the men who attacked Officer Vargas Retana, it seems the men who attacked local authorities in this instance received no punishment. In fact, no official documents exist on the incident, suggesting the police made no record of what took place. Perhaps the police officers who were involved chose not to file a report with San José because of the humiliating reality that they were unable to maintain the peace. Or perhaps a report was filed, but sometime in the following sixty years, it was destroyed, misplaced, or misfiled. Regardless of whether or not local police filed a report, this event was part of the intense political turmoil that would only calm after the 1948 Civil War, the subject of chapters 4 and 5.

In sum, Tarrazú's cantinas, pool halls, and political clubs were not only venues where men met and discussed issues, forged alliances, and sometimes came to blows, they were also spaces that defined manhood. The ability to enter these spaces, participate in discussions, and consume liquor was a rite of passage for many men and a central component of masculine identity.

Women's Spaces, Domestic and Gendered Violence

The position of women and their children on the lowest rung of Tarrazú's social hierarchy was enforced in many ways, including outright violence. In the late 1950s, nurse and midwife Cecilia Jiménez Rojas arrived in San Marcos de Tarrazú to head up the local birthing clinic. Jiménez was originally from the Central Valley town of Turrialba. Though also a rural community, in comparison to San Marcos, Turrialba boasted infrastructure such as electric power and paved roads.[46] While the "dusty . . . streets" and the lack of electricity made her job difficult, the region's gendered relations proved the most trying part of Jiménez's job. As a nurse, she was expected to offer her patients information and access to birth control. However, "women had very little control [over their bodies], . . . and they feared their husbands," so most women refused to become informed, let alone to use contraceptives.[47]

Moreover, for Jiménez, who had studied nursing and was an independently employed woman who believed in gender equality, living in Tarrazú was isolating and restrictive. She suggested that, with the exception of Catholic Church services and the annual civic festivities, *all* of San Marcos's public social spaces were exclusively masculine spaces.[48] Women were "expected to be quiet, serve their husbands, and not leave the home without them." Additionally, women in the region "accepted infidelity and beatings from their drunken husbands."[49] Not only were Jiménez's social activities limited in the community, her access to other women with whom to socialize was restricted as well, since decent women were expected to largely remain within their homes. When women did leave their homes, it was often to go to Mass and to attend the occasional social event, such as the dances that were held to celebrate the patron saint of each community or weddings that both men and women would attend.[50] At these events, women and men would dance, but men would also drink among themselves, excluding women.

The presence of women at social activities did not preempt the chance that violence would break out between men but only changed its trigger. Retired Resguardo guard Socorro Galera Solera recalled attending dances as a youth in the 1950s: "When I danced with a woman, . . . it was not unheard of for another man to take out his knife because I was dancing with *his* [dance] partner."[51] According to Galera, oftentimes the women were not even aware that a particular man had decided that she was his partner. Perhaps this had much to do with the courting rituals of the time. As Lourdes Gamboa of Carrizal de León Cortés, who was born in 1924, explained, "back then, we never looked the boys in the face. I did not know the color of my husband's eyes until after we were married. . . . Back then, we [young women and young men] were scared to look each other in the face. . . . When we danced, the boys would put handkerchiefs in their hands to not touch us. . . . Those were other times."[52] At the few social events that women attended, husbands, fathers, brothers, and other familial males were always present. The presence of familial men was critical to protecting women's reputations and, in turn, familial honor.

Tarrazú's patriarchal society not only restricted women to limited social spaces and activities outside of the domestic sphere, but also made it difficult for women to establish independent identities. Instead, women were understood as the property or as an extension of their fathers, husbands, and sons. As sixty-something Luz Berta Monge explained, "when I was little, I was Matías Monge's daughter; when I married, I became Tista Naranjo's wife; and now, as a widow, I am Froylan Naranjo's mother."[53] For Monge, it was an issue of pride that her identity within the community was always linked with that of a man's, since in her estimation all of these men were honorable, honest, and hardworking.[54] However, for other women whose fathers and husbands were abusive or alcoholics, the power these men exercised over their lives and that of their mothers, siblings, and children left a painful legacy.

Drunken men often terrorized their families on returning home from a night of drinking with other men, and some men drank their wages away, leaving women and children to suffer hunger and other deprivations. Moreover, because drunken men often engaged in physical fights, women often spent Saturday nights "difficultly," as they worried about the state in which their husbands would return home.[55] Domestic violence resulted from other causes besides drinking. As retired school teacher Fany Jiménez of San Marcos de Tarrazú told it, "back then, men were told that to be men they had to hit women. Women were educated to have children, do the housework, and accept being beaten."[56] The passage from boyhood to manhood in Tarrazú comprised three components: (1) the ability to drink in the cantina; (2) the exercise of absolute control over women and children in the household; and (3) the ability to engage other men in violent confrontations. So, while a boy, just like a girl or woman, was the potential victim of older men's violence, a mature man was defined by his ability to mete out violence against weaker members of *his* household. Thus, liquor, gender, and power came together centrally in the definition of manhood in Tarrazú.[57]

While public acts of drunken disorder were a cause for concern among Tarrazú officials, the violence that took place behind closed doors was of little interest to the state. In fact, what men did or did not do to their wives and children within their homes was deemed strictly of familial concern. The lack of state and societal concern over domestic violence provided men with a green light to physically, emotionally, and sexually abuse their wives, children, servants, and other inferiors. The transition to coffee production (which led to the socioeconomic debilitation of many of the region's small- and medium-scale farmers) likely led to an increase in cases of domestic violence. Men attempted to increase their sense of agency within the home as their ability to provide for their families decreased. It was arguably the women and children who bore the brunt of the negative consequences of Tarrazú's masculine drinking culture.

In the mid-1950s, for instance, a man brought to San Marcos the "mutilated" corpse of his twenty-three-year-old wife, stuffed into a "coffee sack."[58] The young woman, Clara Casa, reportedly died of a heart attack.[59] Casa's childhood friend, Juana Fernández, who was selected to prepare the body for burial, however, adamantly denied that her friend's life came to a natural end. According to Fernández, Casa's husband had a reputation for being excessively violent with his wife when he drank. Moreover, Fernández claimed that Casa's body was covered in bruises and her neck was broken and exhibited clear strangulation marks. Frightened by what she discovered, Fernández confided in the parish priest before her friend's funeral. The priest warned her to keep quiet, suggesting that "saying something would not help anyone, it would just cause problems for Clara's 'poor' widower."[60] Fernández asserted that although Casa's passing was especially difficult for her because they were friends, "there were many Claras."[61]

Even when violence against women did not end in homicide, it impacted the whole family. Catalina Muñoz of San Lorenzo de Tarrazú related that when she was "a child, my father drank a lot and owed everyone money. He drank whatever he earned. [In the summer,] he would take us all [Muñoz and her siblings] to pick coffee, and whatever we earned picking, he would take to the bar. We went hungry a lot."[62] Making matters worse, Muñoz's father was a violent drunk who frequently beat her, her siblings, and their mother. Apparently, his main justification for beating them was that they had eaten too much, leaving him hungry, or that not enough food had been prepared.[63] However, it seems that the true issue was that Muñoz's father spent the vast majority of his wages on liquor, leaving insufficient funds to feed the family.

Muñoz, who was born in the 1950s, explained that she had forgiven her father for the "beatings and drinking, since that was what men did then."[64] Nonetheless, she could not forgive the fact that he constantly allowed drunken men to sleep on the earthen floor of their one-bedroom wooden shack. Muñoz recollected that on the nights that her father went to the bar, he would sometimes make some money to pay for the next day's drinking by "renting" out his floor to any man who did not want to go home that night. For Muñoz, who shared a small bed with three of her sisters, the nights drunken men spent on their floor were nights of terror. Muñoz recalled that the men "would try and climb into bed with us girls and we would scream. They would touch us and our mom would light the candle and they would lie back down on the ground. It was really terrible."[65]

The most interesting aspect of Muñoz's recollection is the fact that it was her mother and not her father who stopped the houseguests from entering the girls' bed. The men who made these attempts were not only making a move against the girls' honor but were also placing into question their father's position as patriarch. The senior Muñoz's reputation and honor would suffer irreparably were his daughters to have become pregnant out of wedlock, be it by choice or force.[66] Moreover, Muñoz was well within his legal and socially prescribed right to throw out his houseguests for their attempts to defile his daughters. That being the case, one might assume that Muñoz's father would have acted when he heard his daughter's screams, but he did not. Maybe the Muñoz patriarch was too drunk or too soundly asleep to hear his daughters' screams. The houseguests were either extremely reckless to attempt to sexually abuse another man's daughters while he slept a few feet away, or Muñoz's reputation as a drunkard was such that his houseguests had no respect for him or his dependents. Unfortunately, for the Muñoz girls, the latter was likely the case.

In Tarrazú, a man's reputation could go a long way. In fact, up until the 1930s, labor contracts, property sales, and loans were often "signed" by an exchange of beard hairs between men.[67] The hairs were not kept but thrown to the wind as a way of saying that each man was confident that the other would uphold his end of the bargain. With no written contracts, a man's word and reputation were often all he had to go by. Perhaps this practice was rooted in the fact that few residents could write much more than their names or that there was a lack of local attorneys, but the end result was that considerable social weight was placed upon a man's reputation. Thus, the drunken houseguests who attempted to enter Muñoz and her sisters' bed almost certainly would never have tried to do the same had they been staying in the home of a more respected member of society. In fact, the daughters of drunks, women who had been abandoned by their husbands, unwed mothers, and widows and their children were the most vulnerable members of Tarrazú society. Their susceptibility came not only from a precarious economic situation but also because of moral and social scorn. So, although the Muñoz girls' experience was not the norm, since few men would allow drunken men to sleep on the floor beside their young daughters, unfortunately, the Muñoz girls were far from the only children of humble means in Tarrazú who at some time or another fought off or became victims of the advances of sexual predators. While a man's social clout might have dissuaded other men from meddling with his wife and children, given the fact that many women and children suffered from this type of abuse, something more than just patriarchal position was likely at play.

The very nature of domestic labor in the countryside placed young women and children of both sexes in a vulnerable position. Most of the region's residents lived on farms, and there was some distance between their homes and those of their neighbors. Moreover, from an early age, children were often required to take on tasks outside the home with little adult supervision.[68] Children frequently collected firewood, weeded their family's vegetable gardens, and walked long distances to attend school and to run errands for their families, and young girls also laundered their families' clothing in streambeds.[69]

Magdalena de Muñoz, who was born in the late 1940s in the small community of San Lorenzo de Tarrazú, recalled that her mother, Mireya Vega, was extremely protective of her and her sisters and never allowed them to go anywhere unaccompanied, not even to their nearest neighbor's house.[70] Vega's concern and protective attitude toward her daughters likely stemmed from her own experience as a young girl in the 1920s. According to de Muñoz, her mother came from an extremely poor family. Her father, Ernesto Vega, was a landless peon on a wealthy neighbor's farms.[71] Mireya Vega was the oldest and often worked as her mother's assistant, helping to care for her younger siblings and bringing water to the home each day.[72]

One afternoon, after twelve-year-old Mireya had filled her water pail at the riverbed, she took the path up to her family's shack and was grabbed from behind and thrown to the ground. The man who had pulled her to the ground was the married son of her father's employer. De Muñoz related that the man raped her mother, "after shoving his handkerchief in her mouth and warning her that if she told anyone what had taken place he would kill her and her family."[73] Terrified, Vega ran home and did not initially tell anyone. A few months later, however, when Vega began to show that she was pregnant, she confided in her grandmother what had taken place. The family chose not to notify the authorities or to bring the crime to the attention of their employer out of fear that Ernesto Vega would lose his job and the home they rented. Mireya Vega gave birth to a small boy before her thirteenth birthday. By the time she was fourteen, she also knew the tragedy of losing a child, as the little boy apparently died of a fever.[74]

For de Muñoz, her family's poverty was critical in explaining what happened to her mother and the lack of consequences for her assailant.[75] Her grandfather's position as a landless peon, dependent on his employer to provide his family with both a home and sustenance, left him with little recourse and few alternatives. The family's inaction might have been read by the larger society and by Mireya Vega's attacker as complacency on the part of the Vega family; however, it might also be read as what historian Steve J. Stern has described as "tacit yet false consent."[76] Stern's examination of gendered relations in late-colonial Mexico suggests that subaltern men were frequently unable to defend the honor of their wives, daughters, and lovers from the desires of elite men. A similar dynamic seems to have been at play in Tarrazú, that is to say, socioeconomic inequalities shaped the ability of victims and their families to seek out legal justice or other forms of retribution against their assailants.[77]

Yet, the same rules clearly did not apply to girls of a higher socioeconomic background. Unlike the daughters of poor peasants, wealthy girls rarely if ever had reason to worry that unsupervised excursions might invite sexual victimization. Witness the case of Luz Berta Monge, Tobías Umaña Jiménez's great-niece, who lived just ten kilometers from where Mireya Vega was raped, in the community of Guadalupe de Tarrazú. Monge, who like Vega, regularly gathered water for her family, recounted that she was a very innocent child and never worried (nor does she today think she ever had reason to worry) about sexual predators.[78] As a little girl Monge and her sisters "walked unaccompanied to school," and in the summer, they "picked coffee together" without direct adult supervision. Moreover, as a young unmarried woman she walked nearly five kilometers each day to her great-uncle's beneficio, where she was employed. Today, as a great-grandmother, Monge recognized that many "terrible things" happened to girls and young women whom she knew when they were little, but she quickly noted that she did not know of these things until she was married and had children of her own.[79] For Monge, whose father had his own coffee farm (and whose grandfathers and uncles all had sizable holdings, and whose grandmother was Umaña's younger sister), her family's socioeconomic position was an effective deterrent to ill-intentioned men.

A family's socioeconomic status was also important because it could determine whether a young woman would have to seek employment outside of her home, dramatically increasing her risk of sexual, physical, and emotional violence. In Tarrazú and other areas of Costa Rica both rural and urban, it was not uncommon for adolescent girls from humble families to seek employment as domestic laborers for wealthy neighbors and relatives.[80] On the face of it, employment of young girls as domestic helpers was a great boon to their poor families. The girls received free room and board, reducing the families' monthly expenses, and the girls' wages could be used to purchase food and other goods for the whole family. Ideally, domestic labor also gave girls extra experience in cooking, cleaning house, caring for children, sewing and washing laundry—experiences they could use in their own homes once they were married.

Nonetheless, many families did whatever they could, despite their weak economic situation, to avoid sending their daughters to work in other families' homes. There is the case of Margarita Mora, whose widowed father struggled economically to make ends meet throughout her childhood but who refused to let any of his four daughters work as domestic laborers.[81] Mora claimed that she suggested a couple of times that she could help the family out by working as a domestic, but her "father did not like the idea of us working outside the home."[82] Mora did not know why her father was so opposed to the idea, but perhaps he knew of the stories of young women such as Sonia Ugalde Madriz of Guadalupe de Tarrazú. Ugalde worked as a domestic servant for several years for a wealthy family in San Marcos but returned home to her parents before her eighteenth birthday in shame after she became pregnant.[83] While Mora and her sisters never labored as domestic laborers during their adolescent years, they did pick coffee during the summers and sought employment at Tobías Umaña Jiménez's coffee processing mill as selectors.[84] Mora's father was not opposed to his girls working, just their working as domestic servants.

The Mora sisters were an exception. Many young women of humble means sought employment at one time or another as domestic servants.[85] In many cases, however, a familial bond united the young domestic worker to her employers. Perhaps this was done by design to limit physical and sexual abuse of young girls. But blood ties did not always serve as a deterrent to abusive men.[86] In 1929, for instance, thirteen-year-old Lidia Angulo Araya of San Pablo de Tarrazú was sent to assist her paternal aunt with domestic work after the aunt had a baby.[87] Angulo's aunt married one of the region's wealthiest men, Ramón Blanco, who owned a coffee mill. While Angulo enjoyed working alongside her young aunt in the home's large kitchen, she feared her aunt's violent husband, "Don Ramón." Angulo recalled that one afternoon she sat in Blanco's favorite chair for a small rest between chores, and Blanco lifted the chair with her still seated. He then tossed the chair with the girl down a flight of steps. When both came to a stop at the end of the staircase, Blanco retrieved the now-empty chair.[88] As young Angulo sobbed and attempted to make sense of what had just happened, Blanco told her: "This is *my* chair, do not ever sit in *my* chair."[89]

Blanco's violence toward his niece is unsettling. Yet, in many ways, Angulo was fortunate, since a number of her contemporaries who labored as domestic workers endured physical, emotional, and sexual abuse. Eva Fernández of Santa María de Dota, who was sent off to work for a wealthy family in San José when she was just thirteen years old, provided a case in point. Seven days a week, Fernández worked from 6:00 A.M. to 9:00 P.M., caring for the family's three young children. This work schedule was demanding, but Fernández claimed that she largely enjoyed caring for the young children.[90] However, Fernández's employment came to an end just a few months after it began because of her male boss's inappropriate behavior. Apparently, her male employer repeatedly attempted to crawl into her bed at night and she would push him off. This went on for several months with the "old man" apologizing each time, stating he had been "sleepwalking." The final straw came one morning when the man asked her to bring a cup of coffee to his study. Fernández claimed she knocked on the door and he told her to come in. She found her boss standing naked before her. Having never seen a naked man before, the sight frightened her so much that she screamed and dropped the coffee cup, which broke into pieces. Her screams brought the man's wife, who slapped Fernández across the face, called her a "whore," and threw her out of the house with no pay, supposedly because her wages were needed to cover the cost of the broken coffee cup. Fernández feared that her father would beat her for returning home empty handed and for acting like a "whore." She explained how, at the time, she did not see herself as the victim and believed that the incident was her fault.[91] Her fear of punishment led her to not relate the incident to her father but instead to claim that the family did not have the money to pay her wages so she had been forced to return home.[92]

Victims of sexual violence tended to come from the lowest rungs of Tarrazú's socioeconomic ladder, but their assailants were often men with some position in the local community. Indeed, sexual assailants appear to have calculated their own position and that of potential victims to ensure that their victims and their families would not take action. In fact, most of these assailants seem to have done a good job of assessing the risks, since just two cases of rape or inappropriate touching from the period under study are documented in regional files at the National Archives. Both of these cases are exceptional because victims and their families contested their assailants in the courts. In addition, and perhaps more significantly, in both of these cases the accused crossed social boundaries that were considered taboo by the larger society, sparking considerable outrage, not just on the part of the victims and their families. In short, the value in these cases lies in their exceptionality since they effectively proved the rule. As such, they offer a window into what Tarrazú society considered acceptable and unacceptable behavior. They also highlight the limited local resources available to contend with pedophiles and rapists.

In 1958, Víctor Manuel Álfaro and Basilio Vega Valverde of San Andrés de Tarrazú wrote a letter to the Department of the Interior (Ministro de Gobernación) requesting that San José officials fire the local chief of police.[93] The two men wrote that the chief of police had "committed infractions with various . . . nine and ten year-old . . . girls" at the local elementary school. The letter writers' daughters were among the victims. The men, however, were moved by more than just their own family's pain and were writing on behalf of "the whole community," which hoped for "a return to tranquility" that would only be possible with this man's removal. The letter writers claimed the situation had become so dire that the community's men determined that until the chief of police was removed from his post they "would not send their girls to school."[94]

The sense of agency on the part of these families is particularly interesting and suggests that something made this case different from the majority of incidents of sexual abuse in the region, which went unrecorded. Perhaps the fact that the chief of police attacked various girls of the community in a public building—the local schoolhouse—meant that there were multiple witnesses to what had taken place. Moreover, numerous families shared the outrage over his alleged actions. This meant that individual victims and their families were part of a collective and, as such, were less intimidated by the police chief's authority. Ultimately, it is unclear whether the parents' actions resulted in the removal of this abusive official. No response from the Department of the Interior has survived to the present day. Perhaps the police chief was summarily fired. Then again, maybe this letter was filed away without any action being taken. Whatever authorities did or did not do in San José, the letter makes clear that, at least in one instance, families united against a recognized pedophile and refused to be intimidated into silence by the assailant's position of power.

The second case that is recorded in the National Archives is that of ten-year-old Ricardo Ugalde Madriz, of Guadalupe de Tarrazú.[95] On October 27, 1964, Lieutenant Mario Robles Mena and Resguardo Fiscal guards Francisco Mora Flores and Rafael Padilla Morales observed as young Ugalde disappeared into a coffee field alongside thirty-one-year-old Edgar Fallas Robles.[96] It is unclear why these Resguardo guards followed Ugalde, who was returning home from school before being sidetracked by his adult companion. Perhaps they suspected that Fallas was producing contraband liquors and the fourth grader was assisting him in some way. Regardless of what they suspected, it is unlikely they were prepared for what they came across that afternoon: Fallas raping young Ugalde in the coffee field.

The Resguardo Fiscal escorted both parties to the local police headquarters in San Marcos, where each was required to provide his testimony. The young Ugalde told his interrogators, "For the past fifteen days [Fallas] has been doing this to me. . . . He takes me to this field and he takes off my pants and makes me do what you saw."[97] Apparently, Fallas coaxed Ugalde into the coffee field the first time by offering him the considerable sum of "two colones," which at the time was two day's wages for a day laborer such as Fallas.[98] Perhaps because the authorities caught him red-handed, Fallas did not deny raping the boy and paying him a sum of money each time he did so.

The financial element of this case is particularly interesting and disturbing. Whereas most women who were victims of rape in the region claimed that they and their families were silenced into inaction by a combination of threats and fear, Fallas does not appear to have threatened his young victim but rather secured his submission through considerable economic rewards.

This tactic likely had less to do with the victim and more to do with the assailant. As the son of an unmarried woman who had become pregnant while employed as a domestic servant, Ugalde was in many ways an ideal victim for this type of crime. The young boy's birth had not only brought shame to his mother and her family but had also cost his mother her employment.[99] In fact, the pair had resided with Ugalde's maternal grandparents since her pregnancy became known.

While Ugalde and his mother were reliant on his grandparents' charity, his mother's family were far from poor. In fact, one of the mysteries of the case is why Sonia Ugalde had sought work as a domestic laborer in the first place. Regardless of the reasons behind that decision, the young victim's grandparents and great-grandparents owned some of the largest coffee farms in Guadalupe.[100] In stark contrast, the unmarried Fallas owned no lands and lived precariously as a wage laborer.[101] While the court documents do not reveal who his employer was at the time of his arrest, Fallas probably worked for a wealthy landholder in the region. Perhaps he was even employed by Ugalde's family and this is how he first came to know his young victim. So, although Ugalde and his mother may have been the black sheep of their family, their family occupied a considerably better socioeconomic position in the community than did Fallas. This disparity arguably forced Fallas to employ incentives rather than threats to induce his victim's silence and compliance.

Still, the most salient element of this case is the fact that Fallas was not only a pedophile but one who targeted little boys. The victims' gender should not be minimized, especially since the Resguardo guards who discovered the crime, as well as the judge who presided over the case, were men. As former little boys, these officials likely felt sympathy for Fallas Robles's young victim. Additionally, Fallas's sexual proclivities made his actions both a legal crime and a moral sin in this highly Catholic community. However, the primary reason why this case made it into the historical records, as in the case of San Andrés, was the fact that there were multiple witnesses to the crime. Had the Resguardo guards not followed Fallas and Ugalde, it is unlikely there would be any record of this crime. Yet they did, and Fallas was convicted of raping a minor younger than "twelve years of age."[102] While the penal code determined this crime merited between ten and twenty years imprisonment, because this was Fallas's first brush with the law, the local judge sentenced him to six years and eight months of prison. This punishment seems small, given the clear physical, mental, and emotional repercussions this crime would have on young Ugalde, but the sentence is significant. In fact, Fallas appears to be the only man from Tarrazú who was tried, let alone sentenced to jail, for the crime of rape during this period.

Conclusion

While the Costa Rican legal system held Fallas Robles accountable for his crime, his trial and conviction had an exceptional outcome. Tarrazú authorities and local society largely ignored, dismissed, and justified physical, sexual, and emotional abuse, particularly when these took place in a domestic context. Authorities were largely unconcerned with what happened in citizens' homes, and victims rarely came forward to authorities. Moreover, in cases where assailants were not victims' fathers and husbands, the assailant almost always held a position of social, political, or economic power over the victim and his or her family. In other words, the less privileged elements of Tarrazú society were the region's easiest prey and the most likely to have suffered physical, sexual, and emotional violence.

To look at domestic violence alone, however, is to ignore the root causes of this social ill: namely, the emasculation many men felt as their power to provide for their families decreased amid the polarization and instability that accompanied the region's transition to a coffee economy in this period. Dependence on international markets, coupled with a reliance on local creditors, meant that in years of low coffee returns, families could lose landholdings and become wage laborers rather than independent farmers. As men were less able to provide economic security for their families, they turned to other means to assert themselves as men. For some, this meant drinking liquor at home or in a bar. For others, this meant engaging in politics or fistfights. For still others, this meant beating members of their families, and for a select few, it might have meant thinking that they could more easily get away with taking sexual advantage of those in a more vulnerable position than themselves. As many men lost ground socioeconomically, they often asserted violent control over their dependents and socioeconomic inferiors.

In this period of economic instability, where alcohol became increasingly central in defining manhood locally, the Costa Rican state, in the form of the Resguardo Fiscal, took steps to undermine men's access to spirits. While the state did not wish to decrease alcohol consumption, but rather merely encourage consumers to purchase FNL-produced liquors, for many men such liquors were prohibitively expensive. Hence, the Resguardo's activities were viewed as an attack on poor men's right to drink and also as the state bolstering the local socioeconomic status quo headed up by Umaña, the primary seller of FNL-produced liquors in the region. Moreover, the interrogation and search tactics employed by the Resguardo, including home invasions, property searches, and the physical torture of men and boys, all served to humiliate men and undermine their ability as family patriarchs to protect themselves and their dependents.

In sum, violence in its many forms—physical, psychological, sexual, and economic—maintained a constant presence in Tarrazú society. While drunken brawls, the production of homemade liquors, and the loss of properties in times of economic decline are part of a shared memory by men and women in Tarrazú, only women seem willing to remember domestic violence. A tradition of violence is acutely felt by women who suffered at the hands of their fathers and later their husbands and other men of the community and who have watched their own mothers and daughters and other female family members suffer similar fates. Some men were victimized as children, but perhaps their own experiences as men in a position of agency has helped them to suppress what they witnessed as children. In sum, state violence, socioeconomic control, domestic violence, and even fistfights between men all served to maintain the social order and ensure that patriarchal authority was respected.

Starting in the 1930s, however, local men would begin to challenge the precarious nature of state authority. Political tensions in the 1930s and 1940s were a product of economic declines on the global coffee market, the embrace of new political ideas on the national stage, namely Communism, and increased national insecurity as World War II broke out. As local men experienced economic decline and uncertainty, their interest in politics expanded and the traditional linkage between masculinity and the right to vote became ever more important. In this political context, government authorities, desperate to retain the order and their grasp on political power, increasingly relied on violent repression of opposition supporters and candidates. These attacks were read by local men as an attempt by the state to emasculate them and would (with outside leadership) lead to the formation of a strong local opposition that would determine to take up arms in 1948 following elections that were marred by blatant electoral fraud by both sides. The hundreds of Tarrazú boys and men who went to war against state authority were motivated by a desire to ensure that their votes were counted and in turn their masculine rights as Costa Rican citizens were respected. The next two chapters delve more deeply into the catalysts of the 1948 Civil War, seeking to explain why this conflict broke out in the Tarrazú Valley and also examine the consequences of this violent political transformation for both Tarrazúceños and the nation as a whole.

4

Revolt in Tarrazú

On March 14, 1948, fourteen-year-old Fany Jiménez noticed a group of "a hundred or so men dressed in khaki" quietly moving on the road that linked her San Marcos home to the city center. Days later, she learned that the men had attacked the schoolhouse with rifles, handguns, rocks, and sticks only minutes after they passed her home. The town's jefe político, civil servants, police officers, Resguardo guards, physician, and the parish priest had been awaiting the rebel attack in the schoolhouse and responded with rifles, handguns, and the town's sole cannon.[1]

While San Marcos officials attempted to defend the schoolhouse, it soon became evident that they were not only surrounded but also outnumbered. They capitulated before the gun battle could produce casualties. The khaki-clad men and their leader José "Pepe" Figueres's seizure of San Marcos that March morning was their second of three victories that day. Hours earlier, they had taken the neighboring town of San Pablo without firing a single bullet. Figueres and his "National Liberation Army" surprised San Pablo's only police officer and Resguardo Fiscal guard, both of whom surrendered without a struggle.[2] With both San Pablo and San Marcos in rebel hands, Figueres's troops moved on to Santa María de Dota, which, like San Pablo, surrendered without a fight.[3] By sunset, National Liberation forces controlled Tarrazú's three most populated communities.

Upon seizing control of these towns, Figueres's numbers increased dramatically. News of the uprising quickly spread, and hundreds of men and boys from throughout Tarrazú volunteered to assist Figueres in his quest to topple the state, a feat they accomplished just forty-four days later.

This chapter explores the local political realities of the 1940s that created the conditions for revolt in Tarrazú. This insurgency would impact the entire nation's political, economic, social, and cultural development, but my analysis focuses on the geographic core of Figueres's movement during the civil war: Tarrazú. Indeed, the communities of Tarrazú provided Figueres with critical material and personnel. The war itself and its political, social, and cultural consequences are the subject of chapter 5; here, however, I analyze key political events at the local and national levels that prepared the climate for revolt. Scholarship on the 1948 Civil War largely centers on celebratory examinations of Figueres as the founder of the Second Republic and as the primary political force behind the nation's decision to abolish the military.[4] This chapter focuses more on some of the reasons why Tarrazú farmers, small business owners, and hacendados put their lives on the line to overthrow the Costa Rican state.

I posit that, because of the establishment of universal male suffrage, Costa Rican men considered the vote a fundamental element of manhood by 1940.[5] Critical to this development are a series of electoral reforms in the mid-1920s that made Costa Rica an effective democracy, by requiring all voters to register before election day and provide a voter identification card before voting, and most importantly the secret ballot was instituted.[6] These reforms effectively empowered the nation's Hispanic adult male population, regardless of their socioeconomic position, with the opportunity to shape the national political future at the ballot box while also limiting (though it did not end) elite politicians' abilities to run blatantly fraudulent elections.[7] Arguably, this meant that by 1940, Costa Rica had a well-established suffrage system, which permitted the nation's Hispanic men to feel invested in their political system and to see the vote as an integral part of their masculine identity.[8] Moreover, in the context of widespread economic hardship, brought about by the Great Depression and World War II, as men in these decades struggled increasingly to provide for their families' needs, a traditional masculine responsibility, the vote's weight in establishing masculinity arguably increased.[9] The growing symbolic importance of the vote meant that men viewed any attempt to keep them from voting as an effort to emasculate them. Voting became increasingly important to Costa Rican men, and as this chapter details, the national political stage became increasingly polarized in the 1930s and 1940s, helping create the political and social conditions for armed rebellion.

Although Tarrazú was far from the nation's governmental center (San José), local residents made a concerted effort to be politically informed. A number of Tarrazúceños not only read San José newspapers and magazines but also, more importantly, took it upon themselves to keep their neighbors abreast of national events in the political clubs they often founded and managed in the region. Within these clubs, men (owners of small- and medium-sized coffee farms) discussed political theories, candidates' merits, recently passed legislation, and current events. In turn, these clubs served to create a local political consciousness. In other words, national political ideas and events, mediated locally, significantly shaped the way locals understood political realities. While Tarrazúceños were aware of national political events, the real catalyst for revolt was resentment toward local authorities who repeatedly overstepped their authority, not only by beating and imprisoning local oppositionists but also by attempting to rob local men of their right to vote. Tarrazú authorities' attacks on men's suffrage rights produced deep-seated resentments toward both local authorities and the national government, grievances that in 1948 would provide Figueres with a community of thousands ready and willing to revolt.

The Origins of Tarrazú's Opposition Movement

On March 15, many of Figueres's rebel forces were peons, or wage laborers, and their sons, who worked at his *cabuya* hacienda.[10] Fittingly named La Lucha Sin Fin (The Endless Struggle), the hacienda was located just four kilometers to the south of El Empalme de Dota, in the community of San Cristobal de Desamparados.[11] Many of Figueres's employees were Tarrazúceños and their familial connections within Tarrazú unquestionably assisted Figueres's ability to recruit soldiers for his cause. While Figueres found substantial support throughout Tarrazú, arguably his key supporter was Marcos Chanto, coffee farmer turned local politician and then leader of the opposition.

Chanto headed the local oppositionist political club in San Marcos and was an avid reader who made it a point to order copies of the monthly magazine *Surco* and the daily *El Diario de Costa Rica* from San José.[12] Both of these publications were extremely critical of the contentious and fraud-ridden elections of 1944 and 1948, as well as of the governments of Rafael Ángel Calderón (1940–44) and Teodoro Picado Michalski (1944–48), who they accused of extreme acts of corruption and dictatorial tendencies. Armed with ideas from these publications, Chanto "indoctrinated [the community of San Marcos] one person at a time," according to his son, Juan Chanto. For most of the 1940s, Chanto reportedly took newspaper and magazine clippings with him to Mass each Sunday and after the service would find a spot on the church's steps to discuss political ideas, events, and candidates with other Marqueños exiting the service. In this way, he helped "organize the community for the [1944 and 1948] elections" and for the Civil War that rampant electoral fraud ultimately inspired.[13]

Chanto's entrance into oppositionist politics began in 1943 when he renounced his post as San Marcos de Tarrazú's jefe político. According to Juan Chanto, his father left his influential position within the local government and founded a political club in San Marcos to support the "opposition candidate, León Cortés Castro," believing that then president Calderón was directing the nation "towards communism."[14] During his presidency, Calderón aligned himself repeatedly with Vanguardia Popular (PVP), the nation's Communist party, to pass his Social Guarantees in 1941 and again in 1943 to pass the Labor Code, which together established a strong social security system for the nation's workers.[15] Yet, according to Juan Chanto, his father did not oppose either of these radical reforms or any specific actions taken by Calderón in alliance with PVP.[16] This suggests that, more than taking issue with Calderón's coalition with the Communists, Chanto surrendered his political post over his loyalty to former president León Cortés, Calderón's predecessor and the man who initially appointed Chanto to his post as Tarrazú's jefe político in 1936. Chanto's 1943 resignation, after seven years of public service, reflected the power of patronage bonds and the fragmentation of the ruling National Republican Party (Partido Nacional Republicano, PNR) during Calderón's presidency, which would eventually create the conditions locally and nationally for Figueres's military rebellion.

Despite the fact that constituents of the PNR elected both Cortés in 1936 and Calderón in 1940 to the presidency, these men were never political allies. In fact, Cortés initially refused to back Calderón's candidacy, relenting only after he secured Calderón's promise to back him for the presidency in 1944.[17] Calderón broke this commitment to Cortés, however, after purging the government of high-ranking *cortecistas* (Cortés supporters). This process began on May 1, 1941, when Calderón successfully backed Deputy Teodoro Picado to become president of Costa Rica's Legislative Assembly, which resulted in Deputy Otto Cortés Fernández, the ex-president's son, losing his prestigious post. Cortés and his supporters did not stand idly by as Calderón took steps to weaken their political power. Deputy Cortés Fernández accused President Calderón of profiting politically from governmental corruption, namely by selling German and Italian ships (captured as part of Costa Rica's alignment with the United States against these Axis powers during World War II) at below-market prices to his supporters.[18] As the PNR fractured into cortecista and *calderonista* camps, Calderón forged an alliance with the nation's Communists to maintain a majority in the Legislative Assembly. This move, however, also served to overlay a high-profile ideological cleavage onto the once very personalized political divide. As cortecistas' political power waned, they began emphasizing this ideological shift, dubbing the government "caldero-comunismo," a term that suggested that Calderón's coalition government was a Bolshevik-leaning dictatorship riddled with corruption. In 1943, when Cortés announced his run for the presidency and Calderón backed Picado, the division between cortecistas and calderonistas was completed.[19] For Chanto and many others, Picado's nomination was the final straw.

The presidential campaign and election of 1944 was a heated affair, with each side claiming victory in the national press days before polling stations opened, and with clear, often successful, attempts at voter fraud perpetrated by both sides. In Tarrazú, local campaigning efforts, the election itself, and its official outcome would serve to underscore deep-seated local support for Cortés and to spark distrust of the voting process as well as of local and national authorities.

After resigning as jefe político, Chanto began campaigning for his candidate each Sunday morning after Mass, running a "friendly" political discussion session among neighbors. According to Juan Chanto, his father was extremely successful in garnering local support for Cortés because many in the community respected him as the former jefe político but, even more importantly, because Cortés was arguably the region's most popular president.[20] Cortés, or "Don León," as many in the region affectionately refer to him even now, reportedly was the first president to visit Tarrazú, and this simple act of regional acknowledgment won the hearts and minds of many in Tarrazú.[21] His local esteem, however, largely stems from his 1937 decree that created the Juntas Rurales de Crédito Agrícola, or Rural Committees of Agricultural Credit.[22] Financed by the Banco Nacional de Costa Rica, the Juntas Rurales provided farmers with access to small, low-interest loans, which augured greater agency for small-scale coffee farmers in their dealings with coffee processors. Effectively, Cortés gave Tarrazú's coffee farmers the means to combat the near-total control the region's principal beneficiador exercised over their lives.

As seen in chapter 2, by the 1940s Tarrazú's primary coffee processor, or beneficiador, was Tobías Umaña. Given local farmers' dependence on Umaña, both to purchase their crop and provide them with credit or loans, farmers had very little bargaining power over the purchase price of their crop or the interest rates of their loans. Chanto, who was both a coffee farmer and Tarrazú's jefe político, recognized the potential power a Junta Rural would provide coffee farmers, and he petitioned and secured the establishment of a local Junta Rural in 1939.[23] The opening of Tarrazú's Junta Rural weakened Umaña's economic hold on local coffee farmers. For many farm families, Cortés's creation of the Juntas Rurales and Chanto's successful politicking tangibly improved their lives by weakening Umaña's economic power, ensuring them greater profits on their coffee. Local farmers repaid Chanto and Cortés with their political support in 1944.

Primarily calling on local farmers, Chanto soon amassed a sizable group of Cortés supporters. As the local cortecistas' presence became increasingly evident, local authorities attempted to persuade Chanto to reconsider his allegiance to Cortés. According to Juan Chanto, his father was not only "offered money" to "not head Cortés's campaign" but also "promised political positions" if he would switch allegiances. Despite this offer, Juan asserted that his father's loyalty to former president Cortés and his "principles" made it impossible for him to support Picado's run for the presidency, and he remained faithful to Cortés to the end.[24]

Having failed in their efforts to co-opt Chanto, local authorities took a more strong-handed approach in an attempt to silence cortecistas. The local police in San Marcos and Santa María, the region's two largest communities, began assaulting and imprisoning oppositionists who made open statements of support for Cortés, namely "*vivando*," or yelling "long live León Cortés," on the streets. Ramón Solís Solís, of Santa María de Dota, recalled how one evening his friend Miguel Montero called out "*Viva León Cortés!*" on his way home from a night out at the local bar, when a policeman approached him and "for no other reason" began "beating him with a 'blackjack'" before "throwing him in jail for the night." Solís noted that the police consistently attacked oppositionists whom they spotted "vivando" Cortés but never took action against those who "yelled '*Viva Calderón!*' or '*Viva Picado!*'"[25]

For Solís, the local police's selective use of violence against cortecistas suggested that the police were not so much concerned with employing their authority to maintain order but rather to "abuse cortecistas."[26] This sentiment of distrust for governmental authority had deep historic roots in the region stemming from decades of physical and psychological abuses on the part of the Resguardo Fiscal. As seen in chapter 3, the Resguardo's activities not only threatened the economic activity of local liquor distillers, their labors signaled an attack on the region's poorest men's ability to assert their masculinity via the consumption of spirits. This, in turn, engendered a violent environment, prompting local men's anger against state authorities, which often led to violent attacks against the police and other state authorities.

While the Resguardo were not primarily charged with keeping the peace, between 1944 and 1948 members of this agency, alongside the local police, reportedly beat oppositionists, who were caught "vivando" their candidates.[27] In this way, oppositionists viewed the local and the national state working collaboratively to suppress democracy locally. Local police and the Resguardo did not limit themselves to beating men who cheered for opposition candidates after a night of drinking; they also threatened to keep known oppositionists from voting. Carlos Elizondo of Santa María de Dota recalls how on the date of the presidential election of 1944—February 13—several police officers and Resguardo guards "formed a line" in front of the local schoolhouse, which was also the local polling station, "waiting" for any provocation to arrest or beat local cortecistas. The sight of armed government agents allegedly kept some men from turning out to vote and filled those brave enough to do so with fear, including Elizondo's then-seventy-seven-year-old grandfather. Elizondo claimed his grandfather "spent the whole morning [standing] in front of the school, and did not vote until after noon, out of fear of the authorities." According to Elizondo, local cortecistas responded to authorities' attempts to "obstruct the vote" by taking advantage of their large numbers in the community. He recalled that his grandfather and the other men who arrived that morning waited until a couple hundred voters had gathered before they lined up to vote.[28] Santa María's cortecistas gambled on the fact that the local authorities would not attack such a large contingent of oppositionist voters.

Although authorities intimidated voters, at least most cortecistas in the town of Santa María ultimately cast a vote. Those of San Marcos de Tarrazú were not so lucky. According to Juan Chanto, his father received word the night preceding the 1944 election that local authorities planned on "destroying cortecistas' ballots" and replacing them with ballots marked for Picado. In an attempt to foil this alleged plan of electoral fraud, Chanto urged Tarrazú's cortecistas to abstain from voting and instead turn over their government-issued electoral identification cards to him. This move would make it nearly impossible for local *picadistas* to switch cortecista votes, since at the time local polling stations were required to record voters' signatures and identification card numbers in a registry, and the number of ballots counted needed to match the registry. In other words, without cortecistas' signatures in the polling station's registry, government officials could not "steal" votes. By nightfall on election day Chanto reportedly gathered over five hundred cortecista electoral identification cards, which he stuffed into a couple coffee sacks and tied to his horse's saddle before taking off "at a full gallop for Don León's home in San José" (fig. 4.1). Chanto turned over the electoral identification cards to Cortés as proof of local Tarrazúceños support for his candidacy. Chanto's action kept cortecistas from the polling booths, arguably hampering local government supporters from "stealing" their votes. This action, however, also cost Cortés hundreds of votes. All the same, Juan Chanto claims that upon arriving in San José with the identification cards Cortés lamented to his father that all of his supporters had not done the same, as a means of later contesting "the fraud [perpetrated] by the communists, Picado, and Calderón."[29]

Figure 4.1. Marcos Chanto Méndez on horseback as San Marcos de Tarrazú's jefe político, unknown date. (Courtesy of Juan Bautista Chanto Méndez)

It is uncertain to what extent fraud took place in the cantons of Dota and Tarrazú or the rest of Costa Rica. Recent scholarly analysis of the presidential election, however, suggests that even if all thirty-eight recorded cortecista accusations of fraud had, in fact, taken place, Picado still would have won the presidency by a wide margin.[30] Indeed, although the opposition claimed that 99 percent of the ballots cast in 1944 ought to be impugned because of electoral fraud, these numbers were not nearly enough to have altered the final outcome. In truth, Picado had no reason to commit fraud, since he appears to have walked away with 90,403 out of 136,806 votes—twice as many votes as Cortés garnered.[31] In short, despite voting irregularities, Picado was the clear victor in 1944's national elections.

Nevertheless, careful analysis of the officially recorded voting results combined with oral histories raise doubts about Picado's official victory margin in the region. In fact, a close examination of the sources suggests three important conclusions: (1) Chanto orchestrated a successful cortecista boycott; (2) Cortés potentially might have won a fair election in the region; and (3) the number of picadistas and cortecistas was extremely close in Tarrazú.

The official vote count reveals that 46 percent of Tarrazú's registered voters did not vote in 1944.[32] These figures back up Juan Chanto's claim that his father carried over five hundred electoral registration cards to San José.[33] Similarly, a close look at the recorded results for Tarrazú and Dota reveal that although Picado officially secured victory in both of these cantons, had the election not been marred by authorities' threats—to beat cortecistas in Santa María and to destroy their ballots in Tarrazú—Cortés may well have won the presidential race in the region.[34]

The 1944 presidential race was extremely close; however, Picado won a clear majority of the nation's votes. The reasons for voter discrepancies in this region can largely be ascribed to the way certain policies were implemented. Both Calderón and, in turn, Picado, counted on the unyielding support of banana laborers on both coasts, as well as urban and landless rural workers throughout the Central Valley who acquired disability, retirement, and maternity benefits under Calderón's presidency.[35] At the local level, however, Picado's support would have been lukewarm at best. As seen in chapter 2, many local residents in Tarrazú saw limited economic benefits and perhaps even lost out under Calderón's administration. As discussed in chapter 2, local hacendado Tobías Umaña responded to the passage of the Labor Code and the Social Guarantees by strategically hiring and firing employees to avoid having to pay into the newly formed Caja. This meant that many of the region's landless peons not only did not benefit from the new legislation but also could no longer count on being employed year-round. This experience meant that local workers did not view Calderón's administration in the same light as many urban workers or even rural workers in other parts of the republic. So, while Calderón's social reforms may have won his endorsed successor—Picado—a majority of the nation's votes, this was not the case in Tarrazú; in fact, it is doubtful he could count on even fifty percent of the local population's support.

Tarrazúceños' support for Cortés, coupled with the fact that local governmental officials had taken or threatened to take steps to rob local oppositionists of their votes, gave rise to a local myth that Cortés not only won a majority of the region's support but a majority of the nation's support. This local myth was based on the premise that Calderón and Picado "robbed" Cortés and his supporters of their victory.[36] Today, some sixty years later, Carlos Elizondo summed up the sentiments of many in the region who recalled the heated election of 1944 when he stated that "the people of Costa Rica put up with Picado's 'victory,' but we knew the declared results were incorrect because nobody, but nobody, voted for Picado." This national "injustice," allegedly perpetrated by the Costa Rican state, left Elizondo and many others Tarrazúceños "not at all happy" with Costa Rican politics.[37] Chanto and Figueres would later channel local discontent and distrust of the state into political support for Otilio Ulate Blanco's presidential run in 1947–48 and eventually into the armed rebellion of 1948.

Costa Rica's Postwar Democratic Opening and Vanguardia Popular

Local anger over the issue of electoral fraud and intimidation on the part of Tarrazúceños places into focus the fact that by 1940 there was widespread faith in the constitutional ideal of republicanism. Although Costa Rica's political structures had been dominated by coffee elites since the nineteenth century, by the 1940s the nation had a firmly established democratic tradition. Deep-seated faith in republican ideals was the result of four decades of universal male suffrage.[38] In fact, starting at the turn of the twentieth century, intensely competitive and regularly held electoral contests (though frequently marred by fraud) progressively became a necessary step to assume state office.[39] Costa Rica was a nation where democratic principles had been at least formally honored for decades, but in the early 1940s, voters of all political stripes in this Central American republic demanded a greater political opening. In fact, during the final years of World War II, Costa Rica—as in much of the rest of Latin America—experienced massive political mobilizations and the rise of leftist politicians, ideas, and legislation.[40] Scholars of Latin America have largely attributed Latin America's vibrant democratic political climate in the 1940s to the Allied victory over the Axis powers, which also marked the triumph of democracy over fascism. Moreover, the United States began putting direct pressure on Latin American governments to democratize during the final years of the war.[41]

Communist parties throughout the region took advantage of the postwar democratic opening as well as the Soviet Union's short-lived but immense prestige in the wake of their alliance with the victorious Allied forces. The 1940s would see the peak of Communist Party membership and influence in most Latin America nations, including Costa Rica.[42] Indeed, Costa Rica's Communist Party, the PVP, acquired unprecedented political power and influence in the 1940s, winning between ten thousand and fifteen thousand votes (10–15 percent of the national electorate) in national elections.[43] While the apex of Communist power was between 1943 and 1948, the PVP's ascension onto the national stage was the product of years of calculated political decisions made by its leadership, namely Manuel Mora Valverde. In 1932, just one year after the Communist Party was established, Mora denounced the goal of revolution and instead asserted Costa Rican Communists' commitment to enacting reforms through the electoral process. To this end, the party successfully secured the election of two legislative assemblymen, including Mora, in 1934. Perhaps, however, the most fruitful action Mora made was in June 1943 when he stated on behalf of the PVP that he supported then president Calderón's Christian Socialist philosophy.[44] This statement secured a letter from Archbishop Victor Sanabria Martínez, which gave Costa Rican Catholics permission to join the PVP's ranks.[45]

The commitment of the PVP's leadership to reform, coupled with their willingness to collaborate, allowed this party to join an unusual coalition with Calderón's ruling PRN and the Costa Rican Catholic Church. Together these diverse institutions would forge a social welfare state during President Calderón's administration (1940–44). The relationship these disparate organizations founded served to permanently amplify the role the state played in regulating the economy. While the coalition had a lasting impact on Costa Rican politics, its unified hold on power would prove short-lived. Cold War global political realities and heightened political polarization at the national level ultimately set the stage for the nation's civil war.

Beyond the Cold War's reframing of political realities, Costa Rican peasant farmers historically rejected Marxist inspired policies and ideologies. As other scholars' research on Costa Rica's highland peasant farmers has demonstrated, even impoverished peasants were as a whole deeply committed to capitalism.[46] The reason appears to be access to land, namely legislation that consistently permitted the nation's rural poor to settle government owned lands, and if they could prove that they had cultivated or otherwise improved the lands, they could legalize their holdings. Thus, even when peasant farmers held such small tracts of land that they were required to labor on the farms of wealthier neighbors for wages, they saw themselves principally as landowners and committed to protecting private property rights. This meant that just like their elite neighbors, many poor peasant farmers were deeply threatened by Communists' declared desires to eliminate private property to forge a more equitable society. This discomfort with Communism created a widespread "anti-labor, anti-Marxist doctrine of social change and national liberation" that was embraced by a large percentage of Costa Rica's rural poor.[47]

Even if Calderón's collaboration with the PVP and his split with Cortés upset Cortés partisans, the nation's elites, and placed many peasant farmers on edge, the passage of the Labor Code and the Social Guarantees ultimately secured him tremendous popular support. In fact, the president's commitment to progressive reforms earned him the adoration and respect of the nation's urban workers and banana laborers on the coasts.[48] In stark contrast, accusations of corruption and postwar inflation—greatly reducing workers' purchasing power—damaged the popular support of his successor, Teodoro Picado.[49]

Although Picado clearly won the popular vote in 1944, widespread electoral inconsistencies throughout the country served to both place into question his electoral victory and invalidate Costa Rica's electoral system in the eyes of many in the opposition. The perceived weakness of the Picado administration emboldened opposition factions that became increasingly militant and attempted to destabilize the state through acts of terror. Disenchanted citizens, such as José "Pepe" Figueres, began coordinating violent attacks against key government targets, including two failed assassination attempts against former president and then presidential candidate Calderón.[50] Radical oppositionists successfully assassinated PNR club leaders in several Central Valley towns, and they perpetrated the deadly bombing of the progovernment daily *La Tribuna*, destroying much of this newspaper's printing capacity.[51]

Pepe Figueres's Political Vision

Figueres's entrance onto the national political scene began in 1942 shortly after Calderón's administration had declared war against Germany in solidarity with the United States, following the Japanese attack on Pearl Harbor. On the evening of July 2, 1942, a United Fruit Company ship, the S.S. *San Pablo*, was torpedoed by a German U-boat while docked at the Atlantic port of Limón. Twenty-four dockworkers, the ship, and its cargo of bananas were the immediate casualties of this submarine attack; however, the national political repercussions would be far-reaching.

Two days after the incident, the PVP organized a demonstration in San José that quickly turned violent. On July 4, 1942, angry crowds, armed with rocks, attacked stores and businesses owned by German, Italian, and Spanish (seen as pro-Franco) families.[52] Amazingly, the San José police made no attempts to restore order until late in the evening, after a majority of looters had dispersed and all of the capital's "enemy owned" businesses had been sacked.[53] Additionally, the next morning Calderón announced the opening of concentration camps that would house the nation's German citizens and their descendants as a means of protecting the nation from a possible fifth-column attack.[54]

The government's inaction against the vandals and the systemic persecution of Costa Rican citizens whose only crime was having a German surname outraged many, including Pepe Figueres, who was the son of Spanish immigrants. This future president's indignation with then president Calderón's quiescence—which Figueres read as the government's tacit support of the mob's attack on San José businesses—led him to purchase airtime from a radio station and critique the government's inaction. This deed at a time when Costa Rica's support for the Allies in the war had justified strict censorship led immediately to Figueres's arrest and earned him two years in exile.[55] Additionally, however, it paved the way for him to become a nationally renowned oppositionist.

While exiled in Mexico, Figueres would pen a couple of articles and essays, publishing his writing in the oppositionist magazine *Surco*, which secured him a national audience for his ideas and afforded him the opportunity to change the way Costa Ricans understood the role of government in their lives. Perhaps Figueres's most well-read and celebrated writing is his essay "Palabras gastadas" (Worn out words), which *Surco* published in January 1943. In this essay, he analyzes three words that he thinks have been "worn out" by the Calderón government's flawed use of them: democracy, socialism, and freedom.[56]

In "Palabras gastadas," Figueres seeks to revive the ideals that he believes these three words ought to stand for while also subtly critiquing Calderón and his administration. To this end, he celebrates democratic states for providing their citizens with the greatest amount of freedom before asserting that "to live in a country governed by a despot is unnatural to rational beings." The association he makes between freedom and democracy is critical because it allows him to suggest that Calderón's government (though democratically elected) was not democratic, since individuals, such as himself, had their freedoms limited. Additionally, the image of Costa Ricans living unnaturally because of the current government suggests the need for political change. While his actions in the 1940s do not always reflect his beliefs, his early writings make clear that Figueres was a firm believer in the democratic process.

Last, Figueres presents himself as a champion of socialism, favoring government intervention to more equitably disperse financial resources; however, he is quick to add that he is a passionate opponent of Communism. Figueres takes issue with Communists' focus on class war as a means to redistribute wealth. This young revolutionary asserts that capitalism and class are not the sources of poverty, hunger, and unemployment but that economic resources are not being fully developed or exploited. Thus, he suggests that large-scale businesses and farms hold the key to increasing productivity, which will create more jobs and serve to lessen poverty. For Figueres, then, the Communists' aim to overturn the capitalist system and their attacks on the wealthy will not only fail to improve the lot of the poor but these actions might arguably serve to increase their poverty. To make his point about the self-destructive nature of Communists' class struggles, he compares capitalism to a cow, noting that just because the cow is incapable of "giving milk to all" does not mean it is necessary to "kill the cow." In "Palabras gastadas," Figueres outlines his political goals as the establishment of a democratic socialist government. This essay resonates with some of the reforms Figueres would implement as head of the victorious junta, namely the nationalization of Costa Rica's banking system. However, his commitment to democracy and personal freedoms would be tested early on, as we will see in the subsequent chapter. First, however, I examine Figueres's political trajectory after his time in exile, as well as the civil war itself.

Violence in the Central Valley and the Cold War

Following his election, Picado clearly recognized that there was a sizable oppositionist movement organizing against him. In light of this, he seems to have determined his best bet was to distance himself from the PVP and Mora, since the alignment between the PNR and the PVP were a central theme in oppositionist critiques of Calderón's administration. He also began to make policy concessions and changes to appease the opposition. This arguably began with his 1944 invitation for Figueres to end his exile and return to Costa Rica. On May 21, 1944, Figueres accepted Picado's invitation. Returning home did not calm Figueres's oppositionist fervor. Indeed, in 1945, he and his supporters decided to leave Cortés's Partido Demócrata to form the more ardently anti-Communist Partido Democrático Social (PDS), which in a real sense served to split the opposition among supporters of Cortés, who sought to gain power via the electoral process, and partisans of Figueres, who had a political party but believed that offensive assaults and ultimately an armed uprising were the only means by which the opposition would gain power.[57]

As Figueres and his supporters sought to overturn the state, some government supporters responded with their own militancy. In fact, in 1943, progovernment forces, namely members of the PVP's "*brigadas de choque*," or shock brigades, began to regularly police the streets to confront oppositionist youth. The brigadas were initially formed to defend Communists from oppositionists' attempts to break up their meetings and marches, as well as to keep marchers in line during large demonstrations and to protect their leader, Manuel Mora, who had survived two opposition bomb attempts.[58] The brigadas were a well-organized force; members reportedly received military-like training five days a week. While they were not issued firearms, brigadistas were infamous for the "blackjacks" (leather-wrapped clubs consisting of a coil spring shaft with a lead weight on one end and a cord on the other end) that they carried and used to beat up oppositionists.[59] Self-defense may have sparked the brigadas' creation, but brigadistas did not always wait to be attacked: they allegedly beat oppositionists without provocation and destroyed private property.[60]

Increased political violence on San José's streets in many ways reflected larger contemporary political alignments on the global stage, namely the start of the Cold War. As the relationship between the United States and the Soviet Union began to cool, the opposition increasingly criticized the Costa Rican government's alliance with the PVP. Pointing repeatedly to linkages between both Calderón and Picado and the nation's Communists, the antigovernmental press suggested that these men had placed the nation on a troublesome political trajectory. Despite (or perhaps because of) these critiques, Picado did not pass any new labor or social reform bills during his presidency. Moreover, in April 1947, Picado, alongside the heads of state of Nicaragua, Guatemala, El Salvador, and Honduras, signed an anti-Communist pact in which all signatories agreed to share information about Communist activities in their respective countries with one another and to restrict the movement of known Communists across their borders.[61] This gesture demonstrated that despite Picado's alliance with the PVP, his administration would not support international Communist organizing within Costa Rica but would adopt a politically moderate stance.[62] Yet, for many, namely the opposition daily *El Diario de Costa Rica*—as well as for US political observers—this action was insufficient to counteract Picado's continued relationship with the PVP. The pages of *El Diario de Costa Rica* repeatedly linked Picado not only to his predecessor, Calderón, but also to the PVP and trumpeted electoral irregularities that suggested that Picado and Calderón were indistinguishable and had effectively installed a Communist dictatorship. Articles in *El Diario de Costa Rica* served to stoke the flames of the opposition's anger, and throughout Picado's presidency, the newspaper published articles by oppositionists who supported the idea of an armed rebellion to restore Costa Rican democracy.[63]

As political violence escalated in Costa Rica's streets, Cortés's unexpected death on March 3, 1946, dealt the opposition a powerful blow.[64] The opposition leader's sudden death in his home of natural causes propelled the movement he headed into chaos as members attempted to settle on a presidential candidate to take on their most despised foe, former president Calderón, who announced his commitment to run in 1948. The choices came down to the more radical Figueres, who believed that only violence could secure state control, and the more moderate Otilio Ulate Blanco, the editor and co-owner of *El Diario de Costa Rica*, who remained committed to the democratic process. On February 13, 1947, nearly a year of internal turmoil within the opposition came to an end when Ulate was selected as the opposition's presidential candidate. Ulate would run under the banner of the newly formed Partido Unificación Nacional, or National Unity Party, and Figueres was selected to lead Ulate's political campaign as his *jefe de acción*.[65] Figueres's sincere disinterest in the democratic process, however, led him to resign from his post just two months later; he preferred to dedicate himself to smuggling weapons and organizing an armed struggle against the government. While Ulate was not a proponent of revolution like Figueres, unlike Cortés, he sought to ratchet up tensions between the opposition and the government to gain political power. This is evident not only in Ulate's often acidic stump speeches but also in the articles he published in the pages of *El Diario de Costa Rica*.[66]

Political tensions in the Central Valley neared the boiling point on July 22, 1947, when opposition-owned businesses throughout the metropolitan area shut their doors for twelve days in *la huelga de los brazos caídos* (a sit-down strike). The precise trigger of the strike is a question of debate among historians, but the dramatic political impact that the strike had is clear.[67] It left thousands of workers without a source of income, with their workplaces shut down, and in many cases without a place to purchase food and other necessities. Anger against oppositionist business leaders for closing their doors, and against the government for not remedying their difficult plight, resulted in looting, attacks against the police, and organized marches. On August 3, 1947, the strike came to an end after the government conceded to the demands of oppositionist organizers of the strike and signed a nine-point agreement that in essence was a pledge by both sides to accept the results of the newly formed Tribunal Nacional Electoral in the upcoming 1948 presidential election and not seek an appeal regardless of the outcome. Moreover, the government relinquished the power to name all three of the Tribunal's magistrates and permitted its opponents to name the head of the Registro Civil, or the Electoral Registry.[68] These electoral concessions would come back to haunt the government in February 1948.

Tarrazú on the Eve of Figueres's Uprising

Tarrazú did not suffer from the more dramatic consequences of increased political polarization, namely the bombings and assassination attempts that defined life for many in the Central Valley during Picado's presidency, but this rural region was far from free of incidents of political violence. Attesting to Tarrazú's violent and politically charged masculine culture, the region witnessed a large number of intense evening confrontations between local authorities and members of the opposition, often outside of bars. In the local context, where drinking, brawling, and politics were critical to the way the local community defined manhood, as discussed in chapter 3, officials' attempts to restrict local men's access to the vote in 1944 were seen not only as an abuse of power but as a direct affront to local individuals' masculinity. So, although political conflicts may have been less dramatic than in the Central Valley, they were arguably just as heated.

In fact, on June 25, 1947, a month before la huelga de los brazos caídos, street politics in Tarrazú made national news when *El Diario de Costa Rica* published an article based on a telegram from Chanto to presidential candidate Otilio Ulate (also the newspaper's editor). The article described how, on the night of June 23, 1947, the police in San Lorenzo de Tarrazú had injured an unnamed man after they shot seven bullets into a crowd of young men who had been "vivando" Ulate.[69] The police additionally were accused of arresting two members of the crowd, both sons of Tobías Navarro Zúñiga. The article presented local authorities in Tarrazú as little more than violent brutes who attacked innocent youth for calling out the name of a presidential candidate.

Perhaps unsurprisingly, local officials involved in the incident had a rather different interpretation of what had taken place. On June 26, Jefe Político Ezequías Umaña sent a report to Costa Rica's secretary of state, Arístides Baltodando, regarding "the information published in el diario [*sic*]" in which he relayed that at around 8:00 P.M. on June 22, he and the local head of the Resguardo Fiscal had asked "a large group of drunks [who were vivando] Ulate and insulting [local] authorities" to disperse and that "all but three individuals" obeyed their orders. After the crowd dissipated, Navarro's two sons, Isaac and Floríndo, purportedly attacked another member of the disorderly crowd, Marcos Navarro Cordero, "with a 25-inch work knife" for unspecified reasons. In an alleged move to save Navarro's life, Umaña wrote that Resguardo guard Juan Pedro Valverde had "whipped" Floríndo while another officer shot two bullets in the air. The police and Resguardo then arrested the brothers before their father bailed them out of prison on the June 25.[70]

While Chanto's letter to Ulate portrayed the arrest as an act of political repression against innocent youths, Jefe Político Umaña described the "victims" as two drunken youths who began fighting after equally inebriated members of the opposition had gathered on the street. Despite the inconsistencies between descriptions of these events, their two accounts when taken together provide insight into how local officials and members of the opposition understood citizens' rights and abuse of authority in this period. In particular, Chanto makes no mention of alcohol, knives, or violence of any sort on the part of oppositionists. In contrast, Umaña claims that the crowd was drunk and making a scene. Given the clear political motives of both politicians—to inculpate the other side and portray their own side as acting well within their rights—each man had reason to portray the crowd and ensuing events in ways that benefited his objectives. While the truth likely lies in between these two extremes (with some of the men in the crowd intoxicated and causing a disruption while others soberly expressed their political support for Ulate), read together these two narratives suggest that for both men it was acceptable for citizens to gather peacefully on the street to "vivar," as long as they were not making a commotion.

Additionally, this incident shows that a full seven months before the elections of 1948 were held, large numbers of men took to the street to express their political sentiments, and authorities cracked down on these politically directed gatherings. Lastly, this incident underscores Chanto's leadership of the Tarrazú opposition.[71] Not only was he the head and founder of Tarrazú's Partido Democrático Social political club, affiliated with Ulate's campaign; he took an active interest in defending the rights of other oppositionists, such as the Navarro family in this case, when they suffered alleged abuses for their political ideals.

Chanto was eager to help his neighbors stand up to the abuses of local authorities, but he and his family suffered the strong-handed tactics of the local authorities as well, as a legal case between Tarrazú police officer Raimundo Picado Álvarado and Chanto's adult sons demonstrates. On the morning of July 21, 1947, San Marcos de Tarrazú's jefe político Ezequías Umaña sent a telegram to San José officials alleging that the previous evening, police officer Picado had been beaten and disarmed by four of Chanto's sons. The brothers were later arrested and taken to trial on charges of "assaulting an officer."[72]

While the court case against his sons played out, Chanto responded with his own legal offensive: taking Picado to trial, charging him with "injuries and abuse of authority."[73] On November 18, 1947, Chanto penned a letter that accused Picado of being "the only provoker . . . responsible for what took place . . . with his arbitrary and aggressive attitude, as my sons were flogged . . . receiving considerable injury especially to my son Rodrigo . . . the wounds—[he] received on his head—were grave and blood gushed" from his wound.[74]

In this case, as in the previous one, Chanto and his sons characterized local authorities as violent, oppressive, and responding with an unwarranted excess of force. The young Marcos, who was accused of inciting the skirmish that July night, claimed the incident began when he suggested to Picado that the act of "vivando" was not a crime. For Marcos, this incident was about local authorities' attempts to violently strip local men of the right to freedom of expression. In his official testimony, Marcos claimed that he and his brother Rodrigo entered and quickly left Dagoberto Solís Mora's bar after the owner warned them that the officer was present and had threatened to arrest anyone he overheard "vivando" Ulate. To avoid trouble the pair left, but Picado allegedly followed them out, and "once in the street," he warned them that "he would arrest [them] if [they yelled] viv[a] Otilio Ulate." Marcos testified that he retorted "it is not a crime to vivar Otilio Ulate" and that Picado responded by taking out his baton and striking him and then his brother Rodrigo, who sought to intercede on his brother's behalf. As Picado attacked the Chanto brothers, a crowd quickly assembled and threw themselves on Picado and "disarm[ed]" the officer to halt the perceived "injustice" that he was perpetrating against the Chantos.[75]

Police officer Picado's testimony about this incident differs dramatically from Marcos's in regards to the catalyst of the altercation, but it also places him in Solís's cantina when Rodrigo and Marcos Chanto entered, suggesting that the brothers were not the only participants who were drinking the night of the encounter. Picado testified that when the brothers entered the bar, he informed them that they were welcome so long as they did not vivando "any candidate." Marcos, according to Picado, responded by exiting the bar, whereupon he "hurled a viva for 'Otilio Ulate.'" Picado claimed Marcos's disobedience left him "obligated to detain" him. When he made his plans known, Picado alleged that Rodrigo responded by "throw[ing] himself upon" him. At this point, in an act of "self-defense," Picado admitted flogging Rodrigo before an angry mob gathered and "succeeded in throwing me to the ground, hitting me, and removing my revolver and club."[76]

The intense violence alleged by both sides in this incident highlights just how high political tensions in Tarrazú ran in the months leading up to the 1948 presidential race between Calderón and Ulate. Furthermore, the centrality of politics in constructing masculinity and vice versa is evident in this confrontation. Given Tarrazú's repressive political climate in 1947, "vivas" were an assertion of the traditional form by which local men performed their masculinity and also an act of political protest. Additionally, the very personal power struggle between Picado and the Chanto family puts into relief the tenuous nature of the local police's authority on the eve of the civil war. In fact, although the brothers were eventually arrested, this occurred only after Picado had suffered the humiliation of being disarmed by a crowd of drunks.

The young Marcos's eagerness to challenge Picado and his brother's readiness and other men's willingness to attack and disarm this officer reflect deep-seated anger on the part of local men toward the state.[77] Perhaps, however, what most angered members of the opposition were the concrete measures taken by officials in 1944 to strip them of the right to vote. As seen, universal male suffrage had been established at the turn of the century, and by the 1940s, elections had become a part of Costa Rican political life. Although the stain of electoral fraud—as in the 1940s—frequently tainted elections, universal male suffrage at least theoretically provided men of all socioeconomic backgrounds with a political voice. Moreover, since women and children were barred from voting, the right to vote was seen as something of a rite of passage for men, one that arguably was more important for men of humble means, who had fewer avenues to assert their masculinity publicly. This was likely more the case in the wake of deep economic hardships experienced by coffee farmers, during the Great Depression and World War II, which limited coffee farmers' abilities to provide for their families' needs, a traditional keystone of masculine identity. So, when police officers and Resguardo guards attempted to keep men in Santa María from voting and when government officials in San Marcos allegedly schemed to "steal" oppositionist votes, men in Tarrazú felt as though the state had attempted to emasculate them. Local men's desire to prove themselves as men, in a context of globally induced financial declines, which limited their access to other modes of (re)constructing their masculinity, partly explains why they consistently embraced violent tactics whenever local authorities attempted to silence them. The local code of masculinity may also have informed many men's decision to take up arms against the state when Figueres began orchestrating his armed uprising.

These particular local realities serve to frame broad-based antigovernment support in the region, but by 1947, political violence was a national issue. The partisan media, coupled with calls by both Mora and Ulate for their respective partisans to take to the streets to demonstrate their political force and will, arguably served to normalize the idea of using violence to express and defend political beliefs.[78] Additionally, as violence between government supporters and oppositionists increased in intensity and frequency, the social conditions that made violent rebellion appear a reasonable proposition began to take shape. That rebellion is discussed in the next chapter, but first, I examine the 1948 elections that helped detonate the revolt.

The 1948 Presidential Elections

On February 8, 1948, men from throughout Costa Rica made their way to polling stations to cast their votes. As in 1944, accusations of fraud tainted the electoral process. However, whereas in 1944 members of the opposition accused government officials of taking steps to destroy ballots and intimidate members of the opposition to abstain from voting, in 1948 accusations of fraud did not come from the opposition, but rather from *government* supporters. The nine-point agreement, signed between Picado, Calderón, and Ulate in August of 1947 to conclude the huelga de los brazos caídos, had in essence placed control over the electoral process in the hands of the opposition. The opposition had selected the three magistrates of the National Electoral Tribunal, who were charged with declaring the final outcome of the election. More importantly, the opposition's choice for the post of supervisor of the Electoral Registry was none other than Benjamín Odio Odio, Figueres's friend and supporter. The registry not only issued voter registration cards (cédulas) but was expected to verify that voting lists were accurate. Such responsibilities included purging the lists of deceased voters, adding new voters to the rolls, registering voters who had moved into new districts, and deleting them from their previous districts. The registry also enlisted observers at each polling place. This last measure ensured that all registered voters were permitted to exercise their right to vote and that no irregularities took place.[79]

Scholars have repeatedly pointed out that there was a dramatic decrease in the number of tallied votes between the 1944 and 1948 presidential elections. In fact, the National Electoral Tribunal declared Otilio Ulate the victor with 54,931 votes to Rafael Calderón's 44,438 votes.[80] These results meant that just 101,060 of the 176,979 officially registered voters actually voted in 1948. In stark contrast, 136,806 votes were counted in 1944, when the electorate was officially made up of 163,100 men.[81] Immediately following the closing of polling stations, calderonistas began accusing the Electoral Registry of purging thousands of their names from the voting rolls.

The claims that calderonistas had been barred from voting went beyond the Central Valley. On February 10, 1948, the head of Tarrazú's PNR, Casimiro Vargas, sent a letter to the Electoral Tribunal in San José accusing the Electoral Registry of committing a "scandalous fraud" against "hundreds" of Tarrazú's calderonistas. Vargas asserted that "more than three-hundred" calderonistas had not been "permitted to vote," despite the fact that they had been "properly inscribed" within the registry, because they were not issued voter registration cards or the cards they were issued had been "intentionally altered," making them invalid. Vargas also accused local poll observer Nelson Chacón Pacheco, who was under the employment of the *ulatista*-controlled Electoral Tribunal, of behaving as an "enraged . . . ulatista" rather than a nonpartisan "judge" on election day. According to Vargas, Chacón had "confiscated the National Bank's jeep," which he employed to transport "ulatistas from [remote] districts" to polling centers to vote. Given the fact that similar claims of misconduct surfaced in other rural regions and in various Central Valley communities, it seems that a large number of calderonistas were stripped of their votes in 1948.[82]

Tensions and insecurities over the electoral process mounted after a San José public high school, el Colegio Superior de Señoritas, mysteriously caught on fire at 3:00 a.m. on the morning of February 10, 1948. At the time, the section of the school where the fire occurred was housing a large number of ballots that needed to be counted. The fire was put out before much structural damage had occurred, but nearly all of the ballots were destroyed. The fire raised more questions as to the legitimacy of the February 8 election. Indeed, the fire coupled with the claim by thousands of Calderón supporters that they had been barred from voting led to a protest on February 12, 1948, on the part of disenfranchised calderonistas who flooded the capital's streets, piercing the air with cries of "we want to vote!"[83]

Despite these accusations of irregularities from calderonistas throughout the country, the Electoral Tribunal declared Ulate Costa Rica's president-elect on February 28, 1948, with one magistrate abstaining and two members voting in favor.[84] Because of the fire at the colegio, the magistrates decided the victor in this contest based solely on the signed certificates of poll station observers, such as Chacón in Tarrazú, who coincidently had all been hired by this pro-Ulate tribunal. In response to the tribunal's declaration, on March 1, 1948, Calderón placed a petition before the Legislative Assembly to annul the election, alleging that the registry had failed to process over thirty-seven thousand eligible applications for electoral registration cards. Without a current card, these men were barred from voting.[85]

Calderón's petition was contrary to the nine-point agreement he had signed with Picado and Ulate to end the huelga de los brazos caídos in August 1947. Moreover, since the Legislative Assembly had a calderonista majority in power at that time, this action was seen by the opposition as an attempt by Calderón and his allies to override the democratic process. Not surprisingly, the assembly voted to annul the election two days after the Electoral Tribunal claimed Ulate the winner. This vote was the final straw for many oppositionists, as it confirmed Figueres's claims that the democratic process was not a viable means by which the opposition could secure power. Some scholars have asserted that Costa Ricans had tired of the extreme political violence of Picado's and Calderón's presidencies and therefore voted for a change—in the form of Ulate. If this is the case, then the opposition was justified in its conclusion that the "caldero-comunistas" who controlled the government would only relinquish their grip on power by force.[86] However, since a large number of ballots were burned, it is impossible to know whether Ulate had in fact won the election. Moreover, Costa Rican scholars have recently suggested that the oppositionist-controlled Electoral Registry's elimination of thousands of voters from the electoral rolls (as Calderón claimed in his petition) was sufficient in magnitude to have hijacked the election from Calderón. For these scholars, Calderón ought to have obtained a majority of the nation's support due to his highly popular program of social reforms.[87]

Figueres's National Liberation Army

Amid growing uncertainty over who would succeed Picado as president, a large number of hopeful rebels (mostly men but also a handful of young women) made their way to Figueres's cabuya plantation, La Lucha. Figueres welcomed the recruits and quickly formed what he would later call his Ejercito de Liberación Nacional, or National Liberation Army.[88] Benjamín Odio, the acting head of the Electoral Registry in 1948, was among the most well-known Josefinos, or residents of the Central Valley, who joined Figueres. Odio not only left his post without notice for La Lucha, but he did so before the Electoral Tribunal had declared the election's victor.[89] Josefinos would occupy many leadership positions in Figueres's army and later in his administration. However, these Josefino recruits were relatively few in number. The majority of Figueres's foot soldiers were coffee farmers and peons from the cantons of Tarrazú, Dota, Desamparados, and Pérez Zeledón.

Many who arrived at La Lucha following the February election were motivated by the failure of the electoral process to bring their candidate to power, but Figueres had been plotting to topple the state since before his return from exile in 1943.[90] In fact, he had begun smuggling weapons into the country as early as December 16, 1947, when he signed the Caribbean Pact with Nicaraguan, Honduran, and Dominican exiles in Guatemala. The signers of this pact, who would later be known as the Caribbean Legion, recognized themselves as victims of dictatorial regimes with a shared desire to implement democracy in their respective Caribbean basin nations. The Caribbean Legion's members were moved by a combination of republican idealism, overt anti-imperialism, and anti-Communism. The pact's signers sought to use military force to break open a new path to Latin American economic development and to forge a new type of democratic republic that was neither a US neocolonial holding nor a Soviet-style one-party state.[91]

The legion had a sizable stockpile of weapons in Guatemala for the purpose of regime change.[92] Figueres managed to secure these guns to overthrow the Costa Rican state by promising that once Calderón and Picado were deposed, the other members of the legion could use Costa Rica as a base to topple dictators Anastasio Somoza García, Rafael Trujillo Molina, and Tiburcio Carías Andino.[93] Members of the legion served as military leaders and advisors under Figueres in the Costa Rican Civil War and played a critical role in his ability to train and arm a successful insurgency.[94]

The importance of the legion's collaboration cannot be understated. In fact, although I would argue that the legion's lofty goals had little if anything to do with Tarrazúceños' objectives, Figueres's alliance with these men would dramatically shape the post–Civil War state that Figueres would help establish, as seen in chapter 5. Figueres's negotiations with the legion also demonstrate that his plan to overthrow the state predates the contentious presidential election of 1948.

Figueres may have been planning to topple the state for months and possibly years, but the majority of men who fought in his National Liberation Army had not been. In fact, by all accounts the vast majority of Figueres's Tarrazú recruits had absolutely no military training; few knew how to shoot a gun, and even fewer owned a firearm when they joined the insurgency.[95] Moreover, for most of the region's population—including young Fany Jiménez, whose description of the arrival of Figueres and his men to San Marcos starts this chapter—the outbreak of a rebellion was largely unexpected. Revolution may not have been on the minds of most Tarrazúceños on the morning of March 14, but the vast majority of people in the region's three largest communities of San Marcos, San Pablo, and Santa María almost immediately jumped onboard to help overthrow the government. Figueres's troops found so little resistance that on the March 14 they were not only able to seize control of these three towns, establishing their barracks in Santa María's schoolhouse, but they also converted San Marcos's schoolhouse into a jail where they placed police officers, Resguardo Fiscal guards, government functionaries, and known government supporters.[96]

Many Tarrazúceños, like their Central Valley counterparts, took up arms in 1948 because they were outraged by the Legislative Assembly's annulment of the election and believed that only by force would the government relinquish power and respect the desires of the electorate. Carlos Elizondo, who had watched his seventy-seven-year-old grandfather waiting for hours to vote in 1944 in defiance of local authorities' attempts to "obstruct the vote," proudly claimed that he was among the first men to join the National Liberation Army after Figueres entered Santa María. Elizondo, who was nineteen at the time, was too young to vote; still, he asserted that he took up arms because he was sick of "living [under] tyranny" and felt "a revolution" was the only way to resolve the "suffrage issue."[97] The democratic process was also central for Álvaro Gamboa of Carrizal de Tarrazú, who was barely seventeen in March 1948 when he ran away from home to join Figueres's troops. Gamboa noted that his mother, who was a widow, had prohibited him from going to war, claiming he was "very new," or too young to fight. Gamboa stated that he disobeyed his mother because at the time he believed strongly that "the Communists wanted to take power" and he had heard that "the communists . . . [would] take away democracy."[98] In a similar vein, Abilio Naranjo Barrantes of San Marcos, who was also too young to vote at eighteen years of age in 1948, recalled that he "fought to defend the right to vote."[99]

The question of suffrage certainly motivated many who took up arms in 1948, but others had their own reasons for joining in. Antonio Umaña Mora of San Cayetano de Tarrazú claimed that he was never "too interested" in politics and "cannot remember who the presidential candidates were when the 'Revolution' began." Despite Umaña's political indifference, a number of his friends were oppositionists, and he recalled how "men from the government," namely members of the Resguardo or police officers, "would [frequently] come to the bars to harass and arrest them." Umaña claimed that while he was not involved in politics, on more than one occasion he too spent "the night, sometimes two nights, in jail" because he socialized with members of the opposition. He recalled that he and the other men who were arrested with him never went to court, which suggests no charges were ever leveled against them and that they were illegally held in the local prison. Given the arbitrary punishment Umaña experienced at the hands of local authorities, alongside the beatings he claimed to have witnessed and heard about in connection with politics, it is perhaps unsurprising that he claimed that he and all of Tarrazú were "waiting for a Revolution to revolt," despite his claimed disinterest in elections.[100]

Anger over what were seen as political injustices played out at the personal level by local and national authorities moved many men in Tarrazú to go to war, but a number went for less idealistic reasons. For instance, Humberto "Beto" Robles Calvo of San Marcos, who was nineteen years old in 1948 and was employed at the National Bank beneficio, explained that because his father had several large barns located near the town's center, his home was "converted into a barrack," and his mother was forced to prepare food "for all the soldiers" staying on their property. Robles recalled that "the house was full of people" and he came home on several occasions to find a soldier in his bed and no food for him to eat. According to Robles, the situation was unlivable and though he knew "the war was between Figueres and Calderón over something, what interested me was getting out of my house; that is why I went to war."[101] So when a group of soldiers in Robles's home began preparing for a mission, Robles claimed he jumped at the chance to escape his difficult domestic situation and volunteered to accompany these same men who had made his home so unwelcoming.

For some combatants, the desire to assert themselves as men largely explains their decision to go to war. Take, for instance, Analías Meza Solís of San Pablo, who was only fifteen years old in 1948. His father and several of his uncles joined Figueres's forces "early" in the conflict, becoming stationed on a mountain just to the south of San Pablo, El Abejonal, where they kept watch for the arrival of government troops. Because he was "a boy," Meza spent most of the conflict with his grandparents, mother, aunts, and other children locked up indoors. However, each day Meza's grandfather would send him to deliver food to his father and uncles. Meza recognized that all of the men were armed, living away from their families, and dressed in uniforms. Like many boys, "what [he] most wanted" was to do the same. So, each day that he dropped off the men's food he would ask his father if he could stay. Every day his father refused until on one afternoon "the captain asked my dad to let me stay," and Meza was given permission to remain. As he recalled, the captain immediately gave him "a gun, new pants, a matching jacket, and a cap with a white 'V' sewn on it." Meza said he felt "very manly" in his new uniform, with his gun. Joining Figueres's army was intimately tied to his desire to be with his father and uncles who were men, and not to stay with the children, women, and other dependents.[102] Similarly, Nino Vargas of San Lorenzo de Tarrazú, who was twenty-two years old in 1948, described his decision to join Figueres as a means of asserting himself as a man. Initially, he had gone with his mother and younger siblings "into hiding in the mountains," while his father had gone off "to fight for 'Don Pepe.'" After "a week hiding in the mountains," however, he asked his mother if he could go and fight and she "gave [me] permission to prove I was a man."[103] Given the established relationship between politics, brawling, and masculinity in Tarrazú, it is unsurprising that both Meza and Vargas understood their entrance into the conflict as a rite of passage for them as young men.

Conclusion

The centrality that masculinity played in the decision of combatants such as Meza and Vargas to take up arms goes beyond the traditional social linkage between war and manhood and extends into the close-knit relationship between suffrage and manhood. In the years between 1902, when universal male suffrage was inaugurated in Costa Rica, and 1948, the ability to vote became one of the cornerstones of poor men's ability to assert their status as men. Arguably, this interrelationship increased in its importance for many men in the context of the economic decline coffee farmers experienced during the 1930s and 1940s. Moreover, as men were becoming more interested in politics in the 1930s and 1940s, the national political stage was becoming more polarized, thanks to the efforts of politicians and news media outlets on both sides of the divide. Indeed, unlike in earlier decades, when the elites were a largely unified block, in the 1940s, government and oppositionist politicians and newspapers alike repeatedly called on men throughout the country to take to the streets, to organize themselves, to use the courts and even force to defend their suffrage rights. And in a nation where, at least theoretically, *all men* had the right to vote, to be deprived of that right was to be deprived not only of a political voice but also of status as a man.[104] The relationship between masculinity and politics explains to a large extent not only why men were willing to go to war over an election but also why men were willing to verbally and physically attack the police and other local authorities in the streets over political ideals in the years before 1948. It is not coincidental that a majority of scuffles between oppositionists and local authorities took place in and around cantinas; drinking socially and brawling (as well as exercising the right to vote) were understood in this period as the key elements that separated men from children and women in Tarrazú and arguably in all of Costa Rica.

Although political participation and going to war were seen as traditionally masculine activities, local men's decision to join Figueres's insurgency would impact all of Tarrazú's residents. As Figueres's ranks swelled, Tarrazú would be transformed into a war zone, and the lives of its men, women, and children would forever be altered. Dozens of Tarrazúceños would die on the battlefield and thousands of residents—civilians and combatants alike—would suffer the pangs of hunger for much of this forty-day conflict. The challenges and consequences of Tarrazú's embrace of Figueres's revolt are discussed in the next chapter.

5

The Civil War and Its Consequences

On May 16, 1948, *El Diario de Costa Rica* published an article penned by Marcos Chanto entitled "Tarrazú in the Revolution." In the article, he sought to celebrate the critical role that Tarrazúceños played in José "Pepe" Figueres's successful revolt. This dedicated oppositionist proclaimed that, in the years to come, "history and future generations" will ask every Costa Rican, "What did you do to save your fatherland from the ignominy and the slavery to which two bad governments [had subjected it] and what did you do to [help] found the Second Republic?" He assured his readers that although some citizens might struggle to defend their actions in the future, Tarrazúceños would have no need to shrink from these weighty questions. Rather, they could be proud of their community's "direct and active intervention . . . in the recent campaign which . . . culminated in the loudest victory of oppositionist arms."[1]

Written nearly a month after the Civil War ended, the article celebrated the key role that Tarrazúceños' heroism and sacrifice played in realizing the rebels' victory. Yet, more than just seeking to inform *El Diario de Costa Rica*'s readers that Tarrazúceños fought in the recent revolt, Chanto sought to convince them that Tarrazú and its people merited special recognition within the national pantheon for their critical role in the revolt's success.

At the geographical heart of Figueres's operations, Tarrazúceños clearly sacrificed more than their fair share for the rebel cause in 1948. In fact, at least a thousand men, women, and children from the region perished during the forty-four-day rebellion, and countless more went hungry as they struggled to survive in a war zone.[2] The experience of Tarrazúceños during the Civil War is the principal subject of this chapter. In addition to relating the hardships civilians and rebels suffered during the war, I look at how combatants and civilians from Tarrazú and the broader Costa Rican nation remember this conflict. I pay close attention to the way public school textbooks represent the nation's official narrative of Costa Rican history and how they have overlooked the Civil War and Tarrazú so as to construct a national narrative of peace and democracy. More than just pointing to the historical inconsistencies in these texts, my analysis foregrounds the reality that Costa Rica experienced a short-lived but violent civil war, which deeply impacted survivors, in the year that the military was dissolved.

The chapter ends with an examination of the local political and socioeconomic consequences of the nation's forgetting the war and the region's contributions to the nation, in particular the formation of local cooperatives. I argue that Tarrazúceños felt empowered after they successfully overthrew the government. Indeed, they recognized that if they worked together, they could accomplish great things without assistance from San José. This sense of empowerment and community strength coincided with the local perception that José "Pepe" Figueres betrayed the war's aims and the community after he rose to power. This sense of betrayal led many in the region to turn inward, focusing their energies on improving their own communities through cooperatives. So, whereas many Tarrazúceños, such as Marcos Chanto, sought the attention, recognition, and resources of the Costa Rican state before 1948, in the decades that followed, Tarrazúceños would begin to look to themselves and their neighbors and not San José to realize change within their communities.

The Armed Struggle for Political Power

Costa Rica's 1948 Civil War lasted just six weeks and registered a low casualty count that most scholars estimate between 1,000 and 4,000 deaths.[3] In a nation with a population of 825,378 inhabitants in 1948, the number of deaths was arguably minimal, with less than 1 percent of the nation's total population perishing in military actions.[4]

However, these numbers do not take into account the fact that most of the fighting was concentrated in the San José cantons of Pérez Zeledón, Dota, and Tarrazú, which meant that a majority of the war's victims were injured and killed in these sparsely populated rural cantons. Men, women, and children in these rural communities were disproportionately impacted by the violence of the Civil War as the victims, witnesses, and perpetrators of many of these deaths. These deaths had a profound impact on Tarrazúceños young and old who witnessed their rural communities transformed into a war zone, with military planes bombing their fields and their schools converted into military barracks and prisons.

Arguably, the people most shaped by what took place in 1948 were the combatants who put their lives on the line for their political ideals. Today, six decades later, many former combatants still struggle to come to terms with what they witnessed and experienced during the war. For instance, for Analías Meza who was just fifteen years old when he joined the rebels, the war was little more than a trauma-filled nightmare. When asked whether he remembered anything about the events of 1948, he responded, "Of course I do. You remember terrible things. And there is nothing more terrible than killing another man, nothing worse than having killed, and that is what I did then."[5]

Although he soldiered for "just the last weeks" of the revolt, he saw his fair share of death. Just a day after joining the rebel forces, he recalled that his squad was ordered to make its way in the evening to a rocky hillside in Santa Elena de Desamparados, where they spent the night. At dawn the next morning, Meza noticed that they were camped above a large "barn where a group of mariachis [slang for government troops] were camped out, ten or so were washing their faces and a large group was around the fire where the coffee was being prepared."[6] The captain of Meza's squad, whose surname was Araya, told the men "they're going to have coffee without any bread, poor mariachis. I will fix that." At which point, according to Meza, Araya began showering the government troops below with bullets, or "bread." Meza claimed that "Araya killed with gusto, laughing as he fired." In addition, as the soldiers' leader, he "ordered us all to shoot too." Meza recalled he "began shooting with [his] eyes closed out of fear," but when he realized that the bullets the mariachis fired could not reach him or his companions, because of their rocky shield, he "opened [his] . . . eyes and the fear went away, but it was terrible, it was a massacre." Emphasizing his point, he added "some fifty mariachis, maybe more, died that morning, no one in our group was even injured. It was really terrible."[7]

On another occasion, Meza claimed that he and the members of his squad participated in one of the bloodiest battles of the Civil War, which took place on a rise alongside the Inter-American Highway, known as La Sierra, just a few kilometers south of El Empalme de Dota. Meza's recollections of the battle of the Sierra clearly haunt him. He recalled emotionally that "we killed so many men that we could not move the vehicles down the highway. They had to bring in a tractor. . . . They pushed the bodies into a ditch and covered them with dirt. . . . There were a lot of bodies. . . . At least some two hundred meters of the road were full of bodies. . . . It was terrible. I was so frightened. I had lost track of my father at this point. I was surrounded by bodies."[8]

Certainly, the magnitude of death he claimed to have witnessed on the Inter-American Highway must have been a shocking sight.[9] Meza stated that his account does not match "official" recollections of the Civil War, noting that "they say it is not true. They claim things like that never happened, but I saw it. I was there, and I did not make this up. My uncles and father were also there, but they are long dead. Everyone who was there is dead. I was 'the newest' there, and now, I am the only one left; the only one who remembers what it was really like."[10]

Other former combatants also noted that their memories do not jibe with the "official narrative" of the Civil War. For instance, Álvaro Gamboa, who was seventeen when he fought, witnessed "horrible things" that he believed "people would rather forget took place."[11] Foremost among those events that haunt this former rebel soldier were the actions of other rebels following the surrender of government troops in El Tejar, a small town located just to the south of Cartago.[12] The men on both sides of the battle recognized the strategic importance of El Tejar as the first community the rebels attacked in the Central Valley, and what followed was "a battle with many men dying from both sides." While the battle itself was a bloody affair, for Gamboa the most troubling thing he witnessed during the war occurred after the rebels' victory in El Tejar. Gamboa claimed that "some of the men on the government's side surrendered . . . [and] placed their guns in the mud." Rather than arrest the prisoners, a group of his fellow rebels approached the surrendered solders and "shot them right there. They killed the prisoners. Not just one or two, they killed several prisoners." Clearly still impacted by what he witnessed decades earlier, Gamboa related "nothing can excuse what they did."[13]

Some men who fought in the Civil War, however, seemed unbothered about what they did and saw in 1948. For instance, Carlos Elizondo recounted that he spent most of the war near El Empalme blocking the passage of government troops on the Inter-American Highway. Elizondo related that on one evening he and two fellow guards "were sent to La Sierra, and on our way there, we came across a soldier from the other side, he stopped and began shooting his gun in the air [apparently to attract fellow government soldiers' attention]. We all three pulled out our guns and shot at him. One of us killed him." He noted that "it is difficult to know if I killed him or not; I do not think much about it. I think he would have shot me had he had the chance."[14]

Aside from the stresses of military combat, rebel soldiers also contended with hunger. For many men, such as Humberto "Beto" Robles, hunger was "the most difficult" part of soldiering. Robles recalled spending "four days without anything to eat" while engaging government troops in and around El Empalme. Allegedly, when he and other rebels found food in a barn or any other place, they "could not risk eating . . . it," as they had been warned that the government "was poisoning food to kill the opposition."[15] Echoing Robles's memories of hardship, former rebel Arturo Valverde of San Marcos de Tarrazú noted that "all of us soldiers went hungry, even Don Pepe [Figueres] went hungry." Valverde claimed, however, that he and his fellow soldiers were not opposed to "robbing farmers" for food.[16]

Civilian Life in Tarrazú during the Rebellion

Not surprisingly, when hungry soldiers stole farmers' crops and livestock, civilians went hungry too. Unquestionably hunger was among the most challenging parts of living in the war zone. Rebel soldiers pillaged farms and fields, and government planes also regularly bombed fields, particularly those nearest the Inter-American Highway.[17] Furthermore, with most of the region's men serving as volunteer soldiers, women and elderly men were left not only to care for their families and homes but also to plant and harvest the fields.

Among the many civilians who contended with hunger was Lidia Angulo of San Pablo, who was then a pregnant thirty-two-year-old mother of five small children. She vividly recalled the challenges of trying to feed her family during the war when "all the food from outside stopped coming in" and her husband left the family to join the rebel forces. As a majority of the region's fields by this date were dedicated primarily to coffee production, the area's farms were far from able to provide enough food for the region's population on a regular basis, let alone during a war when farmland was being bombed.[18] To keep from starving, Angulo explained that her children, nieces, nephews, and sister-in-law would all "wander into [their neighbor's coffee] farms in search of *guineos* [small bananas] to eat. Everyone did the same [until] . . . there was nothing to eat in the trees but lemons and squirrels."[19]

Children obviously suffered from hunger as well. Juana Fernández of San Marcos who describes herself as a "young girl, not yet twelve" in 1948, took on the responsibility of begging for food to feed herself, her mother, and her two younger brothers. Fernández spent the war alongside numerous families from the center of San Marcos at the family farm of Humberto Umaña Parra, Tobías Umaña Jiménez's son. While Fernández claims her family "appreciated" the fact that the Umañas opened their home to them, she also noted that they were not the most generous of hosts and that her family "suffered hardships," namely hunger, while at the Umañas' home. Fernández's eyes teared up as she recalled the sound of her youngest brother, who was just a toddler in 1948, crying himself to sleep each night because the family had no milk to give him.[20]

However, what most upset Fernández was that while she begged her neighbors for table scraps to feed her family, their hosts hoarded large quantities of food. In fact, Fernández claimed that Humberto Umaña's daughter, Nelly Umaña Parra, recruited her and several other children staying with her family "to help her carry cans of food, bags of beans and rice, powdered milk, and other foods from the Umaña's store to a large hole she had us dig where we buried it all." Fernández understood Umaña's decision to bury the food as evidence that she and her family "were tightfisted" and "did not care that people were starving in front of them."[21]

The Umañas' hoarding, coupled with her baby brother's hunger, prompted Fernández to action. She recalled that toward the end of the conflict the baby had become "so weak he no longer cried" and her mother began to say he "might die without milk." Knowing that the milk he needed was buried nearby, Fernández recruited the older of her two younger brothers and "another little boy" to sneak out of the barn where they were staying at "around 1:00 A.M." Under cover of darkness, the trio went "to . . . where [they] had buried the food . . . [and] dug a hole with [their] . . . hands and sticks." Once they uncovered the buried food, the children removed "rice, beans, lard, and lots of powdered milk, but no sweets, because I told the boys God will punish us if we take what we do not need." Nearly sixty years after she stole from the Umañas, Fernández made a clear distinction between what is morally and legally correct, explaining that "stealing is a crime, but it was the right thing to do, since it saved my little brother's life."[22]

Both soldiers and civilians in Tarrazú also worried about what they would do if Figueres's insurgency failed and government troops recaptured their communities. For years before the Civil War broke out, local police officers and members of the Resguardo Fiscal harassed, beat, arrested, and intimidated the region's men over not only issues of politics but also the consumption and production of homemade liquor. As seen in chapters 3 and 4, a pattern of abusive practices engendered considerable ill will toward government authorities, which no doubt facilitated Figueres's recruitment process in the region. However, years of government repression also meant that many in the region feared government retribution if their insurgency was unsuccessful. Fears of government retaliation are perhaps best captured through the stories Tarrazúceños tell of the capture, torture, and murder of a rebel soldier, Ernesto Zumbado of Santa María, by government soldiers.

According to Nelly Barrantes Porras of Guadalupe de Tarrazú, Zumbado's story began "when he was captured by government forces . . . [while] gathering water." Barrantes claimed that when a few of his friends went in search of him they spotted him from a ridge within the government's barracks. Zumbado's friends were allegedly able to overhear the government soldiers asking the captured man to reveal "where the rebels were staying and their [military] plans, but he refused." Barrantes claimed that the government troops began to do "terrible things" to coax their prisoner into speaking. They allegedly "cut off his nose and ears with a machete. . . . Since he still did not want to talk, they took out his eyes and . . . [finally] they cut his tongue out." Barrantes suggested that Zumbado's friends chose not to tell Zumbado's family what they had seen. Moreover, she claimed that "everyone [in Tarrazú] but the family knows what happened to him. . . . They know their son died a soldier, but they do not know how he died."[23]

Barrantes's story is perhaps the most graphic description of Zumbado's torturous demise, but others confirm the story of his death at the hands of government troops. For instance, Analías Meza claims that when Zumbado would not talk "they shot him. Who knows how many bullets they shot at him, but the bullets were so many his body moved like a puppet and would not fall to the ground."[24] For some, such as Carlos Elizondo of Santa María, Zumbado's demise is certain but nothing else. He explained that "he was captured by the enemy, . . . [and] they shot him. Other people say he was tortured before they shot him. . . . I cannot comment on that. I was not there, and I never saw his body." While Elizondo did not want to comment on things he did not know for certain, others who readily remembered the macabre tales of Zumbado's demise, but not his name, were quick to share what they had heard. For instance, Blas Vargas Blanco of Santa María, who was only twelve years old during the Civil War, recalled having "heard of a young man from Santa María, and the men from the government cut his face."[25]

Former combatant Guillermo Villegas Hoffmeister, of the Central Valley province of Alajuela, has written extensively on his experiences as a soldier in Figueres's National Liberation Army and makes passing mention of Zumbado's death, placing himself in the latter's company minutes before his capture by government troops. According to Villegas, while searching for water "he was taken prisoner by some Government soldiers. . . . They took him to Frailes [the location of one of the government's barracks at the time]. They believed that because he was tall, white, and [had] reddish hair, he was a German, and so his captors . . . called him the German."[26] In Villegas's account, the most remarkable facet of Zumbado's capture was the fact that the prisoner was believed to be a foreigner because of his physical appearance. Although providing little detail of Zumbado's death, Villegas instead emphasizes what happened to the boy's remains, writing, "In Frailes they placed him behind the school and there they shot him. They halfway buried him and so later he was taken out of his grave and to the cemetery of the town [and] buried properly. Years later his remains were moved to Santa María." Villegas, however, gives some credence to Barrantes's claim that some of

Figure 5.1. *Hero of 48: Ernesto Zumbado Ureña* statue in Santa María's central plaza to commemorate this fallen soldier. Zumbado cradles four canteens, perhaps recalling the fact that he was allegedly fetching water when he was captured by government troops. (Carmen Kordick)

Zumbado's friends followed his captors, noting that an unspecified person "told us of Ernesto's disappearance and Tuta Cortés, Juancito Camacho, myself and others tried to rescue him but we could not reach them."[27]

The importance of this account of Zumbado resonates with Tarrazúceños who have publicly commemorated this fallen rebel by naming the central plaza in Santa María, the town of his birth, Ernesto Zumbado Ureña Park and also by placing a sculpture, *Hero of 48: Ernesto Zumbado Ureña*, in this park (fig. 5.1). Given the importance Zumbado's memory has for Tarrazúceños and the extremely violent stories of his death told by some, it is curious that the Tribunal de Sanciones Inmediatas did not seek out Zumbado's alleged killers. The tribunal was established to punish crimes committed during both the short-lived revolt and the eight years before the war, when Presidents Picado and Calderón governed. This tribunal heard some 922 cases, including a variety of accusations pertaining to unlawful incarceration and other abuses against members of the opposition before the war and cases of murder, rape, and pillaging during the war.[28]

Perhaps, however, the circumstances of Zumbado's death matter less than the way Tarrazúceños recalled his cruel demise as a means of expressing their fears of what government officials might have done to them, their families, and the rest of their community had the revolt failed. Giving credence to this reading of the local Zumbado mythology, Barrantes alleged that if "Don Pepe and his men had not been victorious, . . . there would be no more Tarrazú, we all would have fallen like Zumbado."[29]

Political Prisoners in Tarrazú

The region's hundreds of government supporters were terrified of what rebels would do to them during the war and after. In rebel-controlled areas, insurgents sought out people associated with the government and imprisoned them in San Marcos's schoolhouse turned into a "concentration camp."[30] While the victors' worries of what might have happened to them had their revolt failed play a central role in the region's collective memory of the events of 1948, government supporters' anxieties have largely been forgotten. One of the reasons for this erasure is the assertion by both government supporters and rebels that in the region no local calderonista prisoners were killed or physically harmed. Another reason for this official omission is that it places into focus some of the less savory and arguably unethical actions taken or considered by the insurgents, in particular the detainment of roughly 150 political prisoners in San Marcos's schoolhouse.

For family members of political detainees, such as Fany Jiménez and Herminía Muñoz, whose fathers had been arrested as alleged calderonistas, the uncertainty of what would happen to their imprisoned loved ones was extremely frightening. Although everyone I spoke with agreed that no one ultimately was killed or injured in San Marcos's makeshift prison, during the length of their imprisonment the prisoners and their families feared they might be killed. Lourdes Gamboa of the small town of Carrizal de Tarrazú is the younger sister of Álvaro Gamboa, and she recalled "as though it were yesterday" when rebel troops discovered "Betón Umaña, a calderonista who had hidden in a home nearby." Gamboa alleged that Umaña "was very frightened and shouted for help because he said they [the rebels who had captured him] were going to kill him."[31]

Betón Umaña was far from the only calderonista who hid or ran, fearing for his life, after Figueres seized control of Tarrazú. Quintín "Kinto" Araya Navarro told how his father, who worked repairing roads for the city of San Pablo, fled with his family to San Isidro de Tarrazú, where they hid out for the duration of the war.[32] Not everyone who had an association with the government, however, had a chance to run and hide. For instance, Fany Jiménez's father was arrested "less than an hour" after Figueres's troops seized control of San Marcos. Jiménez claimed her father, who owned a small blacksmith shop where he fashioned horseshoes, was not actually aligned with any political party. However, because he employed "several well-known calderonistas," he was initially suspect and arrested. Jiménez recalled that the day after his arrest her mother sent her to deliver food to her father. She carried a white flag made out of a tree branch and a white rag. When she arrived at the plaza in front of the schoolhouse "waving [her] white flag," the troops that had amassed there "stopped their target practices," allowing her to make her way to the school gate where she spotted the jailer, "Don Marcos [Chanto] with a Mr. Araya." The two men were arguing about Araya's intention to destroy the prison and kill all of the prisoners, a desire Araya was clearly ready to act on, given the "grenade [in his] hand." Jiménez recalled that Chanto "beg[ged] him not to." Recognizing the gravity of the situation, she "walked up to both men and looked that Araya in the face and begged 'no, please, my father is in there.'" The sight of the young girl seemed to have calmed Araya, who "put his grenade away and walked off."[33] Jiménez's recollection suggests that although no calderonistas reportedly died in the oppositionists' schoolhouse jail, at least one rebel considered killing them all. Most certainly, their fate remained uncertain for the length of the war.

Bernardo Martínez of San Lorenzo was seventeen years old and "had aligned [himself] with the opposition; however, [he still] has problems with what took place then." Politics deeply divided Martínez's family and a brother and two of his uncles, who had "supported the state," were imprisoned. He struggled decades later with the memory of rebel soldiers "grabbing" his uncles "without cause . . . from their farms" to imprison them. Martínez claimed that it was not just men involved in politics, but that several "elderly [men], children and even women" were also jailed, in the "concentration camp." Perhaps Martínez's most difficult memory concerned his brother, who worked as a clerk in the municipality and was also imprisoned by the rebels. Years later, his brother shared that, while imprisoned, "Carlos Gamboa and Colonel Sosa walked him behind the school and told him they were going to shoot him." The men then asked if he had any last words, before shooting a bullet into the wall behind him. Apparently, the men had no intention of actually killing him but simply intended to "frighten" him for their own amusement. For a political prisoner, "the joke" was anything but funny.[34] Just as soldiers Meza and Gamboa asserted that their recollections do not line up with the "official memory" of the Civil War, Martínez explained that "today people deny this happened [that people were imprisoned in the school], but I remember, I was there."[35]

Hacendados, Social Reform, and the Civil War

Some government supporters had no fear of imprisonment during the Civil War. Tobías Umaña Jiménez's son, Humberto Umaña Parra, who gave sanctuary to numerous Tarrazúceños, including Juana Fernández's family, was a steadfast and vocal supporter of the government. He spent the war with his family in his home with little fear of political reprisals. Umaña Parra's son, Helber Umaña Gamboa, stated that though the Civil War was "grave," as he was only twelve at the time, he did not know that people were being killed. It seemed to him "it was a party," with his house "full of children to play with." Although Umaña Gamboa does not have bad memories of 1948, he recalled that his father's political stances made him a target of rebel looters who "sacked [his] father's store."[36] Aside from suffering some property damage, it seems that Umaña Parra suffered little for his political support of the government. Perhaps this was largely due to the fact that Tobías Umaña Jiménez was not only Umaña Parra's father but also a personal friend of Figueres who, like Don Pepe, shared the distinction of being one of the region's large hacendados (fig. 5.2). In fact, class goes a long way toward explaining the relationship between Figueres and Umaña. According to Umaña Gamboa, in 1948, his grandfather was deeply upset by "the social reforms that [he believed] mistreated hacendados." To support the insurrection, which he hoped would do away with the social reforms, Umaña Jiménez opened his home to Figueres, "who spent the war" living in Umaña Jiménez's San Marcos home. He also lent rebel troops "his trucks" and sold the National Liberation Army khaki cloth "to make [troop] uniforms," on credit.[37]

It seems clear why Umaña supported Figueres as well as why a majority of the community (who had voted for Cortés and later for Ulate and believed that their votes had been robbed by the state) supported the revolt. What is less clear to this day is why Umaña Parra "was different than his father and supported the social reforms." His son seems unable to answer this question, but other Tarrazúceños today point as well to the importance of social class in understanding the Civil War. For instance, Elías Montero of Copey de Dota worked as a wage laborer on Emilio Mata's farm in El Llano de la Piedra de Tarrazú in 1948. This Figueres supporter suggested that although suffrage motivated "humble" men, like himself, to take up arms, what encouraged the region's elites, including Figueres, to "lead" the revolt were eco-

Figure 5.2. Tarrazú's two biggest employers, Tobías Umaña Jiménez (*left*) and José Figueres (*middle*), and an unknown man, downtown San Marcos de Tarrazú, 1937. (Courtesy of Juan Mora)

nomic considerations. In fact, he asserted that the "revolution started because bosses like Don Emilio [his employer] and Don Pepe did not want to pay taxes for their employees." The taxes Montero referenced are the social reforms Calderón made into law during his presidency. Montero claimed it was consequential that Figueres started the conflict and that he "owned one of the largest farms . . . and had a lot of employees, and [therefore], lots of taxes to pay." Montero went on to say that "Don Tobías in San Marcos, he gave Figueres a lot of help, you know he too had lots of taxes for his farm."[38]

Although the government his father supported collapsed, Umaña Gamboa claimed that "everything worked out for the best. Don Pepe won, but instead of ending the Social Reforms, he strengthened and amplified them."[39] While Umaña Gamboa suggested that things ended well, Blas Vargas Blanco of San Marcos saw things a bit differently. He claimed that "when the 'Revolution' ended and 'Don Pepe' did not take away the Social Guarantees but taxed employers, Don Tobías . . . [spoke] openly about how much he disliked [Figueres's] government."[40] Umaña Jiménez was likely not only upset that Figueres retained the Social Guarantees but also that he implemented a 10 percent wage increase for agricultural laborers, including coffee pickers.[41] Don Pepe's actions likely felt like a betrayal to Umaña, who had given his support to Figueres's insurrection believing that one of the war's aims was to reclaim their shared economic interests as hacendados.[42]

Politics after the War

Figueres's political decisions in the months, years, and decades following the Civil War would ultimately disappoint more than just the nation's hacendados. In fact, many who supported the revolt, both in Tarrazú and throughout the rest of the nation, would soon think that Figueres betrayed their cause in search of personal political power and glory. The roots of much oppositionist anger with Don Pepe began even before the government capitulated to the rebels on April 19, 1948. On that date, government and rebel representatives signed a peace treaty, the Pact of the Mexican Embassy.[43] With the war over, many oppositionists, including former combatant Arturo Valverde, incorrectly presumed that Ulate would immediately assume the presidency.

As discussed in the previous chapter, for most oppositionists, suffrage was the key issue that led them to support Figueres's call to arms. For many combatants, such as Valverde, Figueres's decision to not allow Ulate to become president in 1948 was nothing short of a betrayal of the revolt's aim. This sense of betrayal is evident in Valverde's words: "I am against Figueres, but I was in favor of the Revolution. . . . We were many who supported the Revolution, but not Figueres." According to Valverde, "as a soldier Figueres was fine, but [after the war ended], he was shameless. I fought for Ulate, not Figueres, but Figueres became the head of the junta."[44]

Although Figueres had stockpiled arms and planned for a revolt for years, before the contentious elections of 1948, that year's election helped him to build an insurgency. Yet placing Ulate in power was arguably never part of his plan. In fact, Figueres was seeking political power for himself. Ever politically savvy, Don Pepe recognized that he needed Ulate's support (or at least Ulate's official acceptance) for him to seize political power without risking the chance of an ulatista uprising against the Figueres-led junta that would install its candidate into the executive branch. And so, on May 1, Figueres and Ulate met and signed the Figueres-Ulate Pact, which officially declared Ulate the victor in that year's presidential race but also called for the creation of a provisional junta, with Figueres as its head, to assume power for eighteen months. The pact called for the disbanding of the Legislative Assembly and for the junta to hold elections in December 1948 to elect a new Legislative Assembly that would be charged with writing a new constitution.[45]

While the Figueres-Ulate Pact called for Ulate to eventually assume the role of president, as head of the junta for eighteen months Figueres secured the power to enact significant changes that would restructure power relations and reshape the Costa Rican republic.[46] One of the junta's most significant accomplishments was the nationalization of the nation's banking system. This action limited the coffee elites' once-dominant economic power and placed considerable control over the nation's economy into the state's hands.[47] This move, alongside the decision to increase agricultural workers' wages and the retention of Calderón's Social Guarantees, brought Don Pepe little support from hacendados. Yet, these initiatives endeared him to many of the men who risked their lives to topple the government—men who might otherwise have been upset because Ulate was not immediately placed in the presidency following the Civil War.

Perhaps, however, the junta's most celebrated action was Figueres's December 1948 announcement that Costa Rica would abolish its military.[48] Figueres declared this momentous decision in a speech he gave fittingly at the nation's most well-known military barracks, San José's Cuartel de Bella Vista. It was there that he proclaimed "the dissolution of the National Army" as "a good police force [is] sufficient for our country."[49] The audience reportedly responded to this unexpected announcement with excited clapping and cheering, though likely also with a measure of disbelief. The irony of the situation was unquestionable, since Figueres had risen to power just eight months earlier after toppling the government in an armed insurgency he had planned for over six years.[50] Couching his actions in terms of these recent events, Don Pepe explained, "We, who have recently shed the blood of a peaceful country, understand the seriousness which these wounds can assume." He continued by promising that this decision would help heal the nation, stating, "The future health of the Nation . . . demands that the wounds heal quickly."[51] He then theatrically demonstrated his sincere commitment to this declaration by ceremoniously taking a sledgehammer to the Cuartel's wall, sending a large chunk of the structure's thick, whitewashed wall to the ground (fig. 5.3).[52] While Figueres proclaimed that he sought forgiveness and healing, the reality would seem far different for many who had supported the previous government and even some oppositionists. In fact, the months and years after the Civil War would deeply disillusion Costa Ricans of all political stripes.

The junta took particularly harsh retaliatory actions against the vanguardistas and the nation's unions. The junta's attack against Communists fits with the opposition's misgivings about Calderón and Picado's alliance with vanguardistas. However, these actions also suggest clear limits to Figueres's apparent commitment to respect the democratic process. Don Pepe's junta moved in dramatic fashion against the vanguardistas and their political

Figure 5.3. José Figueres knocking down a section of the Cuartel de Bella Vista's outer wall, 1948. This action has become emblematic of the nation's commitment to peace. In the decades since the Civil War concluded, Costa Rica's "peaceful" society and culture has been celebrated as a fundamental element of Costa Rican national identity. Yet the soldier with his bayonet in hand serves as a reminder that this event took place at a moment when Costa Rica was far from peaceful. (Courtesy of Costa Rica's National Archives)

leader, Manuel Mora. Not only was Mora's political party outlawed; so was the Confederación de Trabajadores Costarricense, which was both the nation's most important union and largely made up of vanguardistas and therefore seen by many as an extension of the party.[53] Additionally, the PVP's ten highest-ranking leaders, after Mora, were imprisoned in December 1948. Five were executed the evening of December 20, 1948, outside of Limón and plans were made to execute the other five who were in San José. The Central Valley's Communist leaders were spared when news of their impending execution reached Archbishop Sanabria who immediately intervened to spare their lives.[54] Not satisfied with these attacks on the nation's Communists and the labor movement, the junta went on to dissolve some sixty unions, exiled three thousand vanguardistas, and executed at least fourteen in its first twelve months in power.[55] These actions would serve to permanently reduce the nation's once-powerful Communist Party and, in turn, reshape the political balance of power.

The junta also fired hundreds of government functionaries without cause and provided these workers with no chance to appeal the loss of their posts. Additionally, the junta gave private industry the unofficial go-ahead to fire workers who were perceived as politically problematic. While vanguardistas lost the most after the war, many calderonistas also suffered.[56] In the Central Valley as late as the mid-1950s, individuals and their children who were associated with the Calderón and/or Picado administrations were persecuted, taunted, and stigmatized.[57]

The political repression Figueres unleashed after the Civil War was far from contained to the Central Valley, as is evident by the actions taken against Tarrazú's calderonistas.[58] Fany Jiménez, who watched her father unjustly jailed and accused of being a calderonista during the war, recalls that her cousin, Carlos Monge Solís, was a "dyed-in-the-wool [*envenenado*] calderonista," and his politics made him a frequent victim of physical attacks by former insurgents. Jiménez related that one evening, "after the fighting had ended," she was at her grandparents' home and watched in disbelief alongside her crying grandmother as Figueres supporters "dragged . . . [my] cousin by the arms from the Red Cross to my grandparents' house [four blocks away] to beat him before us." Jiménez claimed that the men gave her cousin a "good beating" despite her grandmother's protests. She had little doubt as to why her cousin was beaten that day, explaining, that he "offended the *liberacionistas* [supporters or members of Figueres's Liberación Nacional Army and later political party] constantly." Jiménez saw that the Civil War had not ended political oppression but rather simply shifted "who was in charge and who was beaten" because of their politics.[59]

Echoing Jiménez, Emilio "Eli" Rojas Ureña, of Santa María, describes the civil war as "the most horrible thing in the world, because I was a calderonista." Rojas, however, was not just a calderonista but Calderón's campaign secretary in the canton of Dota. For the length of the conflict, Rojas lived in hiding alongside his mother and several cousins on a farm they owned in "the mountains near Quepos," which is a port city on the Pacific coast. When Rojas returned to Santa María after the war's conclusion, he discovered that he "was now a local political enemy," and "like all . . . poor calderonistas" he was "without food or work." Rojas lost his post as a municipal clerk and could not so much as find work "as a peon" locally. Thus, Rojas made his way on foot some eighty kilometers south along the Inter-American Highway to the community of San Isidro de El General de Pérez Zeledón, where he found employment as a carpenter. He claimed that he was lucky to find a man who admired his woodcarving skills and "who never asked" why he had left Santa María. Rojas stated that for "several years" he was "exiled" from Tarrazú because of the heated postwar political atmosphere.[60]

The political animosity that followed the insurgency not only upset calderonistas but also a few dedicated oppositionists, such as Marcos Chanto, who organized the local opposition movement.[61] Figueres repaid Chanto's fealty by designating him Tarrazú's jefe político, a post he held until 1953, when he retired.[62] Although Chanto had been a dedicated oppositionist, he quickly fell into "disfavor" with many because he refused to support "the persecution of . . . [local] Calderón" supporters. Juan Chanto, his son, recalled that after the Civil War, many residents began "attacking . . . Resguardo Fiscal [guards], throwing rocks at their homes," and his father had the police arrest the vandals. Chanto noted that although his father did not necessarily agree with the actions Resguardo guards had taken before the revolt, he strongly believed they "had the right to live in peace." Despite Chanto's attempts to "protect the rights" of local calderonistas from persecution, "many people lost everything: their jobs and home," and many, like Emilio Rojas, "had to leave."[63]

Forgetting the War

The tragic repercussions of the war—the deaths of civilians and combatants, the hunger suffered by young and old, the destruction of private property, and the persecution of calderonistas and vanguardistas after the war—are as much a part of the Civil War's history as is Figueres's abolition of the military, yet these dismal aspects of the war are not given equal weight in the official narrative, including the version taught in the nation's public schools. While the violence both during and after the Civil War has largely been overlooked, the photograph of Figueres defacing the Cuartel de Bella Vista is arguably the most iconic image of 1948. By focusing on the abolition of the military, the public school system created and encouraged the promulgation of the idea that Costa Rica is a nonmilitarized society because the national character is innately pacific.

Looking at official civics textbooks used in public schools from 1948 to the present, it is evident that the nation's public education has underscored the centrality of peace and democracy to the national narrative. Although Figueres's dissolution of the military is frequently presented in Costa Rican exceptionalist works as a key, if not the primary, piece of evidence that Costa Ricans are committed pacifists, the nation's myth of peace was not born immediately after the military's dissolution in 1948.[64] Civics textbooks from as late as the mid-1970s, which hardly describe the nation's politicians as committed to the "politics of peace" and "neutrality," provide a case in point. These textbooks make no mention of the military's abolition and the political violence that preceded it, nor do they propose that Costa Rica has a deep-rooted history of pacific resolution of conflict.[65]

In fact, 1970s textbooks such as Oscar Aguilar and Carlos L. Fallas Monge's seventh-grade social studies textbook, *Estudios sociales para 7° grado: Geografía, historia y cívica de Costa Rica*, make no mention of the events of

1948.[66] Yet, these authors do note that the nation's current constitution dates back to 1949, without explaining why a new constitution was so recently drafted. The absence of the actual narrative of the Civil War likely implies that these historians had yet to decide how they wanted to interpret the events of 1948 into the larger Costa Rican narrative. However, this silence does not reflect a desire to present Costa Rica as a historically pacifist nation: instead, these textbooks are dotted with references to coups, attempted coups, civil wars, and other political conflicts in the nineteenth and early twentieth centuries.[67]

Sometime in the late 1970s the narrative of Costa Rican pacifism entered the nation's civics textbooks. This shift coincides with an escalation in militarization and violence throughout Central America in the 1970s and 1980s. In these decades, Costa Rica stood alone as Nicaragua, El Salvador, and Guatemala all experienced bloody civil wars that left thousands upon thousands displaced.[68] Many who fled the violence of their war-torn nations migrated to the United States, and thousands of Nicaraguan and Salvadoran refugees also made their way to Costa Rica.[69]

I suggest that the arrival of political and economic refugees fleeing the terror of their nation's militaries, anti-insurgent militias, guerrilla forces, and death squads caused Costa Ricans to pause and contemplate their nation's history in a different light. It did not take long for scholars, educators, and politicians to point to the fact that Costa Rica alone of the Central American republics did not have a military and had not been plagued by a civil war in the second half of the twentieth century.

As scholars focused on the 1948 demilitarization, they began reexamining Costa Rican history in such a way as to emphasize a tradition of peace. Thus, for example, the authors of a 1988 textbook declare that Costa Rica's commitment to peace dates back to the republic's first president, Juan Mora Fernández. The book's authors cite an 1829 speech Mora gave before the Costa Rican Congress regarding tense relations between the various members of the Federal Republic of Central America, of which Costa Rica was a member at the time. Mora is recorded to have assured the congress that although "the whole . . . Central American Republic appears divided, consumed and covered in blood, . . . Costa Rica presents a [small] painting . . . illuminated . . . by the rainbow of peace."[70] Mora may have promised congressmen that Costa Rica would not go to war in 1829, but Costa Rica had suffered a civil war just six years earlier in 1823, and a second civil war would divide the nation in 1835, and of course a third in 1948. Additionally, Costa Rica would declare war against the US filibuster William Walker in Nicaragua in 1856 and against Panama in 1921 over a border dispute. The nation also suffered several coups and coup attempts in both the nineteenth and early twentieth centuries. These historical realities certainly serve to complicate the textbook's attempts to suggest that, since Mora's speech, Costa Ricans have embraced democracy, peace, and neutrality.

Indeed, the nation's textbooks written in more recent decades repeatedly downplay historical incidents that might arguably place into question the idea of Costa Rica's commitment to peace.[71] For instance, the 1992 pedagogical text *Educación cívica costarricense* makes brief mention of Costa Rica's first civil war in 1823. However, this textbook explains the event to readers within a larger pacific narrative: "The fact that . . . this first Civil War [occurred] . . . should not impede us [Costa Ricans] from recognizing the natural pacifism and equilibrium of our nation. . . . Our preoccupation with . . . the law and peace are exemplary and are the cause of great pride to us."[72] In a similar vein, this same textbook describes the events of 1948 in a celebratory manner that almost entirely overlooks the war that took place before the Second Republic was formed: "Paradoxically, the final period [of Costa Rican democracy] began with an armed struggle, that of 1948. The Civil War consolidated . . . democracy. . . . From this moment forward, follow[ed] regularly perfect governments."[73] As this quotation suggests, the war itself is presented as an aberration in a larger tradition of democracy and peace. In this and other civics textbooks, the war and its impact on participants and civilians alike are ignored in favor of celebrating the nation's "peaceful traditions." These ideals go beyond the late 1970s and 1980s; they continue today, as is evident in the civics textbook *Educación Civica: IX año*, published in 2005, which declares "peace" to be the first of fifteen Costa Rican national values.[74]

When discussing the events of the 1940s, many Costa Rican scholars also follow suit, providing no more than a passing reference to the actual war, focusing instead on the events that led to its outbreak and its consequences, namely, the dissolution of the military. The decision to abolish the military dramatically shaped how scholars interpreted Costa Rican history by encouraging a Costa Rican exceptionalist myth, highlighting Costa Ricans' innately peaceful, democratic, and conciliatory national character, in stark contrast to their more "violent" and less civilized Central American neighbors. Many of these post-1948 historical works whitewash Costa Rica's past to suggest that the nation's commitment to peace and democracy date back to the nineteenth century. Take, for instance, Constantino Urcuyo Fournier and Chester Zelaya Goodman's *Democracia costarricense: Pasado, presente y futuro*.[75] Contributors to this edited volume posit that Costa Rican democracy dates back to 1889 and point to 1948 as the culmination of the democratic process because the conflict saw the establishment of the current democratic constitution and because demilitarization eliminated war as a possible solution to conflicts.[76]

One need look no further than the experiences of Tarrazúceños in the years before, during, and immediately after the Civil War to recognize that Costa Rica was no peaceful paradise. In addition to inaccurately presenting Costa Rica's history, these texts ignore the critical role that Tarrazú played in the formation of Costa Rica's Second Republic. In fact, Chanto's 1948 hope that Tarrazú would be privileged within the nation's historical narrative was never realized. Instead, the "official" historical narrative isolates Tarrazúceños because their experiences of hunger, imprisonment, death, and injury do not fit within a peaceful rendition of the nation's past. This sense of exclusion is evident in the way that former combatants such as Meza and Gamboa repeatedly mentioned how their memories contradict "what is said" to have taken place, or perhaps more accurately, what is not said about Costa Rica's past.[77]

Additionally, this inaccurate presentation of Costa Rica's past by the nation's education system and pro-Figueres scholars serves to downplay one of Costa Rica's most significant historical transformations: the nation's development during the second half of the twentieth century into a democratically stable nation that avoided militarization and war during the Cold War, unlike its neighbors. Indeed, this might arguably be one moment where Costa Rica merited its exceptionalist image in the region. If scholars wish to explain the roots of Costa Rica's exceptionalism in the twentieth century within the isthmus, they must be willing to "remember" the state violence and political repression of the pre-1948 period. Moreover, they must reinsert the role of Tarrazú in realizing the violent birth of the current political order.[78]

The Civil War and the Arrival of "Progress"

Even though Costa Rican textbooks have overlooked the hardships Tarrazúceños suffered before, during, and after the nation's Civil War, the region's residents recognized their own contributions to the nation. In fact, the events of 1948 demonstrated to many the power that they had to accomplish dramatic change if they worked together. That is precisely what they would do during the 1950s and 1960s. During these two decades, the region would experience what Juan Chanto today describes as "progress coming to Tarrazú." He, like other Tarrazúceños, pointed to several events and developments that took place in these decades—in particular the arrival of electric power, the opening of Tarrazú's first high school, and the creation of a coffee cooperative—when asked about evidence of such "progress."[79]

Others confirmed that things improved after the Civil War. Former combatant Carlos Elizondo of Santa María de Dota proudly proclaimed that "the cultural and socioeconomic changes that took place in Santa María after the revolution were tremendous. Before there were few, maybe five or six people who owned the whole town, . . . but with the Revolution we saw a great opening. The nationalization of the banking system and the formation of the [coffee] cooperatives . . . made it possible for people to take out loans and purchase farms, . . . which resulted in [an increased] distribution of capital and land within the community."[80]

Government supporters, many of whom suffered loss of jobs and were socially ostracized in the months immediately following the Civil War, also note that in the following two decades they generally saw an improvement in their quality of life. Kinto Araya, whose father worked for San Pablo's municipal government in the 1940s and was persecuted during and after the conflict for his association with the government, provides a case in point. Despite hardship the Civil War brought his family, he felt that "after the war, the nation improved." For Araya, the key difference on the national level was that "after the war, they rid [the nation] of the army, . . . and regardless of one's political stripe, people could live in peace."[81] Additionally, although Araya's father lost his government job in 1948, this loss translated into his father "beginning his own business" as a "coffee farmer," which ultimately proved more lucrative for the Araya family. According to Araya, his father saved some money over the years in the hope of "one day" purchasing a farm; however, the loss of his job encouraged this fiscally conservative man to finally take that economic risk and purchase a small farm in the remote community of Trinidad de Tarrazú. Because of the opening of the local coffee cooperatives, the Araya family was able to establish themselves as coffee farmers, and Araya suggested that his family ultimately saw an improvement in their financial standing in the post–Civil War period.[82]

Women in Tarrazú also attest to dramatic improvements after the Civil War. Flora Villa, for instance, noted that "women were given the vote in 1949," which she believes "placed us on a plan towards equality." On a more personal level, Villa also claimed that after 1948 her "life improved most [significantly] with the arrival of electricity and running water," which allowed her to "do the domestic work" of washing and ironing clothes, as well as cooking food, without having to gather firewood or water from the nearest stream.[83]

The almost universal consensus that Tarrazúceños' quality of life improved after 1948 is backed up by concrete facts. Yet, despite Tarrazúceños' recollections, which celebrate the local initiative that permitted these material developments, the community only realized these noteworthy accomplishments in the 1950s and 1960s because San José policy makers passed laws and allocated funding to support cooperative formation and provide educational and credit opportunities for farmers to embrace Green Revolution techniques and chemicals.[84]

In 1955, fewer than 5 percent of farmers in the canton of Tarrazú reported employing chemical fertilizers on their crops and even fewer owned an electric generator or motorized vehicle.[85] These figures, although considerably lower than the national average, reflect widespread rural poverty throughout the republic, an issue that the post-1948 government would make a concerted investment in altering.[86] Critical to the government's push to encourage farmers to embrace the Green Revolution was the Ministerio de Agricultura y Ganadería (Ministry of Agriculture and Livestock). In 1952, this ministry established an office in San Marcos and its functionaries immediately began visiting the region's farms to provide advice and education on different agricultural practices and technologies that could increase coffee yields. At the same time, this institution also organized educational meetings for farmers to learn about new coffee varieties, herbicides, fertilizers, methods for their use, and potential benefits.[87] The opening of a ministry office in San Marcos reflected a clear commitment on the part of the post-1948 state to advance the economic position of Tarrazú's farmers. Additionally, and most significantly, this agency's efforts likely improved the lives of many rural families, by increasing their ability to produce greater quantities of coffee on their lands. In fact, by 1963, over 50 percent of the region's farmers were using chemical fertilizers and herbicides.[88] Moreover, coffee production rates dramatically increased with farmers producing on average 6.6 fanegas of coffee per hectare of coffee planted in 1963, which was higher than the national average of 6.3 fanegas.[89]

San José policy makers' largest contribution to local farmers was, however, without question their support of cooperatives. Indeed, starting in early 1949, the new government passed legislation and began to invest tax revenues to facilitate the establishment of cooperatives throughout the republic. Critical to this venture was the nationalization of the banking system, which ensured that cooperative ventures had access to loans to help jump-start their formation. Additionally, the rural credit agencies, or Juntas de Crédito Rural, saw increased funding in the 1950s that allowed them to provide farmers with low-interest loans to purchase the chemical fertilizers and herbicides that they were learning about through the initiatives of the ministerio's programs.[90] Of importance too was the 1969 Law of Cooperative Associations, which critically provided newly incorporated cooperatives with a decade-long exemption on all import duties for machinery, equipment, and parts. This proved critical to the ability of members to purchase the newest equipment for their mills and gave them a considerable edge over their private competitors.[91] Also noteworthy, in 1949 when women were granted voting rights, they also secured access to loans, allowing them to also participate in the new cooperative ventures.

Taking advantage of San José's support of cooperative ventures, local farmers came together to organize coffee cooperatives that would provide increased access to credit and, more importantly, a higher price for their crop than that offered by private processors, namely the Umaña family. The success of the coffee cooperative would be followed by many of these same farmers working together to bring electricity to the region through an electric cooperative, which not only secured federal aid but also funding from the United States, through the Alliance for Progress.[92] Furthermore, the region's first high school opened its doors in San Marcos, providing Tarrazúceños for the first time with the chance to receive more than a sixth-grade education. These three developments—the creation of coffee and electrical cooperatives and the opening of the local high school—clearly improved the community and the lives of men, women, and children of the region.

The coffee and electrical cooperatives formed through a combination of local collaboration and organization as well as critical governmental support. Interestingly, however, many, such as Noe Lopéz of San Marcos, do not credit the government in any way for the cooperatives and the benefits they rendered the community. Moreover, when speaking of the cooperatives, residents frequently celebrate the idea that the community—and not the government—was the purveyor of change. Lopéz described the years after 1948 as the moment when "progress arrived, that is to say, when the cooperatives were formed."[93] This sentiment is echoed by Elías Montero, who explained that "the people of Los Santos have worked hard to bring progress here through the cooperatives and the government has done little to aid" this cause.[94] Similarly, Misael Monge Álvarado, who served as the director of the region's electrical cooperative, claimed the government, in the form of Figueres, actually stole from Tarrazú and in this way tried to restrict Tarrazú's "development into a modern community."[95]

Although Monge was only eleven years old in 1948, he recalled that, days before the Civil War broke out, the municipality of Tarrazú received a long-awaited shipment of pipes that would provide San Marcos with plumbing. Monge alleged, however, that the pipes were never installed because "Don Pepe took the pipes with him when he left San Marcos [after the Civil War] and gave them to another town." Many were justifiably infuriated by this action, and in 1952, when Figueres visited San Marcos during his run for the presidency, he was met by a crowd of "angry men who screamed, 'Pipes! Pipes! Pipes!'" This candidate's decision to return to Tarrazú seeking votes, but without the town's pipes (and not even prepared to promise that he would replace those he had taken), understandably angered many. In fact, Monge suggested that Figueres's actions marked a turning point in the community, which in that moment "recognized that the government would not help us, and so, if we wanted something, we would have to do it ourselves." Additionally, although the angry crowd's shouts of protest forced Figueres to leave without making his speech, "it took us another ten years to get the plumbing we should have had in 1948, which is why even the liberacionistas here do not trust the government to help."[96]

According to Monge, Juan Chanto, and many others, this disappointment with the government would soon lead Tarrazúceños to look to one another and "cooperatively bring progress" to the region. Although both the electrical and the coffee cooperatives were created with a combination of local community support and governmental loans, most portrayed the cooperative's establishment as a local act in the face of what Tarrazúceños perceived as San José's disinterest in their region.[97]

Crucial to the cooperative ventures that transformed the region and to local pride in these institutions was the challenge of implementing a successful strategy for local men to pool their resources and ideas to realize positive change. According to both Misael Monge and Juan Chanto, the strategy came in 1954 with the arrival of Father Rodrigo Jiménez, who Chanto claimed "instilled [the idea] that . . . [farmers] join in a cooperative . . . from his pulpit."[98] Under Jiménez's guidance, a committee was formed that included ten coffee farmers, Father Jiménez, and the town's physician, Gumercindo Velásquez.[99]

The twelve-man committee decided that to create a coffee cooperative they required members, money, and a beneficio. With these three goals in mind, the committee began discussing the merits of a coffee cooperative in open community meetings with skeptical farmers, as well as collecting funds from the farmers, who would be associates of the cooperative.[100] In 1956, the committee began meeting with the Banco Nacional's recently formed Cooperative Department to see about establishing a coffee cooperative.[101] For four years, this committee negotiated terms with the Banco Nacional to purchase the bank's coffee beneficios in San Marcos and Santa María.[102] In 1960, the committee and the bank settled on a price for the two beneficios, and a vote was held on October 13, 1960, in San Marcos's schoolhouse. In the same building where twelve years earlier political prisoners were detained, Coopetarrazú was formed with 228 associates.[103] Just a few days later, a similar vote was held in Santa María, and local farmers in this community created their own coffee cooperative, Coopedota.[104]

Although Tarrazúceños recalled the coffee cooperatives establishment as a local project that functioned without governmental support, San José played a key role in encouraging the formation of agricultural cooperatives. Calderón first encouraged cooperatives, and Figueres and subsequent presidents retained the favorable tax policies that his administration established for these organizations. The success of these tax policies in encouraging cooperatives is evident in the fact that, by the late 1970s, an incredible one-third of all the nation's agricultural producers belonged to a cooperative.[105] Moreover, the Banco Nacional and its cooperative department, which provided Tarrazúceños with the loans and the sale of the beneficios, were both state entities. The cooperatives also depended heavily on the Instituto de Café (ICAFE) to publicize and help secure a market for their coffee internationally.[106] The benefits provided to cooperative members created political capital that politicians were quick to exploit. In the 1960s and 1970s, for instance, Figueres's Liberación Nacional Party would build political support networks around and within the nation's cooperatives. Ultimately, however, it was farmers at the local level who formed and governed the various cooperatives.

The local element of the coffee cooperatives excited many in the community, who quickly realized that the cooperatives had the potential to revolutionize the region's economic relations, as profits benefited "the community" of coffee producers rather than a single individual (fig. 5.4). The concept of community moved men such as Marcos Tulio Blanco Valverde, who worked for thirty years at Coopetarrazú after having labored several years at the Umaña beneficio.[107] Blanco was a wage laborer for Tobías Umaña Jiménez's son, "Tobís" Umaña Parra, and he claimed he knew little about "the benefits of a cooperative" when he took his job at Coopetarrazú. Blanco asserts that he changed employers initially because they offered to pay him five colones more each month. Moreover, where he had been "a regular peon" at the Umaña beneficio, he was hired as the manager's assistant by the cooperative.[108] Although self-interest initially encouraged Blanco to abandon his post with the Umañas, he explained that after working at the cooperative for a few months, he began to see "that the cooperative was a beautiful concept. . . . It is the community helping itself, and in that moment [the cooperative's opening in 1960], the region changed." Blanco noted that José Zúñiga Calvo, who headed the cooperative, was "so dedicated to the ideals of the cooperative" that on more than one occasion he "used his own money to pay the workers, such as myself. The cooperative worked because he and others sacrificed for it."[109]

Local faith and commitment to the cooperatives would be seen also in Tarrazú's quest for electrical power. Whereas the coffee cooperatives transformed the economic position of the region's coffee farmers, electricity would dramatically improve and change the lives of all Tarrazúceños. A

Figure 5.4. Meeting of coffee farmers in San Marcos, 1950s. The farmers are seated on the outside steps of this town's church discussing the benefits of creating a coffee cooperative. Most men seated are barefoot, reflecting the region's poverty. Father Rodrigo Jiménez is the third man from the left in the front row, wearing shoes. (Courtesy of Juan Mora)

key player in bringing the region electric power was Misael Monge, who worked as an accountant for Coopetarrazú for "five rewarding years," while simultaneously sacrificing his weekends and workday evenings "to sell the community on the need to form a cooperative to bring electric power" as a volunteer for the nascent Coopesantos. Monge's dedication to the cooperative model and the drive to bring Tarrazú electricity earned him the prized position as Coopesantos's first director, a post he held when electric power was inaugurated in San Marcos in 1968.[110]

For Monge, Coopesantos, like the region's coffee cooperatives, "work for the progress of the community" and not "individuals," which is evidenced by the fact that "today all of the region's homes have electricity. No one was left out. Everyone in the region belongs to Coopesanto, everyone." Monge, like many Tarrazúceños, believed cooperatives not only demonstrated the local community's strength but the uselessness of involvement in partisan politics. Monge claimed that the cooperatives were "not political" in the sense that they are not tied to any political party. The nonpolitical nature of the cooperatives was "critical to their success," since "people distrusted political projects, . . . and politicians never brought us anything but [empty] promises."[111]

Conclusion

Regardless of political stripes, Tarrazúceños recognized that the assistance their region provided Figueres was critical to his successful 1948 uprising. In the first months after the Civil War, Tarrazúceño rebels such as Marcos Chanto believed that the contribution their region had made to Figueres's successful insurgency had earned them a special place within the national narrative and with Figueres in particular. Chanto's May 1948 *El Diario de Costa Rica* article, with which the chapter opened, proclaimed that the critical role Tarrazúceños had played in that year's successful revolt merited national recognition. Aside from seeking a place for Tarrazú in the national narrative, this article sought to lay the groundwork for Tarrazúceños to make demands on the Costa Rican state on the basis of their service and sacrifice to the nation. Yet, in spite of the assistance Tarrazúceños provided Figueres in 1948, the nation made no real effort to repay the region's contribution to the founding of the Second Republic and did not create a special place for the region within the official national narrative. Moreover, the government made no infrastructure development in the region that it promoted as a means of appreciating Tarrazú's role in the Civil War.

The region, however, was not fully forgotten, as many recalled. Rather, the post-1948 state put into place legislation and policies that allowed Tarrazú and other rural communities to work together as a community with the state to create cooperatives to increase profits at the local level for farmers and also provide rural residents with greater services, in this case, electrical power. Although the national government provided critical support allowing for the establishment of coffee cooperatives, the opening of a local high school, and the creation of a communal electrical power source, local residents have largely forgotten, or chosen to overlook, the labors of state agencies and agents in these processes. Indeed, in their recollections of the past, Tarrazúceños tended to emphasize the local character of post-1948 projects that benefited their community, which engendered not only pride in local community unity and capacity to effect change but resentment with San José. Moreover, many forged and maintained a local narrative that bitterly described the nation as having "forgotten" the role that their community played in the formation of the Second Republic. This narrative refueled deep-seated resentments of the state that reach back to the violent tactics historically employed in the region by Resguardo guards against illegal liquor production and consumption. As the face of the federal government, Resguardo guards helped seed a historical distrust of government. While rebels sought to reformulate regional-state relations after the Civil War, San José's disinterest in commemorating Tarrazúceños' sacrifice served to stoke local suspicions of the federal government. Nonetheless, this post–Civil War reality created the ideal conditions for successful collective and cooperative actions.

In the late 1950s, as Tarrazúceños began to construct a narrative that suggested that the state had not and would not reward their community for the political and material assistance they provided in 1948, residents banded together to create cooperatives to bring about change. By the close of the 1960s, the region's cooperatives proved to be not only successful agents of change but powerful motors for communal empowerment. Although the government played a key role in bolstering conditions that permitted cooperatives to be formed, for many the cooperatives served to emphasize state disinterest in facilitating change and, in turn, the strength and unity of their community. Thus, ironically, in the 1950s and 1960s, as Tarrazúceños secured access for the first time to services that had for decades been exclusively available to Central Valley residents with the opening of the region's first high school, the arrival of electric power, running water, and the creation of a coffee cooperative, locals were also becoming more and more disinterested in national politics and courting the favor of San José officials.[112]

Certainly, since 1948, local resentment toward the government has arguably increased rather than decreased as Tarrazúceños lost faith in federal officials as agents willing and capable of realizing successful projects for their community. Thus, by the time Costa Rican civics textbook authors began to rewrite the nation's history in such a way that it downplayed not only the violence of the Civil War but also the region's contribution to these events, Tarrazúceños had already given up hope in the government repaying their sacrifice with infrastructural projects, national renown, or any other appreciative gesture.

While the cooperatives have unquestionably improved the lives of many Tarrazúceños, not everyone has benefited. In fact, the postwar period did not result in greater economic opportunities or wages for landless peons. Take, for example, Francisco Madrigal of San Lorenzo, whose father was a landless peon. Madrigal noted that "after the coffee cooperatives opened, many men were able to make a better and more reliable living, but for those of us without land, the cooperatives changed nothing." Madrigal and his family were in a real sense "left behind" by the post-1948 progress many experienced, as they remained dependent on the wages their landholding neighbors paid them. Yet this family, and many like them, did not sit idly by; instead, Madrigal and two of his brothers made a dramatic decision. They took out a loan from a local money lender for six thousand dollars, "more than we could ever hope to save up in Costa Rica," and traveled without documents across the US-Mexican border in the 1970s with the help of a "coyote." In the United States, the brothers eventually started a construction company, and with the money they made remodeling homes they repaid their debt and purchased homes and even farms in Tarrazú. From the United States, they helped their family transcend the steep divide separating landless peons and landholders. The Madrigals' experience is far from unique; these brothers are part of a larger process of emigration that links Tarrazú to the United States economically, culturally, and socially beginning in the late 1960s. That process is the subject of the next two chapters.[113]

6

Migration and Shifting Class, Racial, and National Identities

In 1969, Martín Cárdenas, the son of landless laborers from the outskirts of San Marcos de Tarrazú, boarded an airplane in San José bound for New York City. Shortly after securing employment in a small diner in Union City, New Jersey, Cárdenas began sending money back home, exciting many Tarrazúceños about economic opportunities in the United States. Cárdenas's flight would forever transform his life and the development of the entire Tarrazú Valley. In the years that followed, Cárdenas became a local living legend for his generosity to other migrants in the United States, providing new arrivals with a couch to stay on, a winter coat, help in finding employment, and anything else he could.[1]

By all accounts, Cárdenas's decision to emigrate secured economic prosperity for him, his family, and many more Tarrazúceños. In fact, when Cárdenas died in 1997, he had established himself in New Jersey, where he owned his own home, but additionally, he had helped his parents and the three (of his twelve) siblings who had not come to New Jersey become economically independent landowners in Tarrazú. As the son of landless laborers without a high school degree and with few skills, it is difficult to imagine how Cárdenas might have secured anywhere near that level of economic prosperity and stability had he remained in Costa Rica. Although Cárdenas's story and those of countless Tarrazúceños who have since traveled to the United States suggest that emigration is an excellent means of escaping the poverty of landlessness in the region, many Tarrazúceños have their reservations about the large-scale out-migration that began in the late 1960s. Many note dramatic changes in US migration policies in recent decades, and so securing a tourist, let alone a work, visa to the United States is not as simple today as it was in 1969. As is the case for their Central American and Mexican counterparts, for most Costa Ricans today, this decision requires them to cross the US-Mexican border without documentation and face all the related dangers associated with that journey.

Since the late 1960s, when Tarrazúceños began emigrating, hundreds have been arrested and deported on both sides of the US-Mexican border.[2] Almost everyone in the region has heard the frightening stories of emigrants such as Orlando Navarro, who was robbed along with the seven other Tarrazúceños after the group was "badly beaten" by Mexican police officers in Tijuana.[3] Additionally, many have heard tales, repeated only in hushed tones, from sisters and neighbors who were raped during their journey by coyotes, crooked police officers, and members of the border patrol.[4] The stories Tarrazúceños relate about emigration suggest that most people in the region recognize that crossing the Mexican border without legal documentation is a risky venture. Nonetheless, many continue to take this gamble. They do so owing to decreasing prices for coffee at the global level and the generally positive experiences of family and friends who have gone before them. Many, like Cárdenas, have succeeded in accomplishing their family's financial goals through emigration. Their success has motivated others to take the same risks.

When Costa Ricans leave their nation of birth in search of economic opportunity, their actions might be read as an indictment of the failures of the Costa Rican government to create an economy capable of providing for its citizens' needs. Ironically, however, migration has strengthened Tarrazúceños' connection to the nation-state by altering local socioeconomic realities in such a way that it has increased the number of families who can identify with the nation's archetype: the yeoman coffee farmer. Migration has decreased the number of landless peasants and expanded the ranks of yeoman coffee farmers. While earnings made abroad have benefited many, they also altered local class relations; increased wealth in the hands of once-poor individuals who emigrated; and recalibrated socioeconomic hierarchies, threatening the position of the region's traditional elites. These shifts are a source of social anxiety, particularly among traditional elites. Another unexpected repercussion of this mass out-migration of the region's workforce is the annual influx of thousands of indigenous Panamanian coffee pickers. The arrival of foreign indigenous workers for the annual harvest at once highlights local insecurities about migration while also affirming Tarrazúceños' racialized image of themselves as a "white" (i.e., nonindigenous but European) community. Given Costa Rica's whiteness myth, the presence of foreign indigenous laborers bolsters the region's claims to whiteness and allows locals to reaffirm their membership in the nation-state.

Emigration as a Threat to the Traditional Socioeconomic Order

The origins of the migratory circuit linking Tarrazú to New Jersey date back to the 1960s, almost immediately after the formation of the region's coffee cooperatives.[5] As seen in chapter 5, the cooperatives provided regional landowners with a better price for their crop and increased access to low-interest credit options; they did nothing, however, to improve the wages or job security of Tarrazú's landless agricultural workers. Moreover, the cooperatives served to widen the socioeconomic divide between landless, rural workers and their smallholding neighbors.[6] In these changing circumstances, ambitious children of landless agricultural laborers, such as Martín Cárdenas and eight of his siblings, left for the United States believing that, as Martin's sister Beatriz put it, "the only way to do something in order to not live so badly, so poorly . . . [is] to leave."[7] Like the Cárdenas siblings, starting in the 1960s and continuing to this day, many of Tarrazú's young adults choose to leave their homes in search of employment opportunities.[8]

The migratory flow out of Tarrazú increased noticeably in the 1980s when global coffee prices began dropping precipitously.[9] Without the avenue of emigration, living standards for many smallholders might have followed suit. In 1977, the average coffee producer in Costa Rica earned $1.39 per kilo of Arabica coffee produced; in 1983, this had gone down to 56¢ per kilo; and in 2006, farmers brought in an average of just 42.91¢ per kilo.[10] During this same period, land, fertilizers, insecticides, and fungicides all experienced repeated price increases.[11] Declines in global coffee prices meant that, since the 1980s, a single poor coffee harvest can easily plunge a farmer into a level of debt that he is incapable of repaying. Given the economic success of countless emigrants, in these tough economic conditions, emigration has become a popular option for men who do not wish to lose their farm to debt and who also seek to meet their "manly obligations" to provide for their families.[12]

Local critics of emigrants suggest that emigration is a choice, which implies that emigrants are greedy, placing their economic concerns over the well-being of their family. These critiques reflect deep-seated anxieties over the way that emigration is transforming local socioeconomic hierarchies, but still, the critics are arguably right: many men who emigrated to save their farms could have chosen to simply accept the loss of them. However, this would be a very difficult "choice" for most smallholders to make, especially when they know that if they emigrate they could likely save their farm and also potentially expand it to improve their children's socioeconomic position.[13] Given Tarrazú's deeply patriarchal society, emigration is arguably often not seen as an option but rather as an obligation for men who feel compelled to provide for their families in a decreasingly profitable coffee market.[14]

In addition to coffee farmers who fear losing their farms, thousands of landless agricultural workers, such as Pedro Sánchez, have followed the example of the Cárdenas family and traveled to the United States in the hope of either becoming landholders or escaping agriculture altogether. But after living abroad for nineteen years, Sánchez was torn by these two possibilities. He did not believe his "children will return to Costa Rica. And so, I think I will have to stay here, though I would love to return, buy my own coffee farm, and grow coffee. It would be great to have a more peaceful life in San Pablo caring for my coffee plants."[15] Despite Sánchez's belief that he will not return to Costa Rica, his desire to live a "more peaceful life" as a cafetalero suggests an idyllic view of coffee growing that does not reflect the stresses that unstable market prices place on farmers trying to support their families on coffee sales alone. Perhaps Sánchez's idealistic portrait of coffee reflects the fact that he was never a farm owner but an agricultural laborer, and thus he perceived that Tarrazú landowners lived a more carefree life than he.[16]

Then again, perhaps Sánchez's romantic idea of coffee farming reflects the impact that emigration has had on Tarrazú's coffee industry and class relations. Dozens of once-landless agricultural laborers such as Orlando Navarro, who spent "eight years or so" washing dishes and cutting lawns in New Jersey, have returned to Tarrazú as landowners. Navarro used his earnings abroad to purchase a small coffee farm and several head of cattle. Additionally, Navarro was able to set his younger brother up with his own small coffee farm. Moreover, when Navarro married (after returning from New Jersey), he built himself a three-bedroom home using some of his savings from his time abroad. Even after such economic accomplishments, Navarro still has "something small saved up for bad years."[17] His story is exceptional: in under a decade, he not only escaped the life of a wage laborer but also helped his brother do the same. While Navarro accomplished his goals in a relatively short time, he is one of many once-landless laborers who eventually joined the region's landholding class through earnings made abroad.

Navarro's and other emigrants' successful entrance into the landholding class, coupled with their ability to retain that position with savings made in the United States, suggests three critically important phenomena related to emigration: (1) Emigration is generally not seen as an opportunity to "escape" Tarrazú but rather as a means for men and their families to remain and/or return. In other words, Tarrazúceños emigrate with the hope that their time abroad will allow them to improve their family's socioeconomic position and financial stability *within* the community. (2) The instabilities of the international coffee economy have required many smallholders to seek alternative economic sources in years of decline. Emigration is the route of choice for the region's farmers and landless workers seeking to either supplement family earnings or substitute entirely for meager local incomes. (3) Emigrants' ability to save considerable sums of money (by Costa Rican standards) in a short period of time has upset traditional socioeconomic hierarchies. In fact, many of the once most economically precarious families, who were reliant on wage labor, are today not only landowners but often have more liquid capital than their former employers.[18]

The economic realities of the coffee market and emigration have created some paradoxical relationships. Take, for instance, the relationship between the Madrigal and Villegas families of San Lorenzo. The Madrigals lived on the Villegas family's coffee farm for "over ten years" and the Madrigal family patriarch, Manuel Madrigal, had a year-round position as a peon charged with caring for the Villegas's coffee plants.[19] In the late 1970s, however, three of his sons took out a loan from a wealthy neighbor and made their way to Paterson, New Jersey. The Madrigal brothers proved extremely successful immigrants. After just fifteen years, they not only legalized their status but also owned a lucrative construction company with over sixty employees.[20] In the mid-1990s, Madrigal's two oldest sons returned to San Lorenzo. During their time home they spoke with Luís Hernán Villegas, their former boss's son, and convinced him to sell them a portion of the Villegas family's farm.[21] With this purchase the Villegas and Madrigal families became neighbors once again, but with a critical difference: both families were now landowners.[22] What makes this story particularly distinctive, among many others like it, is that the Madrigal brothers purchased land from their former employer. Additionally, a few years after the Madrigals became coffee farmers, Luis Hernán, who was then struggling to keep his farm profitable, asked the Madrigals if they would give him a job were he to make it to New Jersey.[23] Today, Villegas works as a painter for the Madrigal brothers in New Jersey six months out of the year and spends the rest of the year in San Lorenzo caring for his coffee.[24]

While the Villegas family appears to have embraced the economic success of their former employees, this is an unusual response. In fact, most landholders resent what they describe as the idleness of their former agricultural workers and their children. Take, for instance, San Pablo's largest landholder, Manuel Castro, whose great-grandfather founded the region's third-largest town of San Pablo in the mid-nineteenth century.[25] He summed up the region's labor problem in two words: "laziness and greed." He explained that "all the men have gone to New Jersey, and the youths do not want to work [on the] coffee [farms]. The coffee would rot on the bushes if we had to rely on the townspeople to pick it." Castro argued that the primary issues involved young Tarrazúceños who are unwilling to accept low wages because their "expectations have changed. Before people just wanted a job, a home, and food. Now everyone . . . thinks they deserve a cellular phone and a car. You cannot buy that picking coffee, so they would rather just not work."[26] Others, besides the old guard of coffee farmers, resent how returned emigrants and their children do not want to work as agricultural laborers. Martín Madrigal, who purchased his farm with earnings he made abroad, for instance, complained that "when I was young, I picked coffee. . . . I worked hard for my wages. Today, no one wants to work. Everyone just wants to go to New Jersey. . . . All my coffee pickers . . . are foreigners."[27]

Even emigrants' family members portrayed their loved ones as motivated by greed and not necessity. For instance, Elías Velásquez, whose son Rolando emigrated in 2000, maintained that "envy and money . . . is why they go." When I asked Velásquez whether his son was any different, he smiled and said that "he has been there five years now, and he makes good money."[28] For Velásquez's father, money was the only cause and measure of his son's success in New Jersey. In addition to the repeated tropes of laziness and greed, many Tarrazúceños had no shortage of opinions and stories that described emigrants' actions as illogical and even fatalistic in nature. Herminía Muñoz, whose husband was a landless peon, insisted that there are plenty of economic opportunities in Tarrazú. To make her point, Muñoz explained how her two sons "with hard work and no vices . . . have made a decent living and have even built me a home . . . without going to the United States." Ironically, Muñoz's sons are construction workers who have made a living by building homes for émigrés and their families. All the same, they have not emigrated, which is what mattered to Muñoz. At the heart of Muñoz's critiques was her belief that emigrants' avarice encourages them to place their own lives on the line. Making clear reference to the physical dangers emigrants face crossing the US-Mexican border, she stated that no economic opportunity is worth the risk of returning home "in a box to be buried."[29]

Costa Ricans in northern New Jersey are aware of the negative opinion that their families and former neighbors have of them, but many are quick to explain that they did not view emigration as a choice, given their families' economic realities. Almost without fail, Tarrazúceños in New Jersey seemed noticeably upset by the suggestion that anything short of economic necessity motivated them to leave their loved ones and nation behind. New Jerseyans repeatedly explained that emigration was necessary if they wished to retain their coffee farms. Whereas many in Tarrazú would suggest that émigrés are not "traditional," the migrants themselves would argue precisely the opposite. Almost without exception, migrants related that they arrived in

New Jersey with concrete goals that involved the preservation of their family's (and the region's) traditional economic activity: coffee. Work trucks, farmland, rainy-day funds, and the construction of a home in the town of their birth were the most common reasons émigrés gave for emigrating.[30]

Ethnicity, Race, and Migration

The exodus of thousands of Tarrazúceños to the United States has created a local labor shortage, particularly during the annual coffee harvest. Beginning in 1987, thousands of indigenous Ngöbe-Buglé (sometimes also called Guaymí) laborers, whose reservation straddles the Costa Rican and Panamanian border, began making an annual migration to Tarrazú to pick coffee.[31]

Although Ngöbe-Buglé families' presence during the annual coffee harvest is a relatively recent phenomenon, this indigenous group is not new to the cash-based economy. Ngöbe-Buglé men first began finding seasonal wage labor in the late nineteenth century on ranches and coffee farms owned by nonindigenous Panamanians. Then, beginning in the 1930s, when the United Fruit Company began growing bananas near Ngöbe-Buglé territory, thousands sought better-paid wage work on banana plantations on both sides of the Costa Rican–Panamanian border.[32] Ngöbe-Buglé families began spending increased time laboring for wages off the reservation, possibly becoming more reliant on the cash economy because of natural population increase and a corresponding reduction in the amount of arable land available to individual families. By the early 1980s, indigenous families began picking coffee on the Costa Rican side of the border, primarily in the community of Coto Brus, between the months of August and November.[33] Shortly after they started harvesting coffee in Costa Rica, they enlarged their picking zone to include Tarrazú, a two-hundred-kilometer bus ride to the north of Coto Brus. Tarrazú has a later coffee harvest than Coto Brus, thanks to a dramatic change in elevation between the two communities.[34] Tarrazú's November through February harvest provides Ngöbe-Buglé families with the opportunity to double their time and, in turn, their earnings as coffee pickers in Costa Rica (fig. 6.1).

As Ngöbe-Buglé families have spent increased time living and working among nonindigenous Panamanians and Costa Ricans, many have *ladinoized*, or assimilated into nonindigenous society. Nonetheless, most have become only marginally integrated into the wage economy and continue to spend at least several months a year engaged in subsistence farming on their familial lands on the Ngöbe-Buglé reservation.[35] Moreover, the process of ladinoization has important and clearly visible gendered overtones, with women taking on the role of cultural "guardians." So, although most Ngöbe-

Figure 6.1. Ten-year-old Ngöbe-Buglé boy picking coffee on a San Marcos farm, 2008. This captures another paradox in Tarrazú's modernity: the continued use of child labor. (Carmen Kordick)

Buglé men have abandoned their traditional brightly colored cotton pants and shirts, almost all Ngöbe-Buglé women and girls continue to wear their traditional colorful cotton dresses replete with ornately embroidered collars and sleeves. Similarly, most men are bilingual, speaking both Ngöbere and Spanish (though for most the native Ngöbere language remains their dominant tongue); however, very few women speak any Spanish.[36]

The process of modernization, reflected by the impact of collapsing coffee prices within a globalizing economy and the ability of Tarrazúceños to emigrate for work for nonunion jobs in the United States, has had an important and positive local gendered effect. In fact, modernization has empowered numerous Tarrazú women, who already exercised a degree of power vis-à-vis the Costa Rican nation-state as enfranchised Hispanic citizens. Using earnings they or their spouses have made abroad, women have established small local businesses that have given them a level of economic independence.[37] At the same time, however, this modernization has dramatically disempowered Ngöbe-Buglé women by making them more dependent on their spouses, brothers, and male children who speak Spanish and are therefore able to navigate multiple economic and political systems. Consequentially, Ngöbe-Buglé women have become both the "guardians" of their indigenous culture and, unwittingly, secondary players within the global economy (fig. 6.2).

Figure 6.2. Ngöbe Buglé women and their children standing in the doorway of the small wooden shelter where they were residing for the coffee-picking season, 2008. (Carmen Kordick)

The Ngöbe-Buglé's culture and physical appearance, coupled with the fact that many members of this ethnic group are Panamanian citizens, is another cause of local unease. In recent years, the arrival of some nine thousand Ngöbe-Buglé men, women, and children to Tarrazú during the annual harvest evoked considerable social anxiety about the local consequences of emigration.[38] For many, such as Elías Velásquez of Santa María, the region is racially transformed each summer when these workers arrive to pick the coffee on local farms. Velásquez explained that in July Santa María is "a peaceful place," but in January, at the height of the coffee harvest, his community is unrecognizable. He observed that on Sundays during the picking season the central plaza becomes "so dark it is almost black—because of the hundreds of Indians" that gather there on weekend afternoons.[39] Velásquez's use of the term "black" clearly suggests his unease with these outsiders, whom he viewed as "nonwhite" racial inferiors. Echoing Velásquez's discomfort with the influx of thousands of Ngöbe-Buglé laborers each year, the owner of a small business in San Marcos de Tarrazú, José Ramírez, observed, "It is shocking to see the region invaded. . . . I look out the window and if fifty people pass by I may not recognize even one of them—they are all Guaymí."[40]

Figure 6.3. Ngöbe-Buglé couple cooking plantains on a fire they made on a large wooden table in their Tarrazú dwelling, 2008. (The woman's face was deformed in a stroke she suffered during childbirth.) This cooking area was shared with three other families. Note the earthen floor covered with ultrathin self-adhesive vinyl flooring and the floor's incline. (Carmen Kordick)

Tarrazúceños' concerns over the Ngöbe-Buglé as nonwhite foreigners are often expressed in terms of fear that these workers carry disease, owing to poor hygiene habits. In general, local residents did not blame the workers' dirtiness on poor living conditions and inadequate access to a clean water supply (fig. 6.3) but, rather, the personal or cultural failings of the workers themselves. For instance, the widow Lourdes Beatriz Ugalde Madriz, who employed three Ngöbe-Buglé families on her San Marcos farm for the 2007–8 coffee harvest, claimed that "the *Inditos* [infantilizing diminutive of Indian] are dirty, and that is a problem when they come to the farm." Evidence of their dirtiness, in Ugalde's mind, was the fact that the two-year-old daughter of one of the couples laboring on her farm had to be treated for scabies.[41] Ugalde explained to me that the little girl's parents did "not bathe her or wash her clothes," which is why she was infected with scabies.[42] However, the wooden structure Ugalde provided her workers did not have a shower, let alone a washing machine, which meant that their clothing had to be washed by hand and the children needed to be bathed in the river or with buckets in the single sink provided to all the laborers. Given that the couple had six children, and both husband and wife (alongside their three oldest children who were aged eight, seven, and five) worked picking coffee from sunrise to sunset, this was not an easy task, and it likely made daily bathing and the washing of all the children's clothing unfeasible.[43]

Figure 6.4. Young, unmarried Ngöbe-Buglé worker posing near a cooking fire that has been made on a large wooden table in the dwelling that he shares with two couples and their children, 2008. (Carmen Kordick)

Ugalde's perception that when the Ngöbe-Buglé are in the region there is more sickness is backed up by the tragic deaths of three Ngöbe-Buglé infants in San Lorenzo in 1998. The three perished due to a contagious pulmonary infection that also left dozens of Ngöbe-Buglé children ill.[44] Yet, these deaths are the direct consequence of the living conditions that Tarrazú coffee farmers provide for laborers. Like Ugalde, many local farm owners do not provide pickers with indoor plumbing, let alone a shower and toilet. Moreover, it is not uncommon for several families to be housed together, thereby increasing the spread of disease. For instance, on Ugalde's farm in 2007, two couples and their thirteen children as well as an unmarried young man and his nephew all cooked and slept in a two-room wooden structure (fig. 6.4).[45]

While these more "typical" conditions leave much to be desired, many Ngöbe-Buglé families suffer in even more primitive shelter during their time in Tarrazú, as coffee worker Mirna Rodríguez Palacios explained. A Ngöbe-Buglé woman who arrived with her husband to the town of San Pablo in the mid-1990s, Rodríguez decided to remain in Tarrazú after her husband was offered year-round employment on a farm. Her permanence in Tarrazú, coupled with her excellent Spanish, enabled her to become an unofficial advocate for her community. She is proud of the fact that she served as a translator on numerous occasions when Ngöbe-Buglé migrant workers were denied medical care at the community clinic or experienced inhumane living conditions on farms. In 2007, she was called to a farm located on the outskirts of the small hamlet of San Martín to help a family that was terribly distressed by the housing provided them. With horror, she encountered a situation in which the farm's owner placed the family in a barn that was strewn with cow dung and still housed several cows.[46]

The deplorable living conditions that Tarrazú's coffee farmers regularly provide Ngöbe-Buglé workers and their families reveal much about the way Tarrazúceños understand themselves and their position in the nation. Indeed, the entrance of non–Costa Rican workers in such large numbers, over the past three decades, has effectively "racialized" coffee picking into a demeaning form of labor.[47] Moreover, the fact that a majority of the region's seasonal (and full-time) agricultural laborers are Ngöbe-Buglé today has dramatically shifted local power relations.[48] Up until the early 1980s, most of the region's landless laborers were Tarrazúceños and class was the primary measure of power.[49] Today, the equation of poverty and landlessness with indigeneity and foreignness has deepened the relationship locals perceive between "whiteness" and the Costa Rican nation. Race and class status are arguably more intertwined than ever before.

As poverty and perceived cultural "backwardness" in the region increasingly become associated with foreignness and indigeneity, deep-seated ideas about civilization, whiteness, and Costa Rican national identity found renewed meaning in the minds of many Tarrazúceños. In fact, many prefer to adopt a "blame the victim" approach to justifying poor housing and living conditions for Ngöbe-Buglé workers rather than to suggest any change. According to Andrea Cordero of San Pablo, for instance, the Ngöbe-Buglé would only ruin or misuse material resources if they had access to them. She related that "the Indians are not accustomed to [having] a mattress, and if you buy them . . . [one], they will throw it in the dirt or put their babies—who do not even wear diapers—on it, and that is the end of the mattress. It is the same thing with the bathrooms. . . . They are from the mountains, they are not accustomed to . . . latrines, let alone toilets. It . . . makes no sense to give them things that they do not know how to use and do not even want."[50] In short, there is nothing to be done.

Additionally, labeling the Ngöbe-Buglé as "uncivilized" provides local employers with the opportunity to validate their own "civilized" state and generously teach their employees about the benefits of hygiene. Thus, several Tarrazúceños, such as Tobías Umaña (Tobías Umaña Jiménez's great-grandson), are proud of the way they educate Ngöbe-Buglé laborers on their farms about the benefits of "more civilized" behaviors. Umaña declared that "many Guaymís in their time here [in Tarrazú] have been reformed by what they see their employers do. . . . We [coffee farm owners] have educated them culturally during their time with us."[51] While Tarrazúceños are confident that Ngöbe-Buglés benefit culturally during their time in the region, they are equally confident of the fact that the Ngöbe-Buglé are not influencing local culture. According to José Antonio Astuas, "the Indians have not impacted our culture because they are here for a short time [each year]. And while they are not very hygienic, when they are here, they see the doctor, and we try to educate them about [the importance of] bathing."[52] In other words, although the time the Ngöbe-Buglé spend working in Tarrazú is supposedly insufficient to impact local culture, it is believed sufficient to better the Ngöbe-Buglé's culture.

At the root of Tarrazúceños' portrayals of the Ngöbe-Buglé as dirty, unclean, and in need of basic hygiene education are deeply entrenched ideas of Costa Rica as an educated, civilized, and white (i.e., nonindigenous but European) nation. Today, most historians, physical anthropologists, and geneticists assert that the vast majority of Costa Ricans are mestizos (some combination of European, Indian, and/or African ancestry).[53]

As introduced earlier, despite this historical and genetic reality, Costa Ricans have embraced a historical narrative that rejects the idea that they are mestizos in favor of a national origin story that asserts that Costa Ricans are white.[54] A critical player in disseminating Costa Rica's whiteness myth has been the nation's public education system. Costa Rica's founding myth has been encapsulated in the nation's social studies textbooks since the mid-twentieth century. A prime example of a nationalistic textbook that embraces the official narrative is a third-grade geography textbook from 1958 that narrates how Costa Rica's allegedly idyllic precoffee past forged a peaceful, white, democratic, and egalitarian national present:

> The white race clearly prevailed. . . . Costa Ricans descend almost entirely, from . . . Spaniards that settled in . . . the sixteenth century.
>
> Costa Rica, despite its name [which means Rich Coast in Spanish], did not offer great riches to those who came to inhabit it; so . . . [only] a small number of [Spanish] families . . . attracted by a delicious climate and fertile soil . . . isolated from the rest of the world, in the center of the country and without quick modes of communication . . . conserved purely their customs and blood.
>
> In this way in Costa Rica a sober, simple, moral, hardworking, robust and sane nation was formed[.] Never have citizens of a republic been more democratic[.] There are almost no distinctions of birth,

> fortune, or position [and instead] men are judged for their aptitudes and their conduct[.] Respect for the established order and [private] property have reached their highest level [as] the Costa Rican [citizen] obeys the law with submission . . . and is peaceful, generous, [and] an ardent patriot . . . proud of his liberty.[55]

This excerpt succinctly encapsulates the centrality of Costa Ricans' alleged ethnic purity to the nation's official narrative.[56]

Despite the fact that the majority of Costa Ricans are mestizos, the mythical whiteness narrative, widely propagated by the nation's schools, is widely accepted by the populace. Tarrazúceños repeatedly cited this myth to me with only slight variation. A number of them proudly related that they were both culturally and genetically very different from the Ngöbe-Buglé. Perhaps, however, the Tarrazúceño who most concisely explained the nation's historical whiteness myth within a local context was coffee farmer Rafael Naranjo Barrantes of La Sabana. According to Naranjo, in the nineteenth century when Tarrazú's first settlers arrived, "Indians passed through but never stayed. They did not mix with the Europeans since logically they already had . . . families just like us [the settlers from Desamparados]. You know, Costa Rica was unique in this, ours was the only [American] nation without Indians. You know half the population of Guatemala, Mexico, Nicaragua, and Panama is Indian, but here, there were only fifteen thousand Indians during the colonial period. Costa Rica was very poor, despite its name, and the little gold the Indians had was not of any value, so there were few people here."[57]

The idea that Tarrazúceños, and Costa Ricans more generally, have no indigenous origins is a constantly repeated trope. Tarrazúceños frequently point to phenotypic evidence of their whiteness. For instance, José Antonio Astuas explained that "as in many parts of Costa Rica, we have European blood. . . . Many people . . . [have] light [colored] eyes. We call them 'pretty eyes.'" Despite Astuas's description of his Europeanized beauty ideals, he insisted that in Tarrazú "there is no racism." Yet he just as quickly qualified this assertion by noting that "if a black person were to arrive, . . . everyone would notice because there are no black people here. . . . When the Indians [first started arriving], many people were shocked. We were unaccustomed to seeing Indians in our town."[58] Astuas's description of how nonwhite outsiders garner attention suggests how the Ngöbe-Buglé's arrival each summer serves to reconfirm local ideas about themselves as uniformly and primordially white.

Tarrazúceños might be unsettled by the Ngöbe-Buglé's annual influx; however, the presence of poor, nonwhite, and mostly non–Costa Rican labor-

Figure 6.5. Ngöbe-Buglé coffee picker with her child awaiting her husband who is having the coffee they picked that day measured, 2008. (Carmen Kordick)

ers also serves to confirm Tarrazúceños' claims to their whiteness, civilization, and in turn their rightful claims to Costa Rican nationality. This has all taken place in the context of local anxieties over changes in class structure. Paradoxically, Tarrazúceños are also reassured by the presence of the Ngöbe-Buglé. Their poverty and generally poor Spanish language skills make them a largely compliant labor force. This is in stark contrast to local landless men, who increasingly refuse to work in agriculture, preferring to emigrate—an act that landholders read as defiance of their traditional socioeconomic position. Thus, the Ngöbe-Buglé's acceptance of low wages and substandard housing allows the landholding class to assert its traditional socioeconomic position as Tarrazú's primary employers and most "Costa Rican" residents.

Moreover, the Ngöbe-Buglé's labor allows Tarrazú's farmers to continue to grow and to harvest their crops, despite the massive out-migration of local landless laborers and the reluctance of the region's youth to pick coffee (figs. 6.5, 6.6, and 6.7). This situation highlights the central role international migration plays in the region's contemporary coffee industry. In recent years, the twin processes of emigration and immigration have become critical to the survival of the region's coffee economy and, by extension, of regional rural culture and society. The steady decline in coffee prices makes it difficult for coffee farmers to make ends meet in years when there is a low cof-

Figure 6.6. Ngöbe-Buglé coffee pickers awaiting their turn to have the coffee they picked that day measured, 2008. (Carmen Kordick)

Figure 6.7. Ngöbe-Buglé men delivering the coffee that they, their wives, and children picked that day to be measured by the farm owner, so as to determine their pay, 2008. (Carmen Kordick)

fee yield or global prices decline. Emigration and wages earned abroad provide farmers with the capital necessary to weather poor years. Additionally, earnings made abroad allow farmers to diversify their agricultural production; increasingly farmers are growing avocados, passion fruits, apples, and grapes in the hope of improving their economic viability. The transition to other crops can be costly, however, and money earned in New Jersey certainly helps ease this transition.[59]

Conclusion

Tarrazúceños have been connected to the global economy at least since the late nineteenth century, when they began growing coffee for export. In the past fifty years, however, Tarrazú has become increasingly tied into the global economy through the process of international migration. Today, Tarrazú's economy depends on both the remittances of Tarrazúceños in New Jersey and on the labor of thousands of indigenous Panamanians. As Tarrazú is increasingly dependent on both emigration and immigration, the community is becoming a transnational migration hub, defined by the constant influx and outflow of people and money. Tarrazú's new global reality stirs up considerable concern and anxiety as Tarrazúceños struggle to understand what emigration and immigration mean for class relations and for their traditional agriculture-centered lives. While the flow of people and ideas disquiets many, the economic situation suggests that Tarrazú's future as an agricultural region will depend on the community's ability to diversify agricultural production and attract outside laborers—both of which require capital, which continues to be easiest to secure by working abroad.

The economic factors that have prompted thousands of Ngöbe-Buglé families to seek work in Tarrazú and just as many Tarrazúceños to immigrate to the United States cannot be minimized. Undoubtedly, if Ngöbe-Buglé workers could make as much money laboring on or nearer to their reservation, they would. Likewise, if Tarrazúceños had the opportunity to make wages in Tarrazú or elsewhere in Costa Rica that were comparable to those they earn in New Jersey, the flow of Tarrazúceños to New Jersey would ebb dramatically. These economic realities illustrate that Tarrazú's position as a transnational migration hub is the product of a series of global economic relationships, most notably steep price declines on the world market for agricultural export commodities, namely coffee, and the dramatic economic inequalities among nations on the American continent.

Although wage disparities within the hemisphere play a key role in pulling and pushing migrants away from their natal communities, economics alone does not determine where migrants will go in search of employment.

Interpersonal relationships that link individuals across political borders are critical to understanding why migrants settle in particular communities. In the case of Tarrazúceños, the settlement of a large portion of the Cárdenas family in New Jersey during the 1960s and 1970s laid the groundwork for a now well-established human network that ties Tarrazú to New Jersey. The importance of personal relationships in directing migrants' destination is evident in the fact that almost all of the Tarrazúceños in the United States reside not just in the state of New Jersey but specifically in and around the town of Paterson, New Jersey. While economic circumstances often motivate emigration, personal relationships usually determine where migrants choose to settle. The social, cultural, economic, and human linkages between Tarrazú and northern New Jersey are the subject of chapter 7.

7

National Belonging and Exclusion beyond Costa Rica's Borders

On a late July evening in 2000, Rolando Velásquez arrived home in Bergenfield, New Jersey, to find his roommate and cousin, Pablo Fernández, collapsed and bloodied on the living room floor. He had suffered a massive heart attack, shattering a mirror on his fall, and had cut his hands and face as he fell unconscious. Velásquez promptly dialed 911 and explained to the Spanish-speaking operator that an ambulance was needed. A few minutes later, an ambulance arrived and the paramedics scooped up Fernández's body, took him to a hospital, and managed to resuscitate him.

Coincidentally, that night ended with Velásquez also losing consciousness in his living room but under very different circumstances. Indeed, likely because Fernández's face was cut and there was considerable blood on the floor, a pair of police officers, who arrived along with the paramedics, decided to question Velásquez. The officers, however, did not speak Spanish, and Velásquez's English was limited to "a few words" including the single phrase he used that evening to respond to the police's questions, "I do not speak English."[1] Rather than call in a translator to help them interrogate him, Velásquez claimed that the police officers simply "asked their questions in a louder voice," which did not help clarify what they were asking for or make Velásquez more capable of responding. His silence appeared to have frustrated the officers to the point of violence. Velásquez alleged that an hour or so into their unproductive exchange, one of them "punch[ed]" him with such force he was knocked out of his chair. Once he was on the ground, the officers began "kicking" him in the face and torso until he lost consciousness.[2]

The linguistic gap that limited Velásquez's ability to understand and be understood by the police officers that night was blatantly obvious to him.

Yet, he suggested that perhaps the police officers did not appreciate it, believing that he pretended not to understand their questions, since "people always think I speak English." For Velásquez, the problem that day (and on other occasions in the United States) likely stemmed from the fact that with blue eyes and a balding head of sandy blond hair, he felt he could "pass for 'macho.'"[3] Costa Ricans use the term *macho* colloquially to describe individuals with "white" skin and/or blond hair, including European and North American foreigners with these features. Velásquez thought he was often not seen as a Hispanic immigrant, but rather as a "white," English-speaking "American." In Velásquez's estimation, "passing for 'macho'" as an undocumented immigrant, has made living in the United States easier for him than for many of his compatriots and other Latino immigrants who phenotypically fit Hispanic stereotypes. Velásquez joked that if immigration officials were to show up at his workplace, he would not run like the other undocumented kitchen staff, as the officers "would never even ask to see my papers. That makes it easier for me, you know?"[4]

Velásquez's encounter with the police demonstrates, however, how "whiteness" coupled with poor English skills can create misunderstandings with violent consequences. It also forces them to "keep quiet." Moreover, regardless of their physical appearance, which permits them to "hide" in plain sight, undocumented immigrants such as Velásquez fear deportation and therefore are unlikely to lodge formal complaints or seek legal redress when they are the victims of unsafe or exploitative work conditions or police brutality or suffer other abuses.[5] This was certainly Velásquez's response to the beating he received from the police in 2000, which left him with a bruised face and torso, and two "cracked . . . ribs."[6]

Following the incident, Velásquez considered securing legal counsel. His fear, however, that he might be fired from his job or deported ultimately persuaded him not to seek legal redress. Moreover, he never even considered contacting the Costa Rican consulate in New York City for legal or other aid. He seemed shocked by the notion that the consulate might have helped him, stating that "if the consul cannot renew my passport in two months, how could [he] possibly help me in a situation like this?"[7]

Velásquez's rhetorical question reflects a widely held opinion among New Jersey's Tarrazúceño community, which is centered in the city of Paterson. For them, the Costa Rican consulate is an inefficient agency incapable of lending assistance to its citizens. Costa Ricans who suffer discrimination and other injustices in the United States rarely seek the assistance or support of their consular officials. Nationalist ideals have dissuaded some officials in both San José and the United States from politicizing the plight of Costa Rica's growing population abroad. Indeed, the existence of a community of impoverished and undocumented workers undermines traditional nationalist understandings of Costa Rica as a bountiful nation that effectively supports its own population and even receives poor and politically oppressed migrants from without.

Emigration not only draws attention to fractures in Costa Rica's nationalist mythology as a stable middle-class republic, it also sheds light on the limits of nationalist racial ideals that have served to "whiten" Costa Rica's historical figures and its past. In fact, for Tarrazúceños like Velásquez, their experiences as undocumented and fair-skinned immigrants draw attention to how citizenship and language can trump the stereotypical phenotypes of race in the United States.

Issues of race, identity, and discrimination in the United States, however, are far from limited to Tarrazúceños who are capable of "passing" for white. In fact, most Tarrazúceños have darker complexions, brown eyes, and brown or black hair. Hispanic immigrants and "white Americans" often assume that these "darker" Costa Ricans are from Mexico, Peru, or some other Latin American nation. The experience of being confused for a citizen of another Latin American republic can be jolting, since it places into question the deep-seated belief of most Costa Ricans that they are "white" or at least "whiter" than other Latin Americans. Many Costa Ricans perceive their Latin American neighbors as racial inferiors, so when they are mistaken for a citizen of one of these other nations, it arguably forces them to question what it means to be a Costa Rican outside the nation's political boundaries. Even as they struggle to understand their positions within US society and the Costa Rican nation, immigrants have made concerted efforts to retain linkages to Costa Rica. This chapter explores some of the challenges Tarrazúceños living in New Jersey face as undocumented, Spanish-speaking laborers, as citizens of a nation that has done little to address their needs working abroad, and as individuals whom their adoptive society read as nonwhites. Additionally, it examines the complex process by which Tarrazúceños struggle to sustain a sense of national belonging via nationalist-oriented consumption in the United States.

Northern New Jersey

Paterson, New Jersey, is that state's largest city and also home to the largest number of Costa Rican émigrés in the area of study and the social and cultural center of the local Costa Rican community.[8] Although Paterson's recorded Costa Rican–born population of 1,241 is arguably small, it has a visible presence.[9] Paterson is home to four Costa Rican–owned restaurants and three bars that cater to Costa Rican clients who live and work in the area. Much of that community is from Tarrazú. Indeed, Paterson has one of the highest concentrations of Tarrazúceño migrants in the United States.[10]

The neighboring towns of Bloomfield, Haledon, and Prospect Park also have a palpable Costa Rican presence.[11] Indeed, Prospect Park and Bloomfield are each home to Costa Rican–owned restaurants that serve as cultural centers for these communities. Costa Ricans in northern New Jersey mostly work in the area's more affluent communities of Montclair, Upper Montclair, Glen Ridge, and North Caldwell, cleaning homes, cutting lawns, caring for children, and working in restaurant kitchens. The communities where Costa Ricans work and live, respectively, are quite near to one another, but they are culturally and economically quite distinct. The average annual per capita income in Paterson between 2008 and 2012 was $15,592; in Bloomfield it was $33,570; in Haledon $23,893; and $23,926 in Prospect Park. In stark contrast, the per capita income of Upper Montclair was $78,135; in Glen Ridge, $68,122; and in North Caldwell, $76,174.[12] The dramatic income discrepancy among these communities within a ten-mile radius creates ideal circumstances for migrants, since it simultaneously offers affordable housing and easy access to service jobs in affluent areas.

Emigration as a Threat to Traditional Understandings of the Costa Rican Nation

In 1999, five hundred Costa Rican elementary and high school students were asked to describe their nation using metaphors.[13] Students' descriptions repeated two central tropes: Costa Rican political values (namely the nation's commitment to nonmilitarism and its stable democratic political system) and foreign tourists' appreciation of the nation's natural environment.[14] The narrative of political exceptionalism in the students' writings was largely unsurprising, as it reflected the emphasis of these values in the nation's textbooks.[15] What was unexpected was that 28 percent of students defined their nation by mentioning foreign tourist's appreciation of Costa Rica's natural environment. The repeated emphasis on foreign tourists' appreciation of the nation's ecology suggests that the ecotourism industry is radically impacting the way Costa Ricans understand their nation. Additionally, the children's focus on the tourists' gaze points to the fact that the nation is constructed by both internal (Costa Ricans') and external (foreign tourists') understandings of the nation.

These tropes also shape the way government functionaries and elected officials define the nation, its citizens, and their problems. Immigration seemingly places into focus the limits of the Costa Rican state to provide for the economic well-being of its citizens and questions the exceptionalist image of Costa Rica as Central America's prosperous and stable republic. Indeed, most Costa Ricans imagine their nation as not only a place tourists visit for pleasure but one where political and economic refugees have come in search of a better life. This idea emerged in the context of the Cold War, when civil wars and the social dislocation they wrought inspired hundreds of thousands of Nicaraguans and Salvadorans to seek sanctuary in Costa Rica during the 1970s and 1980s.[16]

To this day, over 215,000 Nicaraguans live in Costa Rica. Moreover, Nicaraguans today are the primary labor source on Costa Rica's coffee, banana, pineapple, and sugarcane farms. Additionally, a majority of the nation's construction workers are Nicaraguans.[17] That so many Nicaraguans come to Costa Rica to accept the lowest-paying jobs is read by many Costa Ricans as a testament to the superiority of their economy and political institutions and, in turn, of their nation's superiority to Nicaragua and, indeed, to all of Central America. Since the 1990s, scholars have asserted that Costa Rican national identity is increasingly being constructed in opposition to Nicaraguans, who are racialized and "othered."[18]

Because Costa Ricans imagine their nation as a nation that *receives* immigrants desperate for better economic opportunities, the idea of Costa Ricans emigrating in search of financial security seemingly flies in the face of Costa Ricans' perceptions of themselves. In this context, it is likely that many Costa Ricans were taken aback in 2005 when Costa Rica's primary daily published a series of articles by investigative reporter Hazel Feigenblatt that asserted some 220,000 (or roughly 5.5 percent) of the nation's then roughly 4 million citizens resided in the United States, the majority of them undocumented. Additionally, Feigenblatt noted that emigrants sent ₡110,000 million in remittances in 2004, more than the total return of coffee exports for that same year.[19] These figures suggest both a sizable Costa Rican community abroad and its palpable impact on the nation's economy. Feigenblatt's description of émigrés' living and working conditions was likely even more shocking. She explained to readers that most Costa Ricans resided in overcrowded apartments, worked long hours, and as undocumented workers lived in constant fear of deportation. Recognizing the paradigmatic reverberations of her exposé, she noted, "The belief that *ticos* [the colloquial term for Costa Ricans] do not emigrate or . . . only do so legally is part of the past."[20]

For traditionalists who embrace the image of Costa Rica as a prosperous Central American nation that attracts immigrant workers and eco-tourists, rather than exports laborers, Feigenblatt's articles presented an unsavory vision of an increasingly transnational Costa Rican economy that had much in common with the economies of its neighbors, like Nicaragua and El Salvador. Among those unsettled by Feigenblatt's articles was Costa Rica's then consul general, Alejandro Cedeño, who responded in an open letter questioning both Feigenblatt's figures and her representation of the émigré community as mostly composed of undocumented workers.[21]

Cedeño's letter questioned the "claim that 220,000 illegal Costa Ricans are in the United States. This assertion is unsupported and does not conform to the U.S. Department of Justice figures that calculate 17,000 Costa Ricans with an irregular migratory status." Reiterating the idea that there are few undocumented Costa Ricans, Cedeño added that just 198 Costa Ricans were deported and 32 were detained attempting to illegally enter the United States in 2005. He added that official US government data "allows us to see that the number of Costa Ricans that enter illegally [to the United States] is very small."[22]

Cedeño's position that the émigré community is perceived as not only small in its overall size but as one dominated by legal immigrant workers, at first seems odd. Indeed, why would a government official charged with serving Costa Rican nationals in the United States argue that this community is minute? Moreover, why would it be important that the Costa Ricans he serves be presented in the Costa Rican press as residing legally, or not, in the United States?

A close reading of Cedeño's open letter provides some answers to these questions. Indeed, he asserts that the figures Feigenblatt published not only "attack the credibility of responsible US institutions," but also potentially endanger the "security of undocumented Costa Rican workers." Strikingly, Cedeño stated that Feigenblatt's articles "might place U.S. immigration authorities on high alert and encourage them to initiate a relentless search for the thousands of nonexistent illegal Costa Ricans . . . to the detriment of the many, who are today exposed to [the threat of] deportation."[23] Cedeño's suggestion that US officials would read *La Nación* is difficult to understand. Even more difficult to imagine, however, is that these articles could on their own reshape US agencies and official treatment of undocumented Costa Ricans.

Cedeño's words suggest—as did the survey of Costa Rican schoolchildren from the late 1990s—an increasing preoccupation among Costa Rican nationals with how the world perceives their nation. Indeed, Cedeño's plead to not draw attention to the suffering and hardships of his fellow nationals as they might bring US official attention to this community flies in the face of the policies and actions of other Latin American governments with sizable émigré communities that are quick to discuss the injustices their nationals suffer in the United States and advocate for better treatment of their citizens within the broader context of diplomatic negotiations. This same idea was brought up by Feigenblatt in her response to Cedeño, where she caustically retorted, "It is lamentable that the Consul is not in contact with Costa Rican groups in the United States and instead blames the media for worsening their situation. Were he in contact with them he would have heard many of them argue that the Costa Rican government, unlike other [Latin American] governments, has not lobbied for better treatment" of Costa Rican nationals.[24]

Feigenblatt and the Costa Ricans with whom she spoke felt abandoned by their government and were not the only ones cognizant of the issues émigrés in the United States face. Moreover, Cedeño's perspective was not the only one within the Costa Rican government. Indeed, Feigenblatt secured her data through conversations she had with consular officials from throughout the United States, whom she questioned about how many Costa Ricans they had recorded (regardless of legal status) who had employed local consular services to renew passports and national identification cards (cédulas).[25] The discrepancies between US governmental data and Costa Rican consular data reflect differing forms of data collection, while Cedeño's response underscores how traditionalist elements within the nation's political elite as late as 2005 presented what seems to be a myth of political, economic, and regional exceptionality, based on the imaginings of foreigners of the Costa Rican nation and its citizens.

Producing Nation, Consuming Costa Rica

In 2005, *La Nación* published numerous articles on emigration.[26] Feigenblatt's six lengthy articles published in March 2005, however, highlighted the plight of undocumented ticos to an extent that had never been seen and has yet to be repeated by the national media.[27] Several of these pieces went beyond simply providing readers with an understanding of the legal and linguistic challenges and economic benefits of emigration and included brief interviews with Costa Ricans living in Bound Brook and Trenton, providing many readers with their first glimpse of what life was like for ticos living in New Jersey.[28] For example, Feigenblatt shared her astonishing discovery that a corner store in Trenton sold Costa Rican sour cream for the shockingly expensive price of $3.25, more than five times the price in a Costa Rican grocery store.[29] She pointed to the sale of this sour cream to suggest that Trenton's tico community was sufficiently large to make the import of this product profitable.[30]

While Feigenblatt was correct in this assessment, she missed the symbolic importance of imported processed foods for New Jersey migrants who are willing to pay to retain cultural linkages to their nation of birth. The import and consumption of processed foods are not limited to the southern New

Jersey communities Feigenblatt visited. Costa Rican sour cream was for sale in the five grocery stores that I visited in Paterson (La Nueva Merced, Teddy's Grocery, and three C-Town Groceries), as well as Costa Rican beer, pasta, condiments (Salsa Lizano), and crackers.

New Jersey émigrés purchase Costa Rican–processed foods because they are familiar and, perhaps more importantly, because they allow them to feel a sense of continuity in a new and often difficult environment. In fact, ticos often go out of their way to purchase Costa Rican foodstuffs. Tarrazúceña Catalina Muñoz, who first arrived in Paterson in 1994, provides a case in point.[31] Muñoz cleans homes in the upscale town of Montclair, where she also rents a one-bedroom apartment that she shares with her two sons. Many of Montclair's restaurants, cafés, small businesses, and homes depend on undocumented Latino laborers. With few Latino residents, Montclair's four principal grocery stores (Whole Foods, PathMark, A&P, and Kings) carry few products targeted for Latino consumers and no processed goods from Costa Rica. Muñoz's home is within walking distance of the PathMark, but she rarely shops there and has never shopped at the town's higher-end grocery stores. Instead, at least once a week she takes the twenty-five-minute bus ride into Paterson to purchase Costa Rican products. For Muñoz, the trip is well worth it because it allows her to cook the same meals for her sons that she would make when they were still living in Tarrazú.[32]

Beyond a desire to raise her sons on Costa Rican cooking, Muñoz clearly sees her purchases as a nationalist act that supports Costa Rica's economy and workers. In July 2007, I accompanied her on a shopping trip to a Paterson C-Town grocery store. As she perused the shelves, Muñoz would point out the preferable Costa Rican brands of canned sardines, candies, and even soda before placing them into her shopping cart. Almost always the Costa Rican brands were located beside comparable US name and generic brand products that were for sale at lower prices. During the drive to the grocery store, Muñoz had explained money was tight and she was looking for new homes to clean. Thus, it seemed odd that she consistently chose more expensive Costa Rican items. When asked why, Muñoz explained that US tuna tastes fine, but because the tuna was fished "by Costa Rican fishermen," for her, the Costa Rican brand, Sandimar, "always tastes better." With that in mind, she happily paid more for it.[33] Muñoz's words revealed that for her the tuna's "taste" was deeply entwined with the idea that it came from Costa Rica and provided income to a fellow countryman.

Muñoz's nationalist consumption practices went beyond processed foods; in fact, they became much clearer when she moved into the produce section. Muñoz carefully examined the stickers on the pineapples and bananas, searching for ones indicating they were grown in Costa Rica. As she picked through the fruits, she explained, "They are tricky. You . . . see a 'Costa Rica' sticker, but it turns out only that bunch [of bananas] is from Costa Rica and the rest are from wherever. So, you have to be very careful. I try always to buy Costa Rican. I grew up on a farm, and I know that if these fruits do not sell, a family goes hungry."[34] Émigré consumers, such as Muñoz, who consciously purchase Costa Rican produced foods, are not only consciously attempting to preserve their culture but also choosing to support their nation's economy.

Nationalist consumption extends to the way Costa Ricans in Paterson spend their leisure time and dollars. There are four restaurants (La Bahía, La Montaña, Las Tejas, and El Típico) and three bars (El Rústico, The Colt Cafe, and Super Corona's) that prepare traditional Costa Rican fare and cater almost exclusively to tico clients.[35] These bars and restaurants are places where immigrants socialize over bowls of *olla de carne* (a typical beef and vegetable stew), drink Costa Rican beers, and collectively create a Costa Rican space for themselves within the United States.[36] The clients, their conversations, the décor, and the items consumed combine to replicate similar spaces in Costa Rica.

In addition to providing a familiar and comfortable space to socialize, these businesses are in a real sense the heart of the community. When Tarrazúceños first arrive in the area, they often visit these businesses to meet up with friends and family from back home, hoping these contacts will help them find employment and housing opportunities. The centrality of these spaces for the community is clear to Paterson restaurant owner Marcos Beltrán. He described his restaurant, La Bahía, as "the community's center. People come in, and they always see people they have not seen in a long time." Embracing the social function that his business plays in many fellow émigrés' lives, on slow weekday afternoons Beltrán often plays cards with his regulars, passes notes and messages between immigrants, and has even organized the "Costa Rican soccer team" that plays against other Latin American immigrant teams organized around their nation of origin at the Turf City Indoor Sports Center in nearby Wayne, New Jersey.[37]

Outside of Paterson's Costa Rican businesses, the community has irregularly organized a very popular celebration of Costa Rica's independence from Spain.[38] The earliest celebrations, which consisted of Paterson's handful of Costa Rican residents and their families getting together over drinks at a compatriot's home, began in the early 1970s. These first nationalist festivities, which ceased in the early 1980s (when two of the event's three organizers returned to Costa Rica), began as small affairs but quickly grew through word of mouth into large celebrations that included performances by popular Costa Rican musicians, most notably the reggae group Marfíl. According to Roberto Vilar, one of the oldest members of the émigré community and one of the primary organizers of Paterson's Costa Rican Independence

Figure 7.1. Costa Rican immigrants and their children visiting stalls selling traditional Costa Rican food, knickknacks, books, and other goods at the September 2007 Independence Day celebration in Paterson, New Jersey. (Carmen Kordick)

Day events, at the final celebration in 1981, over a thousand migrants traveled from as far north as Vermont and as far south as Delaware to attend.[39]

Despite the increasing popularity of these Independence Day celebrations, they ended in 1981, when Vilar became overwhelmed as the event's sole organizer. Decades later, in 2005, he revived the festivities when a young tica asked him to help her resuscitate the event. Between 2005 and 2008, the pair organized the community's largest celebrations (fig. 7.1). After this co-organizer returned home to Costa Rica in 2008, Vilar noted that he had little trouble finding financial sponsors and vendors willing to pay to have a stall; however, he struggled to find anyone willing to take the time to help him secure municipal permits and book the various Costa Rican musical acts. The unwillingness of others to take on responsibilities has prevented the celebration from taking place since.[40]

Despite the recent discontinuation, Vilar hopes another tico will ultimately take on the responsibility of organizing future festivities. His hope is likely shared. The more recent Independence Day events attracted attendees, food vendors, musicians, and retailers from throughout New Jersey, New

Figure 7.2. Vendor at the September 2007 Independence Day celebration selling a number of nonperishable food items, including the Costa Rican condiment Salsa Lizano. He is wearing an Importadora Monge T-shirt, one of the major funders of the event. (Carmen Kordick)

York, Pennsylvania, and Costa Rica. The event's setup, with multiple musical acts and traditional Costa Rican puppet shows, coupled with a plethora of local restaurant owners selling an array of traditional foods, offered something for Costa Ricans of all ages. Additionally, half a dozen vendors offered a dizzying variety of Costa Rican foodstuffs, key chains, jewelry, glasses, mugs, and T-shirts emblazoned with the Costa Rican flag, the nation's coat of arms, tropical birds, and other nationalist and ecological motifs (figs. 7.2 and 7.3).[41]

Perhaps the most interesting booth at these events was run by Costa Rica's largest appliance store chain, Importadora Monge. This retailer has shops throughout Costa Rica, including several in Tarrazú. Importadora Monge's booth provided migrants with the opportunity to purchase computers, televisions, microwaves, irons, and other electronic goods for their families in Costa Rica. Migrants selected the items they wanted, paid the booth attendee, and received a code with their receipt that family members could use to pick up their gift at the local Importadora Monge. This booth not only facilitated migrants' ability to send their family gifts but allowed

Figure 7.3. Young Costa Rican immigrant family enjoying the Independence Day celebration with their baby girl who is dressed in a traditional Costa Rican peasant's dress in the colors of the Costa Rican flag, red, white, and blue, September 2007. The parents wear jerseys for a Costa Rican soccer team, Saprissa. (Carmen Kordick)

this Costa Rican store to profit directly off of migrants. Migrants have traditionally purchased these same electronic goods in the United States and sent them to family members in gift packages. Importadora Monge sought to eliminate the package middleman to make a profit. The sale of goods highlights the transborder flows of goods between Paterson and Costa Rica. Moreover, this booth expands the simple "nation as commodity" dynamic that Catalina Muñoz's grocery shopping trip suggested, demonstrating how Costa Ricans in northern New Jersey actively participate in their national economy beyond their nation's physical borders. Indeed, Paterson provides a prime example of a transnational community, that is, a Costa Rican community beyond the nation-state's borders.

Gender, the Family, and the Dream of Returning

In a survey I administered to 103 immigrants, an amazing 92 percent wrote that they intended to return to Costa Rica.[42] Despite these expressed intentions, it seems unlikely that many will actually do so. In fact, 31 percent of those surveyed had resided in northern New Jersey for over a decade, and over half of this group had spent over fifteen years abroad.[43] An immigrant's

Figure 7.4. Young Costa Rican girl attending Paterson's Independence Day events, September 2007. Children play a pivotal role in determining whether immigrants will return to Costa Rica or remain in northern New Jersey for the long term. (Carmen Kordick)

civil status and the location of their spouse or children appear the principal determinant as to whether an émigré will remain long-term in the United States. Most ticos who had spent at least a decade in the United States were single, divorced, or living with their spouse and children in New Jersey.[44]

Given that families determine in large part whether a migrant will remain in the United States, it is important to consider Costa Rican women émigrés. Women, who made up just 18 percent of those surveyed, all indicated that they planned to return to Costa Rica. However, 75 percent had no plans to return within the next five years. Moreover, for the women who indicated their time in the United States, they had spent at least three years abroad, suggesting that, as a group, women are more likely to settle than their male counterparts.[45] The greater length of time most women have spent in the United States likely reflects the fact that the vast majority of women were married (61 percent), and 100 percent of married women migrants were living with their spouse in New Jersey.[46] The two divorced women in the sample both wrote that they left Costa Rica to be with their husbands and divorced after arriving in New Jersey.[47] This points to another striking tendency among women migrants: 88 percent emigrated not for monetary reasons but to be closer to family.[48] Given that most women emigrated to unify their families, once in the United States they have little motivation to return home, as their arrival signifies the completion of their aim.[49] Moreover, if couples had raised their children in New Jersey, a permanent return seemed less likely, since children acculturate in U.S. society (fig. 7.4).

Although women as a group seem to be more rooted than men to their new country of residence, their cultural relationship with Costa Rica remains strong. Women immigrants consistently pride themselves on the daily cooking of traditional Costa Rican foods for their families.[50] For instance, although in 2007, Tarrazúceña Susana Jiménez of San Isidro had lived with her husband and two sons in Bloomfield for nearly sixteen years, she claimed that she raised her sons in a "traditional Costa Rican home." During the school year, Jiménez spoke proudly of waking by 5:00 A.M. to prepare homemade tortillas, eggs, and *gallo pinto* (a Costa Rican rice and bean breakfast dish) for her family. Additionally, Jiménez prohibited the use of English in her home and boasted that her sons "speak excellent Spanish and English." Although her children were raised bilingual, Jiménez strived to raise them as she would have in Tarrazú, noting that the entire family attends church every Sunday and that her sons had received all of their Catholic sacraments. Additionally, she beamingly noted her sons' academic successes; she believed that they will earn high school diplomas. For Jiménez, the fact that her sons were fully bilingual, good students, practicing Catholics, and by all accounts well-behaved teens reflected the fact that she was a "traditional homemaker" dedicated to "cleaning, cooking and caring" for her family.[51]

Jiménez may have asserted she is a stay-at-home mother, but this was only partially the case. She was home every afternoon baking sweetbreads and other snacks when her children arrived from school; however, each weekday morning she took the bus to the affluent community of Glen Ridge, where she cleaned a large home. Jiménez described her work as challenging but lucrative: she earned as much as eighty dollars per house and could generally clean a four-floor home in five hours. This means that she makes around sixteen dollars an hour, which she quickly noted was "nearly as much as what [her] husband earn[ed] installing [wood] floors." In fact, although most women emigrated in the hope of unifying their families, the economic opportunities they find (primarily as domestic laborers) make many reluctant to return.[52]

Although Jiménez claimed that above all else she "wish[ed] to return to San Isidro and live a rural life," most Tarrazúceñas in northern New Jersey have very different plans.[53] In Haledon, close friends and next-door neighbors Julieta Blanco and Karla Molina offer a case in point.[54] Both originated from Llano Bonito and worked together cleaning homes in the mansion-lined communities of Montclair and Glen Rock while their children attend school. Like Jiménez, they described themselves first and foremost as housewives, but unlike Jiménez, Molina and Blanco revealed that they were happy in New Jersey and had no desire to return to Costa Rica. They enjoyed the economic freedom that working brought them and believed that they would have to give this up if they returned.[55] Blanco stated, "Here I can work. I make my own money. . . . In Llano Bonito, I could not work; there are no jobs for women. . . . I would go crazy stuck at home all day."[56]

In Tarrazú today, there are few employment options for women who, like Blanco and Moreno, lack advanced education.[57] In the past, they might have found seasonal employment picking coffee, but in recent decades, the entrance of indigenous Panamanians into this labor sector has effectively "racialized" coffee picking into a demeaning and unattractive form of labor.[58] Additionally, at about the same time foreign workers began harvesting coffee, the valley's coffee-processing mills (beneficios) purchased coffee-sorting machines. As discussed in chapter 2, the job of hand-sorting coffee was historically considered women's work. With the elimination of coffee-sorting jobs, the only real option for year-round employment for nonprofessionally trained women locally is in the domestic service industry.

Even though Jiménez, Blanco, and Moreno were employed in New Jersey as domestic laborers, they would be unwilling to assume the same type of work in Tarrazú. Their principal concerns would be autonomy and wages. Whereas in New Jersey they all can make $80 to $100 per day cleaning one to two homes, in Costa Rica they would likely make around $265 a month as a fulltime domestic laborer.[59] In other words, they would earn less in a month in Costa Rica than they made in a single week in northern New Jersey.[60] Moreover, in the United States, domestic work has largely undergone a process of depersonalization, with domestic servants rarely interacting face to face with their employers. This process, which is a hallmark of modern economic relations, has been a boon to women's autonomy, the traditional source for this labor. Domestic work, however, is far from depersonalized in Costa Rica. In Costa Rica, domestic servants are expected to work much more than in northern New Jersey. This is primarily because in Costa Rica cleaning homes almost always implies being a live-in maid. Domestic servants are expected not only to clean their employer's home but also to cook meals, help with child care, and do other household chores. Moreover, because domestic laborers in Costa Rica tend to live with their employers, they are often expected to work all their waking hours. In stark contrast, émigré women noted that because they almost always cleaned different homes each day and because their employers were often at work when they were cleaning, they had little contact with their employers. Given the difficult and limited working conditions available to women in Tarrazú, it is not surprising that migrants, who often emigrated to unite their families, would find economic reasons prompting them to remain abroad.

Although Costa Rican women, like men, are generally undocumented laborers in the United States, women who have managed to legalize their status often use their time in Tarrazú to narrate and demonstrate their economic success. This performance of wealth frequently means that migrants live diametrically opposed lives during their time in Tarrazú and in New Jersey.[61] Take, for instance, Emilia Paniagua, who in 2007 was in her mid-sixties and a proud dual citizen.[62] Paniagua spent roughly nine months out of each year in Haledon, New Jersey, cleaning houses while her daughter ran a daycare in the home the two women and their husbands shared. Although in New Jersey, Paniagua claimed she "works every day, even Sundays," cleaning houses and caring for her family, she added that she "never works in San Pablo," the Tarrazú community from which she hails and where she spends several months of every year. Not only does Paniagua not have a job in Tarrazú, but she claimed that she refused to do any cooking or cleaning there: "I do not even want to dry the dishes, I just want to relax. . . . I have a girl who does everything for me. . . . She cooks, . . . and on her day off, we just go out to eat."[63]

In addition to taking a vacation from work during her time in Costa Rica, Paniagua also took a vacation from living in a small cramped home with her daughter and son-in-law. Paniagua had constructed a "large US-style home" in Tarrazú, replete with a dishwasher, which is a rare luxury in a Costa Rican home. The role this home plays in Paniagua's assertion of economic success is evident. After mentioning her dishwasher, she quickly added that when she first built the home, neighbors would stop by "just to see."[64] For Paniagua, life in the United States composed long days, but those days paid off in Tarrazú where she sat back in her large home as her domestic servant cooked and cleaned for her and her family in much the same fashion as she, Paniagua, served her employers in New Jersey. The ironic experience of working as a domestic servant in the United States and having a domestic servant in Costa Rica is not exclusive to Paniagua. In fact, many migrants who are legally able to travel back and forth between Tarrazú and New Jersey often hire others to do the same work they do in the United States.

Most male émigrés surveyed reported that they worked in a restaurant (26 percent), followed closely by those who worked in construction (21 percent) and landscaping (21 percent). Thus, the employment choices Costa Rican men make in New Jersey reveal that many of the jobs they do are either considered women's work (e.g., washing dishes and cooking in a restaurant) or are strikingly similar to the types of low paid wage labor that many, particularly those from the countryside, hoped to avoid at home. There is little difference in terms of labor conditions between working as a peon in Tarrazú, where one is charged with weeding, fertilizing, and picking coffee, and working in landscaping in New Jersey, where one weeds and cuts lawns. Similarly, since many peons also help farm owners construct fences and other structures on their farms, working as a peon arguably also has several parallels with working in the US construction industry. Like their female counterparts, then, men often find employment within labor sectors in northern New Jersey that they would avoid in Tarrazú. Immigrants' willingness to work jobs in New Jersey that they would not work in Costa Rica highlights the economic inequalities within the hemisphere that, along with exchange rates and wage disparities across borders, drive emigration.

In the case of restaurant work, given gendered ideas about the kitchen as a woman's space, it is not surprising that men would not seek this type of work in Costa Rica. In fact, former restaurant workers who have resettled in Tarrazú, such as Gustavo Camacho, make clear they would never work in a Costa Rican kitchen. Camacho, who today owns a coffee farm in El Llano de la Piedra, is proud of the fact that he purchased his farm after twelve years working in northern New Jersey restaurants. Since returning to Tarrazú in the late 1990s, this forty-something son of a landless laborer and former line chef boasted that he had "never [so much as] fried an egg." Instead, he related that his mother and later his wife (whom he met and married several years after returning to Tarrazú) cooked for him since his homecoming.[65] Although Camacho abandoned the kitchen when he left New Jersey, he nostalgically recalled that he "used to make the best omelets with onion, finely chopped ham, and cheddar cheese." Yet, when I asked Camacho whether he ever considered making omelets for his family, he chuckled before explaining, "I think my wife would not like to know I can cook better than she can; I certainly would not want to know if my wife were a better coffee farmer than me." Clearly, for Camacho, cooking is women's work and farming is men's work. Regardless of the gendered denigration tied to working in a kitchen, he was proud of the financial benefits his work in the kitchen has brought: "I was a good chef, but I only ever cooked to be able to buy my farm. If I had wanted to be a cook, I would have stayed in New Jersey."[66] Camacho, like Paniagua, made a clear distinction between his life in New Jersey and his life in Tarrazú in terms of the type of work he did in each location. Moreover, Camacho's shift from New Jersey cook to Tarrazú farmer brings into focus how class slippage has become the norm among returnees. Nevertheless, traditional gender boundaries remain firm in Tarrazú. In fact, migrants such as Camacho arguably have become "increasingly Costa Rican" as they have become yeoman coffee farmers, embracing a discourse of traditional gendered divisions of labor. Paradoxically, the money that was used to secure ownership in the independent coffee class was earned doing "women's work."

Tarrazúceños employed by landscaping companies in New Jersey, who emigrated in the hopes of remaining or becoming landowners (and thereby leaving the ranks of landless agricultural laborers), are in perhaps the most paradoxical position of any migrants. Josue Araña of San Carlos de Tarrazú provides a good case study. Araña emigrated in 2005 in the hope of retaining his family's small coffee farm in the wake of a bad harvest that made him unable to keep up with his mortgage payments. Araña saw emigration as a means of avoiding the degradation of his class position, explaining, "I came to the US so that I could hold onto the farm and not have to work as a peon for . . . my neighbors." While this was his aim, Araña agreed it is ironic that he worked in New Jersey for a fellow Tarrazúceño, Manuel Fuentes, who owns a landscaping company, weeding lawns to avoid weeding his neighbor's farms in Tarrazú.[67]

Araña, however, quickly pointed to the obvious fact that although his work in New Jersey involves the same precise tasks he did not wish to do in Costa Rica, he is paid much better to weed in New Jersey than he would be in Tarrazú. In fact, after paying his rent and other expenses in the United States, the money he sends back to his wife not only pays for his family's needs but also pays the salary of his two peons. Perhaps the most important distinction for Araña, like Camacho and Paniagua, is that their arguably humiliating work in the United States is seen as temporary and as a means to an end: the retention or creation of a better socioeconomic position in Tarrazú as coffee farmers or as affluent housewives. Thus, the dream of returning to Tarrazú and being an independent farmer who employs peons or a housewife who has a maid plays a fundamental role in migrants' willingness to work long hours in difficult and humiliating jobs in New Jersey.

Ideas of Race, Nation, and Belonging from beyond Costa Rica's Borders

Despite steady declines in most sectors of Costa Rica's economy in recent decades, Costa Rica's international standing has remained strong. Many immigrants, such as Gregorio Herrera, assert that this benefits them, particularly in the search for work. Herrera claimed that many of his employers visited Costa Rica, which instilled in them a positive opinion of Costa Ricans. In fact, he related that "when gringos learn I am Costa Rican, they always tell me I am crazy to have left [my] home for New Jersey. All the gringos know how beautiful Costa Rica is and how friendly we ticos are. They also often ask me to come back; I think it is because we ticos are good workers and also we do not have the same reputation as violent criminals that Colombians, Mexicans, and other Latinos have."[68] Echoing Herrera's words, fellow Tarrazúceño Rodrigo Enríquez, who made a living cutting trees, claimed that his boss, "an American," realized several years back that "Costa Ricans are honest and good workers [so he therefore] only hires ticos."[69] Herrera's and Enríquez's words underscore the idea that Costa Rica's exceptionalist image and its tourist-friendly reputation have served to open doors for Costa Rican laborers in northern New Jersey.

As proud as immigrants were of their homeland's reputation and their hardworking character, they were quick to recognize that their nationality did not confer any political benefits in the United States. Moreover, many related that they were just another Latino group in the eyes of US citizens and that their struggles and issues were the same as other émigrés', with one singular difference: they could not call on the Costa Rican state to support them. It is unsurprising that New Jersey ticos feel unsupported. After all, at least one consular official denied the presence of a sizable population of Costa Rican workers, many undocumented, in the United States as late as 2005.[70] Without recognizing this community, the Costa Rican state cannot allocate the funds and other resources to advocates for its citizens who have been victims of injustice in the United States. In stark contrast, the Dominican Republic, Mexico, and El Salvador all make concerted and visible efforts to serve and defend their nationals from abuse, injustice, and exploitation in the United States.

One of the most vexing issues for Costa Ricans in northern New Jersey was the poor and limited service they received from the New York consular office. In fact, émigrés repeatedly expressed their dissatisfaction with the services offered at the local consulate.[71] Like many of her fellow countrymen, Ana Casas was noticeably upset by the subject of the consul, declaring "our government ignores us; they do not have time to renew our passports. We go there [the New York City consulate] to spend the whole day waiting in line. The secretary does not care we have taken the day off from work to spend six hours in line. When it is time to go home she simply tells us 'you will have to come back tomorrow.'"[72] I experienced the challenge to speak with consular officials in New York in the early 2000s. As part of my research, I attempted in 2005, 2006, 2007, 2008, and 2009 to speak with consular staff in New York over the phone but repeatedly encountered busy (or potentially off the hook) phone lines.[73]

In addition to difficulty reaching consular officials and contending with long lines at the New York Consulate, immigrants complained that their government largely (if not entirely) ignored them during presidential visits and political negotiations between the United States and Costa Rica. Informants repeatedly described how presidents from other Latin American nations sought to defend the rights of their nationals in collaboration with their consular offices. El Salvador and Mexico were the two most common examples provided by migrants such as twenty-two-year-old Gabriel Naranjo: "When the president of El Salvador visits, he speaks to the [US] president and he asks for things for Salvadoran immigrants. Our president never does that."[74]

Costa Ricans have reason to covet the services and representation that other Latin Americans receive from their governments in the United States. The Mexican government has a long history of engaging and negotiating with the US government to protect the rights of its citizens. Before 9/11, then Mexican president Vicente Fox was in the process of negotiating an amnesty for his nation's undocumented nationals.[75] Moreover, the Mexican government, through its forty-two consular offices, consistently involves itself in the legal defense and protection of its citizens' rights, even in cases where its nationals participated in illegal or questionable activities.[76]

Mexican consular officials also dedicate considerable man-hours lobbying to improve Mexican nationals' access to services in the United States. Since March 2002, when amnesty talks between the US and Mexican governments broke down, Mexican authorities have been involved in an effort to have consular-issued identification cards recognized as a valid form of identification. While states such as New York and New Jersey do not recognize these identification cards as a legitimate proof of identity, thirteen states, including New Mexico, have done so for the purpose of applying for a driver's license. Furthermore, hundreds of police departments and banks across the nation now accept these cards as proof of identity. While they do not provide their bearers with any legal rights, they have, thanks to consular lobbying, allowed thousands of Mexican nationals the opportunity to enjoy greater access to essential services.[77]

Taking notice of the sizable Costa Rican community in the United States and the success of Mexico's identification card efforts, in August 2006 legislative assemblyman Jorge Eduardo Sánchez Sibaja proposed law 16.323. The law would have established a consular identification card program, similar to Mexico's, for Costa Ricans in the United States. Sánchez's proposal suggested that the identification cards would not only help their bearers to open bank accounts and procure driver's licenses but would also be a source of symbolic capital, allowing ticos to "maintain their dream [of] . . . continu[ing] . . . to feel Costa Rican."[78] Unfortunately for undocumented ticos in the United States, his law never passed.

In 2007, Costa Ricans in New Jersey were well aware of the limitations Mexican nationals often found, with many banks and states refusing to recognize their identification cards as legitimate proof of identity. Still, Costa Ricans were impressed by the fact that Mexico had made a concerted effort to improve the living conditions of its nationals working abroad. As numerous émigrés explained, "something is better than nothing." Representative Sánchez's law certainly would have been a good first step, but since his legislation was not passed, it failed to produce any visible change for the thousands of undocumented Costa Ricans working in the United States.

Since Sánchez's failed attempts to create a consular identification card in 2006, Costa Rican politicians appear to have abandoned any effort to improve the living and working conditions of their nationals abroad. But, in an unexpected turn of events, in June 2010, Costa Rica's Supreme Tribunal of Elections decided to allow Costa Ricans abroad to vote in the nation's forty-four consular offices, which shows that San José has not completely ignored its nationals abroad. Beginning in 2014, Costa Rican émigrés with a valid national identification card have had the chance to vote in their nation's presidential elections.[79] This policy means that Costa Rica has joined the ranks of such Latin American nations as Argentina, Bolivia, Brazil, Colombia, the Dominican Republic, Ecuador, Honduras, Mexico, Nicaragua, Panama, Peru, and Venezuela, all of which have legislation providing their citizens abroad with the same right.[80] The Supreme Electoral Tribunal's decision has the potential to increase emigrants' political power in the nation-state. This, however, did not happen in 2014, as only 9,883 Costa Ricans outside of Costa Rica registered to vote and a mere 32 percent, or 2,271 exercised their right.[81] In 2018, the numbers seemingly improved considerably, which signified a 151 percent increase in potential voters abroad.[82] While the final voting tally of these recent elections has not been calculated, the registration numbers suggest growing interest among the émigré community in voting, and if it continues might possibly (as in the case of the Dominican Republic) encourage future presidential candidates to campaign in the United States for emigrants' votes.[83] Were this to occur, Costa Rican migrants might encounter a president more willing to negotiate on their behalf with the US government.

Costa Ricans were regularly frustrated by the long delays they saw as they attempted to complete mundane bureaucratic transactions, but their irritation quickly gave way to despair when the subject of consular (in)action to defend the basic rights of Costa Rican citizens was brought up. Perhaps one of the most dramatic episodes that reveals how unsupported Costa Ricans in Northern New Jersey feel involves Federico Araya. On the evening of July 14, 2007, while driving his car down Interstate 80 East, Araya pulled over to the side of the road to urinate.[84] While Araya was urinating, a patrol car pulled up and two officers asked to see his driver's license and green card. When Araya produced a New Jersey license but no green card, they realized he was undocumented. Araya soon found himself handcuffed on the ground, lying on the same spot where just minutes before he had urinated. The officers kicked him in the side a couple of times before helping him up and walking him to the patrol vehicle.[85]

Araya's brush with the police differs from that of Rolando Velásquez, whose story opened this chapter, because of their physical appearance and their linguistic skills. While Velásquez spoke almost no English, Araya has considerable command of the English language, though as a nonnative speaker he does have an obvious accent. Araya believes that this was critical to the way the police treated him: "As an Hispanic, they wanted to see a green card or a visa; I do not have one. My driver's license was not enough." As an "illegal Hispanic," Araya believed the police "know they can do [to me] what they want."[86] Both Araya and Velásquez saw language and physical appearance as critical to the way authorities responded to them. In Velásquez's case, the police assumed that he should speak English because of his lighter complexion, whereas for Araya, his accent and his darker complexion suggested to the officers that he was an undocumented Latin American immigrant.

Unlike Velásquez, who recognized the police's actions as unjust and illegal, Araya seemed fully resigned to the idea that the police were entitled to act as they had, explaining that "they are the police; they do whatever they want." When asked whether he had considered speaking to the consul, he echoed Velásquez's response to the same question: "What could the consulate do for me? Nothing."[87] Araya's grandmother, Emilia Paniagua, who has legal residence, wanted him to hire an attorney and press charges, but Araya thought it was useless, explaining his belief that "in the US, if you do not have citizenship, you are no one. The police do what they want, no one cares here, and the Costa Rican government certainly does not care. As an illegal [immigrant] you do not count."[88] Araya clearly perceived himself and other undocumented workers as occupying a powerless space on the political margins of both the United States and Costa Rica, and he is largely correct. In fact, Araya's migration status meant that if he did find legal counsel, his attorney would be required to report his undocumented status, almost definitely getting him deported. Additionally, since the consulate in New York City has done little to demonstrate its willingness and capacity to help its nationals, it is unsurprising that Araya thought that he had no recourse.

Araya's and Velásquez's experiences with New Jersey police officers suggest that undocumented Costa Rican workers need both access to legal services and information about their legal rights. Moreover, their experiences point to the fragility of generalized racial categories and suggest that neither physical appearance nor the ability to speak English can protect immigrants from feeling the brunt of anti-Latino and anti-immigrant violence in the United States.

Aside from evidencing the clear role that phenotype plays in the way individuals are classified in the United States, these two incidents bring to the forefront traditional ideas about Costa Rican whiteness and national identity. In the case of Velásquez and other Costa Ricans who have been able to pass as "white" within US society, the experience of immigrating has arguably affirmed deep-seated ideas about Costa Rica as a white (i.e., nonindigenous, European) nation. Indeed, blue-eyed Margarita Romero, who works in a Franklin Lakes deli (nine miles northwest of Paterson), claimed that clients frequently asked her if she is French or Italian, and "I enjoy letting them know I am Costa Rican." Romero said that she was never surprised by these questions. In fact, she asserted, "Most of Latin America is Indian; Costa Rica is different in that way, but since most people [in the United States] have never been [to Costa Rica], they do not know that."[89] Romero's words suggest that she was not only accustomed to being confused for a European immigrant but saw this as an unsurprising confusion, given the fact that Costa Rica is a "white" nation. Thus, for Romero, and likely for many of her compatriots who have pale complexions, light-colored eyes and have been mistaken for non-Hispanics, the experience of living in the United States has served to bolster their belief in Costa Rica's whiteness myth.

In stark contrast, for individuals such as Federico Araya who have suffered discrimination because of a darker complexion, the experience of living in the United States serves to subvert the idea of Costa Rican exceptionalism and whiteness. This is certainly the case for Tarrazúceño Manuel Fuentes, who began a landscaping business in Wayne, New Jersey, in the early 1990s, after he secured US citizenship through a short-lived marriage to a US citizen. Fuentes, who was thirty-nine in 2007, employed ten full-time workers (all of whom were undocumented Tarrazúceños), owned a "large and very comfortable" home in Wayne, and drove a new BMW, making him one of northern New Jersey's most successful Tarrazúceños. While Fuentes saw himself as having realized and even surpassing his aims when he emigrated, he asserted that his time in New Jersey has been very difficult because of the racial discrimination he suffered.[90]

Fuentes's clients, his former wife, and his neighbors are all "white," non-Latinos, and native-born US citizens, suggesting that Fuentes had largely been accepted into the local non-Latino community. Yet, Fuentes's take on his position differed, as he contended that because he is a *trigueño* (of dark olive complexion), his economic success, US citizenship, and good English skills are not enough to bring him acceptance within the larger non-Latino community. He thought that he had been the victim of discrimination in several restaurants near his home. While he did not wish to elaborate on what took place in these restaurants, the experiences led him to stop eating out in his town of residence. Because Fuentes refused to cook, this meant that each day he drove fifteen minutes to Paterson to eat his breakfast, lunch, and dinner at Costa Rican–owned restaurants, where he felt "respected as a customer."[91] Fuentes believed that the ill treatment he experienced had everything to do with his complexion. He asserted the discrimination would not have occurred if he had light-colored eyes and skin, like some of his countrymen. Highlighting this idea, Fuentes told me that although he and I shared the same legal status, as dual nationals of the United States and Costa Rica, because I have blond hair and blue eyes, we were "treated very differently . . . because . . . I am trigueño." Fuentes's words suggest that in the United States, legality and even socioeconomic position are trumped by his "Latino look." Arguably his experience, like Araya's and those of the countless other Costa Ricans who suffer from discrimination in the United States, poke holes in the idea that Costa Rica is a "white" nation. Indeed, Fuentes opined that the idea that Costa Rica is "Central America's Switzerland" reflected the fact that the nation did have "some machos," but this myth ignored the fact that, in his estimation (and that of most anthropologists and scientists), Costa Ricans had "both Indian and Spanish" origins.[92]

Fuentes was quick to note that Costa Ricans too give preferential treatment to lighter-skinned foreigners over their own nationals. As a dual-national, Fuentes had frequently vacationed in Costa Rica and complained that he often had a harder time than North American and European tourists locating a taxi at the airport, a guide at the beach, and other services. Fuentes noted that although he was confident that he had "as much if not more money" in his pockets as many of the foreign tourists that his fellow nationals jump to serve, because he was Costa Rican and looked the part, they assumed he did not. A trip he made to a San José brothel that was frequented by foreign tourists made this abundantly clear. Noticeably bitter, Fuentes recalled how none of the women in the brothel paid him any attention until he began chatting with some of the foreign clients, who told a couple of women that he "had money to pay." In fact, only after the foreigners intervened, Fuentes claimed, did he get any attention. The whole experience was humiliating.[93] What bothered him the most was the incident's striking similarity to his experiences in New Jersey. Indeed, just as Fuentes's legal status and money were apparently not enough to gain him acceptance in the community where he lived, his money alone could not make him an attractive client in a San José brothel. Fuentes's experience points to a common racial code that transcends US and Costa Rican borders: individuals perceived as "white" almost invariably enjoy more power.

Conclusion

Like many international migrants, Costa Rican émigrés have embraced a transnational vision of their natal nation. Indeed, although ticos in northern New Jersey recognize that they are physically quite far from San José, they continue to understand themselves as a part of the larger Costa Rican nation-state. As loyal citizens, community members have made efforts to retain their culture and pass it on to their children through a number of intentional actions and rituals. Many, for instance, engage in a variety of nationalist-oriented consumption practices, including the purchase of Costa Rican coffee, produce, and processed foods. Additionally, ticos have (like many other émigrés from other nations) sought to retain a sense of belonging to their communities, families, and friends who remain in Costa Rica through the use of remittances, social media, telephone calls, gifts that are sent through various packaging services, and email.

Émigrés' commitment to maintaining strong relationships with loved ones who have not emigrated and to creating a Costa Rican community abroad has not inspired San José policy makers. In fact, perhaps hoping not to draw attention to this community, policy makers have done a poor job of providing these citizens with legal and other services. The state's seeming disinterest in defending its citizens from discrimination and other hardships in the United States highlights the strength of the nation's official mythology. Indeed, the very existence of this community of impoverished and undocumented workers undermines traditional nationalist understandings of Costa Rica as a prosperous nation that effectively supports its own population and even receives poor and politically oppressed migrants from without. Costa Rican bureaucrats have not drawn attention to the plight of Costa Ricans working abroad.

This New Jersey community's experience also places into relief the limits of nationalist racial ideals that have celebrated Costa Rica as the isthmus's "white" republic. In particular, ticos who are read as nonwhites within US society are forced to contend with the limits of their nation's racist mythology and its implications for their own identity. For those ticos whose complexion, hair, and eye color allow them to pass as "white" (i.e., as non-Hispanics) by the broader American populace, their sense of national belonging to Central America's "white" republic is arguably bolstered. At the same time, however, many of these individuals are forced to try to make sense of what it means to be an undocumented, non-English speaking, "white" laborer. In fact, the experience of "white" ticos in the United States arguably exposes the intersectional nature of class, race, and citizenship in the Americas.

Conclusion

Costa Rica's Cold War Exceptionalism

In June and July 2014, Costa Rica's national soccer team, La Selección, became the World Cup's Cinderella story. Indeed, as enthusiasts around the globe watched in amazement, the team from this tiny developing nation defeated both Uruguay and Italy before tying with England and Greece to enter the quarterfinals.[1] Ultimately, Costa Rica was eliminated in their quarterfinals, but few soccer fans—regardless of their nationality or team loyalties—were anything but impressed and inspired by this Central American republic's team that held its own against much more formidable foes.[2] In the face of this international success, Costa Ricans poured onto the streets to cheer their team during the matches and then to celebrate the players with considerable fanfare following their final elimination.[3]

For Costa Ricans, their team's success confirmed their nation's exceptionalist mythology on a global stage. Yet, at the same time, La Selección arguably provided the world with an image of Costa Rica that contradicted the nation's traditional collective vision of itself as a "white" republic. In fact, six of the twenty-three players who took to the field, or over a quarter of the team, were of evident African ancestry. Moreover, all of the players were plainly of mixed indigenous, African, and European ancestry.[4] In other words, there were no "white" players representing Central America's alleged white republic.

Costa Rican success at the most recent World Cup, much like many of the events and historical processes examined in this volume, reveals that there is certainly something special and unique about Costa Rica, its historical development, and its people. At the same time, just like La Selección, the historical and contemporary experiences of Tarrazú Valley residents inadvertently fracture the nation's official narrative and identity. More to the point, Costa Rica's past and present must be considered within an isthmian context. The national soccer team's players are a case in point, since all of the players could have easily been confused with residents from any of the isthmus's five Hispanic republics, which, unlike Costa Rica, embrace a mestizo national identity. Likewise, Tarrazúceños' experience with debt peonage, their active role in successfully overthrowing the First Republic, the long-standing sexual and physical abuse of women and children in the region, and more recently locals' experience with both emigration and immigration all suggest that there are more commonalities than differences between Costa Rica and Central America's other nations.

In fact, this book highlights the limits and shortcomings of various aspects of Costa Rica's official national narrative. Indeed, this work begins by countering the largely accepted myth that the introduction of coffee served to create a prosperous yeoman coffee-farming class throughout Costa Rica that softened the nation's harsh colonial-era socioracial hierarchies. As this work shows, when commercial coffee production took off in the Central Valley during the 1850s, it helped transform Tarrazú, which since the 1820s had been little more than an isolated familial settlement, into a growing rural community. Coffee helped increase Central Valley property values in the 1850s, encouraging some families in and around the national capital, who did not want to become wage laborers on wealthier neighbors' farms, to immigrate to Tarrazú (and other areas outside the Central Valley) in search of new lands and new opportunities for their families. While the families who settled in Tarrazú in the second half of the nineteenth century arguably migrated because of coffee's impact on the socioeconomic order, they were not largely fleeing agrarian capitalism. Indeed, as soon as coffee mills were opened locally in the 1880s, commercial coffee production would take off. Coffee profits in Tarrazú ultimately served to increase, rather than decrease, class divisions and tensions. In sum, the way that coffee capitalism reshaped Tarrazú society pokes holes in the widely accepted narrative of coffee as a great socioeconomic equalizer.

Additionally, this work takes on the most steadfast of Costa Rica's exceptionalist mythologies, which holds that Costa Ricans are innately more peaceful a people than their Central American counterparts. This book takes on this myth by considering state violence in Tarrazú, highlighting confrontations between local men and state authorities over issues of suffrage, as well as state violence against local men who were suspected of producing, selling, and/or consuming illegal homemade liquors. The culture of violence extended, as this book demonstrates, into the household, where men used domestic violence, without fears of social or state sanctions, to establish and maintain gendered power hierarchies. It is in the context of an isolated rural community where state and patriarchal authority were asserted and maintained through violence that rebel leaders, namely, José "Pepe" Figueres, would find support in his successful bid to overthrow the government in the short-lived, but violent, 1948 Civil War. The civil war would result in the establishment of the Second Republic, which would create the myth of national peace following the elimination of the nation's military in 1949 as a means of consolidating political power.

Finally, this work questions the image of Costa Rica as Central America's "white" republic by embracing a transnational framework, which allows for a deep analysis of how Tarrazúceños' racial identities have at once been affirmed and questioned at the local level because of international migration flows. Indeed, the large-scale out-migration of Tarrazúceño workers to the United States, coupled with the mass influx of indigenous Panamanian laborers into the region, have served to bolster local faith in the nation's whiteness mythology. Moreover, for many Tarrazúceños the presence of impoverished, nonwhite, foreign workers in their community has affirmed their sense of themselves as "white," civilized members of the nation-state. For many Tarrazúceños laboring in the United States, whose complexions allow for them to "pass" as white, their experiences further strengthen local faith in their nation's whiteness. Moreover, remittances earned abroad have served to further bolster local families' sense of national belonging, by permitting them to purchase lands for coffee production. This has meant that emigrant families arguably are better able to identify with the national narrative as yeoman coffee farmers by exiting the nation than are their counterparts at home who in many cases have been forced to abandon coffee production. At the same time, life abroad for many Tarrazúceños has served to break apart their faith in their nation and its exceptionalist mythology. Those who are seen as nonwhites by US society and other Latinos question their sense of faith in the nation's alleged whiteness and/or their sense of belonging. Their experiences with Costa Rican US consular officials add to some Tarrazúceños' wavering faith in their nation's exceptionalist mythology. In fact, consular functionaries seemingly are incapable of meeting the basic needs of their citizens laboring abroad and have until recently denied the existence of a community of undocumented Costa Rican laborers in the United States, as discussed in chapter 7. This, in effect, serves to preserve the nation's exceptionalist imaginary.

In sum, this book offers the historical experiences of Tarrazúceños both in their region and in New Jersey to scrutinize the remarkably durable, multilayered, official national narrative that celebrates Costa Rica as the isthmus's peaceful, democratic, white, and egalitarian republic. This myth, which emerged in the context of the Cold War as a means of explaining why

Costa Rica avoided the violent civil wars that rocked the rest of the isthmus in the 1960s, 1970s, and 1980s, undeniably, like all myths, was born of some truth. This conclusion reflects on the truths that undergird Costa Rica's official national narrative.

I argue that Costa Rica's difference is a product of a series of specific national, hemispheric, and larger global circumstances and political realities that came into alignment just before, during, and after World War II. I squarely reject the idea that Costa Rica's democratic society has deeper historical roots that can be traced to either the nation's imagined genetic/racial composition or any other allegedly "special" element of its historical development, during the colonial era or in the early-national period, as the nation's myth-making historians argued for decades. In fact, before the 1930s arguably little significantly separated Costa Rica from its neighbors, and differences did not become palpable until the 1940s and 1950s.

The best evidence that Costa Rica's national trajectory started to deviate significantly from the rest of the isthmus in the post–World War II period can be found in the fact that the nation's exceptionalist national identity myth was forged in the Cold War period, not before. Certainly, all nations have unique national personalities, differing demographic compositions, and geographical features that inspire particular economic, social, and political realities. Arguably, however, before the early 1950s, one would be hard-pressed to make the argument that Costa Rica was more distinct from El Salvador than Guatemala was from Honduras. In fact, all of Central America's republics had agroexport-centered economies based largely on the production of coffee, bananas, cotton, and sugar.[5] Starting in the nineteenth century, the whole isthmus experienced some level of US economic, political, and/or military intervention. Additionally, by the 1930s, all of these republics had well-established political and economic oligarchies that used military and police violence to silence popular opposition to their interests.

These shared realities created a level of political and social instability throughout the isthmus that inspired military coups, rural revolts, labor strikes, and the formation of militant opposition parties, many with communist leanings, during the Great Depression. Events in El Salvador's coffee fields that culminated in the infamous La Matanza massacre received the greatest scholarly attention (and are arguably the most tragic) of these movements during the 1930s.[6] Yet, in this same decade, banana workers on Costa Rica's Atlantic coast collaborated with Communist labor organizers to undertake a bitter, prolonged, and successful strike against United Fruit Company, resulting in better wages, improved working conditions, and other gains for workers.[7] The success of the strike helped Costa Rican Communists secure massive worker support both in the banana fields and in the Central Valley among urban laborers. Moreover, the Communists' popular appeal encouraged mainstream politicians to collaborate with the PVP, the nation's Communist party. Most significantly, as detailed in chapters 4 and 5, President Calderón worked with PVP leaders to pass a series of progressive reforms between 1941 and 1943 that established the nation's Social Security system and provided wage laborers with newly outlined rights.[8] The PVP's prominent role in shaping national policies and political discussions crucially shaped Costa Rica's political and socioeconomic trajectory until 1948.

The political timing of mainstream Costa Rican politicians' embrace of progressive reforms was extremely fortuitous and would be a key element in ensuring the nation's political and social stability in the following decades. Indeed, the Cold War years were marked by US military and political interventions aimed to eliminate any and all Communist influence from the hemisphere. Starting with the infamous 1954 coup in Guatemala, which the CIA planned, the United States took a forceful position against Communism and progressive reform in the isthmus. Therefore, it seems likely that if Costa Rica's two years of massive reform coupled with the alliance between the government and Communists had taken place a decade later, US policy makers would not have stood by idly. Additionally, whereas the connections between the Guatemalan administration of reform-minded Jacobo Arbenz and Moscow seem to most scholars to have been minimal, if not a fantastical fiction, the Costa Rican government was openly collaborating with the nation's Communists. Moreover, the Calderón administration's reforms cut into US corporate profits, namely those of the United Fruit Company—the reason most scholars identify as the driving force behind CIA intervention in Guatemala.[9]

The most beneficial repercussion of Costa Rica's successful implementation of its reform program was that it served to relieve the socioeconomic tensions between the nation's poorest and wealthiest residents in the decades that followed. By increasing wages, legalizing workers' rights to unionize, and providing laborers with improved working conditions, Costa Rica's progressive reform program alleviated the poverty of rural and urban workers alike. Additionally, the reforms established legal channels through which workers could contest perceived injustices by their employers, which served to further decrease class tensions in Costa Rican society. In stark contrast, the US-backed coup of 1954 eliminated legal channels in Guatemala for political and economic reform, ensuring that class tensions remained high. US Cold War–era policy makers would eagerly fund and train Guatemala's military, encouraging it to root out internal threats to political stability and capitalist development and also support the installation of a military regime.[10]

In sum, US political support and funding of the Guatemalan military concretely assured that Guatemala developed a political and socioeconomic landscape very different from Costa Rica's in the latter half of the twentieth century.

If US nonintervention is critical to explaining Costa Rica's relative political stability during the Cold War, it raises the question of why the United States choose to act in Guatemala in 1954 but not in Costa Rica a decade earlier. In the simplest of terms, very different global political realities dictated US policy in 1944 and 1954. Costa Rican politicians undertook their reform program during World War II, when the United States sought to ensure regional support against the Axis threat and therefore invested heavily in cultivating an image of itself as a "good neighbor" in Latin America. Part of the good neighbor policy was a commitment to nonintervention and respect for the democratic process. Moreover, during World War II, despite deep-seated misgivings and diametrically opposed political visions, the United States and the Soviet Union joined together to eliminate the shared threat that the authoritarian imperialists of Eurasia, namely Germany, Italy, and Japan, posed to the established world order. These political and military objectives meant that when Costa Ricans elected a government that established a political alliance with Communists, US policy makers took no action. Moreover, US policy makers did not seek to limit or reduce the social reform programs the Costa Rican government implemented during the war, despite their pernicious impact on US businesses, namely the banana companies.

After World War II's end on September 2, 1945, the global political stage began to rapidly change, and so too did US policies within Latin America. The elimination of the Axis threat brought to the surface deep-seated tensions between the Soviet Union and the United States. As the Cold War began to take shape, US policy makers determined that eliminating communist ideas was a principal priority. This meant that Washington, DC, acted in 1954 when Guatemalan elites and the US-based United Fruit Company both alleged that Guatemala's democratically elected government was aligned with the Soviet Union and embracing communist reforms. Arguably, Costa Rica's progressive government of the 1940s with its ties to the communist intellectuals and politicians would have been an attractive target for US policy makers during the Cold War. Yet, in another example of fortuitous timing, Costa Ricans realigned their nation's political framework to fit emerging US Cold War ideals through the establishment of a conservative government after Costa Rica's violent though short-lived Civil War in 1948.[11]

The rebels, who took up arms and succeeded in unseating the progressive government of Teodoro Picado in 1948, took serious issue with the alliance that Picado and his predecessor, Calderón, made with the PVP.[12] The centrality of anti-Communist sentiment to the rebel movement is evident in the fact that Figueres outlawed the PVP and dissolved dozens of unions because of their association with communism within weeks of his securing political control. Additionally, in the first year after the Civil War, at least fourteen vanguardistas were executed and some three thousand vanguardistas fled into exile.[13] Taken together, these actions effectively eliminated Communist influences and voices from Costa Rica's political scene for the duration of the Cold War. Hence, by the time US policy makers began contemplating meddling directly in Latin American politics to eliminate any Communist influence in the hemisphere, Costa Rica had no Communist Party or even radical labor organizations. More to the point, the post-1948 regime's actions against the vanguardistas ensured that Costa Rica was perceived to be solidly in the US camp by the time the Cold War began to heat up in Latin America.

The Second Republic's firm anti-Communism interestingly and critically did not mean that its political leaders, let alone the mass of rebels that took up arms to place them into power, opposed the progressive reforms Communists helped pass in the 1940s. In fact, as detailed in chapter 4, Figueres, the intellectual, military, and political head of the successful rebellion, was a self-avowed socialist who favored government intervention in the economy to help more equitably distribute financial wealth.[14] Thus, Figueres's ascension to power did not mark the end of progressive reforms but rather their institutionalization. Indeed, Figueres did more than retain the social security network that Calderón and the PVP established in the early 1940s. The nation's post–Civil War constitution of 1949—which he helped write—made the national healthcare system, the progressive labor reforms, and the modern social security system into constitutional rights. Moreover, Figueres's government would invest heavily in supporting the formation of cooperatives and other progressive means of reducing poverty and socioeconomic divisions. Thus, the 1948 Civil War at once freed Costa Rica from the taint of Communist influence in the late 1940s and also marked the expansion of the Communist-inspired reform program that would critically decrease socioeconomic tensions within Costa Rican society in the decades that followed. This ensured Costa Rica's relative political stability during the Cold War, since it reduced economic pressures on the masses who might have inspired the formation of future revolutionary movements, namely those with a Marxist slant.

In the second half of the twentieth century, particularly following the Cuban Revolution's Communist embrace, most of the region's militaries expanded in size and political influence. This was largely due to US investment as part of the US Cold War strategy that called on Latin Americans to seek out and eliminate internal Communist threats, which theoretically freed the US military to protect the hemisphere from external Communist dangers.[15] Scholars of some of the worst Cold War–era human rights abuses in Latin America have repeatedly pointed to how enlarged military might, along with repressive political regimes, and steep socioeconomic inequities, encouraged both state terror and the formation of guerrilla movements. Critically, the closing off of legal political channels for workers and members of the political opposition to express discontent and push for reform, coupled with a well-trained and armed military that was charged with eliminating internal threats to order, encouraged disaffected citizens throughout the region to take up arms against the political establishment. The clear inequity between state forces and oppositional groups inspired the latter to embrace guerrilla tactics. In much of the region, during the second half of the twentieth century, cycles of violence were established with the military and guerrillas employing terror and violence both against one another and against civilians. The nature of guerrilla conflict meant that both sides viewed civilians as both potential enemies and recruits to their respective forces and cause. This scenario did not, however, develop in Costa Rica.

During the Cold War, when powerful militaries were a regional norm, Costa Rica had no armed forces. As discussed in chapter 5, in December 1948 Costa Rica eliminated its military. This action had clear Cold War–era implications for both Costa Rican and US policy makers; namely, the lack of a military forced Costa Rican policy makers to consistently demonstrate to the voting majority that their interests and concerns were a paramount consideration in shaping policy.[16]

The combination of the willingness of state authorities to listen to popular demands and the reduction in socioeconomic cleavages that the reforms of the 1940s inspired helped Costa Rican society to become increasingly democratic during the second half of the twentieth century. Democratic institutions that were receptive to popular calls for justice, reform, and change eliminated any perceived need by citizens to forge guerrilla groups. In other words, as much of the isthmus became characterized by authoritarian regimes that held power through the use of military violence and its threat, Costa Rican society became increasingly democratic. Thus, by the time the final battles of the Cold War were being waged in Nicaragua, El Salvador, and Guatemala during the 1960s, 1970s, and 1980s, Costa Rica seemed clearly out of step with its neighbors.[17] At the very least, Costa Rica escaped from the political violence, impunity, mass dislocations, and other legacies of intense poverty and political repression that much of the rest of the isthmus experienced in this period. Costa Rican elites' ability to decapitate the radical leadership of the nation's major social movements, while simultaneously moderating class tensions, ensured more moderate outcomes and eliminated the opportunity for radical shifts in political and economic policies that might have directly challenged the traditional elites in power.

Costa Rica's post-1948 political stability and strong democratic institutions did not, unfortunately, ensure economic opportunities and prosperity for all of its citizens. Limited labor options and decreasing access to arable land in rural regions led many in the Cold War era and years since to migrate to the Central Valley in search of educational and labor opportunities. Some found the opportunities they sought, but many were forced to enter into San José's informal economy. Similar rural to urban migration patterns and the formation of increasingly visible informal economies occurred in this period throughout Latin America, with similar results. Additionally, in the case of Tarrazú, as chapters 6 and 7 illustrate, decreasing stability in the coffee sector, coupled with limited alternative economic options, led many Tarrazúceños to immigrate to the United States. Countless Tarrazúceños and Costa Ricans from other parts of the republic have realized economic stability for themselves and their families through remittances and savings earned through laboring abroad. Immigration to the United States, San José's growing informal economy, as well as the establishment of democratic governments throughout the isthmus in the post–Cold War years suggest that Costa Rica is increasingly looking like its isthmian neighbors once again. What precisely this means for the way Costa Ricans understand their nation and their exceptionalism is something that will become increasingly clear in the years ahead.

Notes

Preface

1. Faith in the nation's whiteness hinges on a historical narrative that has been taught in public schools for decades. For more on the racial aspects of the official national narrative, see chapter 7.

2. In recent years, social scientists have highlighted the way that Costa Rica's whiteness myths have been bolstered by the presence of Nicaraguans, who the media has continually portrayed as nonwhite outsiders prone to crime and violence. For more on this, see Carlos Sandoval García, *Otros amanezantes: Los Nicaragüenses y la formación de identidades nacionales en Costa Rica* (San José: Editorial Universidad de Costa Rica, 2002).

3. Sandoval García, *Otros amanezantes.*

4. Carlos Sandoval-García, ed., *Shattering Myths on Immigration and Emigration in Costa Rica*, trans. Kari Meyers (Lanham, MD: Lexington Books, 2011).

5. The collapse of coffee prices internationally was sparked by high prices starting in the 1960s that encouraged farmers globally to dramatically increase coffee production. By the mid-1970s, production outstripped world demand and coffee prices took a nosedive. For more on this, see Deborah Sick, *Farmers of the Golden Bean: Costa Rican Households and the Global Coffee Economy* (DeKalb: Northern Illinois University Press, 1999), 12–23.

6. International Coffee Organization, "Historical Data," International Coffee Organization online, accessed December 2, 2005, www.ico.org/asp/display7.asp.

7. Rodrigo A. Jiménez Robles, interview by author, San Marcos de Tarrazú, Costa Rica, January 3, 2006.

8. Rodrigo A. Jiménez Robles, interview. Also, see Elías Rodríguez Valverde, interview by author, Santa María de Dota, Costa Rica, July 13, 2005.

9. Field notes, August 6, 2005, Santa María de Dota, Costa Rica.

10. For more on the origins of and consequences of emigration from and immigration into the region, see chapters 6 and 7.

11. For more on how coffee reshaped cultural, social, and economic relationships

in San José during the nineteenth century, see Lowell Gudmundson, *Costa Rica before Coffee: Society and Economy on the Eve of the Export Boom* (Baton Rouge: Louisiana State University Press, 1986).

12. In addition to coffee production, the construction of the Inter-American Highway, which linked this community to San José, played a critical role in permitting these transformations. For more on the local cultural impacts of this roadway, see Carmen Kordick, "Constructing Costa Rica's Inter-American Highway and Building U.S. Empire: Social, Economic, and Political Change at the Local Level, 1941–1944," *Journal of Iberian and Latin American Studies* 23, no. 2 (Fall 2017).

13. For a detailed examination of how Tarrazú became interlinked with New Jersey through migration, see Carmen Kordick Rothe, "La memoria del viaje: Primeros emigrantes de Costa Rica a Nueva York y Nueva Yersey," in *Inmigración y emigración en Costa Rica*, ed. Carlos Sandoval García and Mónica Brenes (San José: Editorial de la Universidad de Costa Rica, 2007).

14. For more on the way that emigration has reshaped socioeconomic relationships in the Tarrazú Valley, see chapter 6.

Introduction

1. This Cerro is more commonly known as Death Mountain (el Cerro de la Muerte). Its popular name is well earned, as the peak's precipitous incline, thick fog, and freezing temperatures claimed countless travelers' lives in the years before the Inter-American Highway's construction. For more on the highway's construction, see Kordick, "Constructing Costa Rica's Inter-American Highway."

2. Tarrazú is the official denomination of the coffee grown in the present-day cantons of Tarrazú, León Cortés, and Dota. (A canton is an administrative division, most similar to a county in the United States.) The legally defined coffee region of Tarrazú reflects the canton of Tarrazú's political borders before 1924. In this book, Tarrazú refers to the denomination region and/or Tarrazú's political boundaries in 1923.

3. This project is part of a larger field of Central American rural histories that underscore the impact of coffee monoculture on socioeconomic relations. For instance, see Julie A. Charlip, *Cultivating Coffee: The Farmers of Carazo, Nicaragua, 1880–1930* (Athens: Ohio University Press, 2003); Elizabeth Dore, *Myths of Modernity: Peonage and Patriarchy in Nicaragua* (Durham, NC: Duke University Press, 2006); Aldo Lauria-Santiago, *An Agrarian Republic: Commercial Agriculture and the Politics of Peasant Communities in El Salvador, 1823–1914* (Pittsburgh: University of Pittsburgh Press, 1999). Also see David McCreery, "Debt Servitude in Rural Guatemala, 1876–1936," *Hispanic American Historical Review* 63, no. 4 (November 1983): 735–59; Mario Samper Kutschbach, *Producción cafetalera y poder político en Centroamérica* (San José: Colección Ruedo del Tiempo, 1998); and Robert G. Williams, *States and Social Evolution: Coffee and the Rise of National Governments in Central America* (Chapel Hill: University of North Carolina Press, 1994).

4. In 1832, Costa Rica inaugurated the isthmus's coffee revolution exporting thirty-two thousand kilograms of coffee. By the 1890s, twenty million kilograms left Costa Rican ports annually. For more on the nineteenth-century coffee boom, see Gudmundson, *Costa Rica before Coffee*, 3.

5. The nation's Central Valley is the location not only of the nation's capital of

San José but also the provincial capitals of Alajuela, Cartago, and Heredia. Since the sixteenth-century colonial era, this forty-five-by-thirteen-mile region has been the heart of Costa Rican cultural, social, political, and economic life. Williams, *States and Social Evolution*, 44.

6. Although studies on the Central Valley have long dominated the field of Costa Rican studies, there is also a sizeable body of scholarship on the English-speaking enclave built around United Fruit Company's primary Costa Rican port, Puerto Limón. For more on this historiographical division, see Carmen Kordick, "Tarrazú: Coffee, Migration, and Nation Building in Rural Costa Rica, 1824–2008," PhD dissertation, Yale University, 2012, 4–15.

7. Programa Estado de la Nación, "Estadísticas," accessed May 6, 2012, www.estadonacion.or.cr.

8. Critiques of the Central Valley focus of Costa Rican studies emerged in the 1990s; see Alexander Jiménez, Giovanna Giglioli and Jesús Oyamburu, *Costa Rica imaginaria* (Heredia, Costa Rica: Editorial Fundación Universidad Nacional, 1998).

9. In the twentieth century, tensions arose between producers and coffee mill owners over the price mills paid farmers for their unprocessed coffee. In the Central Valley, pressures were relieved by producers' abilities to easily access multiple mills to secure better prices. In Tarrazú, however, by the 1930s, the region's mills were all owned by one man. More to the point, Lowell Gudmundson found that in the Central Valley medium-sized landholders fared much better than both their neighbors with smaller and much larger holdings. In fact, Gudmundson suggests that in the 1920s and 1930s a strong capitalist-centered rural middle class emerged in Costa Rica's Central Valley. Lowell Gudmundson, "Peasant, Farmer, Proletarian: Class Formation in a Smallholder Coffee Economy, 1850–1950," in *Coffee, Society, and Power in Latin America*, ed. Roseberry, Gudmundson, and Samper Kutschbach, 112–50.

10. Fabrice E. Lehoucq and Iván Molina, *Urnas de lo inesperado: Fraude electoral y lucha política en Costa Rica* (San José: Editorial de la Universidad de Costa Rica, 1999); Lehoucq and Molina, *Stuffing the Ballot Box: Fraud, Electoral Reform, and Democratization in Costa Rica* (Cambridge: Cambridge University Press, 2006).

11. Mercedes Muñoz Guillén, *El estado y la abolición del ejercito, 1914–1949* (San José: Editorial Porvenir, 1990).

12. Kirk Bowman, *Militarization, Democracy, and Development: The Perils of Praetorianism in Latin America* (University Park: Pennsylvania State University Press, 2002).

13. Mitchell A. Seligson, "Costa Rican Exceptionalism: Why the 'Ticos' Are Different," in *Citizen Views of Democracy in Latin America*, ed. Roderic Ai Camp, (Pittsburgh: University of Pittsburgh Press, 2001), 106.

14. In 2004 former Costa Rican presidents Miguel Ángel Rodríguez, Rafael Ángel Calderón (both members of the nation's traditionally second-largest party, the Partido Unidad Social Cristiana—PUSC), and José María Figueres (of the dominant Partido Liberación Nacional—PLN) were accused of corrupt business dealings with the French telephone giant Alcatel. For more on this scandal, see Giannina Segnini, Mauricio Herrera, and Ernesto Rivera, "Exdirectivo del ICE declaró ante fiscalía Rodríguez exigió 60 percent del 'premio,'" *La Nación*, October 1, 2004, accessed May 15, 2012, www.nacion.com/Generales/Subsitios/Sucesos/2010/ICEALCATEL.aspx.

15. John A. Booth, Christine J. Wade, and Thomas W. Walker, *Understanding*

Central America: Global Forces, Rebellion, and Change, 5th ed. (Boulder, CO: Westview Press, 2009), 25.

16. Booth, Wade, and Walker, 25.

17. Booth, Wade, and Walker, 25.

18. Booth, Wade, and Walker, 62. The first (of many) US-based scholarly works that promoted Costa Rican exceptionalism was James Busey's classic work on Costa Rica's democracy, *Notes on Costa Rican Democracy* (Boulder: University of Colorado Press, 1962).

19. US Department of State, Bureau of Western Hemisphere Affairs, "Background Notes: Costa Rica," accessed April 9, 2012, www.state.gov/r/pa/ei/bgn/2019.html.

20. US Department of State.

21. Carla Victoria Jara Murillo, *Corpus Digital de Mensajes Presidenciales de Costa Rica* (San José: Universidad de Costa Rica, 2012), accessed May 28, 2012, https://sites.google.com/site/mensajepresidencialcr/home.

22. Jara Murillo.

23. Most notable on this account is Gen. José Tinoco Granados, who in 1917, alongside his brother, José Joaquín, orchestrated a successful military coup. The Tinoco brothers' two-year hold on power (which came to an end in 1919 after they failed to win US recognition) exposes the shallowness of Chinchilla's claims that by the nineteenth century Costa Ricans were committed to peace and democracy. For more on the coup, see Thomas M. Leonard, *Central America and the United States: The Search for Stability* (Athens: University of Georgia Press, 1991), 73–75.

24. With two exceptions, I interviewed all participants on just one occasion. I interviewed two particularly helpful informants, however, on three separate occasions. In one interview session, I spoke with two individuals, a married couple. Otherwise all interviews took place with only me and a single interviewee present.

25. Surveys and pens were placed on dining tables and the wait staff agreed to both invite diners to fill out the surveys and to collect completed surveys, which they placed in a manila envelope. For more on the surveys, see Kordick, "Tarrazú," appendix 1.

26. While more conversations with indigenous Ngöbe-Buglé laborers might have enriched this project, language issues limited these interviews. Both Ngöbe-Buglé informants were selected not only for their willingness to speak with me, but also for their Spanish-speaking skills. The sample size is too small to meaningfully represent the diverse experiences of the region's sizable immigrant labor community, but their interviews do provide a powerful image into the experiences of many Ngöbe-Buglé in Tarrazú. Particularly insightful was my conversation with Mirna Rodríguez Palacios who has lived year-round in Tarrazú with her husband and children for several years and has become a local activist who has used her Spanish language skills to advocate for Ngöbe-Buglé workers in the region.

27. As the book's focus is on Tarrazú's historical development, whenever possible I make a distinction between Tarrazúceños and the larger Costa Rican community.

28. Before each interview began I provided all interviewees with a form that included my contact information (telephone numbers both in Costa Rica and in the United States and my email address). The form explained the topics that I intended to discuss during the interview (their family's economic activities; changes they had witnessed over the years culturally, socially, politically, and economically;

key life events including marriages, births, and deaths; and the impact of emigration and immigration on the region in recent years) and that I wished to interview them to help me learn about the region's historical development for an eventual book I wished to write. The form also explained that if they had any questions about our conversation, any questions about how I would utilize any aspect of what we discussed, or if they wanted to retract anything they had said, or request a pseudonym, at any point after we had finished speaking, they simply needed to contact me with these wishes. I also read the form to them before beginning the formal interview. I did not ask interviewees to sign the form or any formal consent forms because of functional literacy levels in the community. While only one of my interviewees related that he was illiterate, most of the older men and women I spoke with had quite limited literacy and were distrustful of any requests made for a signature.

29. Given the potential risks to undocumented immigrants, I strongly encouraged all immigrants in the United States to not share their surnames with me and to either provide me with a pseudonym or permit me to create one for them. In all cases, undocumented immigrants assented.

30. In all interviews where issues of sexual or domestic abuse came up, I asked the interviewee at the end of our conversation if I could use a pseudonym. In all cases where sexual violence came up and in many cases where domestic violence was discussed, interviewees agreed with my suggestion.

31. In all cases where I followed up my interviews with a secondary visit to clarify questions that arose while transcribing our conversation, I began by explaining the reason for my visit—to clarify a point/question that I had from the day before. I then reminded the interviewee of their rights to not answer questions, to retract any ideas or recollections shared, to discontinue the conversation at any moment, and to request that I provide him or her with a pseudonym, before asking whether I could pose my follow up question(s). After clarifying any questions I had, I reminded the interviewees that they could contact me at any point with any questions and concerns or if they wanted to retract any portion of what we discussed.

32. For more on recent media coverage of Tarrazú, see Kordick, "Tarrazú."

Chapter 1

1. During the colonial period, Costa Rica (alongside present-day Honduras, El Salvador and Nicaragua) was a province of the Captaincy General of Guatemala under the jurisdiction of the Viceroyalty of New Spain.

2. Archivos Nacionales de Costa Rica (hereinafter cited ANCR), JUCA, no. 2703 (1825).

3. My account of this episode is based on the following oral history accounts: Quintín "Kinto" Araya Navarro, interview by author, March 18, 2008, San Pablo de León Cortés; Vela Mina Flores, interview by author, April 21, 2008, San Pablo de León Cortés; Antonio Umaña Mora, interview by author, April 8, 2008, San Lorenzo de Tarrazú.

4. ANCR, JUCA, no. 2703 (1825).

5. Mario Samper's *Generations of Settlers* is an excellent statistically driven examination of the settling of the northwestern fringes of the Central Valley in the decades after independence. Samper's analysis suggests that the Cascante family's move was part of a larger out-migration from populated Central Valley communi-

ties. Rural families initiated this migration in the hopes of securing landholdings to participate in rural capitalism as independent farmers. Mario Samper, *Generations of Settlers: Rural Households and Markets on the Costa Rican Frontier, 1850–1935* (Boulder, CO: Westview Press, 1990). Long before Samper's work was completed, the British geographer Carolyn Hall first articulated the idea that the dream of securing coffee profits in the nineteenth century, following independence, drove emigration from the populated Central Valley to new areas of the republic. Carolyn Hall, *El Café y el desarrollo histórico-geográfico de Costa Rica* (San José: Editorial Costa Rica y Universidad Nacional, 1976), 9–15.

6. A number of scholars have considered how the relationship between government policies, existent labor conditions, and available lands for coffee shaped labor and land tenure during the coffee boom of the nineteenth century. An excellent comparative analysis of the isthmus is Williams, *States and Social Evolution*.

7. My description of the Cascante family's homesteading site and the labor of women homesteaders is based on the following oral histories: Juan Chanto Méndez, interview by the author, April 15, 2008, San Marcos de Tarrazú; Lourdes Gamboa, interview by the author, April 22, 2008, Carrizal de León Cortés; Fany Jiménez Solís, interview by the author, September 14, 2008, San Marcos de Tarrazú; Luz Berta Monge Umaña, interview by the author, February 14, 2008, San Marcos de Tarrazú; and Flora Villa, interview by the author, April 21, 2008, San Pablo de León Cortés; Villa's name is changed at the request of the interviewee to maintain her privacy.

8. Because the Cascante family had no neighbors until the late 1850s, for decades they were fully responsible for producing all of the foodstuffs that they consumed at their remote homestead. Additionally, despite their personal labors on the road that linked their farmed lands to the Central Valley, the road's rudimentary quality coupled with the distance of their home from the capital likely limited their ability to produce goods for sale in Central Valley markets. Almost all agrarian labors were therefore likely centered simply on feeding the familial unit with little interest in surplus production for sale on the market. This does not mean, however, that they rejected agrarian capitalism. In fact, the Cascante family appears to have raised a considerable number of cattle, which likely were transported for sale in San José markets. This is consistent with similar patterns of agrarian expansion in the nineteenth century. In fact, families who relocated to Alajuela from San José in the mid-nineteenth century produced basic grains and raised cattle, in much the same fashion as in Tarrazú, before the local infrastructure for coffee processing and reliable roads were constructed, allowing for the transport of processed coffee and sugar to San José markets. For more on the role that farmers' active participation in agrarian capitalism played in emigration, see Samper, *Generations of Settlers*, 11.

9. Costa Rica. Leyes y decretos. "Decreto XXIV," November 29, 1824.

10. Policy makers and agrarian elites' decision to encourage ambitious families to settle the nation's unpopulated areas and expand the agrarian frontier in the nineteenth century created a pattern that continued well into the twentieth century. The nation's persistent agrarian frontier limited class-centered tensions over access to land. Instead, agrarian struggles historically centered on access to credit and the prices mills paid for unprocessed coffee. For more on this, see Samper, *Generations of Settlers*, 3–16.

11. ANCR, JUCA, no. 2703.

12. For more on legislation designed to keep colonial subjects within particular

geographical areas, see José Antonio Salas, *Liberalismo y legislación agraria: Apuntes introductorias para el estudio de la colonización agrícola en Costa Rica*, vol. 8 of *Cuadernos de Historia* (Heredia, Costa Rica: Escuela de Historia, Universidad Nacional, 1983), 6. To ensure the letter of the law was followed, between 1755 and 1777, colonial authorities repeatedly sent troops to round up families living outside of designated communities, destroying their homesteads, and forcing them to relocate to sanctioned colonial communities. For more on these actions, see Florencia Quesada Avendaño, *La modernización entre cafetales* (San José: Editorial Universidad de Costa Rica, 2011), 4–7.

13. Eugenia Rodríguez Sáenz, *Hijas, novias y esposas: Familia, matrimonio y violencia domestica en el Valle Central de Costa Rica, 1750–1850* (Heredia, Costa Rica: Editorial Universidad Nacional, 2000), 12.

14. Colonial mercantilist policies provided Costa Rica with a monopoly on tobacco production within the Central American isthmus; however, these policies also banned Costa Rican farmers from producing cochineal and indigo. These dyes brought handsome profits to large farm owners in the rest of Central America. Williams, *States and Social Evolution*, 22–26.

15. Salas, *Liberalismo y legislación agraria*, 6.

16. While Casilda and José Miguel shared a surname, they likely had at least four degrees of separation between them, since no record of a dispensation from the Catholic Church exists. Their shared surname, however, does suggest that they were unlikely to be elites. During the early 1800s nonelites tended to marry within their community, which significantly increased the chance of marrying someone with a shared surname. For more information on colonial class relations and marriage, see Rodríguez Sáenz, *Hijas, novias y esposas*, 62–79.

17. ANCR, JUCA, no. 2703. In this land request, Cascante makes note of "*un Sitio de Ganado mayor,*" or "a site with large quantities of cattle."

18. In Costa Rica's first schools, which were under the auspices of the Catholic Church, priests taught multiaged young boys basic reading, writing, and arithmetic as well as religion. For more on these late colonial institutions, see Iván Molina-Jiménez, *La educación en Costa Rica de la época colonial al presente* (San José: Editoriales Universitarias Públicas Costarricenses; San José: Consejo Nacional de Rectores y Programa Estado de la Nación, 2016).

19. Others besides the Cascantes decided to live without legal sanction in unpopulated portions of the young republic in this period. Carolyn Hall found that in the 1820s and 1830s a considerable number of squatters established farms without making any move to legalize their holdings. Carolyn Hall, *Costa Rica: A Geographical Interpretation in Historical Perspective* (Boulder, CO: Westview Press, 1985), 110–11.

20. Costa Rica. Leyes y decretos. "Decreto XXVI," October 6, 1840.

21. ANCR, Juzgado de lo Contencioso Administrativo, no. 2731 (1848).

22. ANCR, Juzgado de lo Contencioso, no. 2731.

23. ANCR, Juzgado de lo Contencioso, no. 2731.

24. Carlos Meléndez, *Historia de Costa Rica* (San José: Editorial Universidad Estatal a Distancia, 1979), 97.

25. Costa Rican elites were the first in Central America to experiment with growing coffee commercially. Colonial Spanish policies limited coffee production to Venezuela, Cuba, and Puerto Rico. These same policies had restricted Costa Rica's elite from growing indigo and cochineal dyes (which had brought elites in the rest

of the isthmus great fortune). Seeking new opportunities after independence and realizing that the rest of Central America was far ahead in the natural dye industry, Costa Rican elites made a sizable commitment to coffee. Coffee was not only a labor-intensive crop, requiring five times the labor needed to grow beans and two times the labor needed to raise cotton and sugarcane, it also required between three and five years of care before plants would produce a harvest. Given the high start-up costs, coffee was initially planted by only a few of Costa Rica's wealthiest landowners. Once the profits of this crop were known, however, coffee bushes were planted throughout the Central Valley by both large- and small-scale farm owners. Williams, *States and Social Evolution*, 22–25 and 105–6.

26. This small first shipment had no European market and the Costa Rican–German exporter Jorge Stiepel was forced to place it in storage for several months before he secured European purchasers, reducing the beans' quality. Once markets were established, however, Costa Rican coffee came to be renowned in Europe, particularly in Germany and Great Britain, for its high quality. Hall, *El Café*, 38.

27. Gudmundson, *Costa Rica before Coffee*, 3.

28. Between the 1840s and the 1890s, coffee became Costa Rica's principal export and this small Central American republic was the first in Latin America to embrace a nearly monocultural coffee-centered export economy. Brazil, Colombia, and the rest of Central America established their coffee export sectors in the second half of the nineteenth century. Coffee's economic dominance drove San José policy makers to sign a series of trade agreements with Great Britain in the early 1840s to ensure a solid market for this critical crop. Hall, *El Café*, 40–41. Near-complete monocultural production of cash crops, like coffee in the Costa Rican context, was only possible with modern global transportation networks, which allowed for the importation of foodstuffs into rural regions that were not producing food. For more on the development of coffee monoculture in the modern period on a global scale, see Mario Samper Kutschbach, "The Historical Construction of Quality and Competitiveness: A Preliminary Discussion of Coffee Commodity Chains," in *The Global Coffee Economy in Africa, Asia, and Latin America, 1500–1989*, ed. William Gervase Clarence-Smith and Steven Topik (Cambridge: Cambridge University Press, 2003), 122.

29. Rodríguez Sáenz, *Hijas, novias y esposas*, 73. British merchants dominated Costa Rica's coffee economy; as late as 1910, 84 percent of the nation's crops were sold to British merchants, many based in Costa Rica. Williams, *States and Social Evolution*, 157.

30. Hall, *El Café*, 39–44.

31. Costa Rica's laws that encouraged squatters to colonize outlying areas coupled with the nation's relatively small population, just 182,000 inhabitants in 1883, meant that labor costs were among the highest in the isthmus and landownership was relatively widespread. Elites did not seek to strip peasants of their lands or ability to acquire new lands, to amplify their own landholdings and secure a large dependent labor-force, as their counterparts chose to do in El Salvador, Guatemala, and Nicaragua, but instead adapted to this situation by dominating the coffee mills, the export markets, and credit resources available to peasant smallholders. Mill owners/elites sought to keep prices paid for unprocessed coffee low, ensuring themselves the greatest profits. This choice not only made the transition to coffee monoculturalism less trying in Costa Rica than elsewhere in the isthmus but ensured greater stability for

elites, who could spread the risks of low prices on the international coffee market to their smallholder sellers. Williams, *States and Social Evolution*, 108–11.

32. This is best expressed in the idealized portraits of Costa Rica's first coffee baron presidents Juan Rafael Mora (1849–59) and José María Montealegre (1859–63), on display today at the National Theater in San José. Both men have whitened complexions. While there are no photographs to compare the likeness of these portraits to the men portrayed, Gudmundson's research highlights how the pair's opponents scorned them for their "obviously mixed racial background," suggesting that the portraits do not reflect their features. Gudmundson, *Costa Rica before Coffee*, 86, and Rodríguez Sáenz, *Hijas, novias y esposas*, 5.

33. Florencia Quesada Avendaño, *En el barrio Amón: Arquitectura, familia y sociabilidad del primer residencial de la elite urbana de San José, 1900–1935* (San José: Editorial de la Universidad de Costa Rica, 2001), 41–42.

34. Gudmundson, *Costa Rica before Coffee*, 87.

35. Quesada Avendaño, *En el barrio Amón*, 41–42.

36. Brunilda Hilje Quirós, *Nuestra Historia: La Colonización agrícola de Costa Rica, 1840–1940* (San José: Editorial de la Universidad Estatal a Distancia, 1997), 9.

37. Before Gudmundson's groundbreaking work on the development of a coffee society, historians such as Rodrigo Facio, Eugenio Rodríguez Vega, and Carlos Monge Álfaro contended that Central Valley coffee production initiated land concentration in the hands of elites for the first time, which—when coupled with extreme population growth—forced peasants to seek out new lands in the hinterlands. Gudmundson has refuted this argument by pointing out that during the colonial period and in the years preceding coffee production, firm class hierarchies already defined Costa Rican society. Additionally, his examination of census and baptismal records demonstrates that population growth did not proceed but rather followed migration out of the Central Valley. Gudmundson, *Costa Rica before Coffee*, 85–87.

38. Rodrigo Facio, *Estudio sobre economía costarricense* (San José: Editorial Costa Rica, 1975); Carlos Monge Álfaro, *Historia de Costa Rica* (San José: Libreria Trejos, 1979); Eugenio Rodríguez Vega, *Apuntes para una sociología costarricense* (San José: Editorial Universidad Estatal a Distancia, 1979).

39. Historically, coffee permitted some peasant smallholders to acquire great fortunes for themselves and their families. For instance, in 1896, Florentino Castro inherited a five-acre coffee farm and sold his services to wealthier neighbors transporting coffee to the Pacific port city of Puntarenas. By 1907, at the age of thirty, he had managed to purchase numerous coffee farms and even a coffee mill in the outskirts of San José. By 1930, Castro was known as the Coffee King and owned the nation's largest export house. Williams, *States and Social Evolution*, 162.

40. Gudmundson, *Costa Rica before Coffee*, 131.

41. Javier Agüero García, "En busca de nuevas tierras: La colonización de una zona de frontera agrícola en el Valle de los Santos, 1870–1927," master's thesis, Universidad de Costa Rica, 2002, 79.

42. Juan Bautista Chanto Méndez, *Cooperativa de caficultores y servicios múltiples de Tarrazú R.L. veinte años de fundación 1960–1980* (San Marcos de Tarrazú, Costa Rica: Coopetarrazú R.L., 1980), folio 3.

43. Marcos Chanto Méndez, *Tarrazú en su centenario: 1868–1968* (San José: Imprenta Lehmann, 1968), 6.

44. M. Chanto Méndez, *Tarrazú en su centenario*, 6. See also Emigidio Ureña

and Pedro Pérez Zeledón, "Monografía de Santa María de Dota," *Revista de los Archivos Nacionales*, 5 (January 1941): 70.

45. J. Chanto Méndez, *Cooperativa de caficultores*, 8.

46. My research did not seek to prove this assumption, but the popularity of these surnames in the region today supports this assertion.

47. M. Chanto Méndez, *Tarrazú en su centenario*, 13. See also, Ureña and Pérez Zeledón, "Monografía de Santa María de Dota," 73.

48. ANCR, Congreso, no. 8723 (1881).

49. ANCR, Congreso, no. 3014 (1905).

50. Milling and transporting wood for sale in San José appears to have been a particularly lucrative economic activity for the region's earliest settlers. However, most of the earliest migrants dedicated their labors to growing basic foodstuffs, such as corn and beans, for familial consumption and transporting for sale their excess grain production to San José markets. As late as 1913, the production of sawed wood and foodstuffs sold in San José were the principal sources of capital for regional families. For more on this, see Agüero García, "En busca de nuevas tierras," 90–93.

51. For more on how coffee served to make San José and the rest of the Central Valley more rural during the nineteenth century, see Gudmundson, *Costa Rica before Coffee*, 182–85, and Quesada Avendaño, *La Modernización entre cafetales*, 23.

52. Agüero García, "En busca de nuevas tierras," 82–83.

53. When the migration to the valley of El General began, this area was part of the canton of Tarrazú. Perez Zeledón became an independent canton in 1931.

54. ANCR, Juzgado Primero del Crimen, no. 4521 (1895).

55. ANCR, Juzgado Primero del Crimen, no. 4521.

56. M. Chanto Méndez, *Tarrazú en su centenario*, 6.

57. The remains of these divisions are present in an early local history that lists seventeen common surnames in the area from Desamparados and eighteen from Guadalupe, while making no mention of surnames from other Central Valley communities. M. Chanto Méndez, *Tarrazú en su centenario*, 6.

58. Carlos Mora Barrantes, *Cantón de Tarrazú en su centenario: Colección de documentos para una monografía: 1868 a 1968* (San Marcos de Tarrazú, Costa Rica: Municipalidad de Tarrazú, 1968), 97. Mora Barrantes cites Municipal Accord 75, September 9, 1882, which established the post of jefe político. Before 1882 Tarrazú was assigned a justice of the peace from Desamparados, the San José canton to which the region belonged before 1868. According to Juan Chanto, this post was the highest level of regional authority, as the jefe político was charged with communicating the needs of the people of the canton to the government authorities in San José. Juan Chanto Méndez, interview.

59. M. Chanto Méndez, *Tarrazú en su centenario*, 17.

60. The couple's 1856 will called for all assets, after funeral expenses, to be divided equally among their six children (José Mercedes, Juan de Dios, Domingo Miguel, Juan de Jesús, Juan María, and Juana Josefa.) These two brothers, however, appear to have bought out their siblings' interests in the region. See ANCR, San José Juzgado Civil, 1775 (1856).

61. M. Chanto Méndez, *Tarrazú en su centenario*, 6. The Cascante family also sold land to Graciano Solís, Loreto Carranza, Rafael Vargas, Luís Ortiz Fallas, and Juana Retana in the center of San Marcos.

62. Ureña and Pérez Zeledón, "Monografía de Santa María de Dota," 71.

63. Blanca Piedra Blanco, *Historias y Añoranzas de San Pablo de Tarrazú* (San José: Editorial de la Universidad de Costa Rica, 1997), 21.

64. ANCR, Ministerio de Educación Publica, no. 8568 (1891).

65. ANCR, Estadísticas y Censo, no. 914 (1905).

66. Estadistica y Censo, no. 914. The most prevalent crop, however, was corn, which was harvested on a reported 1,081.5 acres in the region.

67. Gudmundson, *Costa Rica before Coffee*, 131.

68. Wet-method coffee mills were extremely costly to construct and run. Considerable capital was needed to purchase machinery and build the facilities for coffee processing. Additionally, *beneficio* owners needed capital to pay the wages of their sizable labor force. Williams, *States and Social Evolution*, 149.

69. A manzana is defined as ten thousand *varas* squared. However, as a vara is an imprecise Spanish colonial measurement that can vary, this measurement is inexact. A good approximation, however, is that one manzana is equivalent to 0.7 hectares or 1.75 acres. For more information, see Jorge Maier, *Antigüedades Siglo XVI al XX* (Madrid: Catálogo del Gabinete de Antigüedades de la Real Academia de la Historia, 2005), 50.

70. Coffee bushes generally require between three and five years before they begin producing fruit. Coffee bushes were thus necessarily planted at least three years before any coffee sales appear on tax or other municipal records. Williams, *States and Social Evolution*, 41.

71. J. Chanto Méndez, *Cooperativa de caficultores*, 2.

72. Juan Bosco Umaña Abarca, *Historia de Tarrazú* (San José: Editorial Nuestra Tierra, 2005), 26–27.

73. ANCR, Estadísticas y Censo, no. 914 (1905).

74. Mill owners processed their own coffee, but they rarely produced sufficient coffee to justify the costs of establishing and running a coffee mill, which means that the region's four owners were confident that their neighbors were growing and would continue to grow enough coffee to justify their investments. The dependency between mills and producers is nicely articulated in Sick, *Farmers of the Golden Bean*, 25–26.

75. Gudmundson, *Costa Rica before Coffee*, 3.

Chapter 2

1. This narrative was part of a larger essay that this Tarrazú native submitted in 1946 as her *bachiller* thesis to secure a degree in pedagogy from the University of Costa Rica. See Umaña Abarca, *Historia de Tarrazú*, 77.

2. Gabriela Monge Álvarado, "Monografía de San Marcos de Tarrazú," bachiller thesis, Universidad de Costa Rica, 1946, 42.

3. Although Monge does not directly accuse Umaña of illegal business practices, he was clearly acting unlawfully, given that Costa Rica's 1943 Labor Code outlawed the use of scrip. For more on the 1943 Labor Code, see Allan Arburola Valverde, *Código de Trabajo: Ley no. 2 del 26 de agosto de 1943* (San José: Litografía e Imprenta L.I.L., 2004), 61–62.

4. Monge, "Monografía de San Marcos," 43.

5. Costa Rica's rural egalitarian myth dates back to Rodrigo Facio's 1942 article series "Estudio Sobre la Economía Costarricense," which was published in the magazine *Surco*. Facio was an outspoken backer of both Costa Rica's 1948 Civil War and increased state intervention in the nation's coffee sector. He argued that the nation's smallholding coffee class was threatened by the exploitative policies of coffee mill owners and lenders (such as Umaña Jiménez in Tarrazú). Facio essentially blamed coffee for creating socioeconomic cleavages. For more on Facio, see Eugenio Rodríguez Vega, *Rodrigo Facio: ¿Quién fue y qué hizo?* (San José: Editorial Universidad Estatal a Distancia, 2006).

6. Central Americanists frequently used Costa Rica (with its sizable smallholding coffee class) as a foil to highlight inequalities in other nations. One recent instance is Lauria-Santiago, *Agrarian Republic*. At the same time, although coffee was principally produced on large monocultural plantations that relied on indebted peons in most of the rest of Central America, in all of the isthmus's republics, scholars have found regions where smallholders persisted. For a good summary of this scholarship and its implications for broader understandings of isthmian coffee development, see Lowell Gudmundson, "On Paths Not Taken: Commercial Capital and Coffee Production in Costa Rica," in Clarence-Smith and Topik, *Global Coffee Economy*, 335.

7. Tensions between mill owners and smallholders became a visible national problem by the 1930s, when the nation's coffee frontier closed. As the possibility of expanding profits through increasing landholdings was eliminated, farmers organized and placed pressure on the state to establish profitable coffee prices. For more on this, see William Roseberry, introduction to *Coffee, Society, and Power in Latin America*, ed. Roseberry, Gudmundson, and Samper Kutschbach (Baltimore, MD: Johns Hopkins University Press, 1995).

8. Recent regional studies by Central American scholars have highlighted rural power relations. For power relations in the Nicaraguan countryside during the coffee boom, see Dore, *Myths of Modernity*, and Charlip, *Cultivating Coffee*. For the case of Guatemala, see Greg Grandin, *The Blood of Guatemala: A History of Race and Nation* (Durham, NC: Duke University Press, 2000).

9. Before coffee, most local farmers grew corn, sugarcane, beans, and other foodstuffs. The production of these foodstuffs provided farmers with food and a meager income source throughout the year, since these crops produced several harvests annually. For more on this, see chapter 1.

10. By 1844, when coffee farming was still young, initially Costa Rican farmers sought to sell their beans in Europe's high-end markets that exclusively purchased wet-method processed beans. This decision was sparked by the high profits secured by Buenaventura Espinach Gaul after he opened a wet-method processing plant and the later successes of other processors who embraced wet-method processing, namely Benito Dengo, who built the second wet-method processing facility near the town of San Joaquin de Flores in 1844. In the years ahead, Costa Rican exporters could expect to receive a 10 percent premium for their wet-processed beans. For more on the early embrace of wet processing, see Hall, *El Café*, 49–50. For more on the financial benefits of wet processing and also the costs of establishing these mills, see Williams, *States and Social Evolution*, 149. Other processing methods were available, and most Latin American coffee producers would adopt a less technically dependent dry-processing method. The relationships Costa Rica's first coffee producers established with high-end merchant houses in Europe and through the wet-

processing mills they built meant that Costa Rican elites, who inaugurated the nation's coffee revolution, arguably forced smallholders to rely on wealthier neighbors with wet-processing mills to purchase their unprocessed crops. This varies dramatically from Brazil and other dry-process dominated republics where smallholders could dry-process their own coffee, expanding their potential purchasers but also arguably reducing the price received per kilo of coffee. For more on the impact of processing methods on the socioeconomic structures of coffee production at the national and regional level, see Roseberry, "Introduction," *Coffee, Society, and Power in Latin America*, 22–23.

11. During the final decade of the nineteenth century, rural elites in El Salvador similarly dominated coffee processing and exports and were the principal source of capital in the countryside. Lauria-Santiago, *Agrarian Republic*, 136–37.

12. In Costa Rica, which in the 1840s became the first country where independent smallholders began coffee cultivation on a massive scale in the Americas, elites quickly came to dominate both the processing of the picked fruit into exportable green coffee beans and the export of this commodity. One of the principal reasons that Costa Rican elites arguably never sought to dominate landownership was the nation's labor shortages and large amounts of uncultivated arable lands, which made labor expensive. Benoit Daviron and Stefano Ponte, *The Coffee Paradox: Global Markets, Commodity Trade, and the Elusive Promise of Development* (London: Zed Books, 2005), 66–67.

13. The Umaña family, who have Umaña Jiménez's accounting books, did not allow me access to these books; however, Tobías Umaña Jiménez's great-grandson, Juan Bosco Umaña Abarca, shared a copy of his notes from a ledger he was leant years ago by Umaña's grandson, Helber Umaña. This section's analysis is based on the information that Umaña Abarca generously provided.

14. In 1948, the Costa Rican *colón* was ₡6.20 to the US dollar. For more on the colón's historic value, see Theodore S. Creedman, *Historical Dictionary of Costa Rica* (Metuchen, NJ: Scarecrow Press, 1991), 96.

15. Agüero García, "En busca de nuevas tierras," 168–69.

16. Agüero García, 174.

17. While most of Central America's coffee was produced on large farms, smallholding coffee growers farmed in the whole isthmus, but they were simply a minority. In sum, Costa Rica had the largest smallholding class of the region. For more on small-scale coffee production in Nicaragua, see Charlip, *Cultivating Coffee*. In the case of El Salvador, see Lauria-Santiago, *Agrarian Republic*.

18. M. Chanto Méndez, *Tarrazú en su centenario*, 11.

19. M. Chanto Méndez, 11. Umaña Abarca, *Historia de Tarrazú*, 28.

20. Umaña Abarca, *Historia de Tarrazú*, 25, 28, 40. Before reaching such prestigious positions, Umaña Jiménez served as municipal treasurer from 1897 to 1904 and the Church Building Commission's speaker in 1899.

21. Fany Jiménez Solís, interview, September 14, 2008.

22. Agüero García, "En busca de nuevas tierras,"156.

23. Agüero García. The present-day canton of Dota split from Tarrazú in 1925. This political division did not impact social, familial, and economic links between these two communities. See Adelia Ureña Elizondo de Fallas, *Reseña Histórica del Cantón de Dota* (San José: Ediciones Serrano Elizondo, 1992), 14.

24. Agüero García, "En busca de nuevas tierras," 156.

25. Agüero García, 166.

26. Agüero García, 156.

27. Víctor Hugo Acuña Ortega, "Clases sociales y conflictos en la economía cafetalera costarricense: Productores contra beneficiadores: 1932–36," *Revista de Historia*, número especial simposio: *Historia, problemas y perspectiva agraria en Costa Rica (1985)*, 189.

28. Acuña Ortega, 186.

29. "Liquidaciones del Café," *El Diario de Costa Rica*, March 29, 1928, 7. The cost of transporting coffee to the capital reduced profits for local mill owners who took their coffee for sale in San José. The cost was passed down to producers who sold their beans to local mills. Additionally, as Lowell Gudmundson has documented, since the 1960s coffee experts have recognized that Tarrazú's altitude, climate, and soil produce Costa Rica's highest-quality coffee beans. Before this decade, however, the region's beans were considered inferior to Central Valley coffee. Indeed, San José–based export houses paid less for all coffee produced outside of the Central Valley, which they believed was intrinsically inferior. Central Valley elitism meant that for decades the producers of the nation's best coffee earned much less for their crops than producers of inferior-quality beans. For more on this, see Gudmundson "On Paths Not Taken," 356–57.

30. "Liquidaciones del Café," 7.

31. Dirección General de Estadística de la República de Costa Rica, *Anuario Estadístico Año 1929* (San José, Costa Rica: Imprenta Nacional, 1930), *Anuario Estadístico Año 1931*, (San José, Costa Rica: Imprenta Nacional, 1932). According to these governmental sources, Costa Rica's annual exports in 1929 totaled ₡72,791,640; in 1931 exports totaled ₡57,116,888.

32. Costa Rica's dependence on coffee (and banana) exports was far from unique. In fact, Cuba's economy was almost entirely based on sugar production. For a brief discussion of single-crop agro-export economies in Latin America, see Bradford Burns and Julie Charlip, *Latin America: An Interpretive History*, 8th ed. (Upper Saddle River, NJ: Prentice Hall, 2002), 226–36.

33. Acuña Ortega, "Clases sociales y conflictos," 190. In indexed numbers, Acuña notes a ninety-point decrease from 1928 to 1936.

34. In 1931, Costa Rican exports were valued at ₡57,116,888. Of this 70.84 percent (₡40,462,562) were coffee exports, and bananas made up 22.23 percent of exports (₡12,699,860). Together, coffee and bananas accounted for 93 percent of export revenues. Dirección General de Estadística, *Anuario Estadístico Año 1931*.

35. Iván Molina and Steven Palmer, *The History of Costa Rica* (San José: Editorial de la Universidad de Costa Rica, 2004), 86.

36. Iván Molina Jiménez, *Anticomunismo reformista* (San José: Editorial Costa Rica, 2007), 106. In response to declining markets for bananas, the US-owned United Fruit Company reduced the price they paid for harvested bananas, despite contracts with farmers. In response, growers reduced banana workers' wages. Under these conditions, Costa Rican Communists organized workers in the Atlantic coast banana strike of 1934, which constituted an unprecedented success both for the concessions workers and banana farmers managed to extract and for the absence of fatalities. For more on Costa Rica's 1934 strike, see Aviva Chomsky, *West Indian Workers and the United Fruit Company in Costa Rica, 1870–1940* (Baton Rouge: Louisiana State University Press, 1996).

37. Molina and Palmer, *History of Costa Rica*, 85–86.

38. Molina and Palmer, 87–96. Costa Rica's laissez-faire economic policies and its embrace of foreign capital investment, namely in the form of US-owned banana companies, mirrored similar relationships throughout Latin America. For more on the impact of bananas on Central American politics, see Héctor Pérez Brignoli, *Breve historia de Centroamerica* (Madrid: Alianza Editorial, 1985).

39. Costa Rica and other countries adopted economic interventionist policies in the wake of the Great Depression. Populist leaders committed to reducing poverty and decreasing the power of foreign companies were elected throughout the region in the 1930s and 1940s. A key example is Mexico's President Lázaro Cárdenas, who nationalized the nation's foreign-owned petroleum industry in 1937, after a heated labor dispute. For more on Cárdenas, see Enrique Krauze, *Mexico, Biography of Power: A History of Modern Mexico, 1816–1996* (New York: Harper Perennial, 1998), 438–80. Also see Adolf Gilly, *El cardenismo. Una utopía Mexicana* (Mexico City: Ediciones Era, 2001).

40. Acuña Ortega, "Clases sociales y conflictos," 188. The Institute for the Defense of Coffee set a precedent of state intervention in the coffee industry on smallholders' behalf that would prove critical in the 1950s and 1960s, when farmers began successfully organizing cooperatives.

41. Molina and Palmer, *History of Costa Rica*, 86.

42. Molina and Palmer, 86.

43. Molina and Palmer.

44. Juan Chanto Méndez, interview.

45. Acuña Ortega, "Clases sociales y conflictos," 189.

46. Acuña Ortega, 187.

47. Acuña Ortega, 187.

48. Although coffee had suffered earlier drops on the global market, the 1930s were a particularly trying decade for coffee farmers. In addition to reduced markets, in 1934, Germany, which was a key purchaser of Costa Rican coffee, embraced protectionist import/export policies that limited the amount of imports from individual countries to the amount of imports they were willing to purchase. For Costa Rica, which had sold some sixteen million marks of coffee to Germany annually, but only had the capacity to absorb three million marks of German goods, the impact was significant. The Costa Rican banking system tried to improve this trade situation with currency controls in 1937, but the overall impact was felt throughout the national economy. Hall, *El Café*, 154–55.

49. Agüero García, "En busca de nuevas tierras," 155.

50. Monge, "Monografía," 50. In 1946, Monge would write that Umaña was "the owner of almost all Tarrazú." The socioeconomic dominance mill owners exercised as the purchasers of raw beans, but also as creditors and exporters, cannot be underplayed. Indeed, until recently in Costa Rica the title of *beneficiador*, or mill owner, was synonymous with wealth and power.

51. Umaña Abarca, *Historia de Tarrazú*, 47.

52. Umaña's ascendency was not a uniquely Tarrazú phenomenon. In fact, Lowell Gudmundson found that the community of Santo Domingo de Heredia went from having fifty-three privately owned coffee mills to just six in the hands of two owners, between 1887 and 1935. For more on this Central Valley case, see Lowell Gudmundson, "Class Formation in a Smallholder Coffee Economy, 1850–1910," in Roseberry, Gudmundson, and Samper Kutschbach, *Coffee, Society, and Power*, 114–16.

53. Umaña Abarca, *Historia de Tarrazú*, 65.

54. Juan Chanto Méndez, interview by the author, June 3, 2009, San Marcos de Tarrazú, Costa Rica.

55. J. Chanto Méndez, *Cooperativa de caficultores*, folio 3.

56. Juan Chanto Méndez, interview.

57. Juan Chanto Méndez, interview.

58. Juan Chanto Méndez, interview.

59. Wilson Picado Umaña, "La expansión del café y el cambio tecnológico desigual en la agricultura del cantón de Tarrazú, Costa Rica, 1950–1998," master's thesis, Universidad de Costa Rica, 2000, 66.

60. Arturo Valverde Navarro, interview by the author, February 9, 2008, San Marcos de Tarrazú, Costa Rica.

61. For more on the widespread use of scrip in coffee plantations, see Manuel Benito Chacón Hidalgo, *Los boletos de café en Costa Rica: Folleto Técnico* (San José: Fundación Museos del Banco Central, 2002).

62. Elizabeth Dore, "Debt Peonage in Granada, Nicaragua, 1870–1930: Labor in a Noncapitalist Transition," *Hispanic American Historical Review* 83, no. 3 (August 2003): 521–59.

63. Dore, "Debt Peonage in Granada."

64. For more on the case of El Salvador, see Patricia Alvarenga, "Auxiliary Forces in the Shaping of the Repressive System, El Salvador, 1880–1930," in Chomsky and Lauria-Santiago, *Identity and Struggle*, 122–50. For more on the impact of coffee on Guatemalan socioeconomic relations, see McCreery, "Debt Servitude in Rural Guatemala," 735–59. For more information on the neighboring case of Nicaragua, see Julie A. Charlip, "At Their Own Risk: Coffee Farmers and Debt in Nicaragua, 1870–1930," in Chomsky and Lauria-Santiago, *Identity and Struggle*, 94–121.

65. Juan Bosco Umaña Abarca, interview by the author, May 8, 2009, San Marcos de Tarrazú.

66. For an excellent synthetic analysis comparing nineteenth-century liberal government policies on coffee production within the isthmus, see Hector Pérez Brignoli and Mario Samper, *Tierra, café, y sociedad* (San José: FLACSO, 1994), 7–49.

67. Agüero García, "En busca de nuevas tierras."

68. Juana Fernández, interview by the author, September 12, 2008, San Marcos de Tarrazú, Costa Rica. At the interviewee's request, her name has been changed to maintain privacy.

69. Juana Fernández, interview.

70. Juana Fernández, interview.

71. Juana Fernández, interview.

72. Quintín "Kinto" Araya Navarro, interview. Carlos Elizondo, interview by the author, January 23, 2008, Santa María de Dota. Lourdes Gamboa, interview. Abilio Naranjo Barrantes, interview by the author, November 20, 2007, San Marcos de Tarrazú.

73. Agüero García, "En busca de nuevas tierras," 156, 167.

74. ANCR, Gobernación, no. 2803 (1911).

75. Santa María and San Marcos had similar population numbers and infrastructure development, namely schools and roads, in this period, yet nothing in the archives suggests that Santa María residents pushed for the division with Tarrazú. In fact, it seems the decision was made in San José. Perhaps policy makers were driven by a desire to improve state authority in the more distant sectors of the original can-

ton of Dota, which included present-day San Isidro de El General, which was known as a center of bootlegging and other clandestine activities.

76. ANCR, Congreso, no. 14240 (1925).

77. Elías Montero, interview by the author, December 7, 2007, El Llano de la Piedra de Tarrazú, Costa Rica.

78. Kiko Vargas, interview by the author, March 25, 2008, San Marcos de Tarrazú, Costa Rica.

79. Molina and Palmer, *History of Costa Rica*, 88.

80. Particularly harmful for Costa Rican producers was the fact that, unlike European consumers, few US consumers valued superior-quality beans. Costa Rican coffee farmers had long earned more for their crop for their beans' overall superior quality (a consequence of wet-method processing, selective picking of ripened berries, and in many cases ideal soil and rainfall conditions). Most US coffee consumers in this period saw cheaper coffee as better coffee and were unwilling to pay any premium for higher-quality beans, further hurting Costa Rican farmers. Hall, *El Café*, 155. The quality of Costa Rican coffee decreased markedly during this period, as producers, mill owners, and exporters recognized that there was no financial reward for improved quality when selling to US markets. In the decades that followed, mills began to produce two qualities of coffee: an inferior-quality bean that was processed with less care, known as, *Chorro Americano*, and a highest-quality bean that was processed with as much precision as possible, known as *Chorro Europeo*. Mario Samper, "The Historical Consumption of Quality and Competitiveness," in Clarence-Smith and Topik, *Global Coffee Economy*, 134.

81. Samper, "Historical Consumption." Not only was the region's coffee sold almost exclusively in the United States during this period but, in exchange for Latin American support of the Allied war effort, in 1940 the United States signed the International Coffee Agreement with fourteen Latin American nations. This ensured coffee-centered republics a market during this conflict and paved the way for high coffee profits in the years immediately after the war. For more on this, see Roseberry's introduction to *Coffee, Society, and Power*, 12.

82. Herminía Muñoz Estrada, interview by the author, December 4, 2007, San Marcos de Tarrazú. Juan Bosco Umaña Abarca, interview. Nino Vargas Picado, interview by the author, November 23, 2007, San Marcos de Tarrazú, Costa Rica.

83. Umaña Abarca, interview.

84. Umaña Abarca, interview.

85. Umaña Abarca, interview.

86. Kiko Vargas, interview.

87. Nino Vargas Picado, interview.

88. Nino Vargas Picado, interview.

89. Luz Berta Monge Umaña, interview.

90. Fany Jiménez Solís, interview, September 14, 2008.

91. Margarita Mora, interview by the author, February 13, 2008, San Marcos de Tarrazú.

92. Margarita Mora, interview.

93. Margarita Mora, interview.

94. Women were the preferred selectors for mill owners in much of Latin America. Although selecting conditions varied little between nations, men were not always employed as women's supervisors. In Veracruz, selectors often worked

under female supervisors. For more on gender in Mexican coffee mills, see Heather Fowler-Salamni, "Gender, Work, Trade Unionism, and Working-Class Women's Culture in Post-Revolutionary Veracruz," in *Sex in Revolution: Gender, Politics, and Power in Modern Mexico*, ed. Jocelyn Olcott, Mary Kay Vaughan, and Gabriela Cano (Durham, NC: Duke University Press, 2006), 162–98.

95. Margarita Mora, interview.

96. Former selectors in Tarrazú uniformly describe their jobs as the most honorable and well-remunerated labor opportunity open to women, yet coffee selecting was a less favorable employment option in other parts of the isthmus. In fact, in 1925, Guatemalan selectors organized Central America's first women's labor strike. Workers demanded higher pay, shorter work hours, and an end to searches of their person by male supervisors. This latter demand suggests issues of sexual abuse. This differs widely from Tarrazú, where the beneficio was seen as a space free of this type of threat for women workers. For more on this 1925 strike, see Ana Lorena Carillo Padilla, "Sufridas hijas del pueblo: La huelga de las escogedoras de café de 1925 en Guatemala," *Mesoamerica* 27 (Junio 1994): 157–73.

97. Luz Berta Monge Umaña, interview.

98. Participant observation, August 6, 2007, field notes of a conversation I overheard between three women from San Pablo de León Cortés and Santa María de Dota in Paterson, New Jersey.

99. Juan Jaramillo Antillón, *Historia y evolución del Seguro Social de Costa Rica: Su primer hospital Dr. Rafael Ángel Calderón Guardia* (San José: Editorial Nacional de Salud y Seguro Social, 2004), 52.

100. Arburola Valverde, *Código de Trabajo*, 61–62.

101. Costa Rica, Leyes y Decretos, "Ley de creación de los seguros sociales obligatorios," La Gazeta no. 17. San José, November 4, de 1941, 2118. See Article 13.

102. Costa Rica, Leyes y Decretos, Article 2.

103. Arburola Valverde, *Código de Trabajo*, 11. The loophole was almost certainly intended to permit large landholders to easily employ their farmhand's wives and children during the annual coffee harvest, without the need to fill out paperwork or pay these temporary workers benefits.

104. Arturo Valverde, interview. As a young boy, Valverde weeded Umaña's field, and as a young man, he managed one of Umaña's beneficios.

105. Herminía Muñoz Estrada, interview.

106. Herminía Muñoz Estrada, interview.

107. Margarita Mora, interview.

108. Herminía Muñoz Estrada, interview.

109. Retired Resguardo Fiscal guard Socorro Galera remembered that a Central Valley union organizer came to Tarrazú in the 1950s and organized an unsuccessful strike to raise wages, but no one else in the region, including former workers at the hacienda and cafetalera, the Umaña family, or any news media from the period corroborate this claim. Socorro Galera Solera, interview by the author, April 14, 2008, San Lorenzo de Tarrazú.

Chapter 3

1. The state's second-largest source of income, just after export taxes, came from the sale of liquor produced by the state-owned National Liquor Factory.

2. Although this chapter focuses on the case of the Tarrazú Valley within a

Costa Rican context, homemade liquor production has historically been outlawed in most of the isthmus. In El Salvador, homemade liquor sparked a violent state response against producers and consumers as recorded by psychologists Michael Gorkin, Marta Pineda, and Gloria Leal. This trio uncovered the story of a rural family defined by illegal alcohol. They relate that rural guards who came to arrest the family patriarch for illegally producing liquor shot him when he attempted to flee. Interestingly, his widow continued illegally producing alcohol to support her family after his death. This Salvadoran widow's home served as a meeting point for neighbors who consumed her liquor. In contrast, in Tarrazú, liquor from one's own or from neighbors' homemade stills were consumed at home. For more on the case of El Salvador, see Michael Gorkin, Marta Pineda, and Gloria Leal, *From Grandmother to Granddaughter: Salvadoran Women's Stories* (Los Angeles: University of California Press, 2000), 97–98.

3. Rafael A. Chavarría F., *Producción de alcohol y licores en Costa Rica: Ciento veinte años después* (San José: Fábrica Nacional de Licores, 1970), 1.

4. Francisco María Núñez, "Estudio histórico sobre la producción y el monopolio de licores en Costa Rica," research report for President Prospero Guardia, 1941, folios 40–43, 77.

5. Núñez, folios 82, 84.

6. Chavarría, *Producción de alcohol*, 9.

7. Núñez, "Estudio histórico," folios 235, 310–11.

8. G. Zúñiga Montúfar, *Manual de Instrucción Fiscal: Conocimientos necesarios para el Resguardo Fiscal, Policía de Orden y Seguridad, Expendedores de Licores y Comerciantes* (San José: Imprenta Nacional, 1950), 5.

9. Núñez, "Estudio histórico," folios 5–18. Yamileth González García, *Continuidad y cambio en la historia agraria de Costa Rica* (San José: Editorial Costa Rica, 1989), 12.

10. Zúñiga Montúfar, *Manual de Instrucción Fiscal*, 6.

11. Núñez, "Estudio histórico," folios 123, 139.

12. Zúñiga Montúfar, *Manual de Instrucción Fiscal*, 4.

13. Víctor Manuel Mata, interview by the author, August 9, 2006, San Marcos de Tarrazú.

14. Víctor Manuel Mata, interview.

15. Núñez, "Estudio histórico," folios 1–3, 21.

16. Núñez, folios 1–3, 21. Additionally, in colonial Mexican villages women commonly sold *pulque*, a fermented drink made from the maguey plant, to neighbors and passersby from their doorsteps. See William B. Taylor, *Drinking, Homicide, and Rebellion in Colonial Mexican Villages* (Stanford, CA: Stanford University Press, 1979), 53.

17. Núñez, "Estudio histórico," folios 1–3, 21.

18. Núñez, folios 25–26.

19. Núñez, folio 13.

20. Núñez.

21. Núñez.

22. Arturo Valverde, interview. Quintín "Quinto" Araya Navarro, interview. Both of these men made their living for several years as *boyeros* (ox herders), transporting goods in oxcarts between San José and the region.

23. Euclides Naranjo, interview by the author, Llano de la Piedra de Tarrazú, August 8, 2006. Before coffee was planted, sugarcane was the region's principal cash

crop. The abundance of planted sugar unquestionably facilitated farmers' ability to produce homemade liquors.

24. Arturo Valverde, interview.

25. Until the 1980s, drinking by women was culturally taboo throughout Costa Rica, and historically, women were prohibited from entering cantinas and bars. See Randall Corella V., "Ellas también alzan la copa," *La Nación*, November 29, 2009. In Tarrazú, many local women, such as Lidia Angulo Araya, view women's drinking in bars as the most surprising cultural change. Lidia Angulo Araya, interview by the author, April 21, 2008, San Pablo de León Cortés. In late colonial Mexico, alcohol was also associated with masculinity. Although women drank in public, they were expected to drink far less than men. Taylor, *Drinking, Homicide, and Rebellion*, 62.

26. Fany Jiménez Solís, interview, September 14, 2008. According to Jiménez, her father was an abusive alcoholic whose alcohol consumption and the degree of violence he meted out to his family increased dramatically in times of economic distress. Jiménez, who worked for numerous years as a schoolteacher in San Marcos, stated that she viewed a similar pattern in the households of her students. Corroborating Jiménez's observations are the recollections of other women, such as Catalina Muñoz. Although Muñoz recalled her father's beatings as a constant in her childhood, she asserted she suffered the worst beating of her childhood the day he was fired by his employer. Catalina Muñoz, interview by the author, July 11, 2007, Montclair, New Jersey, United States. As requested by the interviewee, her name has been changed to maintain privacy.

27. Euclides Naranjo, interview. According to Naranjo, alcohol was the "critical ingredient" for all social activities and that "to be a man one must drink [alcohol]." Luís Hernán Villegas, a reformed alcoholic who had not had a drink in twenty-two years, similarly linked liquor consumption to local ideas of masculinity. In fact, Villegas claimed that his father was an abusive drunk and as a young child he knew he "never wanted to drink." Yet, he explained that at the age of twelve he "began drinking liquor to become a man, [and] by fifteen, I would get drunk almost every night. That was part of being a man." Luís Hernán Villegas, interview by the author, August 1, 2007, Newark, New Jersey.

28. During the late colonial period, indigenous men in Central Mexico frequently blamed liquor for exciting passions and weakening their self-restraint in homicide cases. See Taylor, *Drinking, Homicide, and Rebellion*.

29. ANCR, Gracia, no. 3075 (1954).

30. ANCR, Gracia, no. 3075.

31. Archivos Judicales de Costa Rica (hereinafter AJCR), no. 1946 (1950).

32. AJCR, no. 1946.

33. ANCR, Gracia, no. 3075.

34. Fany Jiménez Solís, interview, September 14, 2008.

35. ANCR, Alcaldía Única, Tarrazú, no. 733 (1912).

36. Rafael "Fello" Padilla, interview by the author, December 5, 2007, San Marcos de Tarrazú. Padilla is a retired Resguardo Fiscal guard who for twelve years conducted searches for clandestine liquor producers, consumers, and sellers. In his tenure as a Resguardo guard, he escorted numerous prisoners to San José for trial and imprisonment.

37. Rafael "Fello" Padilla, interview.

38. In the 1940s, however, Resguardo guards did involve themselves to a limited

extent in putting down large politically motivated street fights. For more on this, see chapters 4 and 5.

39. Juan Chanto Méndez, interview, June 3, 2009, San Marcos de Tarrazú.

40. Juan Chanto Méndez, interview.

41. ANCR, Remesa 1660, no 217 (1947).

42. ANCR, Remesa 1660, no 217.

43. Manuel Castro, interview by the author, April 21, 2008, San Pablo de León Cortés.

44. Manuel Castro, interview.

45. Quintín "Quinto" Araya Navarro, interview. Lidia Angulo Araya, interview.

46. Cecilia Jiménez Rojas, interview by the author, March 15, 2008, San Marcos de Tarrazú.

47. Cecilia Jiménez Rojas, interview.

48. Cecilia Jiménez Rojas, interview.

49. Cecilia Jiménez Rojas, interview.

50. Euclides Naranjo, interview.

51. Socorro Galera Solera, interview.

52. Lourdes Gamboa, interview.

53. Luz Berta Monge Umaña, interview.

54. Luz Berta Monge Umaña, interview.

55. Lidia Angulo Araya, interview. Angulo vividly recalled spending Saturday evenings worrying about her husband's safety and the amount of money he would spend at the bar.

56. Fany Jiménez Solís, interview, September 14, 2008.

57. Tarrazú was far from the only Costa Rican community where men beat their wives/lovers and engaged one another in drunken brawls over questions of honor. In fact, historian Lara Putnam found numerous legal cases between 1870 and 1960 documenting these types of violence in the port city of Limón. Putnam argues that the lack of governmental control and United Fruit's disinterest in regulating society in this relatively isolated Caribbean city led to high levels of violence. My findings in Tarrazú, however, suggest that perhaps Limón did not suffer from greater incidents of violence than other Costa Rican communities but had more women who resisted abuse through the courts. For the case of Limón, see Lara Putnam, *The Company They Kept: Migrants and the Politics of Gender in Caribbean Costa Rica, 1870–1960* (Chapel Hill: University of North Carolina Press, 2002).

58. Juana Fernández, interview.

59. Juana Fernández, interview. Fernández chose not to disclose the real name of the victim and created the pseudonym of "Clara Casa" during the interview.

60. Juana Fernández, interview.

61. Juana Fernández, interview.

62. Catalina Muñoz, interview.

63. Catalina Muñoz, interview.

64. Catalina Muñoz, interview.

65. Catalina Muñoz, interview.

66. Cecilia Jiménez Rojas, interview.

67. Víctor Umaña, interview by the author, December 4, 2007, Guadalupe de Tarrazú.

68. Flora Villa, interview. Luz Berta Monge Umaña, interview. Fany Jiménez Solís, interview, September 14, 2008.

69. Flora Villa, interview. Luz Berta Monge Umaña, interview. Fany Jiménez Solís, interview, September 14, 2008. These child labors were common in many Costa Rican rural communities. In 1979, the Universidad Nacional Autonoma published a five-volume collection of peasant autobiographies where women participants shared how as children they had assisted their mothers and fathers, either in the home and/or on both familial and neighbors' lands. In other words, peasant children worked and they sometimes did so either unsupervised or under the supervision of nonfamilials. For an analysis of these peasant autobiographies, see Zaira Escamilla Gutiérrez and Lorena Vargas Mora, "Peasant Women's Autobiographies: Women's Double Contribution to the Rural Economy," in *The Costa Rican Women's Movement: A Reader*, ed. Ilse Abshagen Leitinger (Pittsburgh: University of Pittsburgh, 1997), 89–97.

70. Magdalena de Muñoz, interview by the author, March 3, 2008, San Marcos de Tarrazú. Interviewee's name, as well as the names of all of her family members related here, have been changed to maintain privacy.

71. Magdalena de Muñoz, interview.

72. For more on the role of oldest daughters serving as their mother's primary assistant in completing domestic labors of all sorts in rural families, see Escamilla Gutiérrez and Vargas Mora, "Peasant Women's Autobiographies," 91–92.

73. Magdalena de Muñoz, interview.

74. The loss of Vega's little boy was a fairly common outcome in this period. In fact, in 1952, the first year we have statistics for infant mortality, 97.95 out of every 1,000 live births in Costa Rica died before their first birthday. Certainly, in the 1930s, these rates must have been comparable if not worse. For more on Costa Rican infant mortality, see Celso A. Porras F., *Costa Rica: Evolución de la mortalidad infantil en los últimos 25 años* (San José: Escuela de Estadísticas de la Universidad de Costa Rica, 1974).

75. Magdalena de Muñoz, interview.

76. Steve J. Stern, *The Secret History of Gender: Women, Men, and Power in Late Colonial Mexico* (Chapel Hill: University of North Carolina Press, 1995), 165.

77. The interrelationship between class, women's vulnerability to rape, and a sense of powerlessness on the part of the victims to report these crimes is not unique to Costa Rica or even Central America; however, other studies that incorporate oral histories in the region have uncovered similar stories. In particular, several cases of poor women disclosing previously unreported rapes in El Salvador can be found in Gorkin, Piñeda, and Leal, *From Grandmother to Granddaughter*, 203–9.

78. Luz Berta Monge Umaña, interview.

79. Luz Berta Monge Umaña, interview.

80. Lowell Gudmundson found that the daughters of poor fathers frequently worked as domestic servants in the homes of wealthier family members in the colonial era. Moreover, Gudmundson asserts that nineteenth-century Costa Rican families could be divided into two classes: those with domestic servants and those who were potential domestic servants. Gudmundson, *Costa Rica before Coffee*, 116–24.

81. Margarita Mora, interview.

82. Margarita Mora, interview.

83. Lourdes Beatriz Ugalde Madriz, interview by the author, February 14, 2008. I have changed the name of this former domestic servant, Sonia Lourdes Ugalde Madriz, her son, Ricardo Ugalde Madriz, and her sister, Lourdes Beatriz Ugalde Madriz, to protect their privacy.

84. Margarita Mora, interview.

85. Nineteenth- and twentieth-century domestic servants in Tarrazú and throughout the Caribbean Basin were often quite young. Nicola Foote's research, for instance, demonstrates that it was common for British Caribbean girls under the age of thirteen to work as domestic laborers, making them particularly vulnerable to employer abuses. See Nicola Foote, "British Caribbean Women Migrants and Domestic Service in Latin America, 1850–1950: Race, Gender, and Colonial Legacies," in *Colonization and Domestic Service: Historical and Contemporary Perspectives*, ed. Victoria K. Haskins and Claire Lowrie (New York: Routledge, 2015), 301.

86. While poor families seem to have sent daughters to work in the homes of wealthier relatives when possible, likely to reduce potential abuses, recollections by Costa Rican and Salvadoran women suggest that if girls were not related by blood to the patriarch of the home where she labored, she could be the victim to both physical and sexual abuse. The Costa Rican Peasant Autobiographies, for instance, include the case of a teenage girl who suffered sexual abuse at the hands of her aunt's husband. For more on this particular case, see Foote, "British Caribbean Women Migrants," 299. Similarly, in the case of El Salvador, a poor elderly woman shared how she had worked alongside her mother in an aunt's home, where they were poorly treated despite their familial linkage to the home's owners. For more on this case, see Gorkin, Pineda, and Leal, *From Grandmother to Granddaughter*, 170–72.

87. Lidia Angulo Araya, interview.

88. Lidia Angulo Araya, interview.

89. Eva Fernández, participant observation conducted by the author, August 6, 2007, Paterson, New Jersey. I changed the name of this former domestic servant to protect her privacy.

90. Eva Fernández, interview.

91. Fernández's decision to not disclose to her family the abuse that led to her loss of employment appears to have been a common response by sexually victimized domestic workers. Foote's analysis of the testimony of a young West Indian woman named Dalia has much in common with Fernández's case. See Foote, "British Caribbean Women Migrants," 299.

92. Eva Fernández, interview.

93. ANCR, Gobierno, Inspección General de Autoridades, no. 40891 (1958).

94. ANCR, Gobierno, Inspección General de Autoridades, no. 40891.

95. ANCR, Ministerio de Economía y Hacienda, no. 34155 (1964), folio 17.

96. ANCR, Ministerio de Economía y Hacienda, no. 34155.

97. ANCR, Ministerio de Economía y Hacienda, no. 34155.

98. Flora Villa, interview. Villa's father worked as a day laborer in this period, earning one colón for a six-hour work day.

99. Lourdes Beatriz Ugalde Madríz, interview.

100. Lourdes Beatriz Ugalde Madríz, interview.

101. AJCR, no. 1004 (1964).

102. AJCR, no. 1004.

Chapter 4

1. Fany Jiménez Solís, interview by the author, April 12, 2008, San Marcos de Tarrazú.

2. Juan Chanto Méndez, interview, April 15, 2008. Also, Analías Meza, interview by the author, June 13, 2008, San Pablo de León Cortés.

3. Carlos Elizondo, interview.

4. Few works interrogate the role of ordinary soldiers, focusing instead on Figueres's triumphant rise from wealthy farmer to revolutionary victor and president. One exception to this is Patricia Badilla Gómez, "Y despues de la guerra seguimos contando la historia: Testimonios de campesinos y campesinas que participaron en el levantamento armado de 1948," bachelor's thesis, Universidad de Costa Rica, 1996.

5. Much has been written about Costa Rican suffrage both insularly and comparatively within an isthmian context. Critical to the exercise of this right was the public education system that created a largely literate populace, initially a requirement for voting. Illustrative of this, by 1909, over half of Santo Domingo de Heredia's landless laborers were also registered voters. In other words, by this date, the liberal education reforms of the 1880s had succeeded in establishing a significant literate and voting citizenry. Gudmundson, "Peasant, Farmer, Proletarian," 130–34. However, the extent of most citizen's literacy was likely quite rudimentary. In fact, recent scholarship by Iván Molina into practical literacy levels has revealed that through the first half of the twentieth century most pupils acquired only very basic reading and writing skills. While Molina's work suggests that Costa Rican liberal policy makers were not as deeply committed to education as these same national myth makers proclaimed, unlike in other isthmus countries, by the early twentieth century, most Costa Rican males could at minimum write their names and read enough to pass the basic literacy test required to vote. Molina-Jiménez, *La educacion en Costa Rica*.

6. These reforms were enacted between 1925 and 1927 and are the basis of Costa Rica's national identification cards, the *cédula*, and seem to have effectively ended the most blatant acts of voter fraud of years past. For more on this, see Lehoucq and Molina, *Stuffing the Ballot Box*.

7. The effectiveness of these reforms in reshaping the political landscape is illustrated in the failed Bellavistazo coup of 1932, which was the first presidential election held after these laws were put into place. On February 15, 1932, a group of young politicians and military men seized the Bellavista Cartel and were forced to surrender four days later. Manuel Castro Quesada initiated this failed coup upon receiving the news that he had lost the presidential election and his recognition, unlike in years past, that with the new electoral reforms, it would be impossible to negotiate with the other candidates for positions of power. For more on this, see Lehoucq and Molina, *Stuffing the Ballot Box*, 77–80. Also see David Díaz Arias, *Crisis Social y Memorias en Lucha: Guerra civil en Costa Rica, 1940–1948* (San José: Editorial de la Universidad de Costa Rica, 2015), 8–10.

8. Women and Afro-Limonenses (Afro-Caribbean citizens of West Indian origins) were not considered a part of the imagined community of citizens until after 1948. The right to vote was in the 1940s very much a testament to Hispanic men's power, regardless of their socioeconomic position. Lehoucq and Molina, *Stuffing the Ballot Box*, as well as Díaz Arias, *Crisis Social*, 340.

9. For more on how masculinity was constructed in the Tarrazú Valley in this period, namely the interrelationship between providing for familial needs and ideas of manhood, see chapter 3.

10. Cabuya is a natural fiber found in fique plant leaves that is used for making ropes, bags, and baskets. Coffee was generally exported in cabuya sacks. For more on cabuya and other natural fibers, see Shannon Okey and Sasha Gulish, *Alt Fiber:*

25 *Projects for Knitting Green with Bamboo, Soy, Hemp and More* (Berkeley, CA: Ten Speed Press, 2008), 8.

11. La Lucha is located in the neighboring canton of Desamparados and many of Figueres's employees were also from this canton. Juan Chanto Méndez, interview.

12. *Surco* was a publication produced by young law students at the University of Costa Rica who imagined themselves as an intellectual vanguard whose scholarly endeavors would make Costa Rican society more equitable, literate, and democratic. Seemingly their interests aligned with Calderón's social reforms. *Surco*'s writers were all members of the self-proclaimed Centro para el Estudio de los Problemas Nacionales (known colloquially at the time as simply the Centro). Like Calderón, and other young politically minded youth in the late 1930s, members of the Centro were seeking a change from the nation's traditional Liberal politicians and their policies. David Díaz Arias has convincingly argued that for Calderón supporters his presidency and the social reforms he enacted were the change they desired. The young men at the Centro, however, wanted to be a part of that change and became antigovernment only after their publications and ideas failed to garner Calderón's attention/interest in bringing them into the government. In sum, jealousy fueled this group's initial displeasure with Calderón's administration. See Díaz Arias, *Crisis Social*, 123–25.

13. Juan Chanto Méndez, interview.

14. Juan Chanto Méndez, interview. The nation's Communists first began attending progovernment rallies related to the social reforms in 1942, which also coincided with increasing fears of fascist threats in the context of World War II. The Communists and government supporters would take their first organized public action on September 15, 1941, Independence Day, in a series of displays of both nationalism and antifascism. On September 22, 1943, the Communists and Republicans would forge an official alliance that they would call the Victory Block (Bloque de la Victoria). In the following years, government supporters came increasingly to see fascism as a potential threat to themselves, the social reforms they supported, and the nation's future. León Cortés's association with fascism served arguably to establish him and his supporters as enemies of the state for government supporters. For more on this, see Díaz Arias, *Crisis Social*, 68–105.

15. Jaramillo Antillón, *Historia y evolucion del Seguro Social*, 52.

16. Juan Chanto Méndez, interview. Farmers, such as Marco Chanto, who disliked their government's alliance with the nation's Communists and were unsure about the benefits of the labor reforms passed in the 1930s, were far from limited to the Tarrazú Valley. In fact, Costa Rica's large smallholding class and relatively small landless peasant class meant that more of the nation's rural poor were employers for at least part of the year, namely during harvest season. Like their latifundio-owning counterparts, many smallholders thus saw the labor reforms as potentially detrimental to their economic well-being. As Gudmundson observed, the nation's smallholding class historically subscribed to "an anti-labor, anti-Marxist doctrine of social change and national liberation." See Gudmundson, "Peasant, Farmer, Proletarian," 112–14.

17. Although most oppositionists I spoke with suggested that they did not vote for Calderón in 1940 and always opposed his presidency, a clear exception is Juan Chanto, whose father served as jefe político both for Cortés and for the start of Calderón's administration. David Díaz Arias argues that most Cortés supporters

almost certainly also voted for Calderón in 1940, as they were candidates for the same party. Yet, as the nation would become increasingly bifurcated, many would choose to recall that they had opposed Calderón from the time of his campaign. This narrative allowed for the opposition to create a false narrative of broad-based anti-Calderón sentiments that preceded his election. Díaz Arias, *Crisis Social*, 153.

18. The corruption allegations centered on the way that Calderón's government appropriated the bank holdings and properties of the nation's German immigrants and their descendants as part of their commitment to the US war effort. Cortés was believed to have profascist leanings and like many in the opposition disagreed with the decision to back the United States in World War II and in the attack against German Costa Ricans and their families. Calderón's government was accused of selling German holdings to his political allies at below-market prices. The attacks on individuals associated with fascism during World War II led many to "other" their neighbors who were associated with the Axis power through blood or marriage, justifying acts of violence, dispossession, and vandalism. This is arguably the start of political violence in this period that culminated in the Civil War of 1948. Additionally, the attacks on German residents and their descendants (many Costa Rican citizens) would forge a devout antigovernment segment of the opposition in the post–World War II period, which would play a major hand in unseating the government in 1948. See Lehoucq and Molina, *Stuffing the Ballot Box*, 215. Also see Díaz Arias, *Crisis Social*, 55, 73–79, and 155–56.

19. Before Calderón backed Picado, he briefly entertained the idea of reforming the nation's electoral laws to permit him to either extend his current term, which was scheduled to end in 1944, or to permit him to run for a consecutive second term. This plan was soon abandoned after students from Central Valley high schools took to the streets in mass protests on May 13, 1943. Responding to the public outcry, Calderón abandoned his plans, endorsed Picado as the PNR nominee, and began campaigning on Picado's behalf. This moment, however, would spark later claims on the part of the opposition that Calderón had dictatorial intentions and did not respect the nation's electoral laws. For more on this protest, see Díaz Arias, *Crisis Social*, 136–39.

20. Badilla Gómez, "Y despues de la guerra," 61–74. This former president's popularity is also evident in the fact that when Tarrazú was divided in 1962 to form two cantons, the new canton would be named León Cortés.

21. Badilla Gómez.

22. Badilla Gómez, 42.

23. Badilla Gómez. Also, Juan Chanto Méndez, interview.

24. Juan Chanto Méndez, interview.

25. Ramón Solís Solís, interview by the author, April 19, 1948, Guadalupe de Tarrazú.

26. Ramón Solís Solís, interview.

27. In many ways, the violence recalled in Tarrazú reflected a broader pattern of increasingly violent confrontations between government supporters and oppositionists in the streets of Costa Rican communities. In the Central Valley members of the PVP and members of the opposition began to train and organize themselves for street confrontations, beginning in 1943. What makes the case of Tarrazú a little different from the broader Central Valley experience is that the major source of political violence was between oppositionists and local police officers. In fact, there seemingly were no private citizens in the community willing to take to the streets to

defend the government. For more on street violence in and around the 1944 presidential election, see Díaz Arias, *Crisis Social*, 73–165.

28. Carlos Elizondo, interview.

29. Juan Chanto Méndez, interview.

30. Lehoucq and Molina, *Stuffing the Ballot Box*, 182. Díaz Arias, *Crisis Social*, 173.

31. Lehoucq and Molina, *Stuffing the Ballot Box*. Díaz Arias, *Crisis Social*.

32. The cantons of Tarrazú and Dota had 1,676 and 600 voters, respectively, registered; however, official tallies suggest that just 900 votes were cast in Tarrazú and 531 in Dota. *La Gaceta Diario Oficial*, January and February 1944.

33. Juan Chanto Méndez, interview. The official record opens the possibility that Marcos Chanto might have taken as many as 776 cards to Cortés.

34. If the number of registered voters who did not vote is added to the government's tallied Cortés ballots, he would have secured a razor-thin victory of thirty-four votes over his opponent. In the case of Dota, this same equation would have seen him lose, but by a very slight margin of just forty votes. While there is no evidence that picadistas did "steal" votes in Dota or even that they would have in Tarrazú, the closeness of this race facilitated unease about election results.

35. National support for the PNR under Calderón was clearly waning as an opposition movement began forming during his presidency. Indeed, Calderón secured nearly 85 percent of the popular votes in 1940. Díaz Arias, *Crisis Social*, xv.

36. Likely adding fuel to the fires of local rage over the electoral fraud that occurred in their community, on February 22, 1948, shortly after Picado was declared the victor in the national elections, an *El Diario de Costa Rica* article declared that Picado had orchestrated a "political coup." Perhaps the article writer wished to express that Picado's win usurped the desires of the opposition, but this article would be later used by *Surco* writers and other members of the oppositionist press to argue that Picado had unlawfully taken power and that his presidency was an undemocratic dictatorship. In sum, although Picado won the elections, he faced an angry opposition that early into his presidency formulated a fictional narrative of Picado as an illegitimate leader. This lie was propagated widely by oppositionist media outlets and political figures and it soon became a common belief for many oppositionists. Díaz Arias, *Crisis Social*, 174. For many Tarrazúceños, moreover, who were deeply upset that they had been stripped of their political voice at the polls in that year's election, this fiction seemed quite plausible and legitimated their antigovernment sentiments.

37. Carlos Elizondo, interview.

38. Universal male suffrage was established in 1902. Eugene D. Miller, "Labour and the War-Time Alliance in Costa Rica 1943–1948," *Journal of Latin American Studies* 25, no. 3 (October 1993): 516. Additionally, direct suffrage was introduced in 1913 and the secret ballot was inaugurated in 1928. Hall, *Costa Rica*, 60.

39. Fabrice Edouard Lehoucq, "Class Conflict, Political Crisis and the Breakdown of Democratic Practices in Costa Rica: Reassessing the Origins of the 1948 Civil War," *Journal of Latin American Studies* 23, no. 1 (February 1991): 37–60.

40. Leslie Bethell and Ian Roxborough, "Latin America between the Second World War and the Cold War: Some Reflections of the 1945–8 Conjuncture," *Journal of Latin American Studies* 20, no. 1 (May 1988): 167–69.

41. Bethell and Roxborough, "Latin America," 172. In 1944, the US assistant sec-

retary of the state circulated a pamphlet to its Latin American embassies asserting that it was US policy to favor democratically elected governments.

42. Post-1959 Cuba under Fidel Castro's leadership would be the clear exception.

43. Miller, "Labour and the Wartime Alliance," 525.

44. The PVP, which was established on June 13, 1943, was a response to the dissolution of the Communist International in Moscow on May 15, 1943. Indeed, when the leaders of the Partido Comunista de Costa Rica (PCCR) dissolved their party and created the PVP, they asserted that more than simply a name change, they hoped to highlight their party's national character. Additionally, it seems likely that Mora also sought to court the votes of workers who were excited by Calderón's social reforms but were hesitant to be grouped together with Communists, who were often associated with atheism. For clarity, I simply use the name PVP when describing the political actions of Costa Rica's Communist parties. For more on the name change, see David Gustavo Díaz-Arias, "Social Crises and Struggling Memories: Populism, Popular Mobilization, Violence, and Memories of Civil War in Costa Rica, 1940–1948," PhD dissertation, Indiana University, 2009, 120–23.

45. While this letter was pivotal in securing mass support not only for the PVP but also for the Communist organized labor movement, it also served to deeply upset firm anti-Communists. Many anti-Communists saw the PCCR's name change and the letter from Sanabria as nothing more than a cheap trick by Mora, which successfully permitted Communists to infiltrate the government and influence policy. Díaz Arias, *Crisis Social*, 99.

46. Lowell Gudmundson's research on popular inheritance practices in Heredia suggests that peasants were deeply committed to capitalism. Similarly, Mario Samper found that peasants who settled the Central Valley's northwest were motivated to leave established communities for the periphery in the hopes of growing crops that would allow them to participate in national and international markets as agrocapitalists. Both Samper and Gudmundson attribute Costa Rica's agrarian frontier, which provided even the poorest landless peasants with the potential to create a future for themselves and their children as independent farm owners, as the source of traditional widespread popular support among Costa Rica's poorest farm owners for a capitalist agrarian model. For more on this, see Gudmundson, "Peasant, Farmer, Proletarian," and Mario Samper, *Generation of Settlers*.

47. Gudmundson, "Peasant, Farmer, Proletarian," 114.

48. For a detailed examination of Calderón's popular support, see Díaz-Arias, *Crisis Social*. This work argues that his populism secured him fanatical popular support, which paralleled that of his contemporaries—Argentina's Juan Perón and Mexico's Lazaro Cárdenas. *Crisis Social* highlights the steadfast electoral support Calderón forged with laborers, both because of the reforms he passed and his alliance with the PVP and national unions. Díaz Arias, however, does not convincingly demonstrate that laborers were as fanatically devoted to Calderón as Peronists or Cardenistas were to their leaders. Indeed, his argument centers on the image of Calderón as a Christlike healer, due to his labors as a physician who cured the poor. While Díaz Arias cites political pamphlets, which might suggest such a construction, he does not provide more than a claim by a fellow historian that her mother believed that Calderón alone could cure her ills. This singular and rather meek piece of evidence, problematic at best, fails to demonstrate a broad-based popular belief that Calderón was more than a doctor turned politician, who earned popular support through the laws he passed that benefited workers and their families.

49. Díaz Arias, "Social Crises and Struggling Memories," 527.

50. See "Los que ponen y imponen el terrorismo en la oposicion," *La Tribuna*, November 6, 1947. Also, see "Historia Revolución," El Espíritu del 48, accessed July 5, 2010, www.elespiritudel48.org/docu/h056.htm.

51. "1 Muerte y 12 heridos," *La Tribuna*, November 3, 1947.

52. This anti-immigrant action is unique in that the victims of the violence were European immigrants and their descendants. Indeed, historically anti-immigrant sentiments centered on Hispanic anxieties over the presence of a sizable Jamaican/West Indian community, which resided around the Port of Limón and made up over one-third of the foreign-born community in 1927. In this same year 10 percent of Costa Rican residents were foreign born. The 1927 census records the largest foreign-born population for the twentieth century. Hall, *Costa Rica*, 68.

53. "56 HERIDOS, saldo de los sucesos de ayer en ESTA CAPITAL," *La Tribuna*, July 5, 1942, 1. For a detailed narrative of the looting actions, see Díaz Arias, *Crisis Social*, 54–57.

54. Díaz Arias, *Crisis Social*. For more on Latin American concentration camps for German citizens and their descendants during World War II, see Max Paul Friedman, *Nazis and Good Neighbors: The United States Campaign against the Germans of Latin America in World War II* (Cambridge: Cambridge University Press, 2003).

55. Calderón's actions silenced Figueres and other dissenters in the short term, but this repression would convert this once unknown agrocapitalist into a recognized national opposition figure. Although most historians have described Figueres as a largely unknown private citizen before his radio appearance, David Díaz Arias counters this argument suggesting that Figueres was seen as a rising politician by the nation's political elite by this date. Díaz Arias, however, provides no evidence aside from the harsh punishment wielded and the recollection of Figueres's first wife, Henrietta Boggs, that she married him partially because she was told that he would one day be president. Díaz Arias, *Crisis Social*, 145–50.

56. José Figueres Ferrer, "Palabras gastadas," reprinted in El Espíritu del 48, accessed July 15, 2012, www.elespiritudel48.org/docu/i02.html. Even though exile would seem sufficient to engender Figueres's anger toward the Calderón government, recent scholarship by Manuel Solís suggests that Figueres's issues with Calderón were deeply rooted in the personal. He was friends with many of the German families who were persecuted by the Calderón administration. Additionally, his father, who voted for Calderón, was fired from his post as the director of a community hospital in the town of Turrialba seemingly to provide a favor to a close Calderón friend. Last, Solís suggests that the two men were in essence polar opposites. While Calderón embraced his Catholic faith and sought to increase the presence of the church in national life, Figueres, who was raised by strict Catholic parents, spent his youth reading books his parents and the church prohibited and otherwise rejecting his Catholic upbringing. Solís suggests that these differences meant that Figueres and Calderón could never conceive of the world in the same fashion. Manuel Solís, *La institucionalidad ajena: Los años cuarenta y el fin de siglo* (San José: Editorial de la Universidad de Costa Rica, 2006), 355–65.

57. John A. Booth, *Costa Rica: Quest for Democracy* (Boulder, CO: Westview Press, 1999), 47.

58. Jacobo Shifter, *Las alianzas conflictivas* (San José: Libro Libre, 1986), 277; Oscar Aguilar Bulgarelli, *Costa Rica y sus hechos políticos de 1948: Problemática de una década* (San José: Editorial Universidad Estatal a Distancia, 2004); Guillermo

Villegas Hoffmeister, *La guerra de Figueres: Cronica de ocho anos* (San José: Editorial Universidad Estatal a Distancia, 1998), 285; and Manuel Mora Valverde, *Discursos, 1934–1979* (San José: Editorial Presbere, 1980), 269–70. Mora first announced the formation of the brigadas in 1941; during the July 4, 1942, looting of San José's Axis identified businesses, he identified it as an organ of the PVP that could defend workers from internal fascist threats. Díaz Arias, *Crisis Social*, 73.

59. They would begin confronting oppositionists in the streets during the run-up to the 1944 election, in particular following an oppositionist rally of peasant supporters for León Cortés held in San José's Plaza Viquez. After the gathering the brigadistas allegedly attacked peasant oppositionists leaving the rally. This confrontation seemingly encouraged the opposition to begin organizing their own bands of violent street fighters. Díaz Arias, *Crisis Social*, 73 and 156. Juan Chanto Méndez, interview.

60. Mora Valverde, *Discursos*.

61. Muñoz Guillén, *El Estado*, 144.

62. Picado's attempt to distance himself from the PVP reflects a larger regional pattern taking shape between 1946 and 1948. In fact, by 1950, Latin American governments had moved decidedly to the right. Communist parties and unions were outlawed and repressed in country after country throughout the region, which largely ended the political vibrancy of the World War II era. Increasing fears of Communism by US policy makers and the United States' unquestioned hemispheric supremacy fostered the emergence of this anti-Communist environment. Although officially preferring democratically elected governments to dictatorships in the hemisphere, after 1947, defending democracy took a backseat to protecting US capital and political interests. See Bethell and Roxborough, "Latin America."

63. Bethell and Roxborough, "Latin America." Also, see Aguilar Bulgarelli, *Costa Rica*, 102.

64. In an analysis of the 1940s, David Díaz Arias echoes my findings and those of Patricia Badilla Gómez that peasants who fought for the rebels spoke adoringly of León Cortés. He suggests, however, that their adoration for this former president likely began *after* the Civil War when the victorious rebels began to construct a narrative of Cortés as a martyr, who seemingly was assassinated (there are no suggestions he died of unnatural causes) by the Calderón regime and whose sacrifice helped found the Second Republic. This argument is interesting and reflects work on the way that memories can be constructed and reshaped. Díaz Arias, *Crisis Social*, 153. The issue with this thesis as it relates to Tarrazú is that veteran rebels, like Juan Chanto, never described Cortés as a martyr, instead portraying him as a strong man who had helped them to stand up to Umaña's economic monopoly in their community, as discussed earlier in this chapter. This suggests that although later events likely shaped local memories and sentiments towards Cortés, his local identity was not part of this martyr mythology.

65. Villegas Hoffmeister, *La guerra de Figueres*, 191.

66. Jeffrey M. Paige, *Coffee and Power: Revolution and the Rise of Democracy in Central America* (Cambridge, MA: Harvard University Press, 1997), 144–45.

67. Scholars have advanced a plethora of reasons for why this strike began. Díaz Arias presents perhaps the most logical explanation for the strike. He claims the strike began in the Central Valley city of Cartago, after a group of oppositionist youth began roaming the city at night to beat up Communists. The city's police chief was a member of the opposition and made no effort to halt the attacks. San

José authorities soon fired the police chief, and his replacement, who supported the government, quickly retook control of Cartago's streets. This band of oppositionists was not ready to relinquish their attacks, and on July 20, 1947, they brutally beat a group of Communists who were vivando their support for Calderón as well as a pair of police officers who were near the gathered Communists. Additionally, in one of the city's poorer neighborhoods, a fight broke out between opposition supporters and the local police just as people were leaving a film at the local theater. Soon innocent men, women, and children found themselves victims of the melee. The next day, in response to the appalling violence, the city's oppositionist businesses chose to strike by not opening their doors. Picado demanded the stores reopen and Ulate agreed, but only after Picado acceded to a series of electoral reforms that benefited the opposition in the upcoming 1948 presidential election. Díaz Arias, *Crisis Social*, 203–11. For alternative arguments, see Charles D. Ameringer, *Don Pepe: A Political Biography of José Figueres of Costa Rica* (Albuquerque: University of New Mexico Press, 1978), 35–36. Ameringer argues that the strike began in Cartago after a confrontation between members of the opposition and local police officers on July 20. Cartago's opposition demanded that the officers accused of attacking scores of civilians be punished and called for a general strike to force the government to act. John Martz alleges that the strike was a response to government soldiers shooting into a crowd of moviegoers with machine guns. John D. Martz, *Central America, the Crisis and the Challenge* (Chapel Hill: University of North Carolina Press, 1959), 212. Iván Molina has described the strike as a move by opposition business owners in the Central Valley to force the government to provide certain electoral guarantees, yet he provides no trigger for the strike. Iván Molina Jiménez, "The Polarization of Politics," in Molina and Palmer, *Costa Rica Reader*, 167. Deborah Yashar, alternatively, blames the strike on the passage of a redistributive tax by the Legislative Assembly. Deborah J. Yashar, *Demanding Democracy: Reform and Reaction in Costa Rica and Guatemala, 1870s–1950s* (Stanford, CA: Stanford University Press, 1997), 17.

68. Miller, "Labour and the War-Time Alliance," 532.

69. "A tiros la policia de S. Marcos contra los que Vivan Ulate," *El Diario de Costa Rica*, June 25, 1947, 4.

70. ANCR, Gobernación, no. 14436 (1947–48).

71. In fact, *El Diario de Costa Rica* described Chanto as the "the opposition leader in the Canton of Tarrazú." "A tiros la policia."

72. ANCR, Gobernación, no. 13119 (1947).

73. ANCR, Remesa 1660, no. 217 (1948).

74. Marcos Chanto wrote his letter with the assistance of San José attorney Eloy Morua Carrillo. ANCR, Remesa 1660, no. 217.

75. ANCR, Remesa 1660, no. 217.

76. ANCR, Remesa 1660, no. 217.

77. Juan Chanto Méndez, interview. Carlos Elizondo, interview. Fany Jiménez Solís, interview, September 14, 2008.

78. For more on how the increasing political violence was experienced and encouraged by both the media and political candidates on both sides, see Díaz Arias, *Crisis Social*, 200. Also, refer to articles in both *El Diario de Costa Rica* and *La Tribuna*, 1947.

79. Jacobo Schifter, *La fase oculta de la guerra civil en Costa Rica* (San José: Editorial Universitaria Centroamericana, 1986), 76.

80. Bowman, *Militarization, Democracy, and Development*, 93.

81. Bowman, *Militarization, Democracy, and Development*. See also Schifter, *La fase oculta*, 80–81, and Lehoucq and Molina, *Stuffing the Ballot Box*, 220. Additionally, see Díaz Arias, *Crisis Social*, 217–19.

82. "A centenares de calderonistas," *La Tribuna*, February 11, 1948, 3.

83. Bowman, *Militarization, Democracy, and Development*, 92. Aguilar Bulgarelli, *Costa Rica*, 147.

84. Max Koberg, the third magistrate, abstained from voting, claiming the colegio fire left him with an incomplete set of ballots to inspect. Koberg thus urged for the Legislative Assembly to determine the election's victor. This recommendation violated the August 1947 agreement brokered to end the huelga de brazos caídos. For more on this, see Aguilar Bulgarelli, *Costa Rica*, 151–54. Also see Lehoucq and Molina, *Stuffing the Ballot Box*, 219, as well as Schifter, *La fase oculta*, 83.

85. Lehoucq and Molina, *Stuffing the Ballot Box*, 219.

86. Aguilar Bulgarelli, *Costa Rica*, 162–63.

87. Lehoucq and Molina, *Stuffing the Ballot Box*, 222. Also see James Dunkerley, *Power in the Isthmus: A Political History of Modern Central America* (London: Verso 1988), 130.

88. See, for instance, Yashar, *Demanding Democracy*, 181. Also see Lehoucq and Molina, *Stuffing the Ballot Box*, 223–24, as well as Schifter, *La fase oculta*, 81–82, and Bowman, *Militarization, Democracy, and Development*, 90.

89. Schifter, *La fase oculta*, 83.

90. Yashar, *Demanding Democracy*, 181. Charles D. Ameringer, *The Caribbean Legion: Patriots, Politicians, Soldiers of Fortune, 1946–1950* (University Park: Pennsylvania State University Press, 1996), 64.

91. The legion's members emerged from a particular set of circumstances that came together in the 1940s. These men were deeply inspired by the Allies' World War II–era propaganda that championed democratic ideals and also frightened by the increasing political sway Latin American Communists had secured through popular elections. Complicating matters further, they were concerned by the growing postwar era political and economic power of the United States.

92. These dissidents first united in mid-1947 to overturn the dictatorship in the Dominican Republic. Their planned coup against Trujillo, however, soured while still being organized in Cuba, and the group was forcefully relocated to exile-friendly Guatemala. Guatemala City was soon hosting dissidents from the Dominican Republic, Honduras, Nicaragua, and Costa Rica. It was here, in December 1947, nearly two months before Costa Rica's contested 1948 elections were held, that Figueres convinced rebels to focus their energies on overthrowing the Costa Rican state. See Ameringer, *Caribbean Legion*, 27–67.

93. Critically Figueres met with Guatemalan President Juan José Arevalo in December 1947, two months before the presidential elections were held, and secured Arevalo's promise for guns in February. See Díaz Arias, *Crisis Social*, 215–16.

94. Piero Gleijeses, "Juan José Arevalo and the Caribbean Legion," *Journal of Latin American Studies* 21, no. 1 (February 1989): 133–45.

95. Juan Chanto Méndez, interview. Analías Meza, interview. Carlos Elizondo, interview. Álvaro Gamboa, interview by the author, March 24, 2008, San Marcos de Tarrazú.

96. Marcos Chanto Méndez, "Primero en la escuela y luego en un campo especial se mantuvieron los presos políticos en Tarrazú," *El Diario de Costa Rica*, June

2, 1948, 3. According to Chanto, the jail initially held 40 prisoners, but by the end of the forty-day conflict around 150 prisoners were housed in San Marcos's schoolhouse.

97. Carlos Elizondo, interview.
98. Álvaro Gamboa, interview.
99. Abilio Naranjo Barrantes, interview.
100. Antonio Umaña, interview.
101. Humberto Robles, interview by the author, April 12, 2008.
102. Analías Mezais, interview.
103. Nino Vargas Picado, interview.
104. Lehoucq and Molina, *Stuffing the Ballot Box*, 41.

Chapter 5

1. "Tarrazú en la Revolución," *El Diario de Costa Rica*, May 16, 1948, 4.

2. As discussed in chapter 4, the precise number of local casualties is uncertain. My estimate of more than one thousand is conservative, based on my interviews with combatants and civilians alike who described seeing dozens of corpses in different locations. Additionally, given Iván Molina's claims that the war cost four thousand lives and most of the fighting took place in and around Tarrazú, this figure seems conservative. Iván Molina Jiménez, "¿Fue una guerra inevitable?," *Ancora*, *La Nación*, March 16, 2008.

3. Bowman, *Militarization, Democracy, and Development*, 74. Also, Alain Rouquié, *The Military and the State in Latin America* (Berkeley: University of California Press, 1987), 189. Iván Molina estimates that by the conclusion of 1948 the war left some 4,000 dead, another 7,000 exiled, and 3,000 political prisoners. See Molína Jiménez, "¿Fue una guerra inevitable?" Additionally, Solís notes that in 1948 Figueres would claim 1,100 combatants perished during the Civil War before revising that number to 1,500 in 1949. Both sums, however, are questionable; the junta made no efforts to count the dead. Solís, *La institucionalidad ajena*, 305. Moreover, the junta published a pamphlet that listed rebel soldiers who perished but made no mention of the deaths of government troops. Díaz Arias, *Crisis Social*, 329.

4. The census does not record any population declines. In fact, the population grew from 803,084 in 1947 to 825,378 in 1948. This growth reflects the nation's high birth rates in this period, which countered any population losses the war caused. Unfortunately, the census does not make note of how many of that year's recorded deaths (9,944) were war casualties. See Centro Centroamericano de Población, *Estadística Anuario de Costa Rica, 1948*, San José: Costa Rica, 1948, accessed July 2, 2010, http://ccp.ucr.ac.cr/bvp/pdf/anuariocr/an1948/index.htm.

5. Analías Meza, interview.

6. The term *mariachi* for government supporters emerged during the huelga de los brazos caídos. When the police proved unable to return order in the face of strikes, looting, and street violence, the government asked for and received the assistance of hundreds of vanguardista volunteers. Hundreds answered the government's call to help restore order. Many came from the coasts where they worked in US banana enclaves and at least some of them were of Afro-Caribbean origins. These two factors meant that many metropolitan residents experienced the vanguardistas' arrival as a foreign invasion. Reflecting these sentiments, *El Diario de Costa Rica* published a political cartoon depicting a group of vanguardista volunteers, who were

clearly unaccustomed to the Central Valley's cool evenings, shivering under blankets they had wrapped around their shoulders. This cartoon's humorous linking of the vanguardistas and Mexican mariachi singers would permanently shape the opposition's narrative. Indeed, government supporters were disparagingly called mariachis by the opposition press until the end of the 1948 Civil War. Additionally, several oppositionists, such as Alberto Cañas, wrote highly racialized, classist, and nationalist critiques of the mariachis, who they described as "Negroes and Communist stevedores . . . without shoes or shirts, presuming to guard the streets of the capital as though they were citizens." For more information on the origins of this term, see Creedman, *Historical Dictionary of Costa Rica*, 170. Cañas's description of the mariachis was translated and quoted in John Patrick Bell, *Crisis in Costa Rica: The 1948 Revolution* (Austin: University of Texas Press, 1971), 26. For a more contemporary analysis of how the opposition dehumanized or "othered" government supporters through highly racialized political cartoons and opinion pieces on the mariachis, see Díaz Arias, "Social Crises and Struggling Memories," 230–31.

7. Analías Meza, interview.

8. Analías Meza, interview.

9. Meza did not want to estimate how many deaths took place at La Sierra, but when asked whether there were more than a hundred corpses he said, "Yes, many more." He would not, however, estimate how many more. Analías Meza, interview.

10. Analías Meza, interview.

11. Álvaro Gamboa, interview. Gamboa, like many rebels, perceived Picado and Calderón as communists because of their alliance with the PVP. See chapter 4.

12. The rebels' seizure of El Tejar was a turning point in the conflict and marked the end of the government's efforts to recapture the south. See Dunkerley, *Power in the Isthmus*, 130.

13. Álvaro Gamboa, interview. Although the El Tejar massacre is not discussed in textbooks or other sources of the official national narrative, several professional historians have conducted oral histories of participants and survivors of the massacre, beginning with Miguel Acuña, *El 48* (San José: Imprenta Lehmann, 1974), 258–59. More recently, an informant of Díaz Arias revealed that rebels killed 225 government supporters after they surrendered and that some injured combatants were burned alive alongside the dead. See Díaz Arias, "Social Crises and Struggling Memories," 263–64.

14. Carlos Elizondo, interview.

15. Humberto Robles Calvo, interview.

16. Arturo Valverde, interview.

17. Lourdes Gamboa, interview.

18. Multiple interviewees mentioned that most of Tarrazú's farms in 1948 were monocultural coffee farms, which meant that the area's farmers could no longer provide for the basic consumption needs of the community. Nino Vargas Picado, interview. Lidia Angulo Araya, interview. Fany Jiménez Solís, interview by the author, April 12, 2008, San Marcos de Tarrazú.

19. Lidia Angulo Araya, interview.

20. Juana Fernández, interview.

21. Juana Fernández, interview.

22. Juana Fernández, interview.

23. Nelly Barrantes Porras, interview by the author, April 19, 2008, Guadalupe de

Tarrazú. Barrantes's claim that Zumbado's family was never told this story of his torturous death is implausible. It is hard to imagine in such a small community, where neighbors gossiped and shared accounts of how Zumbado allegedly died, that the family never heard this rendition of events. It is, however, possible that family members chose to believe another version of Zumbado's death.

24. Analías Meza, interview.

25. Blas Vargas Blanco, interview by the author, March 18, 2008, San Marcos de Tarrazú.

26. Villegas Hoffmeister, *La guerra de Figueres*, 412.

27. Villegas Hoffmeister, 413.

28. Of the 922 cases brought to the tribunal, it seems that 322 individuals associated with the former regime were prosecuted. See Díaz Arias, *Crisis Social*, 305–6.

29. Nelly Barrantes Porras, interview.

30. M. Chanto Méndez, "Primero en la escuela," 3.

31. Lourdes Gamboa, interview.

32. Quintín Araya Navarro, interview.

33. Fany Jiménez Solís, interview, April 12, 2008.

34. Bernardo Martínez, interview by the author, March 25, 2008, San Marcos de Tarrazú. Interviewee's name has been changed to maintain his privacy. At the concentration camp or political prison, located in San Isidro de El General, witnesses recalled that the rebel leader Frank Marshall threw explosive grenades at prisoners and shot at the prisoners' feet "for fun." For more on this incident of prisoner abuse, see Díaz Arias, "Social Crises and Struggling Memories," 282.

35. Bernardo Martínez, interview.

36. Helber Umaña Gamboa, interview by the author, March 17, 2008, San Marcos de Tarrazú.

37. Helber Umaña Gamboa, interview.

38. Elías Montero, interview. Montero is correct that both Figueres and Umaña had a sizable workforce that labored planting and harvesting their cabuya and coffee fields, but these two also owned and ran processing mills for their respective crops. As the region's primary agroindustrialists, these men were potentially natural allies against the social guarantees. Yet, given Figueres's commitment to socialism in his early writings, it seems he was uninterested in reversing the social reforms. A personal grudge against Calderón over his exile and anger over the government's tacit support of mob violence against German, Italian, and Spanish businesses seem more likely drivers.

39. Helber Umaña, interview.

40. Blas Vargas, interview.

41. Bowman, *Militarization, Democracy, and Development*, 99.

42. Umaña and others felt betrayed by Figueres's policies. Lowell Gudmundson asserts that many Costa Rican beneficio owners, like Umaña, had supported Figueres's insurrection because they feared the old regime's alliance with the communists, which they viewed as a threat to their socioeconomic position. While Figueres would destroy the communist presence in the country, as discussed later in this chapter, he and his government would also support the formation of cooperatives and the nationalization of the banking system, which would effectively strip the traditional coffee mill owning elite of their near absolute economic monopoly. Indeed, the national banks and cooperatives would provide smallholders with al-

ternative sources of credit at lower interest rates, breaking smallholder dependence on beneficio owners and also reducing mill profits. Additionally, the cooperatives would provide private mills with competition for smallholders' harvests and in this way destroy this class's once economic dominance over coffee profits as both processors and exporters of smallholder cooperative members' beans. Gudmundson, "On Paths Not Taken," 349.

43. Bowman, *Militarization, Democracy, and Development*. The pact's key negotiator was US ambassador Nathaniel P. Davis, who was asked by Picado's government to help broker a peace settlement. The pact was named for the location where it was signed.

44. Arturo Valverde, interview.

45. For more on this pact, see Bowman, *Militarization, Democracy, and Development*, 94.

46. In 1972, years later, Ulate would admit that he was never in favor of the junta and wanted to immediately take political power. He believed, however, that, since Figueres had both guns and soldiers, he had no option but to accede to Figueres's demands. Of course, Ulate did have some bargaining power since Figueres required his public support to present himself credibly as a legitimate powerholder. Díaz Arias, *Crisis Social*, 285.

47. Yashar, *Demanding Democracy*, 185–86.

48. Figueres's reasons for abolishing the military are an issue of contention among historians. Figueres claimed that his action was not revolutionary but reflected the junta's desire to return Costa Rica to its peaceful roots. The political violence of the 1940s orchestrated by both sides, coupled with the fact that Costa Rica had the largest, best-trained, and best-armed military in Central America from the 1850s through the 1880s, pokes holes into the image of Costa Rica's allegedly peaceful past. See Iván Molina Jiménez, *La campaña nacional, 1856–1857: Una visión desde el siglo XXI* (San José: Museo Histórico Cultural Juan Santamaría, 2000), 61. Historians contend that Figueres was moved less by the desire to return Costa Rica to an idyllic past (that never was) and more by immediate political necessity. Some claim that Figueres acted to boost his waning political popularity in the face of his unpopular economic policies, namely the nationalization of the banks and the creation of an income tax; see Ameringer, *Caribbean Legion*. Others suggest that Figueres sought to sidestep his promise to the Caribbean Legion to convert Costa Rica into the base for subsequent revolutions in the region; see Kyle Longley, *The Sparrow and the Hawk: Costa Rica and the United States during the Rise of José Figueres* (Tuscaloosa: University of Alabama Press, 1997). Kirk Bowman, alternatively, maintains that Figueres feared a military coup; see Bowman, *Militarization, Democracy, and Development*. More recently, Matthew Eisenson argues that Figueres was motivated by a desire to gain US political support, which up until then had favored Picado and Calderón; see Eisenson, "The Myth of Pacifism, the Reality of Politics: The Roots and Consequences of Unilateral Demilitarization in Costa Rica," unpublished senior essay, Yale University, 2009. Clearly, Figueres had plenty of political reasons to be rid of the military.

49. Leonard Bird, *Costa Rica: The Unarmed Democracy* (London: Sheppard Press, 1984), 92.

50. Bird, 92.

51. Bird, 93.

52. Bird, 90.

53. Additionally, the attacks on vanguardistas forced Figueres to renege on a personal promise he made to Manuel Mora on April 15, 1948. Mora, recognizing that the rebels were winning the war, met with Figueres, where he agreed to encourage Picado and Calderón to negotiate a peace treaty in exchange for Figueres's commitment to protect vanguardistas from retribution once the conflict ended. For more, see Eduardo Mora Valverde, *Setenta años de militancia comunista: Recuerdos de Eduardo Mora Valverde* (San José: Editorial Juricentro, 2000). Also see Ameringer, *Don Pepe*, 74.

54. The five men boarded a train headed for San José, but just outside of Limón, they were removed from the train car and shot in a place known as El Codo del Diablo. In San José, Sanabria was not informed of these men's arrests so he was unable to intervene on their behalf. This action coupled with his cooperation and support of not only the Calderón and Picado administrations but also the PVP earned him many enemies in the junta, including Figueres. In fact, the junta would attempt to get Sanabria unseated through backdoor letters to Rome. This plot failed and Sanabria remained a thorn in the Second Republic's side. Díaz Arías, *Crisis Social*, 284–85 and 302–4.

55. For more on this, see Mora Valverde, *Setenta años*. Also see Dunkerley, *Power in the Isthmus*, 131.

56. Yashar, *Demanding Democracy*, 187.

57. Civil servants and applicants for government positions who were believed supporters of the former regime were let go and refused employment well into the 1950s in Central Valley communities. This included high school teachers and University of Costa Rica *professores* who were associated with either the PNR or PVP. Additionally, the children of calderonistas were taunted and teased by other children and even adults as late as the 1950s for their fathers' political associations. Díaz Arias, *Crisis Social*, 309.

58. It is possible that there were vanguardistas in Tarrazú, but they would have been an extreme minority, since no votes for PVP candidates were counted in the region. Moreover, no one I spoke with could recall the existence of a local vanguardista presence. This is unsurprising, since so many local families were landowners, who saw socialism and communism as a greater threat than capitalism to their familial futures.

59. Fany Jiménez Solís, interview, April 12, 2008.

60. Emilio "Elí" Rojas Ureña, interview by the author, April 9, 2008, Santa María de Dota.

61. Elí Rojas Ureña, interview.

62. Elí Rojas Ureña, interview.

63. Elí Rojas Ureña, interview. The violent attacks against former supporters of the toppled government arguably ended, or at least began to decrease markedly, after 1958, when Calderón was permitted to return to Costa Rica, after nine years of exile in Mexico. A few weeks after he and his family returned to Costa Rica, their home was victim to a drive-by shooting. For years, officials in the Second Republic had turned a blind eye to these types of partisan attacks against the former regime and its associates. After this attack, however, the government responded by demanding justice and the prosecution of the assailants. While they were never captured, this event marked a clear shift in the nation's political culture and arguably the end of the long Civil War period. For more on Calderón's return and the attack on his home, see Díaz Arías, *Crisis Social*, 320.

64. The military's abolition did not mean that Figueres was committed to democracy or even peaceful resolutions to political conflict. Recent analysis of the 1950s suggests politicians from both of the nation's main political parties sought to violate democratic principles. In 1953, after Ulate's term concluded and Figueres assumed the presidency, Ulate joined forces with his former enemies, exiled presidents Calderón and Picado, to devise a plan to forcefully oust Figueres. While the plan ultimately failed, it suggests just how tentative these leaders supported democracy, and they were not alone. Indeed, in 1958 when Figueres's fellow liberacionista Francisco Orlich Bolmarcich lost the election, Figueres allegedly considered remaining in power. For more on this, see Kirk Bowman, "Democracy on the Brink: The First Figueres Presidency," in Palmer and Molina, *Costa Rica Reader*, 175–82.

65. Civics textbooks that date back to the 1950s suggest that Costa Rica's mythic democracy has deeper historical roots. See, for example, Juan Trejos, *Geografia ilustrada de Costa Rica con un vocabulario geográfico* (San José: Trejos Hermanos, 1958), 27–29.

66. In the 1970s, Costa Rica's exceptionalist mythology would expand, with textbooks joining peace and democracy as interrelated values with allegedly deep historical origins. Oscar Aguilar and Carlos L. Fallas Monge, *Estudios sociales para 7º grado: Geografía, historia y cívica de Costa Rica* (San José: Libreria, Imprenta y Litografia Lehmann, 1973). These same authors published slightly edited versions of this same text under slightly different titles in 1974, 1975, and 1976.

67. Aguilar and Fallas Monge.

68. Honduras was also extremely polarized in this period, as it was essentially converted into a US military base from which the Contra war was launched.

69. For more on Salvadoran immigration to Costa Rica, see Bridget A. Hayden, *Salvadorans in Costa Rica: Displaced Lives* (Tucson: University of Arizona Press, 2003). For more on Nicaraguan immigration to Costa Rica, see Carlos Sandoval-García, *Threatening Others: Nicaraguans and the Formation of National Identities in Costa Rica* (Athens: Ohio University Press, 2004).

70. Angela Quiróz de Vallejos, Rosa María Durán Aguilar and María Cristina Durán Aguilar, *Estudios Sociales para bachillerato en enseñanza media* (San José: Editorial de la Associación Nacional de Educadores Costa Rica, 1988), 218.

71. More recent historical monographs, as discussed in the introduction, question the argument that stable democracy was established and that demilitarization began in the nineteenth century. See, for example, Muñoz Guillén, *El Estado*, and Bowman, *Militarization, Democracy, and Development*. Although these two works present a more complicated image of Costa Rican politics and the military's role in society before 1948, neither delves into the actual Civil War. So, although these authors together break apart some of the mythology surrounding Costa Rica's traditions of peace and democracy, they fail to examine in detail the greatest piece of evidence in their argument—the violence that occurred during the Civil War. Most recently, the work by David Díaz Arias does consider some of the political violence leading up to the Civil War and some of the recorded atrocities of this conflict.

72. Francisco Antonio Pacheco and Mario A. Houed Vega, *Educación cívica costarricense* (San José: UNED, 1992), 18.

73. Pacheco and Houed Vega, 21.

74. Raquel Bolaños Herrera, Emilia Gamboa Escalante, and German Vásquez Agüero, *Educación Cívica: IX Año* (San José: BIS, 2005), vi.

75. Constantino Urcuyo Fournier and Chester Zelaya Goodman's *Democracia costarricense: Pasado, presente y futuro* (San José: UNED, 1989).

76. A similar argument to that of Zelaya and Urcuyo is presented by Miguel A. Umaña Aglietti, "Militaries y civiles en Costa Rica," licenciado thesis, Universidad de Costa Rica, 1978. Umaña's thesis presents Costa Rica as historically dominated by politicians and characterized by a traditionally weak military. Umaña asserts that the historic strength of Costa Rica's democratic traditions allowed Figueres to easily dissolve the military. A slightly different approach is taken in Ana Luisa Cerdas Albertazzi and Gerardo Vargas Cambronero's *La abolición del ejército en Costa Rica: Hito de un camino de democracia y paz* (San José: Imprenta Nacional, 1988). These authors, with their clear liberacionista leanings, suggest that Costa Ricans were attracted to democracy, but only after Figueres abolished the military was democracy firmly established.

77. The expressed sense of distance that older Tarrazúceños feel to the nation, based on the way that the official national narrative has sidelined their experiences and actions in shaping the political landscape, shares some parallels with the experience of peasants in Chinadega, Nicaragua. Indeed, peasants in this community organized a successful agrarian protest movement in the 1950s and 1960s, which in the wake of the successful Sandinista Revolution of 1979 was quickly forgotten in this nation's postrevolutionary official narrative. Interestingly, however, where Tarrazúceños have largely silenced themselves, choosing not to actively seek to "correct" the record, the Nicaraguan campesinos of Chinadega reportedly approached historian Jeffrey Gould and asked him to record their stories to help them secure a place for their community's actions within their nation's history books. There is little to suggest why Tarrazúceños have not been as eager as the Chinadegans to insert themselves into their respective official national narratives. Jeffrey L. Gould, *To Lead As Equals: Rural Protest and Political Consciousness in Chinadega, Nicaragua, 1912–1979* (Chapel Hill: University of North Carolina Press, 1990).

78. For more on this, see the conclusion.

79. Juan Chanto Méndez, interview.

80. Carlos Elizondo, interview.

81. Quintín Araya Navarro, interview.

82. The formation of coffee cooperatives in Tarrazú was part of a broader transition within the coffee industry following the Civil War. In fact, Carolyn Hall points to the 1960s as the decade of Costa Rican coffee cooperative formation. She notes that between 1957 and 1970 an astonishing twenty-two coffee cooperatives were established throughout Costa Rica. Hall, *El Café*, 163–64.

83. Flora Villa, interview.

84. For more on how legislation in the 1950s coupled with government support of agrarian cooperatives and Green Revolution agrochemicals helped Costa Rican coffee farmers sustain high profits in the 1960s and 1970s, see Mario Samper, "Costa Rica's Response to the Coffee Crisis," *Globalization, Neoliberalism, and the Latin American Coffee Societies*, March 2010, 74.

85. Picado Umaña, "La expansión del café," 70.

86. According to Picado Umaña's statistical research, roughly 20 percent of the nation's farmers were using chemical fertilizers and herbicides in 1955. Picado Umaña, 72.

87. Picado Umaña, 74.

88. Picado Umaña, 88. Tarrazú farmers' chemical use was above the national average, which in 1963 was just 18 percent. This is curious, as it suggests too that on the national level chemical use declined between 1955 and 1963. The causes for this are not discussed by Picado Umaña. However, given that peasants in this period were opening new lands for agricultural exploitation, it is likely a reflection less of decreased use of chemicals than an increase in hectares of land being planted in the republic. In more recent decades, many have come to question the region's heavy investment in agrochemicals, raising concerns over issues of water pollution and its potential impact on human health. In fact, in the 1990s, Tarrazú saw Costa Rica's first successful environmental contamination case when neighbors downhill from a coffee farmer sued him for contaminating their water with his use of agrochemicals on his crops. For more on this court case, see Wilson Umaña Picado, Rafael Ledezma Díaz, and Roberto Granados Porras, "Territorio de Coyotes, Agroecosistemas y Cambio Tecnológico en una región cafetalera de Costa Rica," *Revista de Historia* no. 59–60 (Enero–Diciembre 2009): 121.

89. A combination of chemical fertilizers, insecticides, and the planting of new coffee varieties permitted Tarrazú farmers to increase the number of coffee shrubs they planted on their properties to double or even triple their coffee production, which, in turn, increased their profits. Picado Umaña, "La expansión del café," 107–10.

90. Between 1956 and 1960, the junta provided an annual average of four hundred loans to Tarrazú farmers. Picado Umaña, 89.

91. Sick, *Farmers of the Golden Bean*, 32.

92. Misael Monge Álvarado, interview by the author, April 11, 2008, San Marcos de Tarrazú. For more on the Alliance for Progress's support of cooperatives in Latin America during the 1950s and 1960s, particularly after the 1959 Cuban Revolution, as a means of encouraging procapitalist sentiments among the popular masses in Latin America, see Sick, 31.

93. Noe Lopéz, interview by the author, November 20, 2007, San Marcos de Tarrazú.

94. Elías Montero, interview.

95. Misael Monge Álvarado, interview.

96. Misael Monge Álvarado, interview.

97. Misael Monge Álvarado, interview.

98. Juan Chanto Méndez, interview.

99. J. Chanto Méndez, *Cooperativa de caficultores*, folio 8.

100. Misael Monge Álvarado, interview.

101. This department was formed on September 23, 1953, via Ley 1644. For more information on this law and procooperative legislation, see Martín Quiróz Sánchez, "La responsabilidad civil de las cooperativas de caficultores," licenciado thesis, Universidad de Costa Rica, 1985.

102. These beneficios were formed in the 1930s under Marcos Chanto's leadership, as discussed in chapter 2.

103. J. Chanto Méndez, *Cooperativa de caficultores*, folio 9.

104. Carlos Elizondo, interview.

105. Marc Edelman, *Peasants against Globalization: Rural Social Movements in Costa Rica* (Palo Alto, CA: Stanford University Press, 1999), 56–61.

106. The instituto was formed in 1933 with the aim of improving the relation-

ship between coffee producers, beneficiadores, and exporters. For information on this organization's formation and tensions between these three groups during the 1920s and 1930s, see chapter 2.

107. By the early 1960s, Tobías Umaña Jiménez had died, and his farms, stores, and beneficios were passed on to his two sons, Humberto and Tobías "Tobís." Juan Bosco Umaña Abarca, interview.

108. Marcos Tulio Blanco Valverde, interview by the author, March 25, 2008, La Sabana de Tarrazú.

109. Marcos Tulio Blanco, interview.

110. Misael Monge Álvarado, interview.

111. Misael Monge Álvarado, interview.

112. The opening of the local high school was significant, as it permitted Tarrazúceños for the first time to secure more than just an elementary education in reading, writing, and arithmetic. The relatively late establishment of a secondary school in the region pokes holes in another Costa Rican exceptionalist mythology, which centers on the state's historic commitment to education. Indeed, as the case of Tarrazú illustrates, the Costa Rican state was slow in building secondary schools outside of the Central Valley. Additionally, as the work of Iván Molina on this topic places into focus, state funds for education fluctuated considerably during the nineteenth and twentieth centuries. Furthermore, until the second half of the twentieth century policy makers had little interest in funding education beyond the primary level, especially outside of the Central Valley. For more on this, see Molina, *La educación en Costa Rica.*

113. Francisco Madrigal, interview by the author, July 1, 2007, Newark, New Jersey. By request, interviewee's name has been changed to maintain his privacy.

Chapter 6

1. Beatriz Cárdenas, interview by the author, July 9, 2006, San Marcos de Tarrazú, and Catalina Cárdenas, interview by the author, July 9, 2006, San Marcos de Tarrazú. By request, both interviewee's names have been changed to maintain their privacy.

2. Between January and July 2005, US border patrol arrested over 700 Costa Ricans without proper documentation. This marked a dramatic increase; indeed, in 2004 border patrol arrested 450 Costa Ricans. For more information on these statistics, see Hazel Feigenblatt, "Se dispara en 200% captura de ticos ilegales en Estados Unidos," *La Nación*, October 17, 2005, accessed February 28, 2011, www.nacion.com/ln_ee/2005/octubre/17/paiso.html.

3. Orlando Navarro, interview by the author, January 13, 2008, San Marcos de Tarrazú. By request interviewee's name has been changed to maintain his privacy.

4. Yamileth Monge, interview by the author, April 29, 2006, Paterson, New Jersey. By request, interviewee's name has been changed to maintain her privacy. Jorge Leiva, interview by the author, September 16, 2008, San Pablo de León Cortés.

5. The first Tarrazúceño to immigrate to the United States was Martín Cárdenas's sister, who married a US citizen and paid for Martín's and several other siblings' tickets to New York. For more on her story and the origins of Tarrazúceño immigration to the United States, see Kordick Rothe, "La memoria del viaje."

6. Increasing socioeconomic divisions between smallholders and landless la-

borers in the region were a by-product both of the better prices coffee farmers were provided by the cooperatives and the cooperatives' investment in technical advances. In particular, cooperatives provided members with access to credit and training opportunities, so farmers could terrace steeper terrains, employ chemical herbicides and fertilizers, and adopt new coffee bush varieties, which together permitted local farmers to increase coffee production levels and profits. For more on the way that technical investment and training by the region's cooperatives and by the handful of Cold War–era agronomists assigned to the region by Servicio Técnico Interamericano de Cooperación Agrícola (STICA) reshaped coffee production in Tarrazú and arguably inspired immigration to the United States for some landless laborers, see Umaña Picado, Ledezma Díaz, and Granados Porras, "Territorio de Coyotes," 121.

7. Beatriz Cárdenas, interview.

8. Many also immigrated to San José, where they studied to become professionals or sought work in the service sector. See Kordick, "Tarrazú."

9. Immigration to the United States increased markedly after the 1982 financial crisis; indeed, scholarly observers often incorrectly assert that Tarrazúceños began emigrating in the wake of this dramatic economic downturn. See, for instance, Umaña Picado, Ledezma Díaz, and Granados Porras, "Territorio de Coyotes," 138. Also see Samper, "Costa Rica's Response to the Coffee Crisis," 80.

10. International Coffee Organization, "Statistics," accessed July 8, 2007, www.ico.org. This organization's data collection priorities appear to have changed; they no longer provide data on what farmers were paid for their crop; hence, more current data is not provided. The 1976–77 crop proved the most profitable year for Costa Rican coffee farmers in the twentieth century, when inflation is considered. The 1980s were, like the 1910s, 1930s, and 1940s, a decade of sharp declines in coffee prices. As in these earlier years of downturn, farmers in Costa Rica and elsewhere, who could, responded by increasing production on their lands, which further decreased coffee prices on the global market. For more on broader shifts in coffee prices and farmers' responses, see Samper, "Costa Rica's Response," 75.

11. Froylan Naranjo Monge, interview by the author, December 2, 2007.

12. Emigration has also been embraced by coffee farmers in the neighboring canton of Pérez Zeledón, beginning in the 1980s, as a familial strategy in the face of declining coffee values, increased population concentration, and a reduction in available lands. Unlike Tarrazú, Peréz Zeledón's coffee is not renowned. In fact, the region is reputed to produce the nation's lowest-quality beans. The economic downturns of the 1980s and 1990s hit this region's farmers particularly hard. This likely explains too why emigration not only became a popular option but has not seemingly garnered the same social backlash as it has in Tarrazú. For more on Pérez Zeledón emigration in the 1980s and 1990s, see Sick, *Farmers of the Golden Bean*, 118–20. Certainly, however, emigration was not the only option available that local farmers selected to contend with decreasing coffee prices in the latter decades of the twentieth century. In fact, both Deborah Sick's and Mario Samper's research demonstrates that some Costa Rican farmers responded to low coffee prices in the 1980s by emigrating. However, others interplanted other cash crops in their coffee fields, developed agrotourism in their farms, sold off their lands, invested in education for themselves and their children, and secured better prices for their coffee by selling to cooperatives or by forming small-scale community processing mills (this has been a strategy particularly embraced in Tarrazú). Critically, however, remit-

tances have provided the needed capital for the machinery in many of these cases. Additionally, cooperatives and large-scale exporters/processors sought out and secured new markets, namely in China and internally within Costa Rica, to increase profitability. Sick, 105–20; and Samper, "Costa Rica's Response," 72–92.

13. Coffee prices have historically fluctuated and many third- and fourth-generation Costa Rican coffee farmers have survived by confidently investing in their coffee bushes and farms even when prices declined. In the Great Depression and World Wars I and II, farmers who were able to weather the storm profited handsomely in the boom markets of the 1920s and the 1960s. Those farmers, however, who could not make ends meet and lost their lands to foreclosures or were forced to sell to avoid foreclosures lost dearly historically. In fact, as chapter 3 details for the case of Tarrazú, many men in these decades of hardship went from being independent farm owners to landless laborers, whereas the wealthiest in Tarrazú and the republic as a whole, who had capital on hand, profited greatly from reduced land and labor costs. Costa Rica's coffee farm owners in the 1980s and 1990s undoubtedly learned from their fathers and grandfathers to hold tight to their lands by reminding them of this earlier history. This idea is well articulated by other scholars, namely Samper, "Costa Rica's Response," 73–75, to explain how and why Costa Rican coffee farmers remained committed to their farms and crops even as global coffee prices declined year after year.

14. Nicaragua provides a similar Central American example. See Roger N. Lancaster, *Life Is Hard: Machismo, Danger, and Intimacy of Power in Nicaragua* (Berkeley: University of California Press, 1992).

15. Pedro Sánchez, interview by the author, April 29, 2006, Paterson, New Jersey. By request, interviewee's name has been changed to maintain his privacy.

16. Pedro Sánchez, interview.

17. Orlando Navarro, interview.

18. Carmen Caamaño Morúa also observed coffee farmers emigrating to retain their relationship to the land in her research in the region. See Carmen Caamaño Morúa, "Subjetividades en Contienda: Redes de Solidaridad, Capital Social y Gobernamentalidad de Migrantes Costarricenses en Espacios Transnacionales," PhD dissertation, University of Albany, State University of New York, 2007, 151.

19. Manuel Madrigal, interview by the author, July 2, 2007, Newark, New Jersey. By request, interviewee's name has been changed to maintain his privacy.

20. Manuel Madrigal, interview.

21. Luís Hernán Villegas, interview.

22. Martín Madrigal, interview by the author, July 1, 2007, Newark, New Jersey. By request, interviewee's name has been changed to maintain his privacy.

23. By working on their farms and seeking wage labor work in the United States, Villegas and countless Tarrazúceños embrace both petty bourgeoisie and semiproletarian strategies for class advancement. Carmen Caamaño's work in Tarrazú and in the neighboring canton of Pérez Zeledón analyzes this phenomenon. See Caamaño, *Entre arriba y abajo: La experiencia transnacional de la migración de costarricenses hacia Estados Unidos* (San José: Editorial de la Universidad de Costa Rica, 2011).

24. Caamaño. The phenomenon of emigration of traditional elites such as the Villegas family is seen outside of Tarrazú, of course. In the 1980s, anthropologist Patricia Pessar observed Dominican elites selecting emigration as a means of coun-

tering downward mobility in the face of reduced crop prices and land fragmentation. For more on the Dominican case, see Patricia Pessar, "The Role of Households in International Migration and the Case of U.S.-Bound Migration from the Dominican Republic," *International Migration Review* 16, no. 2 (Summer 1982): 350–52.

25. Piedra Blanco, *Historias y Añoranzas*, 21.

26. Manuel Castro, interview. Remittances and wages earned in the United States have left rural workers throughout Latin America with greater economic expectations, which have sparked tensions between employers and workers. In the Dominican Republic, Patricia Pessar found a community deeply touched by emigration, where rural workers refused to take jobs that offered wages below subsistence levels. In response, landowners complained to Pessar that local workers were "lazy." Patricia Pessar, "Role of Households," 355.

27. Martín Madrigal, interview.

28. Elías Velásquez, interview by the author, July 13, 2005, Santa María de Dota. By request, interviewee's name has been changed to maintain his privacy.

29. Herminía Muñoz, interview.

30. According to a survey I distributed in New Jersey restaurants that cater to Costa Rican clients, of the 103 immigrant respondents, 27 disclosed concrete economic goals that they were saving toward, including the purchase or improvement of a home or farm in Tarrazú. For more information on the survey, see chapter 7. Additionally, a study conducted in the region at about the same time suggested that most emigrants from the region to the United States were young men who owned three hectares or fewer and were seeking to invest in improving and/or expanding their farm. In stark contrast, these same researchers found that when Tarrazúceños immigrated to the Central Valley they tended to abandon farming. In sum, wages earned abroad permitted committed farmers from the region to retain their farms. See Umaña Picado, Ledezma Díaz, and Granados Porras, "Territorio de Coyotes," 139.

31. Rocío Loría Bolaños, e-mail message to author, March 11, 2011. Loría Bolaños is an anthropologist who conducted ethnographic research on the Ngöbe-Buglé in Tarrazú.

32. Philip D. Young, *Ngawbe: Tradition and Change among the Western Guaymí of Panama* (Urbana: University of Illinois Press, 1971), 82–104.

33. Mirna Rodríguez Palacios, interview by the author, September 13, 2008, San Marcos de Tarrazú.

34. Historically, the region's coffee was not only picked by local farmers, their families, and landless laborers but also by pickers from the adjoining southern canton of Pérez Zeledón. Beginning in the 1970s, however, new varieties of coffee were developed that could produce fruit at much lower elevations, including this neighboring region. The growing seasons between Tarrazú and Pérez Zeledón were such that this source of seasonal workers evaporated. Magnifying the region's need for laborers was the out-migration of Tarrazúceños to the United States and the intensification of local coffee production, both as strategies to contend with declining global coffee prices. In fact, between 1989 and 1994, coffee farmers throughout Costa Rica doubled their farms' coffee production (through intensified use of agrochemicals and farmland expansion). In Tarrazú, however, farmers increased production by an incredible six-fold in this same period, which meant that several times more labor was needed than in earlier years. Thus, in the 1990s the Ngöbe-Buglé filled a growing labor need in the wake of increased coffee production and reduced local labor.

For more on this, see Umaña Picado, Ledezma Díaz, and Granados Porras, "Territorio de Coyotes," 142. Also see, Samper, "Costa Rica's Response," 75.

35. Young, *Ngawbe*.

36. Gendered use of traditional dress goes beyond the Ngöbe-Buglé. In an analysis of the K'iche Maya of Quetzaltenango, Guatemala, historian Greg Grandin has analyzed photographs to suggest that by 1900 most elite K'iche men had adopted European dress, but their daughters and wives had not. Grandin attributes this to tensions between a desire to modernize and remain traditional. For the K'iche, like the Ngöbe-Buglé of today, the solution was clearly gendered. Grandin, *Blood of Guatemala*, 185–89.

37. Also see Kordick, "Tarrazú."

38. "Manos indígenas Panameñas y Nicaragüenses recogen café Costa Rica," *La Nación*, April 18, 2006, accessed March 8, 2011, wvw.nacion.com/ln_ee/2006/abril/19/ultima-ce20.html.

39. Elías Velásquez, interview.

40. José Ramírez, interview by the author, January 2, 2006, San Marcos de Tarrazú. By request, interviewee's name has been changed to maintain his privacy.

41. *Sarcoptes scabiei* is a microscopic mite that causes an acute itch and a contagious skin disease.

42. Lourdes Beatriz Ugalde Madriz, interview.

43. Participant observation. These opinions and information are based on my observations and conversations with Ugalde, her neighbors, and others in the community while I was living in San Marcos. I lived in the region continuously between September 2007 and May 2008.

44. Montserrat Solano Carboni, "Otro guaymí muere," *La Nación*, December 17, 1998, accessed March 14, 2011, wvw.nacion.com/ln_ee/1998/diciembre/17/pais6.html.

45. Solano Carboni.

46. Mirna Rodríguez Palacios, interview.

47. Coffee had long been racialized in other areas of the isthmus where elites in the nineteenth century had stripped indigenous communities of their lands to permit them to establish coffee farms and secure labor. This is particularly the case for Guatemala, El Salvador, and Nicaragua. In Costa Rica, however, general government/elite support of legislation that favored squatters' abilities to legalize holdings permitted small farmers to expand into new regions, carve out new farms, and survive as a class without the need to labor on wealthier neighbor's farms even in the face of generational divisions of small plots. The benefit for elites and the state was that the poor opened up new lands and developed them at no cost. Additionally, elites, who quickly came to dominate the processing and export sectors of the coffee economy, secured profits from their smallholder neighbors who sold them unprocessed beans. The downside, for elites, however, was that they had to pay relatively high wages and treat wage earners with respect, if they wished to retain much-needed labor on their farms and in their beneficios. These conditions meant that historically coffee farm work was not racialized or in any other way stigmatized. Williams, *States and Social Evolution*, 128.

48. Today few Tarrazúceños pick coffee or work as farm peons. I had the fortune, however, to casually speak with two local high school students who picked coffee to purchase school supplies. The pair earned the same wages as their Ngöbe-Buglé counterparts.

49. The racialization of coffee picking is relatively recent; indeed, as late as the

1980s, San José policy makers invested in public ad campaigns each year that promoted coffee picking as Costa Rican's patriotic duty, as noted by anthropologist Deborah Sick, who conducted research in the late 1980s. See Sick, *Farmers of the Golden Bean*, 57.

50. Andrea Cordero, interview by the author, January 29, 2008, San Pablo de León Cortés.

51. Tobías Umaña, interview by the author, March 17, 2008, San Marcos de Tarrazú.

52. José Antonio Astuas, interview by the author, December 4, 2007, San Marcos de Tarrazú.

53. Mavis Hiltunen Biesanz, Richard Biesanz, and Karen Zubris Biesanz, *The Ticos: Culture and Social Change in Costa Rica* (Boulder, CO: Lynne Rienner Publishers, 1999), 98. The Biesanzes cite a 1995 research project, conducted by geneticists of the University of Costa Rica, which asserts that the "general population's mix of genes [is] 40–60 percent white, 15–35 percent Indian, and 10–20 percent black. The mix varies according to region and socioeconomic status." Additionally, historical geographer Carolyn Hall in the 1970s classified Costa Rican society as "Mestizo American," within a three-tiered system based on genetic and cultural composition of the community. According to Hall, Costa Rican society was the product of both extreme racial mixing, which eliminated most visible racial lines between Europeans, Native Americans, and Africans. At the same time, Hispanic cultural practices had been fully embraced helping to forge a mixed-race but culturally homogenous Hispanic society. Hall, *Costa Rica*, 61.

54. The origins of Costa Rica's whiteness myth can be traced back to at least the mid-nineteenth century; see chapter 1. By the early twentieth century, notions that all Costa Ricans were white appear to have become widely accepted. Evidence comes in the form of discriminatory legislation intended to "protect" Costa Rica's whiteness from foreign nonwhites. See Clodomiro Picado, "Our Blood Is Blackening," in Palmer and Molina, *Costa Rica Reader*, 243–44. For how Costa Rican racism was instituted on the ground in the first half of the twentieth century, see Putnam, *Company They Kept*.

55. Trejos, *Geografía ilustrada de Costa Rica*, 27–29.

56. This text is a mid-twentieth century version of Costa Rica's official narrative, but the narrative has changed little since then. For more on this, see the introduction.

57. Rafael Naranjo Barrantes, interview by the author, March 16, 2008, La Sabana de Tarrazú.

58. José Antonio Astuas, interview.

59. Emilia Mora, "Cafetales producen angustia y pobreza," *La Nación*, September 13, 2003, accessed March 8, 2011, www.nacion.com/ln_ee/2003/septiembre/13/pais14.html.

Chapter 7

1. Rolando Velásquez, interview by the author, August 25, 2005, Bergenfield, New Jersey. By request, interviewee's name has been changed to maintain his privacy.

2. Rolando Velásquez, interview.

3. Rolando Velásquez, interview.

4. Rolando Velásquez, interview.

5. Diana Walta Hart, *Undocumented in L.A.: An Immigrant's Story* (Wilmington, DE: Scholarly Resources, 1997), 113–16. Hart found fears of being deported encouraged immigrants not to contact authorities when they were victims of crime or were paid below minimum wages.

6. Rolando Velásquez, interview.

7. Rolando Velásquez, interview.

8. The 2010 US census recorded Paterson's population at 145,236, of which 87,398 were Latino. Best known as the largest Peruvian community outside Peru, Paterson is also a primary destination for Costa Ricans. US Census Bureau, "American Factfinder," accessed April 5, 2012, http://factfinder2.census.gov/faces/tableservices. For Peruvian immigration, see Teófilo Altamirano, *Los que se fueron: Peruanos en Estados Unidos* (Lima, Peru: Pontifica Universidad Católica del Perú Fondo Editorial, 1990).

9. According to the 2010 census, Salvadorans (1,292) were the city's largest Central American–born group, followed by Costa Ricans. US Census Bureau, "American Factfinder."

10. My Tarrazú informants repeatedly shared that they had friends and family in Paterson. Additionally, many of the Costa Ricans I met in northern New Jersey were from Tarrazú.

11. The town of Bloomfield, which in the 2010 census had a total population of 47,315, recorded 319 Costa Rican–born residents. Costa Ricans are Bloomfield's largest Central American–born group, although the Puerto Rican population (4,156) is the largest of the city's 11,606 Latinos. Haledon, with a population of 8,318, recorded 95 Costa Ricans and, as in the case of Bloomfield, they were the largest Central American–born group, but also much smaller than the Puerto Rican community (1,185). Just 94 of Prospect Park's 5,865 residents were Costa Rican–born migrants. In all of these cases, Costa Ricans make up a small portion of the total population, but because they tend to cluster together, their presence is much more palpable on the ground. For instance, in Prospect Park, I found two blocks of multifamily homes inhabited by Costa Ricans. US Census Bureau, "American Factfinder."

12. US Census Bureau.

13. For the study, researchers directed 563 students in thirteen schools to write short essays using metaphors to describe their nation. For more, see Sandoval-García, *Threatening Others*.

14. Most students provided a positive image of their nation.

15. For more on the representation of Costa Rican political exceptionalism in textbooks, see the introduction and chapter 6.

16. For Salvadoran emigration to Costa Rica, see Hayden, *Salvadorans in Costa Rica*; for Nicaraguan emigration to Costa Rica, see Sandoval-García, *Threatening Others*.

17. Additionally, as discussed in chapter 6, indigenous Panamanians are the principal coffee pickers in Tarrazú.

18. Sandoval-García, *Threatening Others*.

19. Feigenblatt cited a Costa Rican Central Bank study for her remittance data. More recent studies show similarly impressive findings. In 2008, the Costa Rican Central Bank found that approximately fifty thousand families regularly received

remittances from family members in the United States, providing a case in point. Esteban Oviedo Leiton, "50.000 hogares reciben dinero de ticos en el extranjero," *La Nación*, November 9, 2008, accessed November 12, 2008, www.nacion.com/nacional/hogares-reciben-dinero-ticos-extranjero_0_1012098866.html.

20. Hazel Feigenblatt, "Consulados estiman que unos 220.000 costarricenses viven en EEUU," *La Nación*, March 13, 2005, accessed March 20, 2005, www.nacion.com/nacional/Miles-costarricenses-ilegales-EE-UU_0_744725696.html.

21. Alejandro Cedeño, "Sin sustento," *La Nación*, March 25, 2005, accessed March 28, 2005, www.nacion.com/ln_ee/2005/marzo/24/opinion5.html.

22. Cedeño.

23. Cedeño.

24. Hazel Feigenblatt, "Nota de la redacción," *La Nación*, March 25, 2005, accessed April 1, 2005, www.nacion.com/opinion/sustento_0_746925409.html.

25. Feigenblatt.

26. See, for instance, Feigenblatt, "Entre el 2002 y este año," March 20, 2005; Patricia Leiton, "País recibió $400 millones en remesas y envió $196 millones," February 18, 2006; María Montero, "Mal de Patria: Realizadores ticos a Nueva Jersey," May 31, 2006; Leiton, "Estudio de UCR estima que 28.000 hogares reciben remesas," November 28, 2006; Leiton, "Ingreso y envío de remesas en el país muestra una recuperación," January 6, 2011.

27. Feigenblatt, "Consulados estiman"; Feigenblatt, "Unos viven sueños truncados y otros el 'sueño Americano,'" *La Nación*, March 13, 2005, www.nacion.com/nacional/viven-suenos-truncados-sueno-americano_0_744725715.html; Feigenblatt, "Nacionales entre papeles falsos, miedo y mal de patria," *La Nación*, March 13, 2005, accessed March 20, 2005, www.nacion.com/nacional/Nacionales-papeles-falsos-miedo-patria_0_744725624.html; Feigenblatt, "Hay deportaciones a cada rato," *La Nación*, March 13, 2005, accessed March 20, 2005, www.nacion.com/nacional/deportaciones-rato_0_744725720.html; Feigenblatt, "Difícil volver a Costa Rica," *La Nación*, March 13, 2005, accessed March 20, 2005, www.nacion.com/archivo.html?date=1110693600&sectionId=100.

28. *La Nación* is not sold in print in the United States; however, it has been available online since 1995 and thus is easily accessible to readers throughout the world.

29. On June 12, 2005, I saw sour cream for sale in a Central Valley grocery store (Más por menos in Heredia) for ₡300, which at the time was around $0.63.

30. Feigenblatt, "Miles de costarricenses given illegals en EE.UU.," *La Nación*, March 13, 2005, accessed March 20, 2005, http://wvw.nacion.com/ln_ee/2005/marzo/13/pais1.html.

31. Catalina Muñoz, interview.

32. Catalina Muñoz, interview.

33. This quotation is paraphrased from an entry in my field notebook, July 16, 2007.

34. Participant observation, July 16, 2007.

35. With the exception of Super Corona's, all of these businesses have Costa Rican–born owners. Super Corona's Mexican owners purchased the bar from its original Costa Rican owners. Despite the newest owner's nationality, this establishment continues to cater to Costa Rican clients.

36. Feigenblatt, "Consulados estiman."

37. Marcos Beltrán, interview by the author, June 5, 2007, Montclair, New Jersey. By request, interviewee's name has been changed to maintain his privacy.

38. In Costa Rica, the national holiday is always celebrated on September 15; in New Jersey, however, the event has traditionally been organized for the first Sunday on or after this date, to allow Costa Ricans to participate without having to miss work.

39. Roberto Vilar, interview by the author, June 13, 2011, Haledon, New Jersey. Interviewee's name has been changed to maintain his privacy.

40. Roberto Vilar, interview.

41. This description is based on my field notebook entry, September 3, 2007.

42. The percentage of Tarrazúceños was slightly higher than the whole Costa Rican community, with forty-four of forty-seven Tarrazúceños (93.5 percent) asserting that they planned to return to Costa Rica.

43. For unknown reasons, many respondents chose not to indicate their time in the United States. In fact, forty individuals (39 percent of participants) left this question blank, making this the least-answered survey question. Blank responses were not included within calculations of this data set, since their inclusion makes all other findings in terms of years in the United States numerically insignificant.

44. Among survey respondents, 23 percent had lived in the United States for a decade or more. Of these long-term migrants, only two (10 percent) had spouses in Costa Rica. Another 10 percent had legalized their status and therefore likely traveled regularly between the United States and Costa Rica. However, the vast majority of long-term New Jersey residents were either residing with their spouse in New Jersey (30 percent), were divorced/separated (30 percent), or had never married (25 percent).

45. Like their male counterparts, many women (38 percent) did not indicate how long they had lived abroad. A full 44 percent of male respondents had spent four years or fewer in the United States, and of this group, 73 percent had arrived within the past three years.

46. In contrast, just 33 percent of the men were married and 65 percent of married men did not live with their spouses (who were likely in Costa Rica). Most (70 percent) men lived with other family members and/or friends.

47. An almost equal percentage of men and women (11 percent of women and 12 percent of men) claimed that they were either divorced or separated from their spouse.

48. The 22 percent of women who listed financial goals as their primary motivation for emigrating were all single, suggesting that they arrived with very different priorities from most women migrants.

49. Of course, since these women followed their spouses and/or children who likely emigrated for financial reasons, in a real sense these women's migration was also shaped by economic concerns.

50. All of the married women I met in northern New Jersey noted that they regularly prepared Costa Rican dishes for their families.

51. Susana Jiménez, interview by the author, July 7, 2007, Bloomfield, New Jersey. By request, interviewee's name has been changed to maintain her privacy.

52. Susana Jiménez, interview.

53. Susana Jiménez, interview.

54. Karla Molina, interview by the author, August 17, 2007, Haledon, New Jersey, 2007. By request, interviewee's name has been changed to maintain her privacy.

55. Blanco's and Molina's reluctance to return to Tarrazú because of the increased agency they exercise within their family as wage earners mirrors a similar pattern

seen in New York's Dominican community. For more on how working impacted women's desires to return to the Dominican Republic, see Sherri Grasmuck and Patricia Pessar, *Between Two Islands: Dominican International Migration* (Berkeley: University of California Press, 1991), 156–58.

56. Julieta Blanco, interview by the author, August 17, 2007, Haledon, New Jersey, 2007. By request, interviewee's name has been changed to maintain her privacy.

57. Both Jiménez and Molina have high school diplomas and Blanco has completed some high school studies. Neither has attended college.

58. For the racialization of coffee picking, see chapter 6.

59. The minimum monthly wage for a domestic laborer in Costa Rica in January 2011 was set at ₡131,907.04, which is roughly $265.94. See Confederación de Trabajadores Rerum Novarum, "Lista de Salarios 2010," accessed June 1, 2011, http://rerumnovarum.or.cr/SalariosSectorPrivado/2010/LISTADESALARIORIGE010110.pdf.

60. There is a large disparity in the cost of living in Costa Rica and the United States. In 2008, Costa Rica's Gross Domestic Product (GDP) was US $6,599 per capita, while the per capita GDP in the United States was US $45,230. Furthermore, domestic servants are paid the lowest minimum wages in Costa Rica. A domestic servant's minimum wage is ₡131,907 a month, while workers in all other unskilled sectors are ensured a minimum wage of ₡206,724 a month. In contrast, women in New Jersey earned between $10 and $20 an hour cleaning homes, noticeably more than the $7.25 hourly minimum wage. For more on GDP per capita, see United Nations Statistics Division, "Demographic and Social Statistics." accessed July 3, 2011, http://unstats.un.org/unsd/demographic/products/socind/inc-eco.html. For Costa Rican wages, see Confederación de Trabajadores Rerum Novarum, "Lista de Salarios 2010."

61. Only 17 (16.5 percent) of survey participants had legal permission to work in the United States; of these a much larger percentage were women (28 percent) than men (12 percent).

62. Paniagua legalized her status through her husband, who secured his citizenship through the Amnesty Clause of the Immigration Reform and Control Act of 1986. Emilia Paniagua, interview by the author, July 16, 2007, Haledon, New Jersey. By request, interviewee's name has been changed to maintain her privacy.

63. Emilia Paniagua, interview.

64. Emilia Paniagua, interview.

65. Gustavo Camacho, interview by the author, June 14, 2006, San Marcos de Tarrazú. By request, interviewee's name has been changed to maintain his privacy.

66. Gustavo Camacho, interview.

67. Josue Araña, interview by the author, August 4, 2007, Paterson, New Jersey. By request, interviewee's name has been changed to maintain his privacy.

68. Gregorio Herrera, interview by the author, July 3, 2007, Paterson, New Jersey. By request, interviewee's name has been changed to maintain his privacy.

69. Rodrigo Enríquez, interview by the author, June 5, 2007, Paterson, New Jersey. By request, interviewee's name has been changed to maintain his privacy.

70. I base this on the open letter that Alejandro Cedeño, Costa Rica's former consul general, sent to *La Nación* in 2005 that denied the existence of a sizable community of undocumented Costa Rican workers.

71. Of the 103 immigrants surveyed, 8 expressed their satisfaction with consular

services, 23 stated that they were dissatisfied, and 73 made no comment. Additionally, with few exceptions, in my conversations with Costa Ricans in New Jersey, the subject of the consulate upset immigrants.

72. Ana Casas, interview by the author, July 6, 2007, Montclair, New Jersey. By request, interviewee's name has been changed to maintain her privacy.

73. The situation has seemingly improved over the past decade in New York, but Washington, DC, officials are not necessarily easy to locate. Indeed, in 2017, I was unable to reach the Costa Rican Embassy in Washington, DC, after several attempts by phone (October 23 and 24, November 7, 8, and 14) as my calls were immediately dropped. Providing some explanation to this, the Costa Rican Embassy's website, www.costarica-embassy.org/index.php?q=node/136, noted that the embassy's phone lines were not functioning on October 23. Additionally, an email to the embassy on October 23 inquiring about Costa Rican immigrants to the United States received an auto-reply promising a response in forty-eight hours, but none came. A second email sent to this same email received an auto-reply and no follow-up phone call or email. The New York City consulate office is also challenging to reach but conditions have improved. Although an email inquiry from October 23, 2017, asking where Costa Rican enclaves in the United States are located went unanswered, phone calls to the office on October 23 and 24 and November 7 and November 8, 2017, were all answered by a recording that offered the chance to speak to an operator if one pressed "0." However, each call was dropped immediately after pressing "0." A second email on November 7 (same contents as the first) did receive a helpful and friendly response on November 8 from an employee who asserted that Costa Ricans were concentrated in the New Jersey communities of Paterson, Trenton, Summit, Boundbrook, Elizabeth, and Newark. This employee also noted there were 8,300 registered voters in the tristate area, and although they did not have more figures on the size of the community, it was much larger than that. A follow-up email, which a second employee answered, on changes in consular staff (given my receiving a response for the first time in over a decade of contacting this office), noted that two staff members had been added to the full-time consular staff in the past year. Still, this employee thought that the office was understaffed. This same person did note too that the consulate had gone to an automated online appointment system, which is now the only means by which Costa Rican citizens can create reservations to renew national identity cards and passports or secure other documentation from the consulate staff. Further, this staff member suggested that this had helped streamline work for consular staff, and as many Costa Rican émigrés are young and tech savvy, many immigrants likely welcome this new mode of appointment making. However, the fact that appointments can only be made on the web undoubtedly is a hardship for those without access to a computer, namely elderly immigrants. The New York City consular office's Facebook page documents numerous complaints to this effect, as well as complaints by nationals who have been unable to secure appointments even with this new appointment system, those who have been refused service when arriving five minutes late to an appointment, and others who complain that the staff at the New York office are rude and uneager to assist nationals with appointments. There were also two Facebook posts that complimented the office for a speedy turnaround on a document, but these were a clear minority of posters. Although there is clearly a lot to be desired, the fact that I was (with considerable persistence) able to reach staff at the consulate suggests that the situation is better than a decade ear-

lier. Rolando Madrigal, New York City, to Carmen Kordick, Chicago, November 8, 2017; José Arroyo, New York City, to Carmen Kordick, Chicago, November 8, 2017.

74. Gabriel Naranjo, interview by the author, July 8, 2007, Bloomfield, New Jersey. By request, interviewee's name has been changed to maintain his privacy.

75. Sarah Silver, "Mexico to Campaign for Rights of Migrant Workers," *Financial Times*, November 6, 2002, accessed October 9, 2008, http://are.berkeley.edu/APMP/pubs/agworkvisa/rekindle110602.html.

76. A notable incident took place in April 1996, when Riverside County sheriffs beat two undocumented Mexicans apprehended entering the United States unlawfully. Despite their legal status, Mexican authorities helped their nationals to mount a federal civil rights lawsuit that was settled after the victims were paid $740,000. See "2 Immigrants Settle for $740,000 in Beating," *New York Times*, June 21, 1997, accessed September 7, 2008, www.nytimes.com/1997/06/21/us/2-immigrants-settle-for-740000-in-beating.html.

77. Susan Sachs, "New York, Citing Security, Rejects Mexican ID Cards," *New York Times*, December 28, 2002, accessed September 7, 2008, www.nytimes.com/2002/12/28/nyregion/new-york-citing-security-rejects-mexican-id-cards.html.

78. Asamblea Legislativa de la República de Costa Rica, *Ley de matricula consular*, 2006, expediente no. 16.323.

79. Álvaro Murillo and Irene Vizcaíno, "Consulados comienzan a levantar padrón electoral," *La Nación*, June 21, 2010, accessed May 2, 2011, www.nacion.com/archivo/Consulados-comienzan-levantar-padron-electoral_0_1129887096.html.

80. Carlos Navarro, Isabel Morales, and María Gratschew, "External Voting: A Comparative Overview," in *Voting from Abroad: The International IDEA Handbook* (Mexico City: Federal Electoral Institute of Mexico, 2007): 1–30, accessed June 15, 2011, www.idea.int/publications/voting_from_abroad.

81. Juan Pablo Arías, "Alto abstencionismo destaca en los votos en el extranjero," *La Nación*, February 3, 2014, accessed February 10, 2014, www.nacion.com/nacional/elecciones2014/Alto-abstencionismo-destaca-votos-extranjero_0_1394460665.html.

82. Hermes Solano, "Casi 32 mil ticos votarán en el extranjero en 2018," *Costa Rica Hoy*, November 17, 2017, accessed February 27, 2018, www.crhoy.com/nacionales/casi-32-mil-ticos-votaran-en-el-extranjero-en-2018.

83. Peter Prengaman, "Dominican Candidates Campaign Abroad," *Miami Herald*, May 8, 2004, accessed September 9, 2010, www.latinamericanstudies.org/dominican-republic/abroad.htm.

84. Federico Araya, interview by the author, July 16, 2007, Haledon, New Jersey. By request, interviewee's name has been changed to maintain his privacy.

85. Federico Araya, interview.

86. Federico Araya, interview.

87. Emilia Paniagua, interview.

88. Federico Araya, interview.

89. Margarita Romero, interview by the author, July 21, 2007, Franklin Lakes, New Jersey. By request, interviewee's name has been changed to maintain her privacy.

90. Manuel Fuentes, interview by the author, September 7, 2007, Paterson, New Jersey. By request, interviewee's name has been changed to maintain his privacy.

91. Manuel Fuentes, interview.

92. This is paraphrased from my field notebook, September 7, 2007.

93. Participant observation, September 7, 2007.

Conclusion

1. Kim Tate, "World Cup 2014: Costa Rica Have Surprised Many and Shown They Are Not a Team to Be Taken Lightly," *Telegraph*, June 23, 2014, accessed August 10, 2014, www.telegraph.co.uk/sport/10920129/World-Cup-2014-Costa-Rica-have-surprised-many-and-shown-they-are-not-a-team-to-be-taken-lightly.html; Mark Ogden, "Costa Rica v Greece: Fairytale Continues as Minnows Reach World Cup Quarter-Finals after Penalty Shootout," *Telegraph*, June 30, 2014, accessed August 10, 2014, www.telegraph.co.uk/sport/football/teams/costa-rica/10934743/Costa-Rica-v-Greece-Fairytale-continues-as-minnows-reach-World-Cup-quarter-finals-after-penalty-shootout.html; "Costa Rica, la sorpresa del Mundial y un nuevo grande de la Concacaf," *CNNMexico*, July 5, 2014, accessed August 10, 2014, mexico.cnn.com/deportes/2014/07/05/costa-rica-la-sorpresa-del-mundial-y-un-nuevo-grande-de-la-concacaf; Jorge Oller, "Costa Rica es campeón moral de la Copa del Mundo," *La Nación*, July 6, 2014, accessed August 10, 2014, www.nacion.com/blogs/a_fuego_lento/Campeon-moral-Copa-Mundo_10_1425157475.html.

2. Scott Murray, "Holland v Costa Rica: World Cup 2014 Quarter-Final—As It Happened," *Guardian*, July 5, 2014, accessed August 10, 2014, www.theguardian.com/football/2014/jul/05/holland-v-costa-rica-world-cup-2014-quarter-final.

3. David Kent, "Costa Rica World Cup Squad Arrive Home to Heroes' Welcome after Reaching Quarter-Final," *Mail Online*, July 9, 2014, accessed August 10, 2014, www.dailymail.co.uk/sport/worldcup2014/article-2685575/Costa-Rica-World-Cup-squad-arrive-home-heroes-welcome-reaching-quarter-final.html; Andrés Díaz P., "La Selección será recibida mañana en La Sabana," *La Nación*, July 7, 2014, accessed August 10, 2014, www.nacion.com/deportes/brasil-2014/Seleccion-recibida-manana-Sabana_0_1425257526.html.

4. Oscar Mario Hernández, "Fedefútbol espera anunciar su nuevo técnico a final de mes," *Evergol.com*, January 19, 2015, accessed June 1, 2015, http://everardoherrera.com/index.php/seleccion-2?start=124.

5. A number of academics in the late 1980s and early 1990s produced a series of systemic socioeconomic studies that credited the way elites introduced coffee production to their respective Isthmian nation, engendering strikingly different sociocultural, political, and economic conditions. Scholars have highlighted Costa Rica in these works for its relatively stable and sturdy democratic institutions. For these scholars, Costa Rica's twentieth-century stability was a direct outgrowth of the way the agroexport boom created a broad-based rural middle class because of the nation's sizable agrarian frontier. These structuralist essays, however, fail to recognize that Costa Rica's peace-centered democracy emerged after 1948. Thus, something more than just access to land was arguably needed for Costa Rica to establish a more democratic and stable society. See Roseberry, Gudmundson, and Samper Kutschbach, *Coffee, Society, and Power*. Also see Pérez Brignoli and Samper Kutschbach, *Tierra, café, y sociedad*.

6. There are numerous works in both Spanish and English on this massacre. The definitive work, however, because of its use of oral histories is likely Jeffrey L. Gould and Aldo A. Lauria-Santiago, *To Rise in Darkness: Revolution, Repression, and Memory in El Salvador, 1920–1932* (Durham, NC: Duke University Press, 2008).

7. Chomsky, *West Indian Workers*.

8. For more on this collaboration and the social reforms, see chapters 4 and 5.

9. For more on how Calderón's reforms upset elite and foreign interests, see Bell,

Crisis in Costa Rica. For more on US intervention in Guatemala in 1954, see Piero Gleijeses, *Shattered Hope: The Guatemalan Revolution and the United States, 1944–1954* (Princeton, NJ: Princeton University Press, 1992); Nick Cullather, *Secret History: The CIA's Classified Account of Its Operations in Guatemala, 1952–1954* (Stanford, CA: Stanford University Press, 2006).

10. Greg Grandin, *The Last Colonial Massacre: Latin America in the Cold War* (Chicago: University of Chicago Press, 2004).

11. As early as 1952, in a speech made at Rollins College in Winter Park, Florida, Figueres proclaimed Costa Rica's Civil War as the Western Hemisphere's first successful strike against a communist threat. Díaz Arias, *Crisis Social*, 253. This definition of the conflict highlights the anti-Communism movement that undergirded the oppositionist movement and would define post-1948 Costa Rican society.

12. While anti-Communism was a centerpiece of oppositionist discourse during the 1940s, most peasant smallholders who took up arms did so in response to perceived attacks on their suffrage rights and in recognition of patron-client ties they had with oppositionist candidates. See chapters 5 and 6.

13. For more on this, see Mora Valverde, *Setenta años de militancia comunista*. Also see Dunkerley, *Power in the Isthmus*, 131.

14. For Figueres and his followers, their principal issue with Communism was this philosophy's focus on class warfare. Figueres believed that large businesses (privately, cooperatively, and government owned) were critical to increasing social wealth in societies and improving the socioeconomic outlook of the poorest members of society. He therefore believed that class divisions were necessary to increase the economic well-being of all people. For more on this, see chapter 4.

15. The classic work on US militarization's impact on Central America is Walter La Feber's *Inevitable Revolutions: The United States in Central America*, 2nd ed. (New York: W. W. Norton and Company, 1993). Grandin follows a similar logic in his analysis in both *Last Colonial Massacre* and in his more recent work, *Empire's Workshop: Latin America, the United States, and the Rise of the New Imperialism* (New York: Holt Paperbacks, 2007).

16. Costa Rica's decision to eliminate the military has been repeatedly employed by intellectuals, scholars, and politicians as evidence of Costa Ricans' innate pacifism. Given earlier events, including the nation's violent Civil War that concluded just months before the military was dissolved, it is clear that this vision of Costa Rican society is problematic at best. For more, see chapter 5.

17. The case of Honduras is worth noting comparatively as it counters the widely accepted theory that Costa Rican democracy explains this nation's political stability in the twentieth century. Robert G. Williams convincingly argues that a series of natural disasters that predated the outbreak of political violence in the isthmus during the 1970s, namely the Managua earthquake (1972), Hurricane Fifi (1974), and the Guatemala earthquake (1976), were critical to popular discontent against established regimes. Indeed, Williams notes that when government responses were slow and/or inadequate to the human suffering, peasants and workers organized protests. This was the case in Nicaragua, El Salvador, Honduras, and Guatemala where discontented citizens took to the streets and demanded government assistance in rebuilding their homes, obtaining higher wages, and bringing about land reform. In all of these cases but Honduras, government leaders responded with violent repression and within a few years civil wars broke out. Honduras's military dictatorship,

however, responded to the 1973–75 crisis by raising wages and implementing pro-peasant land reform policies that preserved the social order and managed to quell oppositionist forces. As a military dictatorship that responded to its citizens' needs, the case of Honduras suggests that a responsive state, more so than a democracy, is needed to ensure social stability. Williams, *States and Social Evolution*, 1–5.

Glossary

beneficiadores. Coffee mill owners.

beneficio. Coffee mill where coffee berries are processed into coffee beans ready for export and roasting.

brigadas de choque. Shock brigades.

cabuya. Natural fiber from fique plant leaves, *Furcraea andina*, which has a similar texture to hemp fiber and is used for making ropes, bags, and baskets. Traditionally almost all Costa Rican coffee was exported in cabuya bags.

cafetaleros. Large-scale coffee farmers.

la Caja. Government agency, the Caja Costarricense de Seguro Social, which since its establishment in the 1930s has been charged with ensuring the social security of all Costa Rican citizens.

calderonista. Supporters of Calderón.

canton. Administrative division similar to a US county.

cédula. Costa Rican national identification card that is required for voting.

chicha. Traditional fermented corn drink.

colón. Costa Rican currency.

comisariato. Similar to a general store in the United States but only receives payments in scrip.

cortecista. Supporters of León Cortés Castro, president of the republic between 1936 and 1940. He was the principal oppositionist candidate for the 1944 presidential campaign and for the 1948 elections until his death in 1946.

creoles. The descendants of Spanish conquerors and colonial settlers.

fanega. Spanish colonial-era measurement of grains and other dry foodstuffs, such as coffee. The measure varies greatly throughout the Hispanic world. In Costa Rica, a fanega of coffee weighs roughly 258 kilos and produces 46 kilos of processed, although unroasted, (i.e., ready for export) coffee beans.

FNL. National Liquor Factory.

gallo pinto. Traditional Costa Rican breakfast dish made from leftover rice and beans, generally from the night before, which are reheated with oil and spices.

guarapo. Traditional fermented sugarcane drink.

guineos. Type of small banana that is not sweet and is considered highly nutritious because of its high levels of iron.

hacendados. Hacienda owners.

hacienda. Large estate, which, in Costa Rica, almost always refers to coffee farms.

la huelga de los brazos caídos. Sit-down strike, a key strike that helped set the groundwork for the 1948 Civil War.

jefe político. Highest governmental appointee in most cantons who functions as a combination between a regional mayor and a justice of the peace.

jornaleros. Day laborers; synonym for peons.

ladinoized. Assimilated into nonindigenous society.

liberacionistas. Supporters or members of Figueres's Liberación Nacional Army and later political party.

machos. In Costa Rica refers to anyone with blond hair and/or a pale complexion. Can also refer to foreigners of European ancestry, who may or may not have blond hair and paler complexions, but generally hail from Europe, Canada, or the United States.

maiceros. Disparaging slang term for subsistence farmers, derived from the word for corn (maize).

manta. Raw cotton fabric primarily used for poor farmers' and peasants' clothing in Tarrazú and other rural regions in Latin America, during the nineteenth and early twentieth centuries.

manzana. Measurement of land similar to acres. One manzana equals approximately 1.75 acres.

Marqueño. Resident of San Marcos de Tarrazú.

mestizo. In colonial Latin America refers to those of mixed European and Indian blood, but more contemporarily refers to anyone with mixed European, Indian, or African blood.

mulatto. Those with mixed European and African blood.

Ngöbe-Buglé. Indigenous tribe/nation who reside primarily in Panama, but also in southern Costa Rica.

olla de carne. Traditional beef and vegetable stew consumed throughout Costa Rica.

PCCR. Partido Comunista de Costa Rica (Communist Party of Costa Rica), which would later become the Partido Vanguardia Popular, or PVP.

peones. Agrarian wage workers in Latin America.

perito. Independent property assessor.

PLN. Partido Liberación Nacional (National Liberation Party).

PNR. Partido Nacional Repúblicano (National Republican Party).

pulpería. Small general store.

PVP. Partido Vanguardia Popular (Popular Vanguard Party).

Resguardo Fiscal. Treasury Department's policing agents.

tapa dulce. Crude sugar product.

Tarrazúceño. Resident of Tarrazú.

tico. Colloquial term for a Costa Rican.

trigueño. Of dark olive complexion.

ulatistas. Supporters of oppositionist political candidate and newspaper editor Otilio Ulate, who ran in the 1948 election and served as president, 1949–53.

Bibliography

Primary Sources

Archives and Libraries

Archivos Judicales de Costa Rica (AJCR)
Archivos Nacionales de Costa Rica (ANCR)
    Alcaldía Única, Dota
    Alcaldía Única, León Cortés
    Alcaldía Única, Tarrazú
    Congreso
    Estadísticas y Censo
    Fomento
    Gobernación
    Gracia
    Judicial
    Remesa
    Mapa
    Ministerio de Economía y Hacienda
    Obras Públicas
Biblioteca Nacional de Costa Rica (BNCR)
    Hemeroteca
    Sala de Colecciones Especiales
Juan Bosco Umaña Abarca, private papers of

Oral Histories

Life Histories in Tarrazú (forty-four men and twenty-four women interviewed)
Migration-Focused Interviews in Tarrazú (twenty-one men and sixteen women interviewed)
Migration-Focused Interviews in Northern New Jersey (twenty men and eleven women interviewed)

Web, Multimedia, and Other Electronic Primary Sources

"2 Immigrants Settle for $740,000 in Beating." *New York Times*, June 21, 1997. Accessed September 7, 2008. www.nytimes.com/1997/06/21/us/2-immigrants-settle-for-740000-in-beating.html.

Arías, Juan Pablo. "Alto abstencionismo destaca en los votos en el extranjero." *La Nación*, February 3, 2014. Accessed February 10, 2014. www.nacion.com/nacional/elecciones2014/Alto-abstencionismo-destaca-votos-extranjero_0_1394460665.html.

Cedeño, Alejandro. "Sin sustento." *La Nación*, March 25, 2005. Accessed March 28, 2005. nacion.com/ln_ee/2005/marzo/24/opinion5.html.

Centro Centroamericano de Población. *Estadística Anuario de Costa Rica, 1948*. San José: Costa Rica, 1948. http://ccp.ucr.ac.cr/bvp/pdf/anuariocr/an1948/index.htm.

Confederación de Trabajadores Rerum Novarum. "Lista de Salarios 2010." Accessed June 1, 2011. http://rerumnovarum.or.cr/SalariosSectorPrivado/2010/LISTADESALARIORIGE010110.pdf.

Embajada de Costa Rica en Washington, DC. "Contáctenos." Accessed August 5, 2007. www.costarica-embassy.org.

Feigenblatt, Hazel. "Consulados estiman que unos 220.000 costarricenses viven en EEUU." *La Nación*, March 13, 2005. Accessed March 20, 2005. www.nacion.com/nacional/Miles-costarricenses-ilegales-EE-UU_0_744725696.html.

———. "Difícil volver a Costa Rica." *La Nación*, March 13, 2005. Accessed March 20, 2005. www.nacion.com/archivo.html?date=1110693600&sectionId=100.

———. "Hay deportaciones a cada rato." *La Nación*, March 13, 2005. Accessed March 20, 2005. www.nacion.com/nacional/deportaciones-rato_0_744725720.html.

———. "Miles de costarricenses given illegals en EE.UU." *La Nación*, March 13, 2005. Accessed March 20, 2005. http://wvw.nacion.com/ln_ee/2005/marzo/13/pais1.html.

———. "Nacionales entre papeles falsos, miedo y mal de patria." *La Nación*, March 13, 2005. Accessed March 20, 2005. www.nacion.com/nacional/Nacionales-papeles-falsos-miedo-patria_0_744725624.html.

———. "Nota de la redacción." *La Nación*, March 25, 2005. Accessed April 1, 2005. www.nacion.com/opinion/sustento_0_746925409.html.

———. "Se dispara en 200% captura de ticos ilegales en Estados Unidos." *La Nación*, October 17, 2005. Accessed February 28, 2011. www.nacion.com/ln_ee/2005/octubre/17/paiso.html.

———. "Unos viven sueños truncados y otros el 'sueño Americano,'" *La Nación*, March 13, 2005. Accessed February 28, 2011. www.nacion.com/nacional/viven-suenos-truncados-sueno-americano_0_744725715.html.

Figueres, José. "Palabras gastadas." El Espíritu del 48. Accessed July 15, 2012. www.elespiritudel48.org/docu/i02.html.

Hernández, Oscar Mario. "Fedefútbol espera anunciar su nuevo técnico a final de mes." *Evergol.com*, January 19, 2015. Accessed June 1, 2015. http://everardoherrera.com/index.php/seleccion-2?start=124.

"Historia Revolución." El Espíritu del 48. Accessed July 5, 2010. www.elespiritudel48.org/bio/bio12.htm.

Hughes, Christina. "Those Left Behind: Impacts of Migration on Guatemalan Women." *FOCALPoint: Canada's Spotlight on the Americas*, June 2011. Accessed November 12, 2011. www.focal.ca/publications/focalpoint/463-june-2011-christine-hughes.

Hunter, Brandon, Angela Jenkins, and Susan Orton. *Swimming against the Current: The Teribe People and the Diquis Hydroelectric Project in Costa Rica*. Austin: University of Texas Human Rights Clinic, 2010. Accessed May 11, 2011. www.utexas.edu/law/clinics/humanrights/workhighlights.php.

Immigration and Refugee Board of Canada. "Costa Rica: Information on the Situation of Victims of Domestic Violence; Whether Victims Have Judicial Recourse or State Protection; Whether the Police Intervene in Cases of Domestic Violence; and the Existence of Shelters for Battered Women," August 1, 1996. Accessed May 15, 2012. www.unhcr.org/refworld/docid/3ae6ad9210.html.

Instituto Nacional de Estadistica y Censos de Costa Rica. "Estadisticas Vitales." Accessed June 29, 2008. www.inec.go.cr.

International Coffee Organization. "Historical Data." International Coffee Organization online. Accessed December 2, 2005. www.ico.org/asp/display7.asp.

———. "Statistics." Accessed July 8, 2007. www.ico.org.

Jara Murillo, Carla Victoria. *Corpus Digital de Mensajes Presidenciales de Costa Rica*. San José: Universidad de Costa Rica, 2012. Accessed May 28, 2012. https://sites.google.com/site/mensajepresidencialcr/home.

Kaye, Jeffrey. "Eye on Public Force." PBS, April 4, 1996. Accessed September 7, 2008. www.pbs.org/newshour/bb/law/brutality_4-5.html.

Leiton, Patricia. "Estudio de UCR estima que 28.000 hogares reciben remesas." *La Nación*, November 28, 2006. Accessed November 30, 2006. www.nacion.com/economia/Estudio-UCR-hogares-reciben-remesas_0_869713066.html.

———. "País recibió $400 millones en remesas y envió $196 millones." *La Nación*, February 18, 2006. Accessed February 22, 2006. wvw.nacion.com/ln_ee/2006/febrero/18/economia1.html.

Lopes, Gilberto. "Aquí uno va haciendo su vida." BBC Mundo.com, July 21, 2006. Accessed March 18, 2011. http://news.bbc.co.uk/hi/spanish/specials/2006/tierra_ajena/newsid_5195000/5195890.stm.

"Manos indígenas Panameñas y Nicaragüenses recogen café Costa Rica." *La Nación*, April 18, 2006. Accessed March 8, 2011. wvw.nacion.com/ln_ee/2006/abril/19/ultima-ce20.html.

Ministerio de Relaciones Exteriores de El Salvador. "Embajada de El Salvador, Estados Unidos de América." Accessed August 5, 2007. www.elsalvador.org/embajadas/eeuu/home.nsf/infoservicioconsular.

Montero, María. "Mal de Patria: Realizadores ticos a Nueva Jersey." *La Nación*, May 31, 2006. Accessed June 4, 2006. wvw.nacion.com/viva/2006/mayo/31/espectaculos20.html.

Mora, Emilia. "Cafetales producen angustia y pobreza." *La Nación*, September 13, 2003. Accessed March 8, 2011. wvw.nacion.com/ln_ee/2003/septiembre/13/pais14.html.

Murillo, Álvaro, and Irene Vizcaíno. "Consulados comienzan a levantar padrón electoral." *La Nación*, June 21, 2010. Accessed May 2, 2011. www.nacion.com/archivo/Consulados-comienzan-levantar-padron-electoral_0_1129887096.html.

Navarro, Carlos, Isabel Morales, and María Gratschew. "External Voting: A Comparative Overview." In *Voting from Abroad: The International IDEA Handbook*. Mexico City: Federal Electoral Institute of Mexico, 2007. Accessed June 15, 2011. www.idea.int/publications/voting_from_abroad.

"Obama Immigration Plan Leaves Young Immigrants Hopeful, Skeptical." *Huffing-*

ton Post, June 16, 2012. Accessed June 17, 2012. www.huffingtonpost.com/2012/06/16/obama-immigrants_n_1602406.html.

Oviedo Leiton, Esteban. "50.000 hogares reciben dinero de ticos en el extranjero." *La Nación*, November 9, 2008. Accessed November 12, 2008. www.nacion.com/nacional/hogares-reciben-dinero-ticos-extranjero_0_1012098866.html.

———. "Ingreso y envío de remesas en el país muestra una recuperación." *La Nación*, January 6, 2011. Accessed January 10, 2011. www.nacion.com/economia/Ingreso-envio-remesas-muestra-recuperacion_0_1169883113.html.

Pessar, Patricia. *Women, Gender, and International Migration across and beyond the Americas: Inequalities and Limited Empowerment*. Expert Group Meeting on International Migration and Development in Latin America and the Caribbean, Population Division, Department of Economic and Social Affairs, United Nations Secretariat. Mexico City, November 28, 2005. Accessed October 15, 2011. www.gcim.org/attachments/TP10.pdf.

Prengaman, Peter. "Dominican Candidates Campaign Abroad." *Miami Herald*, May 8, 2004. Accessed September 9, 2010. www.latinamericanstudies.org/dominican-republic/abroad.htm.

Programa Estado de la nación. "Estadisticas." Accessed May 6, 2012. www.estadonacion.or.cr.

Radel, Claudia Anne, and Birgit Schmook. "Migration and Gender: The Case of a Farming Ejido in Calakmul, Mexico." *Yearbook of the Association of Pacific Coast Geographers* 71 (2009): 144–63. Accessed December 15, 2011. http://digitalcommons.usu.edu/envs_facpub/37/.

Sachs, Susan. "New York, Citing Security, Rejects Mexican ID Cards." *New York Times*, December 28, 2002. Accessed September 7, 2008. www.nytimes.com/2002/12/28/nyregion/new-york-citing-security-rejects-mexican-id-cards.html.

Segnini, Giannina, Mauricio Herrera, and Ernesto Rivera. "Exdirectivo del ICE declaró ante fiscalía Rodríguez exigió 60% del 'premio.'" *La Nación*, October 1, 2004. Accessed May 15, 2012. www.nacion.com/Generales/Subsitios/Sucesos/2010/ICEALCATEL.aspx.

Silver, Sarah. "Mexico to Campaign for Rights of Migrant Workers." *Financial Times*, November 6, 2002. Accessed October 9, 2008. http://are.berkeley.edu/APMP/pubs/agworkvisa/rekindle110602.html.

Solano, Hermes. "Casi 32 mil ticos votarán en el extranjero en 2018." *Costa Rica Hoy*, November 17, 2017. Accessed February 27, 2018. www.crhoy.com/nacionales/casi-32-mil-ticos-votaran-en-el-extranjero-en-2018.

Solano Carboni, Montserrat. "Otro guaymí muere." *La Nación*, December 17, 1998. Accessed March 14, 2011. www.nacion.com/ln_ee/1998/diciembre/17/pais6.html.

United Nations Statistics Division. "Demographic and Social Statistics." United Nations. Accessed July 3, 2011. http://unstats.un.org/unsd/demographic/products/socind/inc-eco.html.

———. "UNSD Statistical Databases." United Nations. http://data.un.org/Data.aspx?q=Costa+Rica&d=SNAAMA&f=grID%3a101%3bcurrID%3aUSD%3bpcFlag%3a1%3bcrID%3a188.

US Census Bureau. "American Factfinder." Accessed April 5, 2012. http://factfinder2.census.gov/faces/tableservices/jsf/pages/productview.xhtml?fpt=table.

———. "2000 Census." Accessed April 6, 2012. www.census.gov/main/www/cen2000.html.

———. "2010 Census." Accessed April 6, 2012. http://2010.census.gov/2010census/.

US Department of State, Bureau of Western Hemisphere Affairs. "Background Notes: Costa Rica." Accessed April 9, 2012. www.state.gov/r/pa/ei/bgn/2019.html.

Zamora, Gerardo. "Mujeres Abandonadas por un Sueño." *Siete Días*, Teletica, May 2005.

Published Primary Sources

"1 Muerte y 12 heridos." *La Tribuna*, November 3, 1947.

"56 HERIDOS, saldo de los sucesos de ayer en ESTA CAPITAL." *La Tribuna*, July 5, 1942.

"A centenares de calderonistas." *La Tribuna*, February 11, 1948.

Aguilar, Oscar, and Carlos L. Fallas Monge. *Estudios sociales para 7º grado: Geografía, historia y cívica de Costa Rica*. San José: Libreria, Imprenta y Litografia Lehmann, 1973.

Arburola Valverde, Allan. *Código de Trabajo: Ley no. 2 del 26 de agosto de 1943*. San José: Litografía e Imprenta L.I.L., 2004.

Asamblea Legislativa de la República de Costa Rica. "*Ley de matricula consular.*" Expediente no. 16.323. 2006.

"A tiros la policia de S. Marcos contra los que Vivan Ulate." *El Diario de Costa Rica*, June 25, 1947.

Bolaños Herrera, Raquel, Emilia Gamboa Escalante, and German Vásquez Agüero. *Educación Cívica: IX Año*. San José: BIS, 2005.

Chanto Méndez, Juan Bautista. *Cooperativa de caficultores y servicios múltiples de Tarrazú R.L. veinte años de fundación, 1960–1980*. San Marcos de Tarrazú, Costa Rica: Coopetarrazú R.L., 1980.

Chanto Méndez, Marcos. "Primero en la escuela y luego en un campo especial se mantuvieron los presos políticos en Tarrazú." *El Diario de Costa Rica*, June 2, 1948.

———. *Tarrazú en su centenario: 1868–1968*. San José: Imprenta Lehmann, 1968.

Corella V., Randall. "Ellas también alzan la copa." *La Nación*, November 29, 2009.

Costa Rica. Leyes y decretos. "Decreto XXIV." November 29, 1824.

———. "Decreto XXVI." October 6, 1840.

———. "Ley de creación de los seguros sociales obligatorios." *El Diario de Costa Rica*, November 4, 1941.

Dirección General de Estadística de la República de Costa Rica. *Anuario Estadístico Año 1929*. San José: Imprenta Nacional, 1930.

———. *Anuario Estadístico Año 1931*. San José: Imprenta Nacional, 1932.

Gillepsie Blaine, James. *Political Discussions: Legislative, Diplomatic, and Popular, 1856–1886*. Norwich CT: Henry Bill Publishing, 1887.

Gaceta Diario Oficial, La. November 1941.

———. January and February 1944.

"Liquidaciones del Café." *El Diario de Costa Rica*, March 29, 1928.

"Los que ponen y imponen el terrorismo en la oposición." *La Tribuna*, November 6, 1947.

Melendez Chaverri, Carlos. *Mensajes Presidenciales, 1940–1958*. San José: Imprenta Nacional, 1990.

Monge Álfaro, Carlos. *Historia de Costa Rica*. San José: Libreria Trejos, 1979.

Molina Jiménez, Iván. "¿Fue una guerra inevitable?" *Ancora, La Nación*, March 16, 2008.

Mora Barrantes, Carlos. *Cantón de Tarrazú en su centenario: Colección de docu-*

mentos para una monografía: 1868 a 1968. San Marcos de Tarrazú, Costa Rica: Municipalidad de Tarrazú, 1968.

Mora Valverde, Eduardo. *Setenta años de militancia comunista: Recuerdos de Eduardo Mora Valverde*. San José: Editorial Juricentro, 2000.

Mora Valverde, Manuel. *Discursos, 1934–1979*. San José: Editorial Presbere, 1980.

Núñez, Francisco María. "Estudio histórico sobre la producción y el monopolio de licores en Costa Rica." Unpublished research report for President Prospero Guardia, 1941.

Pacheco, Francisco Antonio, and Mario A. Houed Vega. *Educación cívica costarricense*. San José: UNED, 1992.

Piedra Blanco, Blanca. *Historias y Añoranzas de San Pablo de Tarrazú*. San José: Editorial de la Universidad de Costa Rica, 1997.

Porras F., Celso A. *Costa Rica: Evolución de la mortalidad infantil en los últimos 25 años*. San José: Escuela de Estadísticas de la Universidad de Costa Rica, 1974.

Programa de las Naciones Unidas para el Desarrollo (PNUD). *Atlas del Desarrollo Humano Cantonal de Costa Rica, 2011*. San José: Universidad de Costa Rica, 2011.

Quiróz de Vallejos, Angela, Rosa María Durán Aguilar, and María Cristina Durán Aguilar. *Estudios Sociales para bachillerato en enseñanza media*. San José: Editorial de la Associación Nacional de Educadores Costa Rica, 1988.

"Tarrazú en la Revolución." *El Diario de Costa Rica*, May 16, 1948.

Trejos, Juan. *Geografía ilustrada de Costa Rica con un vocabulario geográfico*. San José: Trejos Hermanos, 1958.

Ugalde S., Patricia. "Solas y valientes: Los Santos lloran." *Perfil*, June 2003.

Zúñiga Montúfar, G. *Manual de Instrucción Fiscal: Conocimientos necesarios para el Resguardo Fiscal, Policía de Orden y Seguridad, Expendedores de Licores y Comerciantes*. San José: Imprenta Nacional, 1950.

Secondary Sources

Unpublished Works

Agüero García, Javier. "En busca de nuevas tierras: La colonización de una zona de frontera agrícola en el Valle de los Santos, 1870–1927." Master's thesis, Universidad de Costa Rica, 2002.

Badilla Gómez, Patricia. "Y después de la guerra seguimos contando la historia: Testimonios de campesinos y campesinas que participaron en el levantamento armado de 1948." Tesis de Bachiller, Universidad de Costa Rica, 1996.

Caamaño Morúa, Carmen. "Subjetividades en Contienda: Redes de Solidaridad, Capital Social y Gobernamentalidad de Migrantes Costarricenses en Espacios Transnacionales." PhD diss., University of Albany, State University of New York, 2007.

Díaz Arias, David Gustavo. "Social Crises and Struggling Memories: Populism, Popular Mobilization, Violence, and Memories of Civil War in Costa Rica, 1940–1948." PhD diss., Indiana University, 2009.

Eisenson, Matthew. "The Myth of Pacifism, the Reality of Politics: The Roots and Consequences of Unilateral Demilitarization in Costa Rica." Senior essay, Yale University, 2009.

Kordick, Carmen. "Tarrazú: Coffee, Migration, and Nation Building in Rural Costa Rica, 1824–2008." PhD diss., Yale University, 2012.

Monge Álvarado, Gabriela. "Monografía de San Marcos de Tarrazú." Tesís de Bachiller, Universidad de Costa Rica, 1946.

Picado Umaña, Wilson. "La expansión del café y el cambio tecnológico desigual en la agricultura del cantón de Tarrazú, Costa Rica, 1950–1998." Master's thesis, Universidad de Costa Rica, 2000.

Quiróz Sánchez, Martín. "La responsabilidad civil de las cooperativas de caficultores." Licenciado thesis, Universidad de Costa Rica, 1985.

Umaña Aglietti, Miguel A. "Militaries y civiles en Costa Rica." Licenciado thesis, Universidad de Costa Rica, 1978.

Published Works

Acuña, Miguel. *El 48*. San José: Imprenta Lehmann, 1974.

Acuña Ortega, and Víctor Hugo. "Clases sociales y conflictos en la economía cafetalera costarricense: Productores contra beneficiadores: 1932–36." *Revista de Historia*, número especial simposio: *Historia, problemas y perspectiva agraria en Costa Rica*, Heredia, Costa Rica, 1985.

Aguilar Bulgarelli, Oscar. *Costa Rica y sus hechos políticos de 1948: Problemática de una década*. San José: Editorial Universidad Estatal a Distancia, 2004.

Altamirano, Teófilo. *Los que se fueron: Peruanos en Estados Unidos*. Lima, Peru: Pontifica Universidad Católica del Perú Fondo Editorial, 1990.

Alvarenga, Patricia. "Auxiliary Forces in the Shaping of the Repressive System, El Salvador, 1880–1930." In Chomsky and Lauria-Santiago, *Identity and Struggle at the Margins*, 122–50.

Ameringer, Charles D. *The Caribbean Legion: Patriots, Politicians, Soldiers of Fortune, 1946–1950*. University Park: Pennsylvania State University Press, 1996.

———. *Don Pepe: A Political Biography of José Figueres of Costa Rica*. Albuquerque: University of New Mexico Press, 1978.

Bell, John Patrick. *Crisis in Costa Rica: The 1948 Revolution*. Austin: University of Texas Press, 1971.

Bethell, Leslie, and Ian Roxborough. "Latin America between the Second World War and the Cold War: Some Reflections of the 1945–8 Conjuncture." *Journal of Latin American Studies* 20, no. 1 (May 1988): 167–89.

Bird, Leonard. *Costa Rica: The Unarmed Democracy*. London: Sheppard Press, 1984.

Booth, John A. *Costa Rica: Quest for Democracy*. Boulder, CO: Westview Press, 1999.

Booth, John A., Christine J. Wade, and Thomas W. Walker. *Understanding Central America: Global Forces, Rebellion, and Change*. 5th ed. Boulder, CO: Westview Press, 2009.

Bowman, Kirk. "Democracy on the Brink: The First Figueres Presidency." In *Costa Rica Reader*, edited by Steven Palmer and Iván Molina, 175–82.

———. *Militarization, Democracy, and Development: The Perils of Praetorianism in Latin America*. University Park: Pennsylvania State University Press, 2002.

Burns, Bradford, and Julie Charlip. *Latin America: An Interpretive History*. 8th ed. Upper Saddle River, NJ: Prentice Hall, 2002.

Busey, James L. *Notes on Costa Rican Democracy*. Boulder: University of Colorado Press, 1962.

Caamaño, Carmen. *Entre arriba y abajo: La experiencia transnacional de la migración de costarricenses hacia Estados Unidos*. San José: Editorial de la Universidad de Costa Rica, 2011.

Carillo Padilla, Ana Lorena. “Sufridas hijas del pueblo: La huelga de las escogedoras de café de 1925 en Guatemala.” *Mesoamerica* 27 (Junio 1994): 157–73.

Cerdas Albertazzi, Ana Luisa, and Gerardo Vargas Cambronero. *La abolición del ejército en Costa Rica: Hito de un camino de democracia y paz.* San José: Imprenta Nacional, 1988.

Chacón Hidalgo, Manuel Benito. *Los boletos de café en Costa Rica: Folleto Técnico.* San José: Fundación Museos del Banco Central, 2002.

Charlip, Julie A. “At Their Own Risk: Coffee Farmers and Debt in Nicaragua, 1870–1930.” In Chomsky and Lauria-Santiago, *Identity and Struggle at the Margins*, 94–121.

———. *Cultivating Coffee: The Farmers of Carazo, Nicaragua, 1880–1930.* Athens: Ohio University Press, 2003.

Chavarría F., Rafael A. *Producción de alcohol y licores en Costa Rica: Ciento veinte años después.* San José: Fábrica Nacional de Licores, 1970.

Chomsky, Aviva. *West Indian Workers and the United Fruit Company in Costa Rica, 1870–1940.* Baton Rouge: Louisiana State University Press, 1996.

Chomsky, Aviva, and Aldo Lauria-Santiago. *Identity and Struggle at the Margins of the Nation-State: The Laboring Peoples of Central America and the Hispanic Caribbean.* Durham, NC: Duke University Press, 1998.

Creedman, Theodore S. *Historical Dictionary of Costa Rica.* Metuchen, NJ: Scarecrow Press, 1991.

Cullather, Nick. *Secret History: The CIA’s Classified Account of Its Operations in Guatemala, 1952–1954.* Stanford, CA: Stanford University Press, 2006.

Daviron, Benoit, and Stefano Ponte. *The Coffee Paradox: Global Markets, Commodity Trade, and the Elusive Promise of Development.* London: Zed Books, 2005.

Díaz-Arias, David Gustavo. *Crisis social y memorias en lucha: Guerra civil en Costa Rica, 1940–1948.* San José: Editorial de la Universidad de Costa Rica, 2015.

Dore, Elizabeth. “Debt Peonage in Granada, Nicaragua, 1870–1930: Labor in a Noncapitalist Transition.” *Hispanic American Historical Review* 83, no. 3 (August 2003): 521–59.

———. *Myths of Modernity: Peonage and Patriarchy in Nicaragua.* Durham, NC: Duke University Press, 2006.

Dunkerley, James. *Power in the Isthmus: A Political History of Modern Central America.* London: Verso 1988.

Edelman, Marc. *Peasants against Globalization: Rural Social Movements in Costa Rica.* Palo Alto, CA: Stanford University Press, 1999.

Escamilla Gutiérrez, Zaira, and Lorena Vargas Mora. “Peasant Women’s Autobiographies: Women’s Double Contribution to the Rural Economy.” In *The Costa Rican Women’s Movement: A Reader*, edited by Ilse Abshagen Leitinger, 89–97. Pittsburgh: University of Pittsburgh, 1997.

Facio, Rodrigo. *Estudio sobre economía costarricense.* San José: Editorial Costa Rica, 1975.

Foote, Nicola. “British Caribbean Women Migrants and Domestic Service in Latin America, 1850–1950: Race, Gender, and Colonial Legacies.” In *Colonization and Domestic Service: Historical and Contemporary Perspectives*, edited by Victoria K. Haskins and Claire Lowrie, 289–308. New York: Routledge, 2015.

Fowler-Salamni, Heather. “Gender, Work, Trade Unionism, and Working-Class Women’s Culture in Post-Revolutionary Veracruz.” In *Sex in Revolution: Gen-*

der, Politics, and Power in Modern Mexico, edited by Jocelyn Olcott, Mary Kay Vaughan, and Gabriela Cano, 162–98. Durham, NC: Duke University Press, 2006.

Friedman, Max Paul. *Nazis and Good Neighbors: The United States Campaign against the Germans of Latin America in World War II*. Cambridge: Cambridge University Press, 2003.

Gervase Clarence-Smith, William, and Steven Topik, eds. *The Global Coffee Economy in Africa, Asia, and Latin America, 1500–1989*. Cambridge: Cambridge University Press, 2003.

Gilly, Adolfo. *El cardenismo. Una utopía Mexicana*. Mexico City: Ediciones Era, 2001.

Gleijeses, Piero. "Juan José Arévalo and the Caribbean Legion." *Journal of Latin American Studies* 21, no. 1 (February 1989): 133–45.

———. *Shattered Hope: The Guatemalan Revolution and the United States, 1944–1954*. Princeton, NJ: Princeton University Press, 1992.

González García, Yamileth. *Continuidad y cambio en la historia agraria de Costa Rica*. San José: Editorial Costa Rica, 1989.

Gorkin, Michael, Marta Pineda, and Gloria Leal. *From Grandmother to Granddaughter: Salvadoran Women's Stories*. Los Angeles: University of California Press, 2000.

Gould, Jeffrey L. *To Lead As Equals: Rural Protest and Political Consciousness in Chinadega, Nicaragua, 1912–1979*. Chapel Hill: University of North Carolina Press, 1990.

Gould, Jeffrey L., and Aldo A. Lauria-Santiago. *To Rise in Darkness: Revolution, Repression, and Memory in El Salvador, 1920–1932*. Durham, NC: Duke University Press, 2008.

Grandin, Greg. *The Blood of Guatemala: A History of Race and Nation*. Durham, NC: Duke University Press, 2000.

———. *Empire's Workshop: Latin America, the United States, and the Rise of the New Imperialism*. New York: Holt Paperbacks, 2007.

———. *The Last Colonial Massacre: Latin America in the Cold War*. Chicago: University of Chicago Press, 2004.

Grasmuck, Sherri, and Patricia Pessar. *Between Two Islands: Dominican International Migration*. Berkeley: University of California Press, 1991.

Gudmundson, Lowell. *Costa Rica before Coffee: Society and Economy on the Eve of the Export Boom*. Baton Rouge: Louisiana State University Press, 1986.

———. *Estratificación socio-racial y económica de Costa Rica, 1700–1850*. San José: Editorial Universidad Estatal a Distancia, 1978.

———. "On Paths Not Taken: Commercial Capital and Coffee Production in Costa Rica." In *Global Coffee Economy*, edited by Gervase Clarence-Smith and Topik, 335–59.

———. "Peasant, Farmer, Proletarian: Class Formation in a Smallholder Coffee Economy, 1850–1950." In *Coffee, Society, and Power in Latin America*, edited by Roseberry, Gudmundson, and Samper Kutschbach, 112–50.

Hall, Carolyn. *El Café y el desarrollo histórico-geográfico de Costa Rica*. San José: Editorial Costa Rica y Universidad Nacional, 1976.

———. *Costa Rica: A Geographical Interpretation in Historical Perspective*. Boulder, CO: Westview Press, 1981.

Hart, Diana Walta. *Undocumented in L.A.: An Immigrant's Story*. Wilmington, DE: Scholarly Resources, 1997.

Hayden, Bridget A. *Salvadorans in Costa Rica: Displaced Lives*. Tucson: University of Arizona Press, 2003.

Hilje Quirós, Brunilda. *Nuestra Historia: La Colonización agrícola de Costa Rica, 1840–1940*. San José: Editorial de la Universidad Estatal a Distancia, 1997.

Hiltunen Biesanz, Mavis, Richard Biesanz, and Karen Zubris Biesanz. *The Ticos: Culture and Social Change in Costa Rica*. Boulder, CO: Lynne Rienner Publishers, 1999.

Jaramillo Antillón, Juan. *Historia y evolución del Seguro Social de Costa Rica: Su primer hospital Dr. Rafael Ángel Calderón Guardia*. San José: Editorial Nacional de Salud y Seguro Social, 2004.

Jiménez, Alexander, Giovanna Giglioli, and Jesús Oyamburu. *Costa Rica imaginaria*. Heredia, Costa Rica: Editorial Fundación Universidad Nacional, 1998.

Kordick, Carmen. "Constructing Costa Rica's Inter-American Highway and Building U.S. Empire: Social, Economic, and Political Change at the Local Level, 1941–1944." *Journal of Iberian and Latin American Studies* 23, no. 2 (Fall 2017): 122–42.

Kordick Rothe, Carmen. "La memoria del viaje: Primeros emigrantes de Costa Rica a Nueva York y Nueva Yersey." In *Inmigración y emigración en Costa Rica*, edited by Carlos Sandoval García, 177–92. San José: Universidad de Costa Rica, 2007.

Krauze, Enrique. *Mexico, Biography of Power: A History of Modern Mexico, 1816–1996*. New York: Harper Perennial, 1998.

La Feber, Walter. *Inevitable Revolutions: The United States in Central America*. 2nd ed. New York: W. W. Norton, 1993.

Lancaster, Roger N. *Life Is Hard: Machismo, Danger, and Intimacy of Power in Nicaragua*. Berkeley: University of California Press, 1992.

Lauria-Santiago, Aldo. *An Agrarian Republic: Commercial Agriculture and the Politics of Peasant Communities in El Salvador, 1823–1914*. Pittsburgh: University of Pittsburgh Press, 1999.

Lehoucq, Fabrice Edouard. "Class Conflict, Political Crisis and the Breakdown of Democratic Practices in Costa Rica: Reassessing the Origins of the 1948 Civil War." *Journal of Latin American Studies* 23, no. 1 (February 1991): 37–60.

Lehoucq, Fabrice E., and Iván Molina. *Stuffing the Ballot Box: Fraud, Electoral Reform, and Democratization in Costa Rica*. Cambridge: Cambridge University Press, 2006.

———. *Urnas de lo inesperado: Fraude electoral y lucha política en Costa Rica*. San José: Editorial de la Universidad de Costa Rica, 1999.

Leonard, Thomas M. *Central America and the United States: The Search for Stability*. Athens: University of Georgia Press, 1991.

Longley, Kyle. *The Sparrow and the Hawk: Costa Rica and the United States during the Rise of José Figueres*. Tuscaloosa: University of Alabama Press, 1997.

Maier, Jorge. *Antigüedades Siglo XVI al XX*. Madrid: Catálogo del Gabinete de Antigüedades de la Real Academia de la Historia, 2005.

Martz, John D. *Central America, the Crisis and the Challenge*. Chapel Hill: University of North Carolina Press, 1959.

McCreery, David. "Debt Servitude in Rural Guatemala, 1876–1936." *Hispanic American Historical Review* 63, no. 4 (November 1983): 735–59.

Meléndez, Carlos. *Historia de Costa Rica*. San José: Editorial Universidad Estatal a Distancia, 1979.

Miller, Eugene D. "Labour and the War-Time Alliance in Costa Rica 1943–1948." *Journal of Latin American Studies*, 25, no. 3 (October 1993): 515–41.

Molina, Iván, and Steven Palmer. *The Costa Rica Reader: History, Culture, Politics.* Durham, NC: Duke University Press, 2004.

———. *The History of Costa Rica.* San José: Editorial de la Universidad de Costa Rica, 2004.

Molina Jiménez, Iván. *Anticomunismo reformista.* San José: Editorial Costa Rica, 2007.

———. *La campaña nacional, 1856–1857: Una visión desde el siglo XXI.* San José: Museo Histórico Cultural Juan Santamaría, 2000.

———. *Costarricense por dicha: Identidad nacional y cambio cultural en Costa Rica durante los siglos XIX y XX.* San José: Editorial de la Universidad de Costa Rica, 2002.

———. *La educación en Costa Rica de la época colonial al presente.* San José: Editoriales Universitarias Públicas Costarricenses; San José, Costa Rica: Consejo Nacional de Rectores y Programa Estado de la Nación, 2016.

———. "The Polarization of Politics." In *Costa Rica Reader*, edited by Molina and Palmer, 163–69.

Muñoz Guillén, Mercedes. *El estado y la abolación del ejercito, 1914–1949.* San José: Editorial Porvenir, 1990.

Okey, Shannon, and Sasha Gulish. *Alt Fiber: 25 Projects for Knitting Green with Bamboo, Soy, Hemp and More.* Berkeley, CA: Ten Speed Press, 2008.

Pacheco, Francisco Antonio, and Mario A. Houed Vega. *Educación cívica costarricense.* San José: UNED, 1992.

Paige, Jeffrey M. *Coffee and Power: Revolution and the Rise of Democracy in Central America.* Cambridge, MA: Harvard University Press, 1997.

Pérez Brignoli, Héctor. *Breve historia de Centroamerica.* Madrid: Alianza Editorial, 1985.

Pérez Brignoli, Hector, and Mario Samper. *Tierra, café, y sociedad.* San José: FLACSO, 1994.

Pessar, Patricia R. *Caribbean Circuits: New Directions in the Study of Caribbean Migration.* 1st ed. New York: Center for Migration Studies, 1997.

———. "The Role of Households in International Migration and the Case of U.S.-Bound Migration from the Dominican Republic." *International Migration Review* 16, no. 2 (Summer 1982): 342–64.

———. *When Borders Don't Divide: Labor Migration and Refugee Movements in the Americas.* New York: Center for Migration Studies, 1988.

Picado, Clodomiro. "Our Blood Is Blackening." In *Costa Rica Reader*, edited by Molina and Palmer, 243–44.

Putnam, Lara. *The Company They Kept: Migrants and the Politics of Gender in Caribbean Costa Rica, 1870–1960.* Chapel Hill: University of North Carolina Press, 2002.

Quesada Avendaño, Florencia. *En el barrio Amón: Arquitectura, familia y sociabilidad del primer residencial de la elite urbana de San José, 1900–1935.* San José: Editorial de la Universidad de Costa Rica, 2001.

———. *La modernización entre cafetales.* San José: Editorial Universidad de Costa Rica, 2011.

Rodríguez Sáenz, Eugenia. *Hijas, novias y esposas: Familia, matrimonio y violencia domestica en el Valle Central de Costa Rica, 1750–1850*. Heredia, Costa Rica: Editorial Universidad Nacional, 2000.

Rodríguez Vega, Eugenio. *Apuntes para una sociología costarricense*. San José: Editorial Universidad Estatal a Distancia, 1979.

———. *Rodrigo Facio: ¿Quién fue y qué hizo?* San José: Editorial Universidad Estatal a Distancia, 2006.

Roseberry, William. Introduction to *Coffee, Society, and Power*, edited by Roseberry, Gudmundson, and Samper Kutschbach, 1–37.

Roseberry, William, Lowell Gudmundson, and Mario Samper Kutschbach, eds. *Coffee, Society, and Power in Latin America*. Baltimore: Johns Hopkins University Press, 1995.

Rouquié, Alain. *The Military and the State in Latin America*. Berkeley: University of California Press, 1987.

Salas, José Antonio. *Liberalismo y legislación agraria: Apuntes introductorias para el estudio de la colonización agrícola en Costa Rica*. Vol. 8 of *Cuadernos de Historia*. Heredia, Costa Rica: Escuela de Historia, Universidad Nacional, 1983.

Samper Kutschbach, Mario. "Costa Rica's Response to the Coffee Crisis." *Globalization, Neoliberalism, and the Latin American Coffee Societies*, March 2010, 72–92.

———. *Generations of Settlers: Rural Households and Markets on the Costa Rican Frontier, 1850–1935*. Boulder, CO: Westview Press, 1990.

———. "The Historical Construction of Quality and Competitiveness: A Preliminary Discussion of Coffee Commodity Chains." In *The Global Coffee Economy in Africa, Asia, and Latin America, 1500–1989*, edited by William Gervase Clarence-Smith and Steven Topik, 120–56. Cambridge: Cambridge University Press, 2003.

———. *Producción cafetalera y poder político en Centroamérica*. San José: Colección Rueda del Tiempo, 1998.

Sandoval García, Carlos, ed. *El mito roto: Inmigración y emigración en Costa Rica*. San José: Editorial U.C.R., 2007.

———. *Otros amenazantes. Los Nicaragüenses y la formación de identidades en Costa Rica*. San José: Editorial Universidad de Costa Rica, 2002.

Sandoval-García, Carlos, ed. *Shattering Myths on Immigration and Emigration in Costa Rica*. Lanham, MD: Lexington Books, 2011.

———. *Threatening Others: Nicaraguans and the Formation of National Identities in Costa Rica*. Athens: Ohio University Press, 2004.

Schifter, Jacobo. *La fase oculta de la guerra civil en Costa Rica*. San José: Editorial Universitaria Centroamericana, 1986.

———. *Las alianzas conflictivas*. San José: Libro Libre, 1986.

Seligson, Mitchell A., "Costa Rican Exceptionalism: Why the 'Ticos' Are Different." In *Citizen Views of Democracy in Latin America*, edited by Roderic Ai Camp, 90–106. Pittsburgh: University of Pittsburgh Press, 2001.

Sick, Deborah. *Farmers of the Golden Bean: Costa Rican Households and the Global Coffee Economy*. DeKalb: Northern Illinois University Press, 1999.

Solís, Manuel. *La institucionalidad ajena: Los años cuarenta y el fin de siglo*. San José: Editorial de la Universidad de Costa Rica, 2006.

Stern, Steve J. *The Secret History of Gender: Women, Men, and Power in Late Colonial Mexico*. Chapel Hill: University of North Carolina Press, 1995.

Taylor, William B. *Drinking, Homicide, and Rebellion in Colonial Mexican Villages.* Stanford, CA: Stanford University Press, 1979.

Umaña Abarca, Juan Bosco. *Historia de Tarrazú.* San José: Editorial Nuestra Tierra, 2005.

Urcuyo Fournier, Constantino, and Chester Zelaya Goodman. *Democracia costarricense: Pasado, presente y future.* San José: UNED, 1989.

Ureña, Emigidio, and Pedro Pérez Zeledón. "Monografía de Santa María de Dota." *Revista de los Archivos Nacionales* 5, January 1941.

Ureña Elizondo de Fallas, Adelia. *Reseña Histórica del Cantón de Dota.* San José: Ediciones Serrano Elizondo, 1992.

Villegas Hoffmeister, Guillermo. *La guerra de Figueres: Cronica de ocho años.* San José: Editorial Universidad Estatal a Distancia, 1998.

Williams, Robert G. *States and Social Evolution: Coffee and the Rise of National Governments in Central America.* Chapel Hill: University of North Carolina Press, 1994.

Yashar, Deborah J. *Demanding Democracy: Reform and Reaction in Costa Rica and Guatemala, 1870s–1950s.* Stanford, CA: Stanford University Press, 1997.

Young, Philip D. *Ngawbe: Tradition and Change among the Western Guaymí of Panama.* Urbana: University of Illinois Press, 1971.

Index

Page numbers in italics refer to illustrations.